BEFORE

HE WAS

BORN

Andrew Perry

and they shall spring up as among the grass,
as willows by the water course

For Nicholas

Published by:

WILLOW PUBLICATIONS
13 St. Georges terrace
East Boldon
Tyne and Wear
NE36 0LU, U.K.

© Seventh Edition, Apr 2020, Revision 1, June 2020

ISBN 0 9526192 0 2

Available from:

www.lulu.com/willowpublications

Other Publications by A. Perry through Willow include:

Head-Coverings and Creation
Demons, Magic and Medicine
Beginnings and Endings
Fellowship Matters
The Book of Job
Demons and Politics
Joel
Isaiah 40-66 (Two Volumes)
Biblical Investigations
Old Earth Creationism
Reasons (ed. T. Gaston)
Story and Typology
One God, the Father (ed. T. Gaston)
More Reasons (ed. T. Gaston)
Who Through Jesus Sleep (ed. T. Gaston)
Just a Minute
John 1:1-18
Paul on Christ (Forthcoming)

Christadelphian EJournal of Biblical Interpretation:

www.christadelphian-ejbi.org

Table of Contents

7

PREFACE

This book was not planned. It just emerged from an exchange of letters between me and a friend who left the fellowship of Christadelphians for the fellowship of an orthodox church. One of the main issues in this exchange was the doctrine that the Son pre-existed *in some way* prior to his birth of the Virgin Mary. The book considers the topic of pre-existence, but it is by no means an exhaustive study. It is meant to be short and it is meant to address those 'problem passages' that encourage many in the churches to believe in the *personal pre-existence of the Son*.

It is difficult to generalise, but it would seem that the vast majority of Christians find the idea of a pre-existent Son quite natural. Most churches believe in a triune God, some believe that the Son of God was the first creature of God's Genesis creation. But these ideas have serious implications for a view that Christ was a **real man**, and this seems to be acknowledged in academic theology.

Christadelphians do not believe that the Son of God had any *personal pre-existence* prior to his birth of the Virgin Mary. Their doctrine does not suffer from the inherent difficulties in the supposition that Christ was the incarnation of God the Son, or that he was the incarnation of a heavenly being. However, their 'difficulties' lie with those 'problem passages' which seem to suggest the Son of God personally existed prior to his appearance on earth. So, whereas academic theologians have doctrinal, metaphysical, and philosophical problems to wrestle with, Christadelphians only have *biblical expositional* problems to handle. Academic theology has become bewitched by its language, whereas Christadelphians have developed expositional strategies that avoid the route travelled by orthodox theologians.

The view of this book is that the 'problem passages' need to be approached at the level of **type and anti-type**. Our thesis is that the proper background to these passages is the Old Testament alone and an appreciation of how the Spirit in the New Testament quotes, alludes to, and echoes the Jewish Scriptures.

Approximately half of the material in this book first appeared as a series in *The Testimony* magazine (Jan 1994-April 1995). I would like to thank Stephen Green for his editorial work on that material. I would also like to thank Trevor Evans for his contribution to Chapter Two. Finally, I would like to thank Arne Roberts for his help in preparing the typescript for publication. *1995*

Second Edition 2007

The second edition of this book remains substantially the same, although it would have been possible to expand the contents at every point. Time has not allowed this more complete revision, and only a light edit has been applied on every page. However, the treatment of Heb 1:10-12, John 1:10 and John 8:58 has been completely altered and re-written. A new chapter (Chapter Nine, on 'God-Language') and a new appendix (A) have been added giving approximately an extra 40 pages. Apart from these changes, the thesis remains unaltered: orthodox interpreters, following Second-Temple leads, read pre-existence *into* texts because they do not read them **typologically**. It is hoped, one day (D.V.), to expand substantially on this topic and engage scholarship.

Third Edition 2010

There was no intention to issue a Third Edition, but my involvement with the background support team for an online debate on the Trinity in 2010 produced extra material on John 1:1 and John 8:58, and this has been incorporated into this edition; a bibliography has been added. It is hoped that in the future that an additional chapter will be added on Jewish Monotheism in the First Century.

Release 2, April 2012

The material on John 1:14 has been changed with a clearer view on 'the Word'. We have also come down in favour of 'became flesh' as opposed to 'was made flesh' or 'was flesh'. Other material on the rest of John 1 has not been changed. It is hoped that there will be a fourth edition with an extra chapter on 'Jewish Monotheism'.

Fourth Edition 2012

The fourth edition has had a new chapter on Jewish Monotheism added; some additional sentences here and there on the topic of incarnation and the bibliography updated.

Release 2, March 2016

This release has had the material on Philippians 2 corrected to reflect a different Adamic typology; slight revisions to the Colossians 1 material for style and clarity.

Fifth Edition – Dec 2016
The fifth edition has had a new chapter added on 'The Divine Name', which is the most academic chapter of the whole book. Some of the material for this chapter (on John 8:58) was transferred from the chapter on 'The Titles of Christ' but a fair amount from that chapter on the exegesis of 'Before Abraham was, I am' was deleted. Hence, the material and approach in this new chapter is different on this text from previous editions. In addition to the new chapter, the whole book has been re-read and little changes made here and there in the manner of a typical fussy author.

When writing the first to the fourth editions of this book, it was felt that something was missing and not quite right about the treatment of John 8:58. With the fifth edition, the book has reached maturity and deficiencies of the earlier editions corrected. With the changes in previous editions to the treatment of Philippians 2 and John 1, this edition overall feels more consistent and coherent in its approach, even if a little uneven in its inclusion of academic material in the chapter on the divine name. God-willing a purely academic sister book entitled 'Paul on Christ' will be released in 2020. Readers with knowledge of the academic literature will find a much fuller treatment of problem passages in that book and engagement with the secondary literature.

Release 2 – March 2017
Corrections to John 8:58 material.

Sixth Edition – October 2017
A new chapter (Twelve) and an Appendix (B) has been added. About 50 pages extra.

Seventh Edition – April 2020
This edition was unplanned. It came about after a five-minute exchange on Facebook about John 1. That exchange sowed a seed of doubt. It suggested I needed to make a distinction clearer in the book, namely, that between 'God saying something and that word becoming flesh directly' and 'God speaking through the prophets and that word of prophecy being fulfilled in a person'. But in doing this, I revisited the biblical concept of 'the word of God' and how 'the word became flesh and tabernacled amongst us'. What was missing in the old exegesis was an emphasis on Jesus as the *ongoing and living* Word of God. So this has been corrected.

As a result I have moved everything on John 1 into one new chapter (it was previously spread over three chapters). I have added new typological exegesis of John 1:1, 10, 14. A major change has been to see in v. 14 the baptism of Christ rather than the birth of Christ.

As I was reading the book, I began also to notice other things that could usefully be adjusted. So, I have updated the material on Col 1:15-20 with regard to 'principalities and powers', coming down in favour of civil authorities present and future, rather than sitting on the fence as previously. I have also added new material on Rom 8:3 as it can be used as an 'incarnation' text. And, inevitably, as I read the book, I changed one or two sentences here and there as my eye alighted on things that didn't look quite right.

All this change justified a **seventh edition** (there are an extra 70 pages). Someone might ask, is this the same book as the first edition. About 50% of the book is the same. Someone might ask, if earlier editions were mistaken, can I trust this one? It is a fair question. We all carry faulty understanding of Bible passages, especially the difficult ones. Trinitarianism has produced a mess of faulty exegesis of the difficult passages. But, while we are alive, we should work at getting them right and, hopefully, as we go through life, our exegesis will get better and for some passages it will become right. For now, I don't think there is anything major to change in the book but, in the future (DV), I might re-work some of the explanations and add a few bits and pieces to the text in the 'Coming Down' and 'Foundation of the World' chapters since I have an inkling that there is something missing from those chapters. (Readers should note that there is some small duplication of 'the world' material from Chapter Seven in Chapter Nine.) Meanwhile, my old exegesis on John 1 is still intact in articles I have written in the past in *The Testimony* and the *Christadelphian EJournal*, it is for the reader to decide whether this edition's new emphasis or that of older articles is the best. All that is asked is an open mind, a complete respect for Scripture, a recognition that the Spirit interprets Scripture with Scripture, and a willingness to stand in the narrow way with God and to forsake the broad way of men.

Revision 1 – June 2020
Added about four pages of stuff and changed the typological reading of John 1:10.

Note on versions and abbreviations:

This study is primarily based upon the standard Greek New Testament (GNT) and mainly uses the Authorised Version (KJV) of the Bible for the English. But we do use other versions and take into account the Majority Byzantine Greek text (BYZ). We sometimes revise versions in line with modern grammar and punctuation as well as our understanding of the Greek.

We follow standard SBL conventions as per *The SBL Handbook of Style* (eds. P. H. Alexander, *et. al.*; Peabody: Hendrickson, 1999).

INTRODUCTION

This book is structured in a sequential manner. We begin in Chapter One by examining some principles of interpretation. It is not essential to read about how we interpret the Bible, because it is something that we do intuitively. However, it may be helpful to lay down some ground rules in interpretation before tackling a controversial subject.

The Christadelphian position is a simple one: Jesus Christ was a man born of the Virgin Mary, a man who had God as his father. In Chapter Two we explain this view and establish that it was part of the purpose of God at creation to have a son. With such a foundation established, we are well able to consider the difficult passages which are used to affirm that the Son of God existed in heaven before his birth.

In approaching the topic of pre-existence, it is as well to map out a route, and preferably a logical one, and we draw this map in Chapter Three. Before we start our journey, we take a digression and look at some of the titles of Christ in Chapters Four. Sometimes the titles of Christ are invoked as points in favour of a pre-existence view. In Chapter Five we examine the divine name and Jesus' 'I am' utterance of John 8:58. This is a common pre-existence text.

Our journey then begins in Chapter Six. Our plan is to start with passages that seem to place the Son in heaven before his birth of the Virgin Mary, and then work downwards. So, we first investigate passages that seem to say the Son of God was doing things in heaven. The main group of texts are those that appear to say that he was the creator of the Genesis creation, and we examine these in Chapter Six. Other texts seem to place the Son in heaven before the foundation of the world, and these we investigate in Chapter Seven. We then consider passages that appear to show that the Son took decisions to become human and then became incarnate in Chapters Eight and Nine. After this, in Chapter Ten, we look at passages which use the language of "coming down from heaven" to determine whether these establish a 'literal' descent of a heavenly being. By the end of this book, the reader should have a grasp of the general solution to 'pre-existence texts, which is to read them in a **typological manner** rather than on the surface and in line with the co-text. We close with a chapter on 'Jewish Monotheism' (11); a chapter on 'Christological Monotheism' (12); a short chapter (13) on God-language; and two Appendices on the doctrine of the Trinity and the only 'proof-text' for the Trinity in the Bible, Matt 28:19.

18

CHAPTER ONE
The Interpretation of the Bible

1. Introduction

It is not necessary to understand anything theoretical about interpretation to follow this book. It is not important to know in advance anything about typology. You can learn about types by "doing them" in this book. Before we embark on this task, it is helpful to think about the interpretation of the Bible. A certain approach to the language of the Bible and its meaning underlies this study on the pre-existence of Christ, and in this chapter, I include a brief explanation of this approach for those who have an interest in such things. Other readers, who favour "getting down to it" and considering the Biblical texts straightaway, can skip to Chapter Two, where the substance of our topic begins.

2. Principles of Interpretation

One principle of interpretation employed in this book, if 'principle' is quite the right word, is that one should seek to extend the context of a Biblical passage by identifying connections to other places in the Bible. Having done this, we can very often see in those other places aspects and features that supply a reason for the *choice* of language in our original passage, and we can thereby be helped to supply an interpretation of our original verse.

> Which things also we speak, not in the words which man's wisdom teacheth, but which the Holy Spirit teacheth, comparing spiritual things with spiritual. 1 Cor 2:13 (KJV)

This principle reflects the view that the meaning of an expression (which may be a word, a phrase or a sentence) lies in its *use*. If we follow this rule, we will naturally look at all the places in the Bible (using Greek and Hebrew where necessary) where an expression occurs. It is not enough to rely on the concordance or lexicon definitions, nor is it enough to rely on the meaning that words have in our own contemporary society. We *have* to look at the whole of the Bible. Following this rule will help us avoid some basic mistakes.

These connections crisscross across the Bible in many ways, and a passage of Scripture can have many links to different parts of the Bible. These connections are made by the same words, phrases, and ideas occurring in other places apart from the passage we are examining. The mere occurrence of a word (in English) from our passage in another place is not sufficient to establish a connection; it all depends on the context surrounding the other occurrence and the underlying Greek or Hebrew. Nevertheless, lexical connections in the KJV (and other versions) are a reasonable guide for identifying parallel passages.

Connections between passages can be drawn out on paper. This helps because a word or phrase in the passage we are studying can occur in several other places, and all of these places might be connected to our passage.

Let us look at an example, see Table 1.

Genesis 33	Isaiah 8	Hebrews 2
Jacob	Isaiah in the house of Jacob	Jesus
Esau	Assyrian King	Devil
Subject to Laban's servitude		Subject to bondage
Fear of death	Fear of death	Fear of death
wrestled with angels		Did not take hold of angels
Took hold of Esau		Took hold of the seed of Abraham
Fell down to ground		Tasted death
I and the children whom God hath given me v. 5	I and the children whom God hath given me v. 18	I and the children whom God hath given me v. 13

Table 1

This example shows how three passages intersect. It helps us appreciate Heb 2:14:

> Since then the children are partakers of flesh and blood, he also himself likewise took part of the same; that through death he might destroy him that had the power of death, that is, the devil. Heb 2:14 (KJV)

Instead of reading this verse as saying that the Son decided to become human, the links with Genesis 33 show that the language is being used in a *typological* way:

20

Someone, be this Isaiah, Jacob, or Christ, is functioning as a priest and delivering children from death and the Devil. In Isaiah's case, he and the nation (children) are placed into the role of Jacob, fertile with children from the Lord, but afraid and fretful of the Assyrian (Isa 8:12), the Devil. In Jesus' case, he did not take hold of angels like Jacob, but rather he embraced the seed of Abraham, as Jacob embraced his brother Esau; and just as Jacob bowed himself to the ground from whence he came, Jesus tasted death on behalf of the children whom he thereby delivered from death.

These connections join certain contexts by sharing out certain family resemblances. We can think of them in family terms. It is like a natural family sharing physical and mental characteristics. An author can set up particular connections between parts of a work: allusions, nuances, overtones, resonances, and puns are a few examples. These connections with the surrounding descriptive detail of their contexts make up types.

As we see from the example of Isaiah 8 and Genesis 33, types are not only a NT phenomenon. The OT was written over a period of some fifteen hundred years, and we should expect that later OT writers saw types of their day in the earlier history traditions of the nation. This is what we find, for example, with the events of the exodus. There are many allusions to the exodus in the Prophets. Isaiah 40-66 sees the plight of the Assyrian deportees of 701 in exodus terms, where the oracles look for a second exodus from deportation and a rebirth of the nation.

In the same way, the author of Hebrews is seeing Christ *in his life* as Jacob embracing his mortal nature and facing up to death, thereby delivering his children from death. Hebrews 2:14 is not about a pre-existent Son, but the courageous decision of a human Jesus.

A second principle of interpretation is to recognise that there are various levels of meaning in a passage. It is difficult to picture this, but one way of thinking about it is to think of a multi-storey car park. Think of a passage of Scripture as such a car park. The passage has a number of levels, and we can examine each level in turn. Lower levels are simpler, while higher levels are more complex. Moreover, the higher levels are built on the foundation of the lower levels.

Another way to approach this diversity is to look at the Scriptures in *different ways*. These different ways will correspond to different levels of meaning. For example, take duck-rabbit pictures. These are pictures that look like a duck's head and also look like a rabbit's head, depending on *how you look* at the picture. So too it is with the Scriptures; there can be different ways to look at a passage. For instance, we can examine Hebrews 2 with an eye on the exodus, we can think of Hebrews 2 with the perspective of the reconciliation of Jacob and Esau, or we can think of Isaiah and Jerusalem — i.e. there are different ways to look at a passage.

The different ways of looking at a passage have their basis in the fact that the NT authors under inspiration have drawn their language from different parts of the Scriptures. This affects how we look at types. When we trace types in the Bible, we should not try to force the type, but we should accept that some details in a passage may not fit the type we are exploring. The other details may very well be part of another type in the same passage. Just as in a duck-rabbit picture, it depends on what point of the picture you take as the reference point in your field of vision.

Recognising that there are levels of meaning in a passage is very important in a study of the topic of 'the pre-existence of Christ'. The main pre-existence texts, drawn mainly from John, are read literally and against Second-Temple writings when they are used to support a pre-existence doctrine. However, if they are read non-literally and typologically, they do not support such a doctrine.

To read passages *typologically* shifts the register in which they are read. It is the OT source text which has a literal level of meaning. The NT is applying this language in a typological way to teach us certain things about Christ. For example, in John 3 Jesus is spoken of as coming from heaven (vv. 31-33). The literal basis of this language is Moses descending from Mount Sinai, where he had met with God and received the testimony of the Law. John is applying this language to describe Christ as someone who has been sent "from above".

The Gospel of John is replete with examples of 'non-literal' language usage, for example, there are many similes such as 'I am the bread of life' or 'I am the true vine' or 'I am the way, the truth and the life', or 'lamb of the world', *and so on*. In addition, there are many types in John, and these are discerned in the patterns of words and phrases from the OT that John uses to construct his narrative. This kind of language-use is a reflection of the fact that Jesus spoke to the disciples in parables pending a future time when he would speak to them more plainly (John 16:25). We shall see that as we approach each pre-existence passage, there is good reason in the text to indicate that a typological meaning is intended rather than a literal meaning.

A third principle of interpretation that we follow is a recognition that the sentence is made up of words and expressions. We also recognise that words and phrases are *put together* to make up stretches of writing, and words and phrases are put together *for reasons*. In order to perceive these reasons we must be flexible in how we think of sentences.

This principle is a truism, but one worth stating. It means that the words and phrases of the original documents are important, and they are not to be treated lightly by translators of paraphrase versions of the Bible. Apart from this point though, it means that we should be careful in how we analyse the text. It is all too easy to concentrate on words as if they are the fundamental unit of meaning. It is better to start with sentences and regard them as fundamental. Words and phrases are put together to make up sentences, and we make a mistake if we do not see the *phrases*. This principle means that we should not necessarily break into phrases but treat them as a whole. In this exercise, the use of computers is of great benefit. They allow quick and easy interrogation of the text in any bite-sized chunk we care to choose. Such searches help reveal two things, which were previously more difficult to find. First, they help us think of the Bible text in terms of sentences and phrases and not just words, and we can quickly find common phrases across different books. Secondly, they help us locate passages which share common vocabulary. These kinds of findings are a great boon to the discovery of types.

A fourth and last principle recognises that we are not just dealing with written language - we are also often dealing with speech. We need to approach speech acts in terms of their pragmatic settings, recognising their *force*. For example, take the 'I am' utterance of John 8:58. Is Jesus citing or repeating, verbatim, part of a divine utterance (Exod 3:14)? Or is Jesus just self-identifying himself as someone?

3. Understanding the Bible
The Bible is written in language, and language is the principal instrument with which we understand each other. God has used language to convey his revelation to man. It follows from this that it is possible to understand accurately what he has to say to us, otherwise there would have been no point in revealing anything to us in the first place.

We succeed in communicating with each other, despite the fact that we misunderstand each other. In fact such misunderstanding proves that in general we do succeed in conveying what we want to say, because we then succeed in correcting any false impressions. If we can succeed in the business of communication, it is certain that an all-powerful God can succeed.

The doctrine we construct from the Bible is not therefore a matter of the unexplainable. We ought to restrict our attention to the conceptual materials that the Bible itself offers us. We should not seek to explain things which are not explained in the Bible. For example, we are not told how miracles occur, we are not told how the dead are raised, we are not told the date of the return of Christ, *and so on*.

The doctrine of the Trinity is not found in the Bible, and if we say that this is a mystery, it is a mystery of our own invention. We have to admit our own impotence when it comes to knowledge of God (Psalm 139). But even though this is true, there are certain facts which God *has* revealed to us, and we should not denigrate our understanding of these facts on any grounds that they are incomprehensible. We should stay within the limits set by the Bible.

Those who argue for the pre-existence of Christ and a Trinitarian view of God often deploy the point that the doctrine is a mystery. Is this a fair strategy? The opinion of 2 Peter on Paul's epistles is that there are in them some things which are hard to be understood (2 Pet 3:16). This is also true of other parts of Scripture, but is the mystery of the Trinity something of man's own invention?

The verses of the NT that are used in discussions about the pre-existence of the Son are not easy passages. The disciples found some of Jesus' utterances 'hard sayings' (John 6:60). Are the creeds like these passages — difficult and perhaps ultimately mysterious? Is it fair for a Trinitarian to argue that no explanation of the incarnation can be offered — it must be just received in faith? *If* the Scriptures presented a doctrine of the incarnation of God the Son, then it may very well be fair to say that this is a mystery, simply because the Scriptures did not *supply any explanation* of the incarnation. But this is a question that ought not to be begged. Does John 1 or Philippians 2, (or any other 'incarnation' text), tell us about an incarnation of God the Son? We cannot deploy the concept of mystery until we have determined at least *something* of what the mystery is supposed to be about. There cannot be a mystery about *nothing*. Is the NT therefore pointing towards a doctrine of incarnation?

4. Conclusion

Many Bible readers are not concerned with semantics, and there is no reason why they should be so concerned. You do not have to know

English grammar to use English, but Bible *students* need to pay attention to the language of the Bible very carefully. The Bible is the most studied book in the history of the world, and there are lots of views about each and every passage. This should not be daunting, but it can be obscuring. The simple approach to the Scriptures, which Christadelphians take, can be obscured by the competing doctrines of the churches. These doctrines start from small mistakes in exegesis, and these build up cumulatively. The end result is a doctrine like that of the Trinity.

On the subject of the pre-existence of the Son, Christadelphians can take the high ground of simplicity. They can eschew the complicated metaphysics of Trinitarian creeds, but to do this, we will need to take the low ground of attention to concordance detail in exegesis. The journey is worthwhile.

It is rarely the case that a doctrine can be knocked down by a single argument or a single text. Generally speaking, doctrines are elaborate positions which have built in defences. Texts which seem to go against the doctrine are given explanations which make them consistent with the doctrine. This can be said of Christadelphians by orthodox Christians and *vice versa*. One objective of any enquiry must be to guard against this pitfall.

As members of a church, with family and friendship connections in a church, it can be difficult to evaluate doctrine in an impartial way, if long held beliefs are at stake. It can be easy to evade difficulties and accept compromises. The attraction of remaining in a community can be strong, and it is not until this attraction wanes that the re-thinking of doctrine can have any effect. If we re-evaluate our doctrine, we need to be careful that our motives are not from any social dissatisfaction with the church of which we are (or were) members.

There are many Christian communities of varying persuasions, and one option is to make beliefs a matter of personal opinion and remain in one's present church. This stance is often coupled with an ecumenical outlook, which says that all Christian churches are in the same broad category. This is a modern approach, but hardly one that is found in the New Testament, where belief is a matter of grave importance. It does matter what you believe in this area; it affects worship. And herein, I think, lies the tragedy of Christendom.

CHAPTER TWO
Creation and the Pre-existence of Christ

1. Introduction

The nature of Christ is a fundamental subject, and our understanding must be based on the whole of God's revelation. Because God's only begotten[1] son is central to the purpose of creation, Christ occupies a unique position in the *whole* revelation of this purpose. Type, symbol, parable, and prophecy are all used in the OT in anticipation of the arrival of the Messiah, and the NT must be seen through these devices. This approach is not taken by those who argue for the pre-existence of the Son, since their case is based more or less wholly on the NT, and in particular the Gospel of John, without generally emphasizing any OT references. Unless we use the OT to help interpret the NT, we shall end up going astray on this subject of Christ's nature.

2. The Son of God

The claim that the Son[2] of God is central to God's purpose is not just hyperbole, and neither is it a claim based solely on the need of all people for salvation. The focal position of the Son of God in God's purpose is secured in Genesis 1 and 2 **before** the fall and **before** the need for salvation.

The Genesis account of creation describes a land transformed from chaos and darkness to one of order and beauty providing the perfect environment for the man who was to be made in the image of God - Adam, the *(son) of God* (Luke 3:38; cf. 1 Cor 11:7).[3] That the concept of *sonship* is connected to that of being an *image* is shown by the later

---

[1] We discuss this translation of the Greek in Chapter Nine. Here we will note that this is one of the meanings given in BAGD.

[2] We treat 'the Son' and 'the Son of God' as titular which is why we capitalize.

[3] There is an arrow going from each name in Luke's genealogy onto the next name in the list: Joseph--->Heli--->Matthat---> [etc]. But for the progression to work for the first name in the chain, i.e. Jesus, it has to work for the individual elements of the chain. Otherwise how does the connection go from Jesus through Adam to God? It follows then that Adam *and* Jesus are called son of God, even though we know from information given to us elsewhere, Jesus is the only begotten son of God, and Adam was created from the dust of the ground.

27

comment in Genesis that Adam 'begat [a son] in his own likeness, after his image' (Gen 5:3).[1]

Adam was unique among the creatures God had made; the mental and moral faculties, with which God had endowed him, set him apart from the rest of creation. While the whole of creation reflected the glory of the creator, man alone was equipped to reflect God's character and be an image of God. In keeping with this exalted role, Adam was given dominion over the works of God's hand. Thus, God made Adam **lord** over his creation to manifest his glory in a unique way.[2]

The requirement for a *son of God* and the requirement for a *lord* are then central to God's purpose as set out in the first two chapters of Genesis. The sonship and lordship of Christ have their roots in the *creative purpose* of God.

Due to the fall, however, a new creation was required. A second man and last Adam was brought into being, Jesus Christ, the Son of God. Jesus Christ is the man at the centre of the new creation of God. This man is the new *Lord* of creation, given from heaven (1 Cor. 15:47). He is then the fulfilment of the purpose of God as shown in the creative actions of Genesis 1 and 2.

The doctrine of the Trinity falsifies this doctrine at its source. It proposes, by contrast, that the Son of God is not the pinnacle of God's *creation*, the *purpose* of that creation, but rather the incarnation of an eternal (and already existent) person of the Godhead. This negates the whole idea of the creation of an image of God, a person[3] imaging God — a Son. It

---

[1] M. G. Kline, *Images of the Spirit* (Grand Rapids: Baker, 1980), 28. K. Børreson, ed., *The Image of God: Gender Models in Judaeo-Christian Tradition* (Minneapolis: Fortress Press, 1991). We could ask whether anything would be a son that did not bear the image of the pro-genitor (Col 1:15)?

[2] Adam is a ruler and therefore *lord* over creation and this is illustrated in the types who follow Adam – antitypes of Adam and types of Christ. It is also illustrated by the Genesis allusions in passages such as Colossians 1 and Ephesians 1, both of which explore Christ's pre-eminence. The allusions trade on the existence of an Adam *with an analogous role and function.*

[3] The term 'person' is a technical term in Trinitarian theology. The word is also used in our ordinary everyday understanding of each other. I use the word in these two ways: when talking of *incarnation* I use it in the Trinitarian sense, but when talking of the Biblical doctrine of Christ as a

achieves this by simply proposing that the person of the Son is not a *created* image,[1] but the eternally begotten second person of the Trinity incarnate — God the Son — come down to earth.[2]

Here we are contrasting a doctrine that says there are three persons in the Godhead with a doctrine that proposes there is only one person. The first doctrine proposes that the second person of the Godhead became incarnate as Jesus Christ. The second doctrine proposes that the *only* person of the Godhead created a person in the person of Jesus Christ.[3] These two doctrinal approaches affect the way we read various texts. For example, take the text, 'Who is the image of the invisible God' (Col 1:15). The doctrine of the Trinity posits an incarnation of God the Son, rather than God the Father (cf. John 14:9). Instead of 'image of God [the Father]' we have 'image of God [via the Son]'. However, the second doctrinal approach proposes that the Son is an image of God the Father, part of his creation — a *begotten* Son.

The doctrine of the Trinity cuts across this *creative* work of the Father in respect of his son. It does so because it claims the Son was eternally begotten, co-equal, con-substantial, and co-eternal with the Father. Trinitarians restrict the creative work of God the Father, God the Son and God the Holy Spirit to the *process* of incarnation, but this is not the *creation* of a Son.

---

person, I use it in the *common* sense. This popular psychological sense is readily understood, but by juxtaposing this sense alongside the Trinitarian sense I am questioning whether the Trinitarian sense is intelligible.

[1] Of course, others go wrong for a different reason, they propose the Son is a created "angelic" being rather than a man. Christadelphians and some other churches share the view that the Son of God was created by God the Father. Christadelphians hold the view that he was *begotten*, while others subscribe to the position that he was the first created being. The birth of the Son of God (of the Virgin Mary) is a special time in the purpose of God the Father, but what is special about the *beginning of time* that required God to create the Son at that point? Such a proposal takes the Son of God away from the sphere of the human, and if you are going to do this, you might as well place him completely in the sphere of the Godhead.

[2] The pre-existence of the Son is ideal, in the mind of God, and not as a person of the Godhead.

[3] Examples of texts useful for establishing that there is one *person* in the Godhead would include Deut 6:4; Mark 12:29; John 17:5; 1 Cor 8:6; Eph 4:4-6; and Jms 2:19.

Rather than considering many texts in the NT which impinge on the doctrine of the Trinity, a consideration of a first principle from the first two chapters of the Bible is sufficient to show its essential falsehood. Without taking into account this context, we shall soon go astray on the subject of the nature of Christ.

When man disobeyed God's command, fundamental changes resulted. The sentence of death was passed upon Adam and Eve, and their natures were changed by God so that their natural thoughts and desires were in opposition to God's ways (Rom 5:19; 8:7). If God's *Genesis 1* purpose (to create a son) was now to be advanced, a new creation would have to be initiated, and a *further* central objective of this purpose would now have to be *the redemption of the human race* (Gen 3:15).

In respect of *the man* of the new creation, Paul writes, 'When the fulness of the time was come, God sent forth his son, made of a woman, made under the law' (Gal 4:4; cf. 3:16), and Luke tells us the means by which the Son of God came into the world. The angel addressing Mary says: 'The Holy Spirit shall come upon thee, and the power of the Highest shall overshadow thee: therefore, also that holy thing which shall be born of thee shall be called the Son of God' (Luke 1:35; cf. Matt 1:1; Acts 2:29, 30).

This introduction of the second man, though, is also different from that of the first. The unique begettal of Christ bestowed upon him a conflicted will:[1] the flesh from his mother, and the spirit from his father. The life of Jesus, during his mortal probation, was one of continual warfare in his will, and because he heeded only the will of his father and denied his own flesh, he experienced intense suffering.[2]

This was not the case with Adam. His probation commenced in the garden when things were very good. Adam's learning was not intended to be through suffering. But the writer to the Hebrews comments that Jesus 'learnt obedience by the things which he suffered', and it was through this

---

[1] By speaking of a conflicted will, this is not meant to imply anything about *divine nature*, as Trinitarian theologians of the fourth century might claim. In terms of his life Christ experienced temptation and proneness to sin, but he was also disposed towards obeying his father. In such terms as these we can understand his life as a conflict from his birth.

[2] See Matt 26:39; John 4:34; 5:30; 6:38; 12:27-28; Rom 15:3; Phil 2:8; Heb 4:15 and 5:7, 9.

suffering that his character was formed (Heb 2:10; 5:8-9; cf. Luke 13:32). That the second man had a probation could be expected from Genesis 2. Adam was placed in a garden and placed under a command. His disobedience led to death. Christ's victory over sin during his probation, however, led to life.[1]

The doctrine of the Trinity strikes at the heart of this *development process* in Christ (Luke 2:52). His character was a true reflection of his father's and it is important to note that Jesus' character had no existence in a person of the Godhead (other than the Father) before his entry into the world, for it was a product of his life as a member of the human race. The doctrine of the incarnation proposes that much (all?) of the character and personality of Jesus Christ was *already* the possession of the Son of God in heaven before his descent to earth.[2] [3]

That Jesus *learnt* obedience and had a probation also goes to the heart of his work as a priest. The work Jesus does as intercessor and High Priest is only possible, because of the direct association he has with the human race (Heb 2:17). He can succour his flock, because he too has suffered their infirmities. When Jesus was raised from the dead, his body changed to an incorruptible one, but the character and personality were the same he possessed as a mortal (Heb 4:15). The doctrine of the Trinity challenges the doctrine that Christ was a priest — *of* the people but

---

[1] God cannot be tempted (Jms 1:13), but Jesus was tempted, and this goes to the heart of his bond with men (Luke 22:28; Heb 2:18; 4:15). A Trinitarian doctrine can only accommodate this fact by saying that Christ was not *fully* God on earth. If this was the case, for a period of 33 years or so, God was not a Trinity, but a duality of God the Father and God the Holy Spirit.

[2] There is a distinction of doctrine here between incarnation and manifestation. A doctrine that says that God the Son became incarnate in the person of Jesus Christ places the person of the God the Son on earth in the body of Jesus Christ. (How does this square with the singleness of God?) The doctrine of God-manifestation retains the position of God the Father *in* heaven, with his character manifested in the person of the Son on earth.

[3] We might pose the following questions to an advocate of real pre-existence: of what (if anything) did Christ divest himself in heaven prior to his departure for the earth? Did Christ have any memory of his heavenly existence at all? Could a single personality combine a truly human consciousness with a consciousness of pre-existent divinity?

towards God (John 1:1).[1] A doctrine that Christ was fully God on earth, the incarnation of the second person of the Trinity diminishes the common bond that Christ shares with mankind, even though the creeds like to claim that he is "fully man".

The doctrine of the Trinity also fails to account for the death of Christ. If Christ were the incarnation of God the Son, then the death of the Son of God must have resulted in the *person* of the Son ascending to heaven while the body hung on the cross. It is difficult to see how this was a *real* death. To be true, there was suffering and pain, and the experience of dying, but was there a real death? And if there was not a real death,[2] where is the *sacrifice*?

The NT witness is that God the Father exalted Jesus. He made him both Lord and Christ (Acts 2:33, 36), and appointed him heir of all things (Heb 1:2). He gave the Son to have life in himself (John 5:26). The doctrine of the Trinity sees Christ's resurrection as a return to heaven, and it is difficult to see how this is a *genuine* exaltation. If Christ were God the Son, maker of the universe, it is difficult to see how God the Father *can* appoint him heir of all things.

There are then some fundamental doctrinal points about *creation* and God's purpose with man that are changed by the doctrine of the Trinity. There are five points in the abstract structure of the doctrine of the Trinity at which we can direct questions, see Figure 1. The first question is how God can be one and yet three; the second question to pose concerns the mechanics of the incarnation - what did the Son leave behind by becoming human, and how can the nature of God be united to the nature of man in one individual; the third question is about the death of Jesus - was this a real death if God cannot die; and lastly, is God the Son both man and God in heaven now? There are many arguments that could be made in addition to these points, but these are sufficient to cast grave doubts on the legitimacy of the doctrine of the Trinity as a development in the history of the Christian church.

---

[1] The Scriptures present Christ as a man in heaven, having performed the work of a mediator (1 Tim 2:5).

[2] On any pre-existence view, did Christ (the person of the Son) cease to exist upon his death on the cross? If not, did the Son of God die for men? In this line of thought we find the *reductio ad absurdum* of any pre-existence doctrine. For if the Son did really die, and if he did pre-exist, how did he view the prospect of his death from the vantage point of heaven?

3. The Creation of the Woman

When did the new creation begin? Some words of Jesus on the *Sabbath* are pertinent. He said in debate with the Pharisees that 'my Father worketh *hitherto* and I work' (John 5:17).[1] In other words, there was no Sabbath of rest for the Father. The work of the Father was a creative work, so Jesus' point is that work of creation had been in progress since Eden, when Adam's sin interrupted God's Sabbath of rest. This sin caused God to begin work again, and this was a *new* work.

The new creation began in Eden when Adam and Eve willingly received coats of skin. Their willingness shows that they wanted to be part of the bride of Christ, and the creation of the bride takes place during the period from the fall to the return of Christ. This creation of the bride takes place in a probationary context. The men and women who make up the bride live out their lives in faith and hope, because they do not receive the fulfilment of the promises in their mortal life. At the return of Christ, those who are judged faithful will receive life and immortality and become the *firstfruits of them that slept*.

In typology, this process of the creation of the bride corresponds to the taking of Eve out of the man. God provided a wife for Adam, formed from the bone and flesh of his own body, and the last Adam is provided with a bride that is bone of his bone and flesh of his flesh (Eph 5:30). The bride owes her very existence to the bridegroom, who gave his life for her, and a *common* bond exists, as a result of this sacrifice and their shared human experience. The doctrine of the Trinity militates against this relationship between Christ and his bride, because it claims that Christ is fully God, and despite their claim that he is also fully man, the common bond of a shared nature between a created man and his wife (taken out of his side), is broken down in their proposed doctrine.

The new creation of the woman begins in Eden and is completed when the bride is resurrected and given life everlasting. With regard to Christ, the new creation of *the man* begins in the same way. The new creation of *the man* began with his birth of the Virgin Mary. A probation followed,

---

[1] Notice the Genesis allusions in the immediate context of John 5:17 - the paralytic man was *made* whole in respect of the chaos of his disease, as Adam had been part of the very good creation made out of chaos. This making good of the man is a second *making good*, and hence Christ says to the man 'sin no more'. These words are spoken only twice by Jesus (the other occurrence is John 8:11), and naturally in the other place where we find the words, they are spoken to a *woman*.

and because of his perfect obedience, he was raised to life and immortality, the firstborn from the dead.

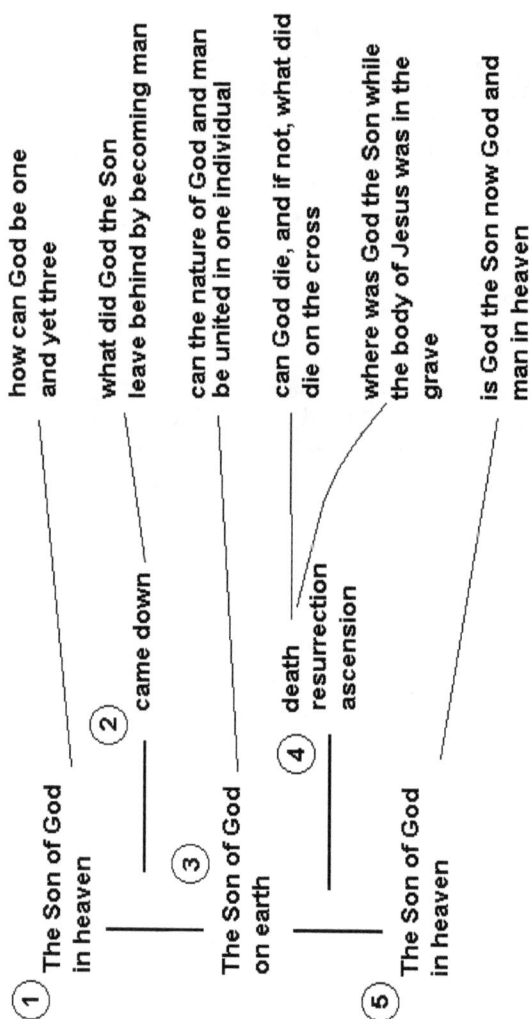

Figure 1

In typology, the new creation of the man Christ Jesus corresponds to the creation of Adam from the dust of the ground. Since the ground is a type of humankind, Christ the second man is created from this dust. With his probation over, and with him raised from the dead, Christ has entered into the heavens.[1]

Christ's position as the firstborn of all creation stems from the fact that he was the firstborn from the dead. Those who are second-born from the dead will be his bride. But in both the cases of the bride and the man, their creation by the Father begins with a period of probation, a period in which the Father works with the dust of the ground. For the bride this began in Eden, for the man this began with his birth of the Virgin Mary.

The bride's origin is similar to the bridegroom's as John writes, 'But as many as received him, to them he gave power to become sons of God, even to them that believe on his name: Which were born, not of blood, nor of the will of the flesh, nor of the will of man, but of God' (John 1:12, 13). The result of this begettal, which is completed at baptism, is that the 'will' of the Father is implanted into the newly born son and, as a consequence, enmity comes to exist between the new born son's own 'will' — the 'will' of the flesh — and the 'will' of God. The significant difference[2] between Jesus and his brethren is that he experienced this conflict from his natural birth, while for the born-again son, this warfare begins when he responds in faith to God. Whilst this enmity remains in the son or daughter of God, the consequent suffering will engender a character that bears the image of the Son. Without the grace of God through Jesus, however, no one can achieve victory over his own will (Rom 7:24, 25).

4. Conclusion

There is an order in the structure of God's creative work. God is from everlasting to everlasting. Before the beginning of time and space, there was God. God then spoke and his creative work began. We cannot conceive of what it is like to be from everlasting to everlasting. We are tempted to ask, *what did God do before he created the universe?* And then we repeat the question, *what did he do before that and before that?* The only

---

[1] This is like Adam being placed in Eden, waiting for his bride.

[2] From birth Jesus was God's beloved son, since from birth he was obedient to his Father. Our first glimpse of his consciousness of his Father is at the age of twelve, when he displayed an already mature awareness of 'his Father's work'. We have no other insight into his early years.

information that we have on such matters is that God is from everlasting to everlasting. Likewise, when we contemplate eternity, stretching out in the future, we fail to grasp its extent. If we ask, *what will we be doing for eternity*, we have no way of knowing. The information has not been given to us.

Sandwiched between the beginning and the end there is our creation of time and space. The creative work has concerned man. For the duration of this creation, until it runs its course, man has been given dominion and a commission to be fruitful and multiply. The fall introduced sin into the world, and God has worked out his purpose despite this happening. In place of the first man, a second man has been begotten, the Lord Jesus Christ. To this man, all power in heaven and earth has been given. His commission is the Adamic commission to be fruitful and multiply for which he needs a woman. When the second man and his bride are united together in the millennial age, the time will have come for them to be fruitful and multiply. The harvest or fruit of the marriage will be realised during the millennium.

Once this has run its course, the Son will hand over the kingdom to the Father. This is the *end* of creation - its goal - its purpose. God will then be all spiritual things in all individuals, one God in a perfect plural manifestation of *images*. The millennium is not the *end* of it all, a figurative time period for an everlasting time with God; the millennium is a period of time in which there will be *work*; the end of *this* beginning is the *end*. Just as things began with *God*, the end finishes with God — **one** God, the Father.

CHAPTER THREE
Approaching the Pre-existence Passages

1. Introduction

Many churches believe that the *person* of the Son, existed in some form in heaven prior to his appearance upon the earth. Some churches believe that he was the principal heavenly being under God the Father, a secondary and derived being. This is roughly the Arian view, so named after a minor theologian of the fourth century (see Appendix A). Others believe in a Trinitarian doctrine whereby it is held that Jesus, as God the Son, is of the same substance as the Father, co-equal and co-eternal with God the Father and God the Holy Spirit (see Appendix A).

The alternative tradition to the above two views affirms that the Son of God *came into existence* through the operation of the holy[1] Spirit upon the Virgin Mary, with the result that there was born a man child who was called Jesus of Nazareth. This view is well represented in the NT, but it becomes largely absent in the early church Fathers from about the second century onwards.[2]

The differences are significant, for they affect the whole of the Christian life, including, for example, worship and praise, prayer, meditation, and reading, and various doctrines such as the doctrine of the atonement. For instance, those who hold a pre-existence position usually stress that no one less than (a) god could save man by coming down to earth to die for him. On the other hand, we might ask, if it were possible, why should the death of (a) god be effective for a man, (after all, the blood of bulls and goats was not efficacious)?[3]

---

[1] Where we refer to the Trinity or quote a version we capitalize, but where we give our view of the adjectival sense of 'holy' we use lower-case.

[2] Some would argue that it is *totally* absent. The historical problem here is that Christian literature from the sub-Apostolic age is slight and much of our knowledge about Christian opinions of the second century derives from 'orthodox' writers. One possible source for the view of this chapter might be in the Jewish Christian groups of the second century, but where we might find agreement amongst them regarding doctrine about Christ, we are more than likely to find odd views on other matters.

[3] The fourth century church father, Athanasius, argues, "For being the Word of the Father and above all, it followed that he alone was also able to re-create everything and to be ambassador for all men with the Father"

Arguing about the nature of Christ is as old as the preaching of the Gospel. 'What do men think of me?' is a question asked by Jesus. When discussing the topic of the deity of Christ, various *kinds* of argument are deployed by orthodox Christians. We can divide these arguments into OT and NT arguments,[1] and our interest is in the NT arguments. A rough and ready list would go as follows:

1) The Son existed in heaven.
2) The Son performed the work of the Creator.
3) The Son did other work from heaven.
4) The Son came down from heaven
5) Jesus was called 'God' by his followers.
6) Jesus bore the titles of God.
7) Jesus was worshipped.
8) Prayer was offered to Jesus.
9) Jesus possessed divine attributes.
10) Jesus exercised divine prerogatives.

These are *kinds* of argument, and by this, I mean each kind of argument uses a key concept and a well-known text or group of texts to argue that Jesus Christ is fully God. We are mainly interested in the first four *kinds* of argument, because these are directly about passages that seemingly involve a 'time' before Jesus was on earth. We are not seeking to discuss the doctrine of the Trinity, or examine the claim that Christ is fully God. Our perspective is strictly limited to those arguments and passages of the NT that have to do with the idea of pre-existence.

A convenient distinction used by some orthodox Christians is this: the name 'Jesus Christ' refers to the incarnation of God the Son, whereas the title 'God the Son' refers to the second person of the Trinity, whether or not that person is incarnate. Our subject then concerns whether Jesus Christ is the incarnation of God the Son, or whether the person of the Son existed in heaven before his birth of the Virgin Mary. Our proposal will be that Jesus Christ is a manifestation of God the Father, not the incarnation of God the Son, and that he came into existence through his birth of the Virgin Mary.

"On Incarnation" in *Documents of the Christian Church* (trans. H. D. Bettenson; Oxford: Oxford University Press, 1944), 47.
[1] The sorts of OT arguments which we will not consider concern such passages as Gen 1:26, Prov 8:22 or Isa 9:6-9. These passages require the idea of a pre-existent Son of God to be *read into* them.

In the last chapter, we looked at the implications of the doctrine of creation for the idea that Jesus had some sort of *personal conscious pre-existence* in heaven prior to his birth of the Virgin Mary. In this chapter, we want to lay out a framework by which we can understand *in general* the arguments put forward by those who argue that Jesus pre-existed as the Son in heaven. This is useful, because it is possible to get lost in all the verses deployed by such arguments and consequently not see the wood for the trees.

2. Passages Quoted in Favour of Pre-existence

There are several kinds of passage used to support the doctrine of pre-existence. We can classify them into six groups. In this chapter, I do not want to approach the passages on a text by text basis. Instead, I want to approach them thematically. We can group the texts in the following way:

1) Passages that seem to talk of Christ existing in heaven before his birth on earth, e.g. *Before Abraham was, I am* (John 8:58).

2) Passages that appear to talk of Christ as *doing things* in heaven prior to his appearance on earth, principally creating the Genesis creation, e.g. *the world was made by him* (John 1:10), *by him were all things created* (Col 1:16).

3) Texts that seem to show Christ taking *intentional decisions in advance* about human nature, i.e. deciding to become human, e.g. *Though he was in the form of God...he took upon himself the form of a servant* (Phil 2:6-7).

4) Statements that indicate an incarnation, e.g. *In the beginning was the Word...and the Word was made/became flesh* (John 1:1, 14; cf. Gal 4:4).

5) Passages about Jesus *coming down* from heaven (e.g. John 3:13; 6:33, 38, 41f, 50f, 58), or *coming forth* from God (John 3:31; 8:42; 13:3; 16:27f; 17:8), and *coming into the world* (John 3:19; 9:39; 10:36; 12:46; 16:28; 18:37).

6) Verses that imply Jesus was *going back* to heaven, e.g. 'Glorify thou me with the glory I had with thee before the world was', or 'what and if ye shall see the Son of Man ascend up where he was before' (John 6:62; 17:5).

So then, the pre-existence arguments fall into six logical groups:

> Existence in heaven
> Doing things in heaven before he was born
> Deciding to become human

Process of Incarnation
Coming down from heaven and being born
Returning to heaven

A powerful set of passages, mainly coming from the Gospel of John (none of the Synoptic Gospels mention Jesus coming down from heaven). But powerful, I suggest, only when we read them on the surface, and with a background awareness of orthodox Christian doctrine, and by making comparisons with other Greco-Roman ideas about gods and with some of the notions to be found in Hellenistic Judaism.

Instead of this background and approach, if we substitute the background of the OT, and read the passages looking for **intra-scriptural reasoning** and **typological patterns of language**, other interpretations present themselves and a different framework emerges. Why go and look for types and patterns? Two reasons: firstly, types *are there* generally in much of the NT and they provide *reasons* for the language under view; and secondly, the arguments against the idea of the pre-existence of Christ, presented in Chapter Two, are too powerful to be gainsaid; they far outmatch the arguments for pre-existence.[1]

By supplying a *reason* for the 'pre-existence' language in the NT, we avoid the temptation to read the passages in a pre-existence framework. This is a real danger when we find ourselves saying, 'I do not think that Christ pre-existed, but I do not know what these 'pre-existence' texts mean'. The types and intra-scriptural reasoning are *there* in each of the texts, the question is therefore: Do the 'pre-existence' passages **also** talk of Christ's literal and real pre-existence? Our answer to this question is that they do not, because this leads to a doctrine of Christ that does not *cohere* with the kind of evidence that we presented in Chapter Two.

But, in all this, the Christadelphian might appear to be at a disadvantage. Types and intra-scriptural patterns are not easy to grasp. With a ready set of ideas, and a surface-reading approach to the pre-existence passages, an orthodox Christian is likely to 'win' the argument. Hence, conversations on this topic can *feel* unsatisfactory. An orthodox Christian can gain the impression that the Christadelphian is playing a game of verbal gymnastics. After all, we often hear (my emphasis), 'It says he came down from heaven, and it means what it says'. But we should insist, *what* can it *actually* mean for a man to come down from heaven?

---

[1] It's not the purpose of this book to directly develop arguments *against* the pre-existence of Christ, beyond those presented in Chapter Two.

The aim of the book is not to give an 'explanation' of each passage in the style of 'Wrested Scriptures', even though this may appear to be the end result. My purpose is rather to illustrate a **general method** which works for all the passages.

My argument can be set out as follows:

- The pre-existence passages draw on OT terms and phrases in order to point up types of Christ and present intra-scriptural reasoning.

- Comparisons[1] with texts outside of the Scriptures are tendentious and uncertain and they obscure the unique scriptural reasoning that binds the NT writings to the OT as Scripture.

- Through the device of typology, the NT passages place Christ into the middle of various OT typological scenarios, showing that 'Christ' is in all the Scriptures. If the NT passage is read separately from the OT background, the reading will be superficial and lead to a pre-existence view. The point of the type is never to show that Christ pre-existed as a person in heaven (God the Son, a divine hypostasis, or an angel) or that he was active in the OT story.

For example, in John 6 Jesus is the 'bread of heaven' which came down from heaven. A comparison with the story of the giving of the manna does not show that the manna 'pre-existed' in heaven, but rather that the manna was *given* by God from heaven.

Typological exegesis seeks to bring out the correspondence between the two Testaments. It takes the history of the OT seriously, and takes as its guiding principle the idea that the events and persons of the OT pre-figure or anticipate the events and persons of the NT

As we look at various passages it is as well to keep in mind our general approach to the exposition of the relevant texts. We will be trying to uncover the OT allusions implicit in the texts. In this way we will be trying to interpret Scripture with Scripture. In the next few chapters we will look at these pre-existence passages and see what they mean.

---

[1] The extent to which we make these comparisons is the extent to which we weaken the status of NT writings as Scripture.

3. The Development of the Idea of Pre-existence

This book is not an historical study of the idea of the pre-existence of Christ, nor is it a study of the doctrine of the Trinity. However, a few brief remarks will help us establish the significance of the idea of pre-existence and see how it was used by the early church Fathers.

After the NT period, the development of doctrine became centred on the *person* of Christ, and this seems to have been in response to various Hellenistic and Jewish currents of thought that impinged on the church.[1] *If* the apostles did not believe in the pre-existence of Christ, then belief in the pre-existence of Christ must have developed in the years after AD70, evolving in the succeeding centuries to result in the crystallization of doctrine in the Nicene (c. 325 CE) and Athanasian creeds (c. 381 CE).[2]

We can discern three periods in this development of doctrine. The first period of the post-apostolic (or sub-Apostolic) Christian church concerns the Apostolic Fathers such as Ignatius, Clement, and Polycarp. Their writing on the person of Christ is not systematic. We have to wait until the next period of church history to get more systematic writing on Christ. This period is known as the period of the Apologists, and includes such people as Justin Martyr, Aristides, and Athenagoras, covering the latter half of the second century. These Fathers developed the idea of Christ as the incarnation of the Word of God. After this period, the doctrine of Christ developed in a Trinitarian direction, as the relationship between the Father, Son and Holy Spirit was elaborated. This is the period of the Pre-Nicene Fathers.[3] A simplified picture of this doctrinal development would be this:

2c. the idea of the pre-existence of Christ as the Word of God is put forward by Apologists

3c. the idea of the pre-existence of Christ develops as a doctrine in the Pre-Nicene Fathers

---

[1] See C. Rowland, *Christian Origins* (London: SPCK, 1985), 244-254.

[2] This hypothesis must remain an 'if' at this stage, because we will not see what the apostles believed until we consider the pre-existence texts in later chapters.

[3] Some scholars talk of *all* the early church Fathers prior to 325 as belonging to the period of the Ante-Nicene Fathers. I use the term 'pre-Nicene' to refer to those Fathers from Irenaeus onwards who illustrate a theological sophistication in the doctrine of Christ that harmonizes with the creed of the Nicene Fathers.

4c. the doctrine of the Trinity triumphs over Arianism at the council of Nicaea (c. 325 CE)

5c. the two-nature (God-man) doctrine of Christ is elaborated

In other words, the early church Fathers first began by presenting Christ as the incarnation of a pre-existent Word.[1] As doctrinal controversies progressed, this idea was elaborated into Trinitarian doctrine as opposed to Arian doctrine. Once the Trinity had been confirmed as orthodox[2] doctrine, subsequent controversies concerned how the human and the divine *could* be united in Christ.

If we look at this development of doctrine *schematically*, the first idea is that of the pre-existence of Christ. It is first introduced as an unelaborated idea, but once it is admitted into the structure of doctrine, you are forced to describe the relationship between the pre-existent Christ and other heavenly persons, particularly the Father.

The church was faced with two choices: either Christ was *on a par* with God the Father, in which case a doctrine is required that preserves the singleness of God while admitting a plurality in the Godhead. (Once the Holy Spirit is brought into view, a Trinitarian doctrine becomes a logical development). Or, Christ was secondary and subordinate to the Father, in

---

[1] It must not be assumed that the early church Fathers agreed about their doctrine of Christ. In the area of Trinitarian thought, each father had his own modes of expression and analogies with which he described the relations in the Godhead. Whether we investigate those pre-Nicene Fathers who were contemporary with one another, or whether we look at each generation of Fathers as they succeed one another, we will see that they differed in the detail of their doctrine. Scholars of the period tend to think of the Fathers as belonging to particular schools of thought depending on the geographical area of the church to which they belonged.
[2] By 'orthodox' doctrine I do not mean to imply that there were those in the first centuries of the Christian era who were orthodox and faithful to the apostles' doctrine. I intend to refer only to that grouping of the church that achieved the majority position towards the end of the fourth century. It was an historical 'accident' that the doctrine of the Trinity achieved its majority status. For times during the late third and early fourth centuries, Arianism was the 'orthodox' view.

which case an Arian doctrine is required.[1] The church chose the Trinitarian option, but we should not allow the basic premise - that Jesus Christ had some manner of personal existence before his birth of the Virgin Mary as the Son. Some examples of this development of doctrine will now show how the early church Fathers used the NT 'pre-existence' texts.

Ignatius (c. 112 CE) in his letter to the Magnesians remarks, 'Jesus Christ who was with the Father before the worlds and appeared at the end of time' (*Mag.* 6.1). To the Ephesians he comments, 'There is only one physician, of flesh and spirit, generate and ingenerate, God in man, true life in death, Son of Mary and Son of God, first passable and then impassable, Jesus Christ our Lord' and '...when God appeared in the likeness of man' (*Eph.* 7.2, 19.3).[2]

> **Comment:** These fragments do not particularly tell us anything about Ignatius' thinking, but he is often cited as an early example of 'orthodox' thinking. The problem with the apostolic Fathers is that their comments are not systematic, and it is difficult to know what their views were on the relationship of the Father to the Son. It's not clear by any means whether they were all pulling in the same direction. One patristic scholar, J. N. D. Kelly, observes, 'The evidence to be collected from the Apostolic Fathers is meagre, and tantalizingly inconclusive'.[3] Nevertheless, it is clear from reading their writings that the pre-existence of Christ has been admitted into the framework of their thought.[4]

Justin Martyr (c. 155 CE) in his *Apology* and in his *Dialogues with Trypho* develops a sophisticated pre-existence doctrine. He is an outstanding example of an Apologist who tries to frame an intellectually satisfying

---

[1] I suggest the Arian alternative is *inferior* to the Trinitarian position, although both are equally wrong. The inferiority stems from the requirement that Arians explain what is special about the *beginning of time* that required the Son of God to be created at that point.

[2] These letters are reprinted in R. Harmer, ed., *The Apostolic Fathers* (London: Macmillan, 1926).

[3] J. N. D. Kelly, *Early Christian Doctrines* (London: A & C Black, 1977), 95.

[4] Of course, we do not know very much about the period immediately after AD70. The writings that have survived may be unrepresentative of the general thinking of the church. They may be writings that have survived because they were useful for the later church to retain.

explanation of the relation of Christ to God, and he does this by using Hellenistic[1] concepts to systematize the doctrine of Christ. He begins, like the other Apologists, with the idea of the pre-existent Word as the thought or mind of the Father. The Biblical starting point for him is therefore the prologue of John. But he develops the idea beyond that of personification to assert that the Word was distinct from the Father, and as the first begotten of all creatures, 'he is adorable, he is God' (*Apol.* 62.4, *Dial.* 63.5). The main thrust of this doctrine was to systemize the relationship of God to the world.

> **Comment:** With the Apologists like Justin, the idea of the Word (Gk: *logos*) is greatly developed. It is this single development, more than any other, which lays down the intellectual foundations for later church Fathers to elaborate into a doctrine that 'preserves' (?) the unity of God along with the pre-existent status of Christ as the Word.[2]

Irenaeus (c. 180 CE), the first of the Pre-Nicene Fathers, in his work *Against Heresies*, III., xviii., comments on the prologue of John, 'Now it has been clearly demonstrated that the Word which exists from the beginning with God, by whom all things were made, who was also present with the race of men at all times, this Word has in these last times according to the time appointed by the Father, been united to his own workmanship and has been made passable man. Therefore we can set aside the objection of them that say, 'If he was born at that time it follows that Christ did not exist before then'. For we have shown that the Son of God did not then begin to exist since he existed with the Father always'.[3]

> **Comment:** The Christadelphian position (expressed by Irenaeus' contemporaries!) is set aside by Irenaeus in favour of a pre-existence view. He does this on the basis of his 'exposition' of John 1.

---

[1] Kelly comments, 'When we pass to the Apologists, the infiltration of secular thought is even more obvious', *Early Christian Doctrines*, 84; and see all of his Chapter 4 for details.

[2] For example, J. D. G. Dunn comments, '...Logos Christology served as a crucial phase in early Christianity's attempts to explain itself to *itself*...[it]...provided the bridge between the earliest Wisdom Christology of Paul and the subsequent Son Christology of the classic creeds.', *Christology in the Making* (London: SCM Press, 1980), 213.

[3] Bettenson, *Documents*, 42.

Tertullian (c. 200) in his *Apology*, xxi., says that, 'We also lay it down that the word and reason and virtue, by which we have said that God made all things have spirit as their substance...This Word, we have learnt, was produced from God, and was generated by being produced, and therefore is called the Son of God, and God, from unity of substance with God...This ray of God...glided down into a virgin, in her womb was fashioned as flesh, is born as man mixed with God.'[1]

> **Comment:** Tertullian,[2] an early church thinker of note, is here using John 1:1 and the idea that the Word was the Reason of God. From the statement that this Reason was begotten, he infers that Reason was a Son and of one substance with God - God of God, as other church writers would later put it. He also refers to Philippians 2 and the *fashioning* of the Word, along with an allusion to John 1:14.

Eusebius (c. 325 CE) at the council of Nicea suggested a creed which was modified by the council and has become known as the Nicene Creed:

> We believe in one God the Father All-sovereign, maker of all things visible and invisible; And in one Lord Jesus Christ, the Son of God, begotten of the Father, only begotten, that is, of the substance of the Father, God of God, Light of Light, true God of true God, begotten not made, of one substance with the Father, through whom all things were made, things in heaven and things on the earth; who for us men, and for our salvation came down and was made flesh, and became man...

And to the creed there are attached some anathemas, one of which affects the Christadelphian body:

> And those that say, 'There was when he was not' and, 'Before he was begotten he was not' and that, 'He came into being from what is not' or those that allege, that the son of God is 'Of another substance or essence', or 'created', or 'changeable', or 'alterable', these the Catholic and Apostolic church anathematizes.[3]

---

[1] Bettenson, *Documents*, 44.
[2] Tertullian is the first father to employ the term 'Trinity' in *Adv. Prax.* 3.
[3] Bettenson, *Documents*, 33-35.

The Nicene Creed was further ratified by councils in c.381 (Constantinople) and c. 451 CE (Chalcedon), with the creeds formulated by these councils addressing, respectively, the doctrine of the Holy Spirit and the two natures of Christ. The Nicene Creed is the most widely used creed amongst the churches of Christendom,[1] admitted as authoritative in both the East and Western halves of Christendom and reinforced by the Reformation churches. Christadelphians are anathematized by the creed, because they say, 'Before he was begotten, he was not'.

> **Comment**: The creed is an amalgam of some pre-existence texts: *came down* (John 3, 6), *was made flesh* (John 1:14), *through whom all things were made, things in heaven and things on earth* (Col 1:16), *only begotten* (John 1:18), and *became man* (Phil 2:6-8).

These examples (many other examples could be cited) from the early church Fathers are useful to illustrate one point: they invariably use some of the 'pre-existence' texts of the NT, with John 1 being the most popular.[2] If the exposition of these pre-existence passages is wrong, then the doctrine constructed upon their foundation will be severely undermined. Indeed, it is not too far-fetched to say that if John 1 had not been penned, then much of the early church's writing (particularly the Apologists) on the nature of Christ would not have been written.

The early church Fathers were men. They were generally the 'university' graduates of their day, no different from the graduates of this day. They were theologians and church leaders, again, no different from such leaders today. They might have made mistakes in their understanding of apostolic writings. They might have been influenced by Greco-Roman ideas about the gods, by the writings of Hellenistic Judaism or by the Rabbis. Each of them might have made mistakes and gone down blind alleys, but could they *all* have been mistaken?

This may have happened because of the **power of tradition**.[3] If the very first church Fathers made mistakes at the expositional level on the subject of Christ, and if these mistakes were embroidered as they developed their doctrine of Christ, then these mistakes could be perpetuated as the tradition of the church. Such mistakes would influence later thinkers to

---

[1] Kelly, *Early Christian Doctrines*, 296.

[2] R. P. C. Hanson, *The Search for the Christian Doctrine of God* (Edinburgh: T & T Clark, 1988), 834.

[3] See for example, Irenaeus, *Adv. Haereses*, III, reprinted in Bettenson, *Documents*, 96-7.

model their doctrine about Christ along the same lines, simply because they wanted to build on a tradition that they could ostensibly trace back to the apostles. This, I suggest, is what happened and the same mistake is perpetuated today: people like to be with a majority and a well-established tradition rather than with a small minority. In the final analysis, the doctrine of the Trinity is grounded on a set of exegetical mistakes.

4. Conclusion

If the early church Fathers held a pre-existence view of the NT witness, were they right? If they developed a Trinitarian doctrine from a pre-existence basis, was this a reasonable development? The early church Fathers read into the NT the ideas and doctrines of their times,[1] but putting this historical thesis to one side, does the NT actually present Christ as having had *some manner of existence* before his birth?

The issue for NT scholars has been whether a *real pre-existence* is to be found in the pages of the NT, or whether it is a post-apostolic and non-apostolic development of doctrine. In this enquiry, it is the fourth gospel that supplies most of the material sustaining a claim that Jesus was pre-existent. Scholars ask whether,

- The NT writers thought of Jesus himself as having some manner of existence in heaven before his birth.

- The NT writers thought of Jesus as the embodiment of a heavenly being.

- The NT writers thought of Jesus as the incarnation of God the Son, the second person of the Trinity.

- The NT writers thought of Jesus as the embodiment of the Wisdom of God and/or the Word of God, i.e. a hypostasized divine attribute.

In answering these questions, NT scholars observe that the NT writers were Jews and they seek to uncover the influences on their thought. Their approach is to investigate the titles of Jesus and other texts, seeking to uncover from them some insight into NT ways of thinking about Christ. It is to traditional topic of the 'Titles of Christ' that we now first turn.

---

[1] See Hanson, *The Search for the Christian Doctrine of God*, ch. 24.

48

CHAPTER FOUR
The Titles of Christ

1. Introduction

Titles often tell us about the *role* of an individual or something about the identity of the person. The Lord Jesus Christ has many titles, including such ones as 'Son of God', 'Son of Man', 'the Word of God', 'The First and the Last'. These titles encapsulate aspects of his identity as well as indicating a role. As such, they can be used in arguments for the pre-existence of Christ. We shall examine these titles in this chapter except for 'the Word of God' which we will look at in Chapter Nine, when we discuss the incarnation in John.

2. Son of God

This title of Christ could be regarded by some as synonymous with the creedal title, 'God the Son'. In the minds of some, to say that Jesus was the Son of God is tantamount to saying that he was God the Son, but this does not follow. In fact, the biblical idea of Christ's sonship is far more down to earth. The creedal expressions of the Trinity describe sonship in philosophical[1] phrases like, *of the substance of the Father, God of God, true God of true God, begotten not made*, and *begotten of the Father before all ages*.[2] But the sense of sonship that Jesus had was more personal, a relationship between two demonstrable *individuals*[3] that began at a certain point in time. It is not clear how this relationship could have come about had Jesus been an incarnation of God the Son.

The NT basis of the title is supplied by Luke. Gabriel's address to Mary was that 'the power of the Highest shall overshadow you, *therefore* that holy thing which shall be born of thee shall be called the Son of God'

---

[1] A recent philosophical treatment of the Trinity is R. Swinburne, *The Christian God* (Oxford: Oxford University Press, 1994).

[2] J. N. D. Kelly, *Early Christian Creeds* (London: Longman, 1972), 215, 297.

[3] The doctrine of the Trinity proposes that the *persons* of the Godhead should not be thought of in demonstrable individualistic terms as three Gods. However, does this strategy work during the period that begins with the incarnation and extends until the end of the millennium? During this *time*, there would appear to be two different individuals, God the Father and the Son of God, acting in separate spheres and in concert together. How does the doctrine that there is *one* God remain intact during this period?

(Luke 1:35; cf. Matt 1:20-21). The reasoning could not be clearer: Jesus is the Son of God in virtue of his divine begettal at a certain point in time. The opposing idea, that he is the Son of God because he is the incarnation of God the Son, the incarnation of a person eternally begotten by the Father, is absent from the birth narratives.[1]

Jesus had an intimate relationship with his father (John 1:18), and this is seen in his use of the Aramaic term of endearment, *Abba,* and in his reference to God as *my Father* (e.g. John 20:17). He had a sense of sonship which matches our own sense of sonship in respect of our earthly Fathers. The use of *Abba* fits the view that Jesus knew himself to be the only *begotten* son of a Father in heaven, a beloved son looking to a Father for support and love in his life (Mark 14:36; cf. Luke 11:2 (R.V.); Rom 8:15; Gal 4:6). But Trinitarianism places the *begettal* of God the Son onto a metaphysical and timeless plane. It does not regard the *birth* of Jesus as **the** begettal of God the Son, but rather the *incarnation* of God the Son (cf. 1 John 4:9). However, the idea of *begettal* has to do with human birth,[2] and it seems natural to follow the reasoning in Matthew's Gospel, which says 'that which is begotten in her is by the holy Spirit' (Matt 1:20). The Trinitarian proposal of an *eternal begettal* elevates the natural process of human begettal to an eternal timeless level, and it's not certain that the language can be stretched in this way (i.e. there is no way to cash out the analogy).[3]

---

[1] The creedal understanding of eternal begettal is that this is a way of describing the metaphysical relationship between God the Father and God the Son. There is no begettal in the sense that humans understand the term. Human begettal is only an analogy on this relationship in the Godhead. By contrast Christadelphians argue that the Son of God was begotten at a specific point in time according to the Scriptures.

[2] Jesus was born of Mary, and he would have been told of his divine begettal by Mary. As a result he believed himself to be the Son of God, but this was still a matter of faith, as we see in his temptations.

[3] One of the main texts used by the early church Fathers to support the idea of eternal begettal was Isaiah 53:8 – "...who shall declare his generation?" (Hanson, *The Search for the Christian Doctrine of God,* 833). But this text has to do with *children,* and in the first instance, Hezekiah's lack of a child when he fell sick. Another text used in the same vein by orthodox commentators is "...without father without mother..." (Heb 7:3), but this is a *typological* application of the lack of parental information in Genesis about Melchizedek. Jesus is being placed into the middle of Melchizedek's encounter with Abraham. The point about Melchizedek having no parents

Obedience is a key idea of sonship. It was integral to Israel's sonship. Israel was the firstborn of God, called out of Egypt (Exod 4:22; Hos 11:1). At his call, Israel made a promise to obey God (Exod 24:7; cf. 4:23). Likewise, Jesus *learned* obedience through the things he suffered (Heb 5:8), and he is declared to be the beloved Son in whom the Father was well pleased. Trinitarian theology often caters for this feature of Christ's life by proposing that in the incarnation, God the Son emptied himself in such a way that He was able to assume a full human life. This requires that the divine attributes be laid aside in some way, but it's not clear that this is *logically possible*. Neither is it clear whether the doctrine of the unity of God can be preserved as soon as we place the persons of the Godhead in different spheres.

We conclude therefore that there is very little mileage in arguments for the pre-existence of Christ that revolve around the title 'Son of God'. A

3. The Wisdom of God

The pre-existence claim surrounding this title is that Christ is the incarnation of the pre-existent Wisdom of God. The argument is based on comparisons between the NT and Jewish and Greek thought about divine wisdom. This thinking personified the wisdom of God and presented Wisdom as a figure alongside God. The argument is that since Jesus is presented in similar language, the apostles would have understood him to have been pre-existent in the same way. What is the evidence for this claim?

In the apocryphal books, Wisdom of Solomon (6:12-11:1), Sirach (24, 51) and Baruch (3:9-4:4), wisdom is personified as a heavenly figure.[1] Wisdom was created before the beginning of the world and made her tabernacle in Israel. Wisdom was the 'maker of all things' and she plays a part in the salvation of men; see Figure 1. Some commentators have proposed that the early Christians thought of Christ pre-existing as the Wisdom of God.[2]

---

is that he contrasts with the Levitical priesthood which was ordered on parental principles; Jesus' priesthood has no parentage.

[1] For the sake of simplicity, we are not offering a discussion of the view that Wisdom is a hypostasis (linguistic or attributive) in Jewish thought.

[2] Paul (1 Cor 1:24, 2:7-8) means that Christ *represents* the wisdom of God, which had been hidden in a mystery before the world, unknown to the princes of that world. Hence, *wisdom* in Paul's thought has to do with a *purpose* rather than a divine figure. As Paul argues, Christ was *made* wisdom

In order to evaluate this argument, we need to decide whether the NT writers use similar language because they *agree* with Jewish or Greek thought, or whether they use similar language in order to express their competing beliefs. I would argue that this latter possibility is in fact the case. If we examine the parallels between the apocryphal Wisdom and Christ, there are several significant differences:

- Wisdom is female, but Christ is male.

- Wisdom is a personification[1] but Christ on earth was a man.

- Wisdom is not a 'god' that is worshipped in Judaism.[2]

- Wisdom is the 'agent' in the Genesis creation, but Christ is the agent in the new creation.

- Wisdom is also spoken of in terms that go against the idea of a heavenly being.

A full examination of the Wisdom literature is not within the scope of this book. But such a study reveals that the Jewish writers used a variety of images, pictures, similes, and metaphors when talking of Wisdom. And alongside such thought, they also wrote of God as the creator and orchestrator of all things. It is doubtful whether the Jews were presenting a view of God that embraced a subordinate heavenly being called Wisdom. One recent scholar observes,

> On the contrary, for a Jew to say that Wisdom 'effects all things', that Wisdom 'delivered Israel from a nation of oppressors', that 'love of Wisdom is the keeping of her laws' (Wisd 8.5; 10.15; 6.18), was simply to say in a more picturesque way that God created all things wisely, that God's wise purpose is clearly evident in the exodus from

---

at a certain point in time, the same time span in which he was made righteousness, sanctification, and redemption (1 Cor 1:30).

[1] Other examples of personifying language include Pss 43:3, 57:3, 85:10f, 96:6.

[2] This is the key point: the Jews were monotheists. Their personification of wisdom in Proverbs, or in the Jewish inter-testamental writings did not compromise their belief in one God.

Egypt and most fully expressed in the law he gave through Moses.[1]

In addition to this, a detailed comparison between the Wisdom literature and the NT parallels shows significant differences in thought. This comes to light when we start to take into account the OT background to the NT, as we will see in later chapters.

A comparison of the 'parallels' between the NT and the Wisdom literature shows what ideas the apostles had to combat. Some of these are set out in Figure 1. These parallels do not show a similarity of theme, but an application of similar language in different contexts. The descriptions of Christ place him as a creator of the new creation, whereas Wisdom is an 'agent' of the old creation.

Wisdom Literature	"From eternity, <u>in the beginning</u>, he created me, and for eternity I shall not cease to exist." Sir 24:9
New Testament	"In <u>the beginning</u> was the Word, and the Word was with God..." John 1:1
Old Testament	"The Lord possessed me in the <u>beginning</u> of his way, before his works of old." Prov 8:22

Wisdom Literature	"<u>With thee</u> is wisdom, who knows thy works and was present <u>when thou didst make the world</u>..." Wisd 9:9
New Testament	"...by whom also he <u>made the worlds</u>..." Heb 1:2
Old Testament	"The Lord by wisdom hath <u>founded the earth</u>..." Prov 3:19

Wisdom Literature	"...the one who created me assigned a place for my <u>tent</u>. And he said, make your <u>dwelling</u> in Jacob, and in Israel receive your inheritance." Sir 24:8
New Testament	"And the Word was made flesh, and <u>dwelt</u> (tabernacled) among us..." John 1:14

---

[1] Dunn, *Christology in the Making*, 174.

Wisdom Literature	"For she is an initiate in the knowledge of God, and an <u>associate in his works</u>. If riches are a desirable possession in life, what is richer than wisdom <u>who effects all things?</u> And if understanding is effective, who more than she is <u>fashioner of what exists?</u>" Wisd 8:4-6 "...and by his word all things hold together." Sir 43:26
New Testament	"<u>All things were made by him</u>; and without him was not anything made that was made." John 1:3

Wisdom Literature	"for wisdom, the fashioner of all things... all-powerful, overseeing all, and penetrating through all ...things. For she is a <u>breath of the power of God</u>, and a pure emanation of the glory of the Almighty..." Wisd 7:22-26
Old Testament	"By the word of the Lord were the heavens made; and all the host of them by the breath of his mouth." Ps 33:6

Wisdom Literature	"<u>Send her forth</u> from the holy heavens, and from the throne of thy glory send her, that she may be with me and toil..." Wisd 9:10
New Testament	"For <u>he whom God hath sent</u> speaketh the words of God: for [to him] God giveth not the Spirit by measure." John 3:34

Wisdom Literature	"For she is a <u>reflection</u> (brightness) of eternal light, a spotless <u>mirror</u> of the working of God, and an <u>image of his goodness</u>." Wisd 7:26
New Testament	"Who being the <u>brightness</u> of [his] glory..." Heb 1:3 "Who is the <u>image</u> of the invisible God..." Col 1:15 "...beholding as in a <u>mirror</u> the glory of the Lord, are changed into the same..." 2 Cor 3:18

Wisdom Literature	"Wisdom went forth to make her dwelling among the children of men, and <u>found no</u> dwelling place" 1 Enoch 42:2
New Testament	"He came to his own, and <u>his own received</u> him not." John 1:11

Wisdom Literature	"Who has gone up into heaven, and taken her, and brought her down from the clouds? Who has gone over the sea, and found her, and will buy her for pure gold?" Bar 3:29-30
New Testament	"Say not in thy heart, who shall ascend into heaven? (that is, to bring Christ down:) Or, who shall descend into the deep? (that is, to bring Christ again from the dead.)" Rom 10:6-7
Old Testament	"It [is] not in heaven, that thou shouldest say, Who shall ascend for us to heaven, and bring it to us...Neither [is] it beyond the sea, that thou shouldest say, Who shall go over the sea for us, and bring it to us...?" Deut 30:12-13

Wisdom Literature	"<u>Draw near to me</u>, you who are untaught... Put your neck <u>under the yoke</u>, and let your <u>souls</u> receive instruction; it is to be found close by. See with your eyes that I have <u>laboured little</u> and <u>found</u> myself much <u>rest</u>." Sir 51:23-7
New Testament	"<u>Come to me</u>, all [ye] that labour and are heavy laden, and I will give you rest. Take <u>my yoke</u> upon you and In view of (1)-(5), we reject the views, a) that 'the Word' is used in v. 1 as or for a linguistic or attributive hypostatization; b) that 'the Word' is a heavenly being; and c) that 'the Word' is pre-existent. Rather, Jesus is the one who now gives effect to God's word and is that very ongoing Word of Life. Jesus had the words of eternal life (John 6:62, 68); these words were given to him by his Father (John 12:44-50); and so, the word of God abode in him (John 5:38). To repeat, the intertext of 1 John 1:1-3 is particularly clear: learn from me; for I am meek and lowly in heart:

55

	and ye shall <u>find rest</u> to your <u>souls</u>. For <u>my yoke</u> [is] easy, and my burden is light." Matt 11:28-30
Old Testament	<u>Come, eat of my bread</u>, and <u>drink</u> of the wine [which] I have mixed." Prov 9:5 "More to be desired [are they] than gold, yea, than much fine gold: <u>sweeter also than honey</u> and the honeycomb." Ps 19:10

Wisdom Literature	"<u>Come to me</u>, you who desire me, and <u>eat your fill of my produce</u>. For the remembrance of me is sweeter than honey, and my inheritance <u>sweeter than the honeycomb</u>. Those who eat me will hunger for more, and those who <u>drink me</u> will thirst for more." Sir 24:19-21
New Testament	"I say to you, except ye <u>eat</u> the flesh of the Son of man, and <u>drink</u> his blood, ye have no life in you." John 6:63 "But whoever drinketh of the water that I shall give him shall never thirst..." John 4:14

If there is a relationship between this Wisdom theology and the NT doctrine of Christ, then it is one of contrast rather than of comparison. The apostles are redeploying some common concepts to elaborate the doctrine of Christ in opposition to contemporary thinking.

4. The First and the Last

This title is used by Christ in the book of Revelation when he says, 'I am Alpha and Omega, the First and the Last: and, what thou seest, write in a book, and send [it] to the seven churches which are in Asia; to Ephesus, and to Smyrna, and to Pergamos, and to Thyatira, and to Sardis, and to Philadelphia, and to Laodicea' (Rev 1:11; cf. 1:17; 2:8). The basis of the title is to be found in Isaiah and in prophecies where the Lord says,

> Who hath wrought and done [it], calling the generations from the beginning? <u>I the Lord, the First, and with the last ones; I [am] he</u>. Isa 41:4 (KJV revised); cf. 44:6; 48:12

The theme behind the title is twofold: Yahweh's foreknowledge of the future and his control of the future. He challenges the gods of the nations (Isa 41:23) to show the things that would be hereafter so that they may be known to be true gods. But, in fact, they cannot declare the end from the beginning; only Yahweh can do this (Isa 41:26), because he is in control. Hence, he is 'the First and with the last ones.' The sense of this title is the same as saying God is the one who knows the end from the beginning, and he is the one who controls the future.[1]

The background to this response of God is the challenge of Babylonian religious beliefs and the associated idols. With this background, we can understand Christ's use of the title, 'the First and the Last'. Christ had said to his disciples, 'of that day and hour no one knoweth, no [man], no, not the angels of heaven, but my Father only' (Matt 24:36). He had also said to them, 'It is not for you to know the times or the seasons, which the Father hath put in his own power' (Acts 1:7). Such statements as these are consistent with the testimony of Yahweh through Isaiah, 'And who, as I, shall declare it, and set it in order for me...?' (Isa 44:6). But these statements raise the question of Christ's *own* knowledge of the future.

The question is resolved in Revelation, where we read, 'The Revelation of Jesus Christ, which *God gave unto him*, to show unto his servants things which must shortly come to pass' (Rev 1:1). This is a book of prophecy *given by the Father* to his son. This makes the Son like his father in one respect: he can declare the end from the beginning. Besides this, all power and authority has been given to the Son (Matt 28:18), and therefore he can declare not only the end from the beginning, but also direct and control affairs to that end. This makes the Son like the Father in a second respect. Because Christ has been given the revelation of the end, and because he is in control of affairs, he also carries the title 'the First and the Last'.

5. The Angel of the Lord

An ancient proposal is that the Angel of the Lord in the OT is the Son of God (e.g. Justin Martyr, *Dialogues with Trypho*, 56.4,10, 58.3, 59.1, 61.1, 128.1). This 'angel' appeared to Hagar (Gen 16:7-12) and to Moses (Exod 3:2). Other passages cited to show the pre-existence of the Son include Abraham's encounter with the three angels (Genesis 18) and Jacob's encounter with the angel at Bethel (Genesis 32).

The problem with such arguments is that the OT gives *no indication* that the beings involved are anything other than angels. Further, in Jewish OT interpretation of these passages there is no indication that they read them in this way. In general angels are viewed as agents of God in both the OT

---

[1] A contrasting analogy can be made with our idiomatic saying, 'he is the *be all and end all* of the...', because we use this saying in many situations where one person thinks he is the main individual.

literature (Ps 103:20) and in Jewish inter-testamental writings. Moreover, the NT writers always place the exalted Christ above the angels (Phil 2:9-11; Heb 1:5). This is to avoid the assumption that he had been exalted to angelic status.

One NT passage is used in this argument. Paul explains a type surrounding Moses and the Angel of the Lord, when he received the Law (2 Cor 3:7ff). Moses' ministry was a ministration of death, even though the Israelites could not behold the face of Moses because of its glory. Consequently, Moses put a veil over his face, thus signifying the unbelief of the nation. Paul states that only when the nation turns to Christ, the Lord (v. 16), will the veil be taken away. In this context, Paul equates 'the Lord' with 'the Spirit' (v. 17) and some argue that he is equating Christ with the Angel of the Presence. But, if so, the equation Paul makes is one of typology, so that the Angel of the Presence is typical of Christ rather than actually being the person of the Son.

6. The Son of Man

This title has been understood by early church theologians to indicate Christ's humanity *and* his divinity. Ignatius of Antioch comments, "Jesus Christ, who after the flesh was of the family of David, Son of Man and Son of God". [1]

Whatever theological use is made of this title, the *biblical* question is whether the Son of Man in Daniel's prophecy was a heavenly being in existence in Daniel's time, and identifiable as Jesus Christ when on earth; this is the pre-existence argument.

The correspondence between Daniel's vision and Jesus' own prophecies establish Jesus as Daniel's 'Son of Man':[2]

> I saw in the night visions, and, behold, [one] like the <u>Son of man came with the clouds of heaven</u>, and came to the Ancient of Days, and they brought him near before him. Dan 7:13 (KJV)

> And then shall appear the sign of the Son of man in heaven: and then shall all the tribes of the earth mourn, and they

---

[1] *Epistle to the Ephesians*, 1.20, repr. in Harmer, *Apostolic Fathers*, 142.
[2] See Dunn, Christology in the Making, 65-67. T. Gaston, "The Son of Man" *CeJBI* (Oct 2007): 3-17.

shall see the <u>Son of man coming in the clouds of heaven</u> with power and great glory. Matt 24:30 (KJV)

Jesus saith to him, 'Thou hast said: nevertheless I say to you, after this shall ye see the <u>Son of man</u> sitting on the right hand of power and <u>coming in the clouds of heaven</u>'. Matt 26:64 (KJV)[1]

However, the focus of these prophecies (and others with the title 'Son of Man') is the future establishment of the kingdom. Daniel shows the timing of this kingdom to be the days of the ten horns (cf. Dan 2:44). There is then no *pre-existence* argument in Daniel. Outside Scripture, in Jewish apocalyptic literature of the period, the title 'Son of Man' is found in pre-existence contexts, for example, the *Similitudes of Enoch*, but it is not certain that this literature pre-dates the NT writings (cf. John 12:34), or if it does, that it is an influence on the NT writers.

7. Conclusion

The titles of Christ are used sometimes to establish the pre-existence of Christ. The general methodology is to relate these titles to contemporary Second-Temple writings which embrace a heavenly existence for the bearers of the titles. However, in each case the NT writers are using the titles differently for their own purposes and these compete with Second-Temple texts. The main battleground for deciding whether Christ pre-existed is whether we see the competing differences of the New Testament.

Endnotes

A. Jesus Christ was the Son of God as well as Son of Man - does this fact make him both God and Man? The Trinitarian argument is that because he was born of God as well as of Mary, he must have had two natures. However, there is no necessary implication in this argument. The possession of two natures, so to speak, is only one possibility out of three: some theologians (now deemed heretical) in the early centuries of the church equally proposed that Jesus had just a divine nature, and others took the opposite view - that he had just a human nature.

Jesus was born of God, born of the Spirit, and that which is born of spirit is spirit. In this process, he was not unique, although his begettal by the holy Spirit was unique. The disciples of Christ are also born of spirit (John 1:12-13, cf. 3:6). This birth of the Spirit is a birth 'from above', and

---

[1] See also Matt 19:28; Mark 13:26; 14:62; Acts 7:56; Rev 1:7, 13; 14:14.

it is contrasted with being 'of the earth' (John 3:6-7, 31). The contrast with being 'of the earth' shows that to be 'of the Spirit' is to have certain *mental dispositions* (1 Cor 15:48, Phil 3:19, Jms 3:15).

As regards his physical nature, Jesus was a man - this was his biological (heart, lungs, brain, etc.) nature. This partly settles the question of his manhood. Can he have been God as well? We do not know the 'physical' nature of God, even if we thought that the word 'physical' was appropriate (John 4:24). Nevertheless, he cannot have shared God's nature on earth, since God is eternal (Heb 9:24) and Jesus was mortal (Rom 6:9). This leaves the *mental life* of Jesus Christ (I speak as a man).

God the Father has thoughts as indeed we do (Isa 55:9); He has emotions, as indeed we do (1 John 4:8); He has attitudes, as we do (Exod 34:6-7); He has a Will as we do (Mal 3:6); He has knowledge and understanding (Ps 39:6), as we do; He forms intentions and purposes (Isa 45:18-23), as we do; He reasons as we do (Isa 1:18); He observes and hears, as we do (Ps 94:9); *and so on.*

In all these aspects of *mental life*,[1] God the Father is not bound by human limitations. Nevertheless, we share these qualities with the Father as we are in His image. With regard to Jesus, his powers surpassed ordinary men, however he was limited in his knowledge (Mark 13:32), and he ascribed his powers to his father (John 5:30). Furthermore, as with other men, he was tempted, although without sin (Heb 4:15), and we know God the Father cannot be tempted (Jms 1:13).

It would seem then that the mental life of Jesus showed greater capacities and abilities than ordinary men. As a result, he manifested the character of his father (John 14:9). But his mental life was not different *in kind* to the mental life of men. As regards the *nature* of Jesus Christ then, there doesn't appear to be a basis for saying that he possessed the *nature* of God the Father in respect of the *nature* of his mental life any more than we do, even though the *content* of his mental life was vastly superior to our own, reflecting that of his father. Furthermore, the sinless perfection of Christ, whilst reflecting the character of his father, was developed in a mental environment where there was temptation. It seems then that Trinitarians get it wrong when they talk of the two natures of Christ. Instead, what we have is an earthly vessel and a heavenly character - the red and the fine-twined linen of the veil.

---

[1] For a resume of the mind, see A. Kenny, *The Metaphysics of Mind* (Oxford: Oxford University Press, 1992).

Prior to the fall, Adam was as much a man as he was after the fall, although differences had occurred. Similarly, Jesus was a man, although no ordinary man. In order for him to live a life of perfect obedience and manifest the sinless glory of his father, he was made strong. This strengthening was necessary to provide a counterweight to the sin-proneness which was part of his nature as a man. This counterweight equalised the testing environment for Jesus to the same extent that it was equal for Adam prior to the fall. It is too simplistic, not to say false, to argue that God the Father begat a God in Jesus Christ, because Jesus was a man, and *this* is what God the Father chose to begat. In any event, Trinitarian theology elaborates the view that the *person* of God the Son became incarnate in Jesus Christ. That this is a fiction is clearly seen in the disparity between the Trinitarian language of the early church Fathers and the language of the Bible.

CHAPTER FIVE
The Divine Name

1. Introduction

The interpretation of the Hebrew *'ehyeh 'asher 'ehyeh* ('I AM that I AM', KJV, Douay, JPS, etc.) has been the subject of contrary opinion in journal articles and commentaries in the latter half of the twentieth century with some scholars opting for a meaning something like "I AM the one who is/exists" (or "I AM he who is/exists"); this proposal is known as the "existential reading" as it sees the significance of the assertion in terms of God's being or existence. The proposal has been most fully defended in Hebrew philological scholarship in the 1954 article of E. Schild, "On Exodus iii 14 — 'I AM that I AM'".[1]

As a proposal for the translation of the Hebrew of Exod 3:14, it is supported in the LXX rendering ("And God spoke to Moses, saying, I am the Being [*'ehyeh 'asher 'ehyeh* translated by egō eimi ho ōn]; and He said, Thus you shall say to the children of Israel: The Being has sent me unto you": Brenton, 1851), and so it is quite an old idea.[2]

As a proposal in Hebrew grammar, however, it was refuted by B. Albrektson in his 1968 article "On the Syntax of *'ehyeh 'asher 'ehyeh* in Exodus 3:14".[3] Nevertheless, the theological proposal that the assertion has something to do with God's existence or being continues to dominate scholarship looking for coherence in Exodus 3. Most translations retain 'I AM that/who I AM' (KJV, RV, RSV, NIV, NASB, and ESV); some include a marginal note offering 'I will be that/who/what I will be' (RV, RSV, NEB, NIV, and ESV). For a Bible student without Hebrew, this weight of supporting testimony is significant. The only question that s/he faces is whether to read the verb as a present "I AM" or a future "I will be", or perhaps juggle both in their mind.

---

[1] E. Schild, "On Exodus iii 14 — 'I am that I am'" *VT* 4 (1954): 296-302.

[2] Philo, *Life of Moses*, 1.75; from C. D. Yonge, *The Works of Philo* (Peabody: Hendrickson, 1997).

[3] B. Albrektson, "On the Syntax of *'ehyeh 'asher 'ehyeh* in Exodus 3:14" in *Words and Meanings* (eds., P. R. Ackroyd and B. Lindars; Cambridge: Cambridge University Press, 1968), 15-28. At SOTS 2007, I spoke to Albrektson and ascertained that the views expressed in his article had remained the same over the years.

The purpose of this chapter is to consider the correct translation. The problem with this task is that the philology of the expression has been carried out by commentators with an eye on the theology of the expression, and this has influenced what they have said about the syntax and linguistics. An obvious illustration of this would be the curious capitalization, 'I AM', which the translators do not follow for the verb elsewhere. The two jobs—linguistics and theology—can and ought to be separated. We should consider the grammar before we look at its broader theological significance, and in this chapter, we will restrict our theological discussion to the most famous NT text with 'I am' – John 8:58.

2. Description and Pattern

On a syntactic level, philology is the study of patterns in sentences and an observed pattern is abstracted and turned into a rule of grammar. The construction *'ehyeh 'asher 'ehyeh* is one that is comprised of a verbal form, *'ehyeh*, with an embedded (prefixed) pronominal element, and a relative clause with the same verbal form and the relative expression *'asher*. The main clause contains no explicit noun or pronoun, and is not, as such, a nominal clause; likewise, the relative clause does not contain a nominal expression.

The above description of Exod 3:14a ("And God said unto Moses, I AM THAT I AM", KJV) is unexceptionable and the question that concerns us is: what else might we say about the construction? While accepting the theoretical possibility of alternative systems of grammar, grammatical description within the discipline of Hebrew Philology seeks to be simple and straightforward and simply a matter of observing patterns of usage. We will start our analysis with two uncontroversial patterns about *'asher*.

Pattern 1

The classic reference Hebrew grammar, Gesenius-Kautzsch (GKC),[1] identifies **dependent relative clauses** and separates main clauses where the governing substantive (e.g. a noun in the main clause) is the subject of the relative clause from those where the governing substantive is the object of the relative clause. Such clauses stand subordinate to the main clause and attribute a quality, state or verbal idea to the main clause.[2]

---

[1] W. Gesenius, *Hebrew Grammar* (ed. E. Kautzsch; trans. A. E. Cowley; 2nd ed.; Oxford: Oxford University Press, 1910); hereafter, GKC.
[2] B. T. Arnold and J. H. Choi, *A Guide to Biblical Hebrew Syntax* (Cambridge: Cambridge University Press), 184.

1) Examples where the governing substantive is the subject of the relative clause:

> ...the water <u>which</u> (*'asher*) was below the firmament... Gen 1:7 (KJV)

This statement has two clauses and it is clear that the subject of the main clause "the water" is the subject of the relative clause.

2) Examples where the governing substantive is the object of the relative clause:

> And on the seventh day God ended his work <u>which</u> (*'asher*) he had made; and he rested on the seventh day from all his work <u>which</u> (*'asher*) he had made. Gen 2:2 (KJV)

This statement has two sentences each with a main clause and a relative clause dependent on the main clause; each sentence relates a noun/object 'work' to a verbal form 'he had made'.

The above subject/object distinction is one pattern of usage for *'asher*; it is not controversial or difficult. It is simply that *'asher* can relate two clauses in a relationship of dependency and the governing substantive may be implied or stated in the subject or object position of the relative clause. We might add that where the governing substantive is a person, *'asher* might be translated as 'whom' as in 'the woman whom thou has placed with me' (Gen 3:12); likewise, if the governing substantive is about a place, *'asher* might be translated 'where', *and so on*.

Pattern 2
Another pattern is one where there is a pronoun implied or stated in the subordinate clause, for example,

> Every moving thing where <u>it</u> (is) alive (*'asher hu' hay*) shall be meat for you; even as the green herb have I given you all things. Gen 9:3 (KJV revised)

We have revised the KJV here to indicate where the pronoun 'it' is in the Hebrew, which brings out its "subject" role. GKC notes that the pronoun is more often present in subordinate negative clauses.[1] Schild observes that it is this feature—the use of a retrospective or resumptive pronoun

---

[1] GKC, 138.

that shows *'asher* itself is not a pronoun.[1] Notice in Gen 9:3 the translators have translated *'asher* as 'where' following the lead of the verb in the relative clause, which indicates a circumstantial qualification of every moving thing—where they are alive.

GKC constructs the rule that for *'asher* constructions, "...if the governing substantive forms part of a statement made in the first or second person, the retrospective pronoun (or the subject of the appositional clause) is in the same person".[2] A typical example would be:

> I *am* the Lord <u>that</u> (*'asher*) brought thee out of Ur of the Chaldees
> Gen 15:7 (KJV)

Here, after the *'asher*, the verbal form for 'brought' is in the first person to agree with the substantive main clause, 'I (am) the Lord'. This rule (the rule of concord) is perhaps trivial, but it is nevertheless a pattern of Hebrew usage. Notice here that the translators have translated *'asher* as 'that' because they see a stress on the fact of "the bringing out of Ur" in the assertion.

Schild qualifies GKC by observing that the agreeing retrospective pronoun need *not* be the subject of the appositional clause. For example, take Gen 45:4:

> I am Joseph <u>whom</u> (*'asher*) you sold me Gen 15,4 (KJV revised)

Schild observes[3] that the implied subject of the relative clause in Gen 45:4 is "the brothers" and the Hebrew is a verbal form of the second person, 'you sold'. The relative clause has a first-person pronoun 'me' which picks up the first-person reference of the main clause, 'I AM Joseph', but the 'me' is in the object position. GKC therefore needs to be modified so that it no longer stipulates that the retrospective pronoun is the subject of the appositional clause (i.e. the bracketed qualification needs to be removed). Hence, Schild proposes a revision to GKC: "If the governing substantive is the subject of a relative clause and is, in the main clause, equated with, or defined as, a personal pronoun, then the predicate of the relative clause agrees with that personal pronoun".[4]

---

[1] Schild, "On Exodus iii 14 — 'I am that I am'" 297.
[2] GKC, 138d.
[3] Schild, "On Exodus iii 14 — 'I am that I am'", 298.
[4] Schild, "On Exodus iii 14 — 'I am that I am'", 298.

Pattern 3

The first two patterns describe dependent relative clauses. We can see that supplementary information is given in the subordinate clause about the subject of the main clause. Another pattern, the *idem per idem* pattern, has instead a focus on *'asher*.[1] There are several examples of this idiom in the Hebrew Bible:

1 Sam 23:13
...[they] went withersoever (*ba'asher*) they went (KJV revised)

2 Sam 15:20
I (am) going where (*'asher*) I (am) going (KJV revised)

Exod 33:19
I will be gracious to whom (*eth 'asher*) I will be gracious (KJV revised)

This pattern repeats the verb on either side of *'asher* and with the same person (1st, 2nd, 3rd person). The statement as a whole is indefinite and the focus is on the relative word *'asher*. This will be translated according to the sense that best fits the verb either side of *'asher* (going/where; being compassionate/whom, etc.). This pattern, unlike the first two patterns, is not about further delimiting a governing substantive (e.g. a noun) in the main clause; rather the pattern involves an **independent relative clause** insofar as the verbs on either side of *'asher* are distinct statements and the two statements are related by *'asher*. As a further illustration of the distinctiveness of this pattern, we can compare Exod 3:14a with 1 Chron 21:17.

1 Chron 21:17

I (am) he (*'ani hu'*) who (*'asher*) has sinned and done very wickedly (NASB revised)

Exod 3:14a

I AM (*'ehyeh*) that (*'asher*) I AM (KJV)

In Chronicles, we have a personal pronoun 'I' coupled with another personal pronoun 'he' in what is a common pattern 'I-he'; translators read this as a simple copula pattern 'I am he'. As Albrektson observes,[2] the pronoun 'I' (*'ani*) serves as a kind of antecedent which governs the verb of

---

[1] Arnold and Choi, *A Guide to Biblical Hebrew Syntax*, 185-186.
[2] Albrektson, "On the Syntax of *'ehyeh 'asher 'ehyeh* in Exodus 3:14", 21, 23.

the relative clause; Exod 3:14a has no such element, being just a first-person verbal form.

In the Chronicles example, *'ani hu'* is a nominal clause with a verbal subordinate clause (predicate). Albrektson's observation is that in Hebrew where the main clause is a nominal clause, and the subordinate clause is a predicate, the antecedent has an explicit noun or pronoun and not just a pronominal concept embedded in a verbal form;[1] accordingly, Exod 3:14a is not part of this pattern whereas 1 Chron 21:17 is part of this pattern.

Schild proposed 'I am the one who is' as the translation for Exod 3:14a and this makes the relative clause into a predicate. In such a case, the patterns of use in Hebrew would lead us to expect a noun or pronoun in the main clause, but we do not have either element. Accordingly, Schild is wrong[2] and the best pattern for understanding Exod 3:14a is the conventional *idem per idem* pattern. This is why B. S. Childs states in his commentary on Exodus, "Schild's denial of the circular *idem per idem* construction is not convincing".[3]

An attempt to rescue Schild has been made by D. J. McCarthy. He concedes that "Albrektson may be right in terms of normal grammar", and he observes that the sentence, 'I am the one who is' would properly be *'ani hu' 'asher 'ehyeh*.[4] However, he speculates that the first *'ehyeh* in *'ehyeh 'asher 'ehyeh* has replaced the normal *'ani hu'* to form an assonance pattern with *Yahweh* in Exod 3:15. Accordingly, we should read the meaning "I am the one who is" even though the grammar is wrong for this meaning.

McCarthy's 1978 article hides a speculative assumption about assonance, namely that another *'ehyeh* is needed and that the first *'ehyeh* in Exod 3:12 and the second *'ehyeh* of Exod 3:14a is not enough to strike a play on words with Exod 3:15 and its *Yahweh*. The choice before the exegete is therefore that God either used normal grammar and an *idem per idem* form or that God felt the need for three uses of *'ehyeh* in quick succession and that normal grammatical rules should be sacrificed. The argument is one from silence and the assonance is struck with three forms; it is just that there is no intended "I am the one who is".

---

[1] Albrektson, "On the Syntax of *'ehyeh 'asher 'ehyeh* in Exodus 3:14", 24.

[2] For the same critique, see A. Gibson, "Our Man in Hell (1)" *The Testimony* (1971): 348-352.

[3] B. S. Childs, *Exodus* (OTL; London: SCM Press, 1974), 50.

[4] D. J. McCarthy, "Exod 3:14: History, Philology and Theology" *CBQ* 40 (1978): 311-322 (316).

3. Existential and Non-Existential Readings

We can be certain that the correct syntax of the Hebrew is as the English translations have it: either 'I AM that/what/who I AM' or 'I will be who/what I will be'. The rendering 'I AM the one who is' is an error based on insufficient analysis of the syntactic patterns of Hebrew. The LXX, 'I AM the Being" (Brenton), is also incorrect for the same reason as it does not translate the Hebrew but is some sort of interpretative guess at the underlying point of the expression.[1] This leaves the question to be answered: are the margins or the main text of the translations right, or are both options right?

There are two issues: the tense of the verb (I am/I will be) and the rendering of the relative word *'asher*; we will first consider the relative word *'asher*. The choice of 'what/that/who' is between an existential and non-existential reading and some have even argued that both readings are legitimate; we now need to explain this choice. In choosing 'that' or 'what' to translate *'asher* in 'I AM that/what I AM' translators direct a reader to think of the assertion in existential terms—God is making a statement about his nature and/or his existence; the assertion is about God's person. The alternative rendering 'I will be what I will be' shifts the focus of the reader to the future and *what God will be* but it is still a statement about his existence/nature.

This is a rough characterization and it is worth qualifying what we mean by "existence/nature". It appears *nothing specific* is said by 'I AM that/what I AM' and the speaker instead relies on what is already known by the other party to the conversation. Hence, nothing is *specifically said* about God's manner of existence or his attributes—his nature. It is a mistake therefore to **select a quality** about God and affirm that he is saying something about that quality. Thus, while God can affirm his existence saying, 'I exist', using the Hebrew verb "to be", this is not what he does in 'I AM that/what I AM'. Further, we might remember that when God wants to affirm that he is the only true God, he does so in Isaiah by saying

---

[1] H. B. Swete, the Septuagintalist, in *An Introduction to the Old Testament in Greek* (Rev. Ed.; Cambridge: Cambridge University Press, 1914) believed that "The translators frequently interpret words which call for explanation . . . .. Occasionally a whole clause is interpreted rather than translated, e.g., Exod. iii. 14 *egō eimi ho ōn*" (326-327). Indeed, there are well-known cases of 'relics of ancient exegesis', not direct translation of the Hebrew Bible, in the LXX. Later (446-447), Swete cites Exod 3:14 as one of many examples listed which "serve to illustrate the exegesis of the LXX in the historical books".

something like, "I am the Lord, and there is none else" (Isa 45:18).[1] Similarly, we cannot expand our analysis and say God is here affirming his "self-existence" or his "eternal existence". This may be good exhortation and true but it is not **exegesis** of 'I AM that/what I AM' simply because it violates the *indefiniteness* of this statement by adding *our specification* of what is said in philosophical and theological terms. If we translate the Hebrew as 'I will be what I will be' we can still make the same mistake if we specify the meaning of the assertion in terms of God's existence or nature; we might mistakenly affirm that God is saying he will always be God, the existent One.

The same point applies if we eschew the notion of existence and think of God's attributes or character, but here the point is more obvious. If we said that by 'I AM that/what I AM' God was saying that he was all-knowing, it would be clear that we were violating the *indefiniteness* of 'I AM that/what/who I AM' by selecting and adding ourselves the attribute "all-knowing". We can see that 'who' readily lends itself to the translation of *'asher* when we read the assertion in terms of God's character, but the mistake is the same as when we use 'what/that' and read the assertion about God's existence or nature.

Existential readings violate the indefiniteness of the *idem per idem* form and they do this by taking a cue from the verb "to be" and offering a gloss along the lines of God's being or existence. This may be good theology, and it can be found in church commentaries, but it is not an exegetical approach. A non-existential reading respects the indefiniteness of the syntactic form and looks to the context to establish the meaning of the relative word *'asher* and the meaning of the assertion as a whole, and this is a quite different approach to the text.

In translating an *idem per idem* form, the relative word *'asher* is rendered in the way that is considered a best fit with the verb; hence, we might have "I will go *where* I will go" or "I will create *what* I will create", *and so on*. The verb "to be" (*hyh*) would fit with 'who', 'what' or 'that' depending on the context; syntax alone cannot settle the correct rendering.

Exodus 3:14 is an answer given by God to Moses in reply to his expectation that the Israelites will not believe or accept him as a messenger. Moses anticipated that the Israelites would challenge his claim

---

[1] Assertions of 'being', that He is, or exists, by God are rare in the Bible. God affirms promises on the fact that He lives (e.g., Num 14:21); when He does so he uses the verb 'to live', rather than 'to be'.

to speak on behalf of God. The anticipated question, 'What is his name?', suggests that he expects they might not accept him as one of their own (John 1:11). The first answer that Moses is given to say involves the verb "to be": "So shall you speak to the Israelites, 'I AM has sent me to you'..." (v. 14b, KJV). The second answer is parallel to the first, "So you shall say to the Israelites, '*Yahweh*...has sent me to you'..." (v. 15, KJV revised).

The first answer, 'I AM has sent me to you' is unusual in placing a verbal form into the position where a name or title might be expected. However, in conversation, a play on words easily accounts for this happening. The play is obvious from the parallel—*'ehyeh* and *Yahweh* are the two words with which God constructs a play. Hence, it is a mistake to assert that *'ehyeh* is a name; lexically, it is a verbal form—nobody says that it is a name in other places. The name of God is *Yahweh*, but it is beyond the scope of this chapter to elaborate upon this play on words and the meaning of the divine name. Our point is simply the observation that there is a play on words in a conversation between Moses and God. This conversational dynamic is set up by the initial *'ehyeh 'asher 'ehyeh*, and this reply is given in response to Moses' hesitancy and self-effacing stance. Such a stance is all about *who* is Moses that he should be sent to Israel. Hence, the reply of God is focused on *who* he can be and spoken to Moses it asserts that God *can be Moses*.

This analysis of the context is not existential; we have not noted elements in the conversation that concern God's existence or his nature. That God is from everlasting to everlasting, that he is self-existent, eternal; that he is good, kind or gracious – none of these aspects figure in the conversation. Accordingly, *'asher* should not be translated by 'what' or 'that' but by 'who' and in this choice, there lies an ambiguity.

In situations of representation and delegation a person acts for and represents another person. In colloquial speech, we might say, "You can be my eyes and ears" or "You can act for me and speak for me in court", *and so on*. In such a situation, the person selected to be a representative, say a junior clerk, might be self-effacing and hesitant. To such a person, a senior solicitor might say, "I can be who I want to be in court; you are to act for me". The 'who' embraces both the senior solicitor and the junior clerk in a relationship of representation, and on this non-existential reading Exod 3:14a is an assertion that states *God can be Moses*.

To sum up: the existential reading elaborates *'ehyeh 'asher 'ehyeh* in terms of God's existence or nature; the non-existential reading leaves *'ehyeh 'asher 'ehyeh* indefinite and seeks to specify the *'asher* from context, and this shows a concern with **who is Moses** and whether and how he can represent God.[1]

3.1 Verbal Aspect

The verbal form *'ehyeh* is not uncommon (55x, BibleWorks), and it is usually translated as "I will be", as it is in Exod 3:12 (KJV). This statistical preference for a future rendering on the part of translators makes this the preferred choice for Exod 3:14a unless there is a reason in the context to prefer "I am".

In teaching grammars, *'ehyeh* will be classified as an "Imperfect" with regard to **aspect** and we need to understand this concept. In their reference grammar (2002), C. H. J. van der Merwe, J. A. Naudé and J. H. Kroeze state,

> Not all languages possess a grammatically realized tense system. In some languages, verbs conjugate primarily to indicate whether an action is complete or incomplete. Languages which have the *grammatical* means of indicating that an *action is complete or incomplete* are described as having an *aspect system.*[2]

Hebrew is described as having a two-aspect system and *'ehyeh*, as an Imperfect, is characterized as signifying incomplete action (with Perfect verbs signifying complete action). However, Van der Merwe, Naudé and Kroeze are careful to state that,

> Various opinions exist as to whether BH [Biblical Hebrew] has a tense or an aspect system. Older Jewish grammarians, like the more recent grammarians, are of the opinion that BH verb system is primarily a tense system.[3]

On this way of describing matters, the Perfect refers to past time and the Imperfect refers to the present and future or "non-past" time. This is how Van der Merwe, Naudé and Kroeze proceed in their grammar and state that "It is not clear whether in BH it is time that assumes aspect, or aspect

---

[1] For a discussion of representation, see N. Wolterstorff, *Divine Discourse*, ch. 3.

[2] C. H. J. van der Merwe, J. A. Naudé and J. H. Kroeze, *A Biblical Hebrew Reference Grammar* (Sheffield: Sheffield Academic Press, 2002), 141-142.

[3] Van der Merwe, Naudé and Kroeze, *A Biblical Hebrew Reference Grammar*, 142.

that assumes time", and "BH speakers and narrators had a choice of describing either the aspect or the time of an action".[1]

The viewpoint presented by Van der Merwe, Naudé and Kroeze is important for our examination of the verb "to be" in Exod 3:14a because commentators, relying on older reference grammars such as GKC, or an older teaching grammar, may mislead by implying that the Hebrew Verb System is all about aspect and not about tense. For instance, the older but still used teaching grammar by J. Weingreen states,

> In Hebrew thinking, *an action* is regarded as being either *completed or incompleted.* Hebrew, therefore, knows of no past, present, or future tenses, but has instead a *Perfect* and an *Imperfect* (which, in a context, lend themselves to a variety of shades in meaning).[2]

This is misleading in that it might cause a reader to deny the presence of tense in the Hebrew Verb System. Hence, a more modern teaching grammar by J. F. A. Sawyer (1976) states,

> Because of this, it is not uncommon to find grammarians nowadays making only one distinction, namely, that between "past" and "non-past".[3]

Accordingly, we can say on a grammatical level that there is tense in the Hebrew Verb System as well as aspect, and that context (and other grammatical features in the context) assists the reader in discriminating the "non-past". Sawyer associates the Imperfect with the "non-past" (present/future) and the Perfect with the "past",[4] but it is important to realise that this is a simplification appropriate in a teaching grammar. B. T. Arnold and J. H. Choi give a fuller picture of the Imperfect and identify that it is also used for customary and habitual action in the past.[5] The tense that the Imperfect contributes towards and participates in could be past or non-past (present or future).

---

[1] Van der Merwe, Naudé and Kroeze, *A Biblical Hebrew Reference Grammar*, 144.
[2] J. Weingreen, *A Practical Grammar for Classical Hebrew* (Oxford: Oxford University Press (Clarendon), 1939), 56.
[3] J. F. A. Sawyer, *A Modern Introduction to Biblical Hebrew* (London: Oriel Press, 1976), 79.
[4] Sawyer, *A Modern Introduction to Biblical Hebrew*, 79.
[5] Arnold and Choi, *A Guide to Biblical Hebrew Syntax*, 58.

3.2 The Verb "to be" in Hebrew

The verb "to be" is very common (3576x, BibleWorks). It might be queried whether this verb is like other verbs; after all, other verbs have been characterized above in terms of *action*, and the verb "to be" does not appear to be a *kind of action*. We should not assume that general descriptions of the Hebrew Verb System apply directly to the verb "to be". Some teaching grammars may single out the verb for special comment. T. O. Lambdin did so in his 1971 grammar,[1] but a full study is that of G. S. Ogden in a 1971 article in *Vetus Testamentum*, "Time, and the Verb *hyh* in O. T. Prose".[2] His opening analysis for the Imperfect of "to be" is interesting:

> In the Semitic languages it is generally understood that the Imperfect represents actions, events, or conditions which are incomplete in themselves. Temporally they may be located in past, present or future time (normally the latter two) but as it is the nature of the action that is more important, the time of its occurrence takes second place.

> The examples of *hyh* in the Imperfect upon examination reveal a temporal reference which is future and in which the nature of the action involved is of considerably secondary importance—in other words, a reversal of the traditional values—for the Imperfect functions primarily as a Future Narrative tense.[3]

Ogden's analysis is useful as a corrective to those who might argue that the verb "to be" is not about tense but about aspect; it is also useful as a corrective to those who argue that the Imperfect cannot be precise with tense: Ogden's conclusion is that it is **primarily a future narrative tense**. In this regard, his conclusion about the Imperfect as a customary and habitual past tense is informative. On this he says "One might therefore be permitted to conclude that this frequentative [his terminology] aspect arises not from within the verb but by association with others".[4] This observation helps to explain the past tense association of some Imperfect forms of "to be" while allowing his conclusion about its primary role as a future tense to stand.

---

[1] T. O. Lambdin, *Introduction to Biblical Hebrew* (London: Darton, Longman and Todd, 1971), 55-56.

[2] G. S. Ogden, "Time, and the Verb *hyh* in O. T. Prose" *VT* 21 (1971): 451-469.

[3] Ogden, "Time, and the Verb *hyh* in O. T. Prose", 456.

[4] Ogden, "Time, and the Verb *hyh* in O. T. Prose", 458.

In any analysis of 'ehyeh, we should tabulate the sentence fragments in which the form occurs in translation (except for Exod 3:14), and this we do for the KJV in the following table.[1]

Passage	Sentence fragment	Speaker
Gen 26:3	and **I will be** with thee	**God**
Gen 31:3	and **I will be** with thee	**God**
Exod 3:12	**I will be** with thee	**God**
Exod 4:12	**I will be** with thy mouth	**God**
Exod 4:15	**I will be** with thy mouth	**God**
Deut 31:23	**I will be** with thee	**God**
Josh 1:5	**I will be** with thee	**God**
Josh 3:7	**I will be** with thee	**God**
Judg 6:16	**I will be** with thee	**God**
Judg 11:9	…shall I be your head?	Jephthah speaking
Ruth 2:13	…though I be not like unto one of thine handmaidens	Ruth speaking
1 Sam 18:18	…that I should be son in law to the king?	David speaking
1 Sam 23:17	I shall be next unto thee	Jonathan speaking
2 Sam 7:6	…have walked in a tent	**God**
2 Sam 7:9	I was with thee withsoever thou wentest	**God**
2 Sam 7:14	**I will be** his father	**God**
2 Sam 15:34	I will be thy servant	Hushai speaking
2 Sam 16:18	… his will I be	Hushai speaking
2 Sam 16:19	… so will I be in thy presence	Hushai speaking
2 Sam 22:24	I was also upright before him	David

---

[1] This table is a list of the straightforward occurrences of 'ehyeh as given in BibleWorks.

Passage	Sentence fragment	Speaker
1 Chron 17:5	...have gone from tent to tent	**God**
1 Chron 17:8	I have been with thee withsoever thou hast walked	**God**
1 Chron 17:13	**I will be** his father	**God**
1 Chron 28:6	**I will be** his father	**God**
Job 3:16	I had not been	Job speaking
Job 7:20	...so that I am a burden to myself	Job speaking
Job 10:19	I should have been	Job speaking
Job 12:4	I am *as* one mocked of his neighbour	Job speaking
Job 17:6	I was as a tabret	Job speaking
Ps 50:21	I was altogether *such an one* as thyself	David speaking
Ps 102:8	...and am as a sparrow	David speaking
Prov 8:30	I was by him	Solomon speaking
Prov 8:30	I was daily his delight	Solomon speaking
Song 1:7	why should I be as one that turneth aside	Solomon speaking
Isa 3:7	I will not be an healer	Anonymous
Isa 47:7	I shall be a lady for ever	Babylon speaking
Jer 11:4	**I will be** your God	**God**
Jer 24:7	**I will be** their God	**God**
Jer 30:22	**I will be** your God	**God**
Jer 31:1	**...will I be** the God	**God**
Jer 32:38	**I will be** their God	**God**
Ezek 11:20	**I will be** their God	**God**
Ezek 14:11	**I may be** their God	**God**

Passage	Sentence fragment	Speaker
Ezek 34:24	I the Lord **will be** their God	**God**
Ezek 36:28	**I will be** your God	**God**
Ezek 37:23	**I will be** their God	**God**
Hos 1:9	**I will not be** your *God*	**God**
Hos 11:4	I was to them as they that take off the yoke on their jaws	**God**
Hos 14:6	**I will be** as the dew unto Israel	**God**
Zech 2:5	For **I**, saith the Lord, **will be** unto her a wall of fire round about, and **I will be** the glory in the midst of her	**God**
Zech 8:8	**I will be** their God	**God**

While we have chosen to represent the KJV in this table, a similar pattern would be presented if we chose, say, either the RSV or the NASB. Examining the table, it is worth observing first the frequency of 'I will be' when God is speaking, and it is perhaps not surprising to see that God would often want to utter 'I will be with you' or 'I will be your/their God'. A second observation is that translators have sensed a tense other than future a few times in the poetic works of Song, Psalms and Job. Thirdly, we have highlighted the five texts when God uses 'ehyeh for continuous action of the past: he was continually walking in a tent and with the people wherever they went (2 Sam 7:6, 9; 1 Chron 17:5, 8); and he treated the people with compassion, like the herdsman that takes the yoke from off the oxen (Hos 11:4).

The five texts where God uses 'ehyeh for continuous action of the past are worth further comment. These are waw consecutive forms and the past tense is partly set by the Perfect verbs in the conversational context:

I have not dwelt…since the time…even to this day… (2 Sam 7:6; 1 Chron 17:5)

…wherever you went/walked (2 Sam 7:9; 1 Chron 17:8)

God had taught Ephraim (Hos 11:3)

Looking at this table as data for the character portrayal of God in the Hebrew Scriptures (under inspiration), we would have to say that God's idiom in speaking using *'ehyeh* is for the future narrative tense unless there are past tense indicators in associated verbs and/or temporal words like 'since' or 'until'.

If we consider the context of Exod 3:14a, its future and forward-looking character is apparent:[1]

> And Moses said unto God, <u>who am I</u>, that I should go unto Pharaoh, and that I should bring forth the children of Israel out of Egypt? And he said, Certainly <u>I will be</u> (*'ehyeh*) with thee; and this shall be a token unto thee, that I have sent thee: When thou hast brought forth the people out of Egypt, ye shall serve God upon this mountain. And Moses said unto God, Behold, when I come unto the children of Israel, and shall say unto them, The God of your Fathers hath sent me unto you; and they shall say to me, What is his name? what shall I say unto them? And God said unto Moses, <u>I will be</u> (*'ehyeh*) who <u>I will be</u> (*'ehyeh*): and he said, thus shalt thou say unto the children of Israel, <u>I will be</u> (*'ehyeh*) hath sent me unto you. And God said moreover unto Moses, thus shalt thou say unto the children of Israel, <u>Yahweh</u>...hath sent me unto you: this is my name for ever, and this is my memorial unto all generations. Exod 3:11-15 (KJV revised)

This future cast is set by the conversation being about Moses ***going*** to Egypt. Accordingly, even if we were to propose that God could equally have said 'I AM with you' rather than 'I will be with you' in his use of *'ehyeh* in Exod 3:12, the cast of the conversation makes 'I AM with you' have an idiomatic future sense. In terms of translation practice, it would be obtuse to propose 'I AM with you' just because *'ehyeh* can be associated with a present tense meaning. The same point would apply if we were to claim that God was saying 'I have always been with you', which would equally be an assurance about the future situation that will face Moses in Egypt.

L. M. Pákozdy notes that the Hebrew equivalent for 'I AM who I AM' would be (better, 'could be'[2]) *'anoki hu' 'asher 'anoki hu'* or *'anoki howah*

---

[1] Ogden, "Time, and the Verb *hyh* in O. T. Prose", 457, gives the same analysis for Exod 3:12.

[2] This change in the modal from 'would' to 'could' avoids giving the impression that Hebrew is inflexible. It would be a mistake to argue that

'asher 'anoki hu' rather than *'ehyeh 'asher 'ehyeh*.[1] He prefers 'I shall be that which I shall be' but usefully draws in the parallel of Hos 1:9 in support of the future tense rendering of Exod 3:14a as it is the only other comparable use of a verbal sentence with *'ehyeh*. It says, *'anoki lo 'ehyeh lakem* which the KJV has rendered "I will not be your *God*". The word 'God' is not in the Hebrew as indicated by the KJV italics and Pákozdy offers 'So I shall not be present for you'. What seems clear is that Hos 1:9 echoes Exod 3:14a in its use of *'ehyeh* without an object word such as 'God'. With the end of the Northern kingdom being prophesied by Hosea, it is appropriate that Hosea would signal the end of God's relationship with his people by reversing the promise implicit in 'I will be who I will be' by saying 'I will not be present for you'.[2]

4. Philosophy of Translation

We have argued that the correct translation of *'ehyeh 'asher 'ehyeh* is 'I will be who I will be'. Moreover, the context of Exod 3:14a is a conversation that revolves around Moses and not the nature of God. Moses' opening question is 'Who am I?' and it is this question of identity that controls the conversation and dictates the rendering of *'asher* as 'who' in 'I will be *who* I will be'. Accordingly, 'I will be *who* I will be' is the translation suggested by context rather than 'I will be *what* I will be' (or even 'I AM *that* I AM').

There are philosophical mistakes that can be made when discussing translation. For example, it is commonplace and uncontroversial to quote foreign language authors in translation. Thus, we might affirm something like, "Descartes **said** 'I think therefore I am'". Notice we have used the notion of *saying* here and no one marking an essay on Descartes would object, "He did not say that; he wrote in French". Likewise, when discussing *'ehyeh 'asher 'ehyeh* we would make a mistake if we stated that

---

exactly the same Hebrew form (*'ehyeh 'asher 'ehyeh*) **would** be used to express 'I am what I am', 'I am the one who exists', or 'I will be what I will be'. Pákozdy shows that Hebrew has alternative ways to express these sentences.

[1] L. M. Pákozdy, "I shall be that which I shall be" *The Bible Translator* 7 (1956): 146-148 (147).

[2] A. Phillips and L. Phillips, "The Origin of 'I Am' in Exodus 3.14" *JSOT* 78 (1998): 81-84 (82) offer the more literal rendering of the Hebrew as "I a no-*'ehyeh* to you" which strikes the link clearly and might be a better option if we wanted to indulge in Engrew or Heblish. Or, given '*Lo-ruhammah*', this could be '*Lo-ehyeh*': "I am '*Lo-ehyeh*' to you" (or: "I am 'Not-I will be' to/for you").

God did not **say** either 'I am that/what I am' or 'I will be what/who I will be' because he said something in Hebrew.

In the same way, we would be overly sceptical towards language if we held the view that languages could not in principle be translated. Obviously, the industry of translation is successful and the discipline of translating dead languages is very much alive and well. Hebrew has a simpler verbal system than English, but this does not mean that translators do not succeed in mapping English tenses to Hebrew tenses. Furthermore, translators may not claim to capture nuance and all the richness in a target language, but they do endeavour to capture basic senses, and it is the basic sense that is disputed when translators propose 'I am that/what I am' and 'I will be what/who I will be' as alternatives for *'ehyeh 'asher 'ehyeh*. Whether God intended a future sense, a present tense, or both, is a definite question which is capable of determination by examining the evidence of context, the import of the conversation, the grammatical form of the verbs that God used, the syntactic form of his expressions, and the wider pattern of his speech. All these points we have laid out in this chapter in favour of 'I will be who I will be'.

It is therefore a mistake to argue that there are many aspects of meaning contained in the Hebrew verb "to be" and that these aspects are somehow there in the word as it exists in any sentence. A lexicon will highlight the range of meaning for the verb (its "fulness"), but it is a fallacy to import this range into each use of the verb. As the verb is used in a context there are selective factors at work which determine the meaning of the verb. As interpreters and translators, we have to make this determination, and as we do the work of translation it is not the case that many aspects of meaning remain "in the word" when we have done the work of translation. The standard dictum is that a word has meaning in a context of use and it is the truth of this dictum that highlights the fallacy of bringing a lexical range of meaning to bear on each use of the verb.

The above fallacy is noteworthy in the argument for an existential reading of Exod 3:14a because the lexical range of meaning for the verb "to be" embraces usage with the past, present and future tense. So, it might be thought, in this connection, that Rev 11:17 is a translation of God's use of the verb "to be" in Exodus because it reads, "O Lord God Almighty, which art, and wast, and art to come" (KJV). This is not a translation of the divine name nor is it a translation of the verb "to be" in Hebrew or the form *'ehyeh*, and this is simply because the contextual use of the verb in Exod 3:14 is specific as to tense (let alone the absence of any "coming" element in the Hebrew verb or the dubious KJV rendering of the Greek).

80

The expression of the future tense in Hebrew is a function of grammatical form, context, and associated verbs. The future tense in Hebrew is not an English future tense; it would be nonsense to say so as an English future tense is an English future tense. Nevertheless, it is important to recognise the future tense in a Hebrew sentence when we have it and translate it appropriately into English. This is where the table of occurrences of *'ehyeh* is important in conveying the likelihood that *'ehyeh* is used in a future sense in Exod 3:14a. There is no *proof* to be had in such tables (to say so would be an error), just an indication of **likelihood** (to deny this is also an error); to this we should add considerations from the context. In this way, we can avoid the fallacy that because a Hebrew verbal form is not *sufficient* to determine tense, Hebrew does not register a distinction between the past, present and future.

Translators will range in their translation from the literal, almost word for word, to the freer kind of paraphrase. If translators thought that there was a clear meaning in *'ehyeh 'asher 'ehyeh* which was about being, existence, eternal existence, self-existence, uncreate existence, then they could have paraphrased accordingly. They did not have to adopt either a future or present tense in their renderings (i.e. I AM/I will be). They could have paraphrased as follows: 'I AM the one who was, who is, and who will be'. It is a significant counterargument to the "God is, was and always will be" interpretation that they have given two alternative choices in the main text and in the margin.

We might ask *why* it is that the translators we have selected have placed 'I AM that/who/what I AM' in the main text and 'I will be that/who/what I will be' in the margin or as a footnote. There isn't an explanation in the versions we have examined and the margin/footnote is presented as an **alternative**. This practice of putting alternatives into the margin/footnote of the Bible is well established. We should note that the margin/footnote is presented as an alternative and this excludes our speculating that the margin/footnote is there because *'ehyeh 'asher 'ehyeh* is not fully comprehended in either the main text or the margin/footnote on their own. If we want to know why translators have made their choices, we have to examine their translators' notes, or in the absence of any specific notes,[1] commentaries and journal articles will supply discussion of the issues at stake from which translators have made their choice.[2]

The influence of church tradition and philosophy should not be discounted in investigating why 'I AM that/who/what I AM' is in the main text. Pákozdy speculates that it is due to the influence of the LXX upon the church Fathers that led to their linkage of the divine name with the concept of Being.[3] McCarthy sketches examples from church theology and observes,

> The passage [Exod 3:14, LXX] "served as the proof text for Christian ontology," and though this may at times have led to an emphasis on static being, there was still plenty of play for the active aspect: God gave because He supremely was.[4]

McCarthy is supportive of the existential approach and says, "The text has a history not only in the scriptures but in the church, and this has not falsified but enriched the meaning of the text".[5] Childs notes that "it was the philosophical implications of the passage which evoked such intense interest in Ex.3.14",[6] and he offers a brief summary of its use in the theology of Eusebius, Augustine,[7] Aquinas[8] and then the Reformers. The Vulgate translates as *EGO SUM QUI SUM*—'I AM who I AM' and this has influenced subsequent church tradition.[9] Moreover, we should also not discount the influence of the Johannine 'I am' statements.

---

[1] For example, L. A. Weigle et al, *An Introduction to the Revised Standard Version of the Old Testament* (London: Thomas Nelson & Sons Ltd, 1952); T. W. Chambers *A Companion to the Revised Old Testament* (London: H. E. Jerrard, 1885); nothing is noted in these volumes.

[2] In addition to the articles discussed in this chapter, the April 1984 issue of *The Bible Translator* has a series of practical papers on translating divine names and titles.

[3] Pákozdy, "I shall be that which I shall be", 147.

[4] McCarthy, "Exod 3:14: History, Philology and Theology", 318.

[5] McCarthy, "Exod 3:14: History, Philology and Theology", 318.

[6] Childs, *Exodus*, 84-87 (85).

[7] See also S. Macdonald, "The Divine Nature" in *The Cambridge Companion to Augustine* (eds. E. Stump and N. Kretzmann; Cambridge: Cambridge University Press, 2001), 71-90 (82).

[8] *Summa Theologica*, Part 1, Q.13, Article 11 in *St Thomas Aquinas: Summa Theologica, Latin Text and English Translation* (ed. T. Gilbey *et al*; London: Blackfriars, 1964), 3:91-93.

[9] See Hanson, *The Search for the Christian Doctrine of God*, 476.

It is entirely plausible to attribute the choice of 'I AM' in the KJV (and later English versions) with the capitalization to such a history of church doctrine. What is surprising is that 'I will be who I will be' has made it back into the margins and footnotes of translations in the modern era. It is a testimony to the strength of the Hebrew patterns of use that this has happened. We might attribute this to the strength of the historico-critical method and its counterinfluence to church tradition on the work of translation today. The church tradition within which a Bible translator works is a potential influence on his/her translation.

We have registered the LXX interpretation "I AM the Being". The early Greek translations of Aquila (mid second century C.E.) and Theodotion (late second century C.E.) render 'ehyeh 'asher 'ehyeh with the future Greek tense *esomai hos esomai*. In doing this, and unlike the LXX, they have produced a translation that is true to the Hebrew text, both with respect to the *idem per idem* form and the future tense.[1] If we examine the Jewish Targums, the situation is mixed. Most editions of *Onkelos* do not translate but merely reproduce the Hebrew. Some editions of *Onkelos* have the translations, 'I will be concerning that which I will be' or 'I will be with whomsoever I will be'. *Neofiti* leaves the phrase untranslated while *Pseudo-Jonathan* has, 'He who spoke and the world was, spoke, and all of it came about'.[2]

In the 20c., M. Buber (a German-Jewish translator) affirmed,

> *Ehyeh* in our passage means precisely what it means in the same story both before (3:12) and after (4:12 and 15): to be present to someone, to be with someone, to assist someone—except that here the verb is used absolutely, without any specification of *whom* the one-who-is-there is there for. God does not by this make any theological proposition that he is eternal or self-sufficient; rather he offers to the creature he has made, to his person and his people, the assurance that they are in need of and that renders all magical feats both void and superfluous.[3]

---

[1] F. Field, ed., *Origenis Hexaplorum quae supersunt* (Oxford: Clarendon Press, 1875), 85.

[2] *Targum Onqelos* (ed., B. Grossfield; Edinburgh: T&T Clark, 1988), 8-9. For a discussion, see M. Buber and F. Rosenzweig, *Scripture and Translation* (Bloomington: Indiana University Press, 1994), 102-104, 190-191, 192-195.

[3] M. Buber and F. Rosenzweig, *Scripture and Translation*, 194-195.

Buber's perspective is not quite our view but it is close and one way of expanding our view. We have said that God is saying *he will be Moses*, i.e. manifest himself in Moses. Clearly, this can be expanded in terms of fellowship: God will be *with* Moses. This is explicit in Exod 3:12 but the change of expression in Exod 3:14a suggests to us God-manifestation and not just redemptive fellowship.

> And the Lord said unto Moses, See, I have made thee a <u>god</u> to
> Pharaoh: and Aaron thy brother shall be thy prophet. Exod 7:1
> (KJV)

Where there is a choice in translation it can be difficult to make that choice. Some may suggest instead that both choices are valid. It may be argued that *'ehyeh 'asher 'ehyeh* has both a future and a present tense—it says *God is* and *God will be*. It might appear that this is an easy option, a way out of conflict, but it is a difficult position to establish in the case of Exod 3:14a. Several obstacles present themselves. First, ambiguity in language use is indicated by context and readers pick up on ambiguity. We cannot just assert that *'ehyeh 'asher 'ehyeh* is present and future, we have to show how *'ehyeh* is conveying an ambiguous tense to readers. It is not enough to observe that the Imperfect can carry the non-past, because this general rule is instantiated in instances that are either present or future. Second, are there other examples of uses of *'ehyeh* where it is both present and future? The table above does not list any such cases on the part of the translators of the KJV. This question concerns pattern—if there is **no pattern of ambiguity** in which *'ehyeh 'asher 'ehyeh* participates as a present and a future tense statement, how can we begin to establish that the tense in Exod 3:14a is both present and future? Finally, the wide-ranging semantic values of the verb "to be" (*hyh*) in Hebrew cannot be cited to establish an ambiguous tense in Exod 3:14a. Any word can have a range of basic senses and a range of subtle overtones, but such are selected in the use of language. It may be good theology to affirm that God is and that God will be, that he self-exists and is always becoming, but this is not strictly linguistic.

By way of a conclusion to our discussion of the philosophy that hangs around grammar, we can say that there are two mistakes to avoid in a discussion of *'ehyeh 'asher 'ehyeh*: we should not rely on grammatical form alone (*'ehyeh*) to assert a future tense; and neither should we rely on the tense ambiguity associated with a grammatical form across a semantic field to argue for the necessary presence of a tense ambiguity in a particular instance of that field, i.e. Exod 3:14a.

5. John 8:58 Before Abraham was, I am

John 8:58 has been given a variety of explanations by commentators which can be set out in a series of alternative bullet points:

- Jesus is saying that
    - before Abraham (was) (born)
        - he existed
        - he is timeless and eternal
        - he is God/divine
    - before Abraham was called 'Abraham'
        - he was to bear the divine name
    - before Abraham was in God's purpose
        - he existed in God's purpose
    - before Abraham is raised to life
        - he has life in himself now

...using I AM from Exodus 3 and/or
...using I *am* He from Isaiah 43

These suggestions can be mixed and matched (and perhaps we could add a few more nuanced choices) but they all have well-known problems which are worth rehearsing before we present our reading. So, (1) had Jesus been saying he existed before Abraham, he would have said 'Before Abraham was (born), I was'. (2) Although many translations render the Hebrew of Exod 3:14 as 'I AM that I AM', this is more down to theology than Hebrew linguistics[1] (the theological giveaway is the capitalization). The LXX has God say, 'I am the Being' and the Hebrew has 'I will be who I will be' (on which see the margins or footnotes in translations). (3) The immediately preceding point in the conversation is about Jesus not being old enough to have seen Abraham, which requires, it would seem, a riposte from Jesus placing himself before Abraham. (4) Jesus could be referring to the naming of Abraham, but if so, he puts it in a rather oblique way and naming hasn't been part of the conversation up to that point. (5) Further, no doubt Jesus is more important than Abraham in God's purpose and before him in this respect, but if he was saying this this he would have said 'I was', (6) Theologians do wax lyrical about John

---

[1] The oldest theologizing here is that of Philo and the Targums, which in various ways develop readings of Exodus 3:14 that relate to existence. In the context of John's 'I am' sayings, these are discussed in M. M. Thompson, *The God of the Gospel of John* (Grand Rapids: Eerdmans, 2001), 89-91. The Hebrew linguistics are set out in Albrektson, "On the Syntax of *'ehyeh 'asher 'ehyeh* in Exodus 3:14".

8:58 and assert that Jesus is claiming to be timeless and eternal and even God or a manifestation of God, but this theology is disconnected from the text; it is less exegesis and more systematic musings. Such theology is dependent on either the thesis that Jesus is using 'I AM' from Exodus 3, or 'I *am* He' from Isaiah 43, but it is not clear how this works textually,[1] nor how it addresses the Jews' arguments. Finally, (7), it is not obvious that Jesus is talking about Abraham being raised in the future, since the conversation/dialogue/exchange (vv. 12-58) hasn't covered the resurrection up to this point.

What we want to do in this section is keep the exegesis mundane and as close to the text as possible, rather than stray into the world of theology. There is doctrine to be had in Jesus' utterance (to do with Exodus 3 and God-manifestation), but this is a deeper layer to an understanding of how the dialogue in John 8 works. There is a much simpler layer to do with ellipsis and the meaning of the promises to Abraham. Our criticism of commentaries and their theology, whether on the Internet, in books, or in papers and articles, is that they leave the text behind and talk about things like Christ's position in the purpose of God, or perhaps his bearing the divine name, or perhaps his pre-existence as a divine being and/or as part of the Godhead, or as a manifestation of God. These kinds of commentary don't explain the conversational dynamics nor the background in the Abrahamic promises.[2]

5.1 Ellipsis in Conversation

A well-documented phenomenon is ellipsis in conversation (see Wikipedia).[3] As conversations flow, speakers will miss out words and phrases because they assume what has gone before in the conversation. Equally, they may also substitute words and phrases for previous ones relying on the hearers picking up the substitution. Misunderstandings and failure to follow the conversation leads to correction. An idiom such as 'I am' is used in self-identifying ellipsis in English. 'Are you the king of France?' and 'I am' work as question and answer because of ellipsis.

---

[1] If Jesus had said 'I am the I AM' or 'I am I am he' we have a clear usage of expressions from Exodus 3 and Isaiah 43, but as it is, we just have an assertion 'I am'.

[2] For example, J. Carter, *The Gospel of John* (Repr. Ed.; Birmingham: CMPA, 1972), 111; Whittaker, *Studies in the Gospels*, (Cannock: Biblia, 1988), 406-407.

[3] G. Yuile, *Pragmatics* (Oxford: Oxford University Press, 1996), 23; A. Georgakopoulou and D. Goutsos, *Discourse Analysis: An Introduction* (Edinburgh: Edinburgh University Press, 2004), 13.

Ellipsis is primarily a conversational phenomenon but then John 8 is a written record of a conversation and so we should expect ellipsis; 'I am' could be elliptical in Greek.

In formal terms, ellipsis is a reduction in what is uttered/written without affecting what is understood. As readers of a written record of a conversation, we can recover what has been left out (or assumed) by examining the potential connections across the conversation. One of the problems with much scholarly commentary on John 8:58 is that 'I am' has been analysed without regard to the phenomenon of ellipsis. Hence, analysis has been theological and involved notions like pre-existence, manifestation, eternal timelessness and deity.

Inter-textual connections within a conversation help to make the conversation a coherent whole. In written discourse, a textual element will mark the ellipsis and direct the reader to what has been elided. It's an empirical investigation and any ellipsis should be recoverable. In 'Before Abraham was, I am' we have a candidate for ellipsis in the use of 'I am'. With 'I am' spoken by Jesus, we need to determine whether it is disambiguated elsewhere in the conversation by Jesus ('I am who/what'). The 'I am' might well be carrying an ellipsis rather than being an assertion of existence (or something more metaphysical). Most scholars have seen an assertion of existence, pre-existence or eternal existence; this overlooks the possibilities of ellipsis.

The candidate ellipses for John 8:58 could be a referring expression or a predicate element. For example, " 'You should join the Pharisees', 'I am' " is an ellipsis involving 'I am', one supplied by the immediate context – '(I am) joining the Pharisees'. Or again, 'I am the promised Messiah, and unless you believe I am he, you will die in your sins' is an ellipsis that would use the Greek 'I am'. How much conversation intervenes between the ellipsis and the prior element can prevent readers seeing the connections, but often the ellipsis is just next door to the elided element.

5.2 Before Abraham was

Commentators look at the expression 'Before Abraham was' and think of the past; they see the person Abraham in the past and they position Jesus before him in time. They might talk about pre-existence and/or eternal existence. The aorist infinitive verb form underlying 'was' is not so cut and dried; instead of 'was' it could equally be prospective and something like 'comes to be' – it depends on how we read the context.

For example,

Your father rejoiced to see my day: and he saw it, and was glad...Before (πρὶν) Abraham was (γενέσθαι), I am. John 8:56-58 (KJV)

And now I have told you before (πρὶν) it come to pass (γενέσθαι), that, when it is come to pass, ye might believe. John 14:29 (KJV)

...telling beforehand the latter events before (πρὶν) they come to pass (γενέσθαι) ... Isa 46:10 (LXE)

These two examples use more or less the same construction of (πρὶν) + (γενέσθαι) and they show how John 8:58 can have a prospective sense. If we widen the list of examples to cover all the verses with the form (γενέσθαι) in John's Gospel (1:12; 3:9; 5:6; 9:27; 13:19), they all happen to be about what will be or what will become or what will come to pass.

The key argument is that the context of v. 58 suggests that we should read before Abraham 'comes to be' as the sense of the verb. However, if we focus on the *person* Abraham and think of his resurrection, we won't have a closing statement by Jesus that fits the argument he has been having with the Jews. Rather, we should ask what/who Abraham *can be or become* and the answer to this question is given in the promises God made to him:

And I will make of thee a great nation, and I will bless thee, and make thy name great; and thou shalt be a blessing Gen 12:2 (KJV)

And I will make my covenant between me and thee and will multiply thee exceedingly. Gen 17:2 (KJV)

And I will make thee exceedingly fruitful, and I will make nations of thee, and kings shall come out of thee. Gen 17:6 (KJV)

There is a difference to mark here between the promise to make nations of Abraham and the promise to make **him** exceedingly fruitful. The point for us is that we have in John 8:58 a statement about what *Abraham* will be/become – namely, a fruitful seed. Jesus' closing assertion is in effect 'Before Abraham becomes a fruitful seed, I am *he*'. This fits the flow of his conflict with the Jews in which they have claimed to be Abraham's seed (vv. 33, 37); we will see below that it forms a fitting closure to what he wanted to say to them.

Your father rejoiced to <u>see</u> my day: and he <u>saw</u> it and was glad…Before (πρὶν) Abraham comes to be (γενέσθαι),[1] I am *he*. John 8:56-58

The allusion here is to the promise of Genesis 17, which records Abraham being glad at the prospect of being a father (Gen 17:17; 21:3[2]) and where we find him re-named. Jesus makes a twofold allusion: he says Abraham rejoiced to see his day and this alludes to the promise of Genesis 17; he then says that he saw it and this seeing alludes to the events on Mount Moriah.[3] Finally, it is worth noting that Paul uses γενέσθαι to talk about Abraham becoming the father of many nations,

> Who against hope believed in hope, that he might become (γενέσθαι) the father of many nations, according to that which was spoken, 'So shall thy seed be'. Rom 4:18 (KJV)

5.3 Self-Identifying

The 'absolute'[4] 'I am' is defined by scholars as a usage where there is no predicate and/or no clear self-identifying idiomatic ellipsis.[5] Some scholars only use the criterion of there being no predicate to define an absolute use, but this is an error because, if we have a self-identifying idiom, 'I am *he*', this equally does not facilitate the theologizing that usually goes with 'I AM'.

Seeing the idiom is a matter of how you read a conversation. Some examples are clear uses of the self-identifying idiom. This is best seen in cases which have not become theologically controversial; there are also

---

[1] This means that readings based on 'was' are wrong, e.g. Before Abraham was born, was your father, was called 'Abraham', etc.

[2] The 'laughter' is his joy which is then commemorated in the name 'Isaac'.

[3] Commentators can mistakenly collapse the two seeing's into one and make a connection only with Mount Moriah.

[4] This is the common scholarly description; see S. Smalley, *John – Evangelist and Interpreter* (Exeter: Paternoster, 1978), 187. C. H. Williams, " 'I Am' or 'I Am He'? Self-Declaratory Pronouncements in the Fourth Gospel and Rabbinic Tradition" in *Jesus in Johannine Tradition* (eds. R. T. Fortana and T. Thatcher; Louisville; WJK Press, 2001), 343-352; Thompson, *The God of the Gospel of John*, 88.

[5] We use the concept of 'idiom' in a broad not a narrow sense; one illustrated in C. F. D. Moule's title 'An Idiom Book of the New Testament'.

clear examples with the corresponding Hebrew idiom which is 'I *am* he'. Interestingly, the Greek idiom (*egō eimi*) has no formal third person pronoun 'he' and the Hebrew idiom ('*ani hu*') has no formal verb 'am'. Nevertheless, the translators of the LXX match the two idioms. A natural translation of the self-identifying Greek idiom in English is 'I am *he*' with 'he' in italics to indicate that it is not formally present in the original Greek (or 'I *am* he' for the corresponding Hebrew), but 'I am' also works as the translation – it depends on the sentence.

Hebrew expressions for identifying are '*ani hu*' ('I *am* he'[1]), and '*atāh hu*' ('You *are* he'[2]); they are verbless but in all cases a present tense verb needs to be supplied in English to capture the sense – 'I *am* he' or 'You *are* he'. A corresponding expression in Greek for '*ani hu*' is *egō eimi*, literally, 'I, I am' but translated in various ways. For example,

> Some said, 'This is he': others, 'He is like him': he said, 'I, I am=I am *he*'. John 9:9 (KJV revised)

> But straightway Jesus spake unto them, saying, 'Be of good cheer; *It is I*=I, I am; be not afraid'. Matt 14:27 (KJV)

There are other places where the expression is translated '*It is I*', where an idiomatic sense is implied equivalent to answering the question, 'Who are you?' - see Matt 14:27; 26:22, 25; Mark 6:50; 14:62; Luke 22:70; 24:39; John 4:26; 6:20;[3] and 18:5, 6, 8. In some cases the idiom is part of a rhetorical question; in other places the questioning is implied by circumstances in a conversational situation.

In two other examples, translators have inserted a proper name to make, 'I am [Christ]' (Mark 13:6; Luke 21:8). These last two cases are interesting because they are part of Jesus' prophecy that false teachers would come in *his name* saying, 'I am'. Translators could have rendered the expression 'I

---

[1] An example in Biblical Hebrew is 1 Chron 21;17, 'I *am* he ('*ani hu*') that has sinned'.

[2] An example in Biblical Aramaic is Dan 4:22 – 'You *are* he ('*ant hú*), O king'.

[3] Williams, " 'I Am' or 'I Am He'? Self-Declaratory Pronouncements in the Fourth Gospel and Rabbinic Tradition", 346, rejects this text as a self-identification text, but she is misled by a mistaken reading of John 6:19 which is a narrator's identification of who they see and not the disciples' recognising it is Jesus. The Synoptics make it clear that they disciples thought they saw a ghost.

am he' in these cases also, since it is used in a self-identifying way and dependent upon a use of Christ's name.

Discussion of whether there are *any* examples of an absolute use of 'I am' centres on John 8:24, 28, 58 and 13:19.[1] We will look at the John 8 texts below, but as for John 13:19, it is a clear self-identifying ellipsis for 'Lord and Master', although often mistakenly taken as an absolute use:

> Ye call me <u>Master and Lord</u>: and ye say well; for so <u>I am</u> (*eimi*). If I then, your Lord and Master, have washed your feet; ye also ought to wash one another's feet. For I have given you an example, that ye should do as I have done to you. Verily, verily, I say unto you, the servant is not greater than his lord; neither he that is sent greater than he that sent him. If ye know these things, happy are ye if ye do them. I speak not of you all: I know whom I have chosen but that the scripture may be fulfilled, He that eateth bread with me hath lifted up his heel against me. Now I tell you before it come, that, when it is come to pass, ye may believe that <u>I am *he*</u> (*ego eimi*). John 13:13-19 (KJV)

As an ordinary idiom of common Greek, there are of course examples of the self-identifying 'I am' outside the New Testament, for example,

(1) *Apocalypse of Moses* 17.2 (1c. BCE – 2 c. CE)

> And bending over the wall, I saw him, like an angel. And he says to me: 'Are you Eve?' And I said to him: 'I am (*egō eimi*).'

(2) 2 Samuel 2:20 (LXX)

> Then Abner looked behind him, and said, 'Art thou Asahel?' And he answered, 'I am (*egō eimi*)'.

---

[1] An absolute use of *egō eimi* is not just a matter of a predicate being absent, or the absence of a participle construction (e.g. 'I am the one bearing witness'). It also has to be shown that we do not have a self-identifying use, i.e. 'I am *he*'. This is why commentators may have more candidate texts – they fail to see how some of their list are self-identifying uses – see W. Carter, *John* (Peabody: Hendrickson, 2006), 123, 203-204 for this mistake.

(3) *Testament of Job* 29:4 (cf. 31:6) (1c. BCE – 2 c. CE)

> Still generally doubting, Eliphaz the king of the Temanites, having turned to me, said: 'Are you Job, our fellow king?' And I, having wept, sprinkling earth upon my head and shaking it, declared to them: 'I am (*egō eimi*).'

The self-identifying idiom 'I am' is elliptical because we have to look to the context to determine who is the 'I'. The presumption should be, going into John 8, is that its uses of 'I am' are self-identifying. The absolute use of 'I am' here is a theological fiction.

And,

(4) *Apocalypse of Abraham* 8:3 (Late 1c. – 2c. CE)

> And he said, 'You are searching for the God of gods, the Creator, in the understanding of your heart. I *am* He.

This Apocalypse exists in a Slavonic translation of what is thought to be a Hebrew original of Palestinian provenance.[1] What is interesting is that the self-identifying use of 'I am He' is clear and that the Apocalypse features an angel communicating with Abraham.

Jesus alludes to Isaiah 43 in his dialogue with the Jews with his use of *egō eimi* — 'I am *he*'. Jesus models his controversy with the Jews in John 8 at the close of the Feast of Tabernacles[2] on Yahweh's contention with the people in Isaiah 43. We should therefore look to the context to determine who Jesus is saying that he is when he says, 'I *am* he'. To take the first example,

> ...for if ye believe not that I am, ye shall die in your sins. John 8:24 (KJV revised)

The self-identification here is with the preceding claims of Jesus,

---

[1] R. Rubinkiewicz "A New Translation and Introduction" *The Old Testament Pseudepigrapha* (ed. J. H. Charlesworth; 2 vols; New York: Doubleday, 1983-1985), 1:681-705 (683).
[2] A. Edersheim, *The Temple* (Repr. Ed.; London: Angus Hudson, 1997), 186.

And he said unto them, Ye are from beneath; I am from above: ye are of this world; I am not of this world. John 8:23 (KJV)

In short, Jesus says 'I am from above...I am not of this world...unless you believe that I am, you will die in your sins'. Generally, elliptical self-identification will be disambiguated near the ellipsis. The best translation here is simply 'I am'.

A second use of *egō eimi* best translated as 'I am *he*' is,

> ...when ye have lifted up the Son of Man, then shall ye know that I am *he*... John 8:28 (KJV revised)

The common suggestion[1] here is that Jesus is identifying himself as the Son of Man; disambiguation will often be a definite description, name or title.

When we look at John 8:58, there isn't an obvious nearby definite description, name or title to disambiguate the *egō eimi*.[2] This is why commentators regard this use as 'absolute', but if this is so, it is unique in John (despite attempts to garner a few more examples). On this basis, commentators then wax lyrical and talk about pre-existence, timelessness, eternity and deity, drawing in Isaiah 43 and/or Exodus 3.

What commentators have rejected from their consideration is the possibility that Jesus is using Abraham's name as a **metonymy** for his seed. Jesus' ellipsis works if 'I am *he*' is about Jesus being (the seed of) 'Abraham' before Abraham becomes a fruitful and multitudinous seed. This identification of Jesus as the **seed 'Abraham'** would become is established by Paul,

> Now to Abraham and his seed were the promises made. He saith not, and to seeds, as of many; but as of one, and to thy seed, which is Christ. Gal 3:16 (KJV)

The multitudinous seed that is 'Abraham' (which the Jews claimed to be) comes to be after Christ, who is the singular seed that is 'Abraham'. The multitudinous seed comes to be through faith in Christ.

---

[1] J. Painter, *The Quest for the Messiah* (Edinburgh: T & T Clark, 1991), 257.
[2] So, 'You are not yet fifty years old...I am' (v. 57) does not work; 'I know him...I am' (v. 55) equally fails to work as an ellipsis; and so on, working backwards.

Before Abraham was glad, this promise was given, and it describes the future work of the Angel of the Lord.

> And I will make my covenant between me and thee, and will multiply thee exceedingly... As for me, behold, my covenant is with thee... And I will make thee exceedingly fruitful... And I will establish my covenant between me and thee and thy <u>seed</u> after thee in their generations for an everlasting covenant, to be a God unto thee, and to thy seed after thee. Gen 17:2-7 (KJV)

It is this promise (and others) that the Jews place their confidence in when they say to Jesus,

> They answered him, 'We be Abraham's <u>seed</u>, and were never in <u>bondage</u> to any man: how sayest thou, Ye shall be made free?' John 8:33 (KJV)

And,

> They answered and said unto him, Abraham is our father. John 8:39 (KJV)

And,

> Art thou greater than our father Abraham, which is dead? and the prophets are dead: whom makest thou thyself? John 8:53 (KJV)

It is against this question that Jesus crafts his reply, "Before Abraham comes to be [a fruitful seed], I am *he*—['Abraham']".

5.4 Abraham

> And when Abram was ninety years old and nine, the Lord appeared to Abram, and said unto him, I *am* El Shaddai; walk before me, and be thou perfect. And I will make my covenant between me and <u>thee,</u> and I will multiply thee exceedingly. Gen 17:1-2 (KJV revised)

Genesis 17 records an incident where Abraham is promised that **he** would be multiplied (v. 2), which a reader would naturally compare with the immediately preceding promise to Hagar. Hagar's seed would be multiplied as well as the seed that would be born through Sarai.

The terms of this promise cover several things:

94

- First, 'I will multiply' is picked up from Gen 16:10, then repeated in Gen 22:17 and then Exod 32:13. The promise is that God would multiply *Abram* and this is what Moses pleads using Gen 22:17 when God proposed instead to make of *him* a great nation (Exod 32:10).

- Second, Abram would be a father of many nations and so his name is changed to 'Abraham'. This 'many nations' element is distinct from the 'multiplying seed' element which pertains to Israel in Egypt:

  > And the children of Israel were fruitful, and increased abundantly, and <u>multiplied</u>, and waxed exceeding mighty; and the land was filled with them. Exod 1:7 (KJV)

- Third, God would establish his covenant with Abraham's seed "after him" (Gen 17:2, 5); he would give the land to his seed "after him" (Gen 17:6). His seed "after him" would be required to circumcise every male child (Gen 17:10). All of these elements are incorporated into the Law (John 7:22; Acts 7:5).

Jesus' "Before Abraham" stands as a natural contrast to the refrain in this promise of what is "after Abraham" (vv. 2, 7, 8, 9, 10). The Jew's confidence in Abraham as their father reflects their position "after him", but Jesus was *before* 'Abraham' would become a fruitful seed.[1]

The Jews had argued as follows,

> They answered him, 'We be Abraham's <u>seed</u>, and were never in <u>bondage</u> to any man: how sayest thou, Ye shall be made free?' John 8:33 (KJV)

Jesus' counter-claim is that if they believed his word, the truth would set them free; the typology is one of *making people* free from bondage.[2] The Jews could point to Abraham as their father but the one greater than Abraham would be the one who was to make him that father both of a multitudinous seed and of many nations.

---

[1] N. Bernard, "BEFORE ABRAHAM WAS, I AM" *The Testimony* (1993): 196.

[2] This is why the ellipsis is neither 'Before Abraham was (Abraham)' nor 'Before Abraham was (your father)' – the naming of Abram pertains to his being the father of many nations rather than his seed being multitudinous. Jesus was sent to the lost sheep of the house of Israel, not the Gentiles.

5.5 Objections

There are four alternatives to our approach to be noted.

(1) The most common interpretation states that 'Before Abraham was' is about a time before Abraham was born (existed). It is said that Jesus' claim is all about a pre-existence in heaven or an existence in eternity.[1] The problem with this reading is that it is dependent on linking 'I am' to either Exodus 3 or Isaiah 43 (or both[2]) but (a) Exodus 3 is about manifestation and not existence; and (b) Isaiah 43 is about self-identification and not existence. Moreover, 'I *am* he' is not about existence but **identity**. Our approach keeps the focus on Jesus' emphasis on identity (v. 25, 'Who are you?') and Jesus' constant assertions about himself – hence, we can properly explain the present tense quality of 'I am *he*' (which the pre-existence reading cannot do).

The argument of Jesus with the Jews is about a present identity and not a past one; Jesus doesn't say 'Before Abraham was, I was'. His thinking is not about his existence as someone (in heaven or on earth) back in the history of the nation.

In order to make a point about Abraham centred on his rejoicing at the promise of a seed and fatherhood, you have to use a prospective tense; hence, Jesus says elliptically, 'Before Abraham comes to be, I am *he*'. Jesus' whole assertion might be regarded as odd because of the mixed tenses, but this is necessary if you are using 'Abraham' as a metonymy for his seed. All Jesus is in effect saying is – **Before Abraham will be made a fruitful seed, I *am* he ('Abraham', that seed).**

(2) A second alternative interpretation is that Jesus does not say 'I am *he*' to refer to what 'Abraham' was promised he would become, i.e. a seed. He is using the divine self-identifying proclamation from Isaiah 43 to

---

[1] You don't have to look far for this idea: C. H. Dodd, *The Fourth Gospel* (Cambridge: Cambridge University Press, 1953), 261; J. Marsh, *Saint John* (London: Penguin, 1968), 371; B. Lindars, *The Gospel of John* (London: Oliphants, 1972), 336; C. K. Barrett, *The Gospel According to St. John* (London: SPCK, 1976), 292; etc. What is astonishing about these commentaries is how very little justification is given for the interpretation; they take it for granted. No doubt part of the reason is that they were unaware in their day of the emerging disciplines of Semantics and Pragmatics.

[2] See B. Lindars, *John* (Sheffield: Sheffield University Press, 1990), 84-86 for a good introduction to the options.

indicate an identity with the God of Israel. The problem with this reading is that it ignores the semantics of the self-identifying idiom 'I am *he*' as it **functions in the real conversation of John 8**. In that conversation, Jesus hasn't previously introduced an identification between himself and the God of Israel, an identification that can then be picked up later by an elliptical use of 'I am *he*'. Further, whereas in a later conversation, the Jews will understand Jesus to make a claim of equality with God (John 10), they make no such reply in this exchange.[1] In essence, this proposal throws the reference of an ellipsis back to Isaiah 43 based on allusiveness in Jesus' reasoning, rather than the more immediate metonymy of 'the seed' of Abraham.

Elliptical self-identifying idioms are common enough and there is nothing intrinsically 'divine' or unique to Isaiah or John about such an expression. For example, to show that there is nothing uniquely Israelite about 'I *am* he', take the following Sumerian hymn to Enlil (c. 1000-1300),

> I am the Lord, the lion of the holy An, the hero of Sumer, I make the fishes of the sea glad, and see that the birds do not fall down, the wise countryman, who ploughs the field, Enlil, I am he.[2]

The conversation Jesus is having with the Jews is about the seed of Abraham, fatherhood, Abraham himself, and his own identity or status. What he has seen his father do in Isaiah, he himself is doing with his identity as the seed of Abraham. Jesus can indeed be alluding to Isaiah 43,

---

[1] It is often argued that the Jews' taking up of stones to stone him requires a recognition on their part that Jesus was using the divine name, claiming it for himself, or referring or alluding to it – see Whittaker, *Studies in the Gospels*, 406-407; Ashton, *Understanding the Fourth Gospel*, 85. If this was their understanding (cf. Lev 24:10-11), this does not mean it was Jesus' intention; they often misunderstood him. Moreover, this reading of the stoning is too narrow. In this exchange, Jesus has said that his opponents can't tell anything about him (v. 14); they judge after the flesh (v. 15); they don't know God (v. 19); they will die in their sins (v. 21); they are of the world (v. 23); they did the deeds of the devil (v. 44); and they were liars (v. 55). It is no surprise that they would take up stones to stone him. In narrative terms, their attempt at stoning obviously stands as an ironic counterpoint to their unwillingness to stone the woman taken in adultery. Jesus has said many things in this discourse to give them cause to stone him.

[2] W. Beyerlin, ed., *Near Eastern Religious Texts relating to the Old Testament* (London: SCM Press, 1978), 101.

but the conversation he is having with the Jews does not itself indicate he is identifying himself directly as the God of Israel (or in contemporary parlance, including himself in the identity of the God of Israel).

(3) The third alternative is that Jesus is using the divine name from Exod 3:14, 'I AM that I AM'. We have already noted that this has more to do with theology than Hebrew linguistics. Simply put, 'I AM' is not the divine name; this is 'Yahweh'.

Nevertheless, Exodus 3 contains a paronomasia between the name 'Yahweh' (*Yhwh*) and the verb form 'I will be' ('*hyh*), and as part of that construction, God instructs Moses to say, 'I will be has sent me unto you' (Exod 3:14). This is distinctive wordplay but not a precedent for John 8. God's use of 'I will be' has a predicate; it stands as a proxy[1] for a referring expression like a name – this is the point of the substitution and how the paronomasia works, which Moses gets, because he was to say that 'Yahweh Elohim has sent me unto you' (Exod 3:15). John is instead an idiom of self-identification 'I am *he*'.

On the other hand, we might well say that 'I will be **who** I will be' is fulfilled in Jesus, and so his use of 'I am *he*' is also designed to show that he is the present tense fulfilment of 'I will be *who* I will be',[2] but this fulfilment is the same as God's presence in the Angel of the Lord before Abraham and at the exodus (i.e. in the Angel of the Presence; Exod 23:20-21; Isa 63:9). Jesus' earlier declaration that he is the Light of the World is how he is claiming in this dialogue to be God manifest[3] in the flesh.

This theology is correct but a more straightforward approach to the discourse of John 8 should at first be established before digging deeper. Whereas scholars usually work with the LXX as their witness for the OG and relate John 8:58 to Exod 3:14's 'I am the Being',[4] this is not how the Spirit quotes and develops its own Hebrew Scriptures. Jesus is a

---

[1] In a wordplay where paronomasia is going on, a unique use of 'I will be/I am' does not create a name in and of itself; there aren't two names of God – 'Yahweh' and 'I will be/I am'.

[2] See A. Gibson, " 'I AM' AND 'I AM HE' " *The Testimony* (1975): 94-95.

[3] Showing God and being a manifestation of God in the flesh is John's theology throughout the gospel. It begins in 1:1, 'and was God', continues through 'has seen the Father' (14:9) and ends with Thomas' confession 'my God' (20:28).

[4] Philo has the same approach as the LXX to the divine name, e.g. *Life of Moses* 1.75.

manifestation of whom God would be, and his 'I am' declarations in John are uttered in part to establish this claim, but we also need to root Jesus' declaration in the conversation that he has with the Jews.

Once *egō eimi* is recognised as a self-identifying idiom, the conversation controls its semantics; it should disambiguate the identification with a more explicit expression of identity such as a name. We are not free to go and look for identities outside the conversation, for example, that Jesus is asserting he is the seed of the woman (Gen 3:15).

(4) The final alternative interpretation[1] is that Jesus is not asserting his pre-existence in respect of Abraham but rather a quality of existence, a timeless eternal existence – he simply *is* ('I am'). He has eternal life in himself and the Jews are just showing their wilful misunderstanding when they accuse him of claiming to be older than Abraham. This interpretation can, of course, be combined with interpretations (2) and/or (3) if it is thought that Jesus is doing more than claiming to have eternal life.

The main problem with this view is that it rejects the reading that *egō eimi* is **a self-identifying idiom**, and so it flies in the face of all the textual evidence for this usage in the NT and the LXX which we have listed. Secondly, it slides together notions of existence and quality of life. A claim to have existed is different from one about having an eternal quality of life. Finally, the interpretation misinterprets what Jesus means when he says that the Father has given to the Son to have life in himself (John 5:26) – this was given upon his resurrection from the dead. The eternal life that Jesus has to give is the light of life (v. 12), a life that is realized through resurrection.

6. Conclusion

In this chapter, we have argued that the correct translation of *'ehyeh 'asher 'ehyeh* is 'I will be who I will be'. This translation fits the focus of God's conversation with Moses, which from our perspective is about **identity** rather than existence and nature. From this point, it would be possible to expand on this basis and show how the idea of God being with someone and being that person through manifestation is fulfilled in other figures in Israelite history and pre-eminently in Jesus Christ. In this sense, Moses is a type of Christ. What we have offered is a contrast—a contrast between the philosophical theology that is imposed on a text, a theology about existence and being, (as if God is concerned to make these points with his

---

[1] Thompson, *The God of the Gospel of John*, 91-92.

servant Moses; that this is *his* need), and an assurance that he *will be* with his servant and in him through the Spirit.

Discussion of John 8:58 has been bedevilled by theology. Failure to see the cut and thrust of a back-and-forth dialogue, making a due allowance for ellipsis, has meant that theologians have wrested the text from its context and plonked it into the middle of musings about existence, eternity and deity. This has been sustained by ancient exegesis of the divine name and Exodus.

The textual evidence for *'ani hu'* ('I *am* he'), and *'atāh hu'* ('You *are* he') and *ego eimi* ('I am *he*') suggests we have a self-identifying idiom rather than, in the case of *ego eimi*, an assertion about existence, eternity or deity. When we investigate who Jesus is identifying himself to be in John 8:58, the conversational context suggests that it is the fruitful seed of Abraham. i.e. what 'Abraham' would come to be.

CHAPTER SIX
Was Christ the Genesis Creator?

1. Introduction

The most commonly quoted passage in favour of the pre-existence of Christ is John 1:1, 'In the beginning was the Word and the Word was with God and the Word was God'. This is placed alongside John 1:14 'And the Word was made/became flesh and dwelt among us...' to affirm the incarnation of the Word. The suggestion is made that the Word was in the beginning creating the world, for John goes onto say that 'All things were made by him' (John 1:3). It is then suggested that at some point the word became flesh.

Another verse usually quoted with John 1 is Heb 1:10, 'And thou Lord, in the beginning hast laid the foundation of the earth, and the heavens are the work of thy hands'; and yet another is Col 1:15-16, '...the firstborn of every creature: For by him were all things created'; or again, Heb 1:2, 'by whom also he made the worlds'.

All these verses involve the idea of a creation and what is made by a creator, who is taken to be the Son or the Father working *through* the Son. The orthodox proposal is that it is the Genesis creation and that the Son is a creator of *that* creation as part of the Godhead.

In this chapter, we want to look at the Hebrews and Colossians passages as *examples* of the kind of texts which are used to affirm the view that the Son was a/the Genesis creator. In Chapter Nine we will examine John 1 in detail as an incarnation and Genesis creation passage.

2. The New Creation

We need to carefully distinguish *what is created*. There are differences in meaning between the expressions 'all things', 'the world', 'worlds' and 'heaven and earth'. Ignoring these differences is a mistake in some writers. For example, the notion of the 'world' is a contrary idea to the notion of 'all things'. The idea of 'all things' in our passages is about a **new creation** (John 1:3) and a **new order amongst existing things** (Col 1:15-16) which is contrary to what commentators claim. The idea of 'the world' (John 1:10), on the other hand, is that of 'the nation of Israel' at that time, and we shall see that other ideas lie behind the 'worlds' of Heb 1:2 and the 'heavens and earth' of Heb 1:10.

In one sense, there is only one creation — the Genesis creation. This was begun in the beginning and has been continuing ever since. However, after the fall God began a work of new creation (cf. the typology implicit in Isa 43:13 and other 'new' texts in Isaiah), and this work was explained to the faithful in OT times in the way their prophets described God's purpose. The language of creation was used and re-used throughout these times to mark endings and then new beginnings in God's purpose. This is also true of the NT period in which, for example, a 'second man' (1 Cor 15:47) appears along with a new 'bride' (John 3:29). The expression 'the new creation' does not occur in the Bible, but this should not blind us to the presence of creative work in OT times and especially the NT period. It is this work which we characterize as part of the new creation (cf. 2 Cor 5:17-18; Gal 6:15; Eph 2:10; 3:9; Col 3:10). We can think of the expression 'the new creation' as a kind of shorthand phrase for the work of bringing about new creatures in Christ. This work is now the work of the Father *and* the Son.

Jesus tells us that the Son can do nothing of himself, but what the Father does, he likewise does (John 5:19). This proves that the Son and the Father are doing the same work; indeed, the Son has the task of finishing the work of the Father (John 5:34). Jesus goes on to say that the Father will yet show the Son greater works than the works he had performed up until that point in his ministry (John 5:20). Jesus characterizes this work as raising the dead for judgment (John 5:21-22). This is a future work, but it has a present beginning, since those who believe in Christ pass from death to life (John 5:24; Rom 6:4-6). This work of bringing people into the church continued after the ascension of Christ(cf. 1 Thess 3:11ff and 2 Thess 2:16-17).

The Father is the source of all creation and pre-eminently **the** creator (e.g. see Phil 1:6; Col 2:10; 3:10), but there is partnership between the Father and the Son (John 5:17; cf. Phil 2:22), and this is shown in several ways:[1]

---

[1] There is a lot of evidence of this partnership; you just look for those passages where the Father and the Son are spoken of *together*. For instance, in the epistles, the opening and closing salutations often have expressions like 'grace be to you and peace from God the Father, and from the Lord Jesus Christ', and this indicates partnership (e.g. 1 Tim 1:2; 2 Tim 1:2; Tit 1:4; 2 John v. 3). In a Jewish framework, this is astonishing because the Jews betray no anticipation of this exalted role for the messiah in their writings of the time.

1) God builds *all things* (Heb 2:10; 3:4; Rev 4:11) and is the architect (1 Cor 3:10); but Christ *also builds* the church (Matt 16:18; Eph 2:22; cf. Eph 4:11; 1 Tim 1:12, 16; 2 Tim 3:11).

2) Christ is our peace, having abolished in his flesh the enmity in order to *make* in himself one new man by reconciling both Jew and Gentile unto God (Eph 2:15-16); but God makes peace through the blood of his cross; and *by* Christ, reconciles all things unto himself, in the body of his flesh (Col 1:19-20). This reconciliation is the heart of Christ's priestly work (Heb 2:17; 2 Cor 5:17-18).

Reconciling men and women unto God is the work of God and Christ. Another way of looking at the work of Christ is to look at its past, present, and future aspects. The past work of salvation, the present work of priesthood, reconciliation and building the church, and the future work of establishing the kingdom. The aspect of Christ's work that we focus on in this chapter is his creative 'building' work.

3. Colossians 1:15-20

Christ is the firstborn of a new creation, and he holds the position of maker of that new creation, working with his father to bring it about. Because it is a new creation, the language used to describe it is closely modelled on the language of the original Genesis creation. It is easy therefore to make a mistake and read those NT passages which talk of Christ as creator with the Genesis creation in our minds. But we shall argue that they should be read with the idea of a **new creation** instead.[1]

One idea shared between the old creation and the new creation is the concept of *all things*. The Greek of the NT is just an ordinary expression and the scope of 'all' is defined in the context.

---

[1] Christ is the 'firstborn' of the new creation by virtue of being the firstborn from the dead, but this does not mean that the new creation began at the point of Christ's resurrection, although to be true, Christ's resurrection is *the* beginning in one sense (Rev 3:14). We argued in Chapter Two that God began his work of new creation just after the fall. With those creatures that make up the bride, their creation has yet to be completed with their resurrection. As with Adam, Christ is the *first* creature to be *completed* in the new creation. Of course, if Christ had not been raised from the dead, he would still be dead, and there would be no discussion about pre-existence or deity.

103

In Genesis, we are taught that God the Father created all things in heaven and earth and the sea (Acts 14:15; 17:24; Rev 4:11; 10:6). We also see that all things were placed under Adam (Gen 1:26; Ps 8:6). Adam was like Noah, given *all things* to eat (vegetable/animal, Gen 1:29; 9:3). He was also given dominion over all the beasts of the field (not the beasts of the earth), having had them first presented as companions (Gen 2:19; Ps 8:6-7).[1] Finally, he was given Eve.[2] We have then the following:

> All things *created* to fill heaven, earth and sea.
> All things placed *under* a man, ordered *by* him.
> All foodstuffs given *to* a man to eat.
> All creatures given to a man for dominion.

The idea of *all* in Genesis embraces *things*, including vegetation, and creatures, including animals; and we cannot exclude Eve from the domain of the idea either, because she was a work of God's hand, given to the man. This kind of usage of 'all things' can be found in the inter-testamental literature

Psalm 8 is an exposition of Genesis 2, and it acts as a filter for the NT usage of "all things". The NT employs the expression from Psalm 8, and through this passage, the creation of Genesis 2 is brought into the NT as a backdrop to the apostolic age and a new creation. Thinking of both the First and the Last Adam, we read:

> For thou hast made him a little lower than the angels, and hast crowned him with glory and honour. thou madest him to have dominion over the works of thy hands; thou hast put all [things] under his feet: all sheep and oxen, yea, and the beasts of the field; the fowl of the air, and the fish of the sea, [and whatsoever] passeth through the paths of the seas. Ps 8:5-8 (KJV)

If[3] the idea of a new creation is valid, we should expect to find the expression 'all things' in connection with a new creation in the NT (and

---

[1] Dominion and companionship is implicit in Genesis 2, because Adam was given the beasts of the field to see *what names he would give them.*

[2] It is usually assumed that when Eve was created, she was the sole *objective* of companionship. This overlooks the fact that, as the mother of all life, Eve would have given birth to a large community of companions.

[3] We should not assume that the concept of a new creation is valid, it requires proof. This can be found in the reproduction of 'creation

the OT). But if we do, we should be on the lookout not only for the idea of *things*, but also for the mention of creatures as well as a mention of the counterpart to Eve — the bride of Christ. Besides the idea of creation, we should be on the lookout for the idea of a man who is placed over the creation and *by (through)* whom the creation is ordered. We should also bear in mind that all things were given *to* the man, so the idea of *giving* should also feature prominently. All these elements should figure in something that was going on in the time of the apostles.

All these ideas come together in Colossians 1:

> Who is the image of the invisible God, the firstborn of every creature: For by (*lit.* in) him were all things created, that are in heaven, and that are in earth, visible and invisible, whether [they be] thrones, or dominions, or principalities, or powers: all things were created through him, and for (*lit.* to) him: And he is before all things, and through him all things consist. And he is the head of the body, the church: who is the beginning, the firstborn from the dead;[1] that in all [things] he might have the pre-eminence. For it pleased [the Father] that in him should all fulness dwell; And having made peace through the blood of his cross, by him to reconcile all things unto (*lit.* to) himself; by him, [I say,] whether [they be] things in earth, or things in heaven." Col 1:15-18 (KJV revised); cf. Eph 1:22-23

This is a difficult passage because it talks of *creatures*, *things*, and a *body*, and seemingly all at the same time. It is difficult to know precisely what Paul is saying about these entities, so we'll split it up into its parts.

The Col 1:15-20 passage is made up of two paragraphs (vv. 15-18a and vv. 18b-20), set out in Figure 1. This paragraph structure is constructed

---

language' in the NT and the application of this language to the work of God at that time. A word study on the word 'new' helps here, see for example, the 'new commandment' given at the beginning (e.g. John 13:34; 2 John v. 5) and compare Adam's commandment; or the new covenant and compare Noah's covenant (e.g. Heb 12:24); or the new man (e.g. Eph 4:24) or new creature (e.g. 2 Cor 5:17). The new heavens and new earth are yet future for when the man and the woman come together (Rev 21:1-2).

[1] Israel was God's firstborn son from the dead (Egypt).

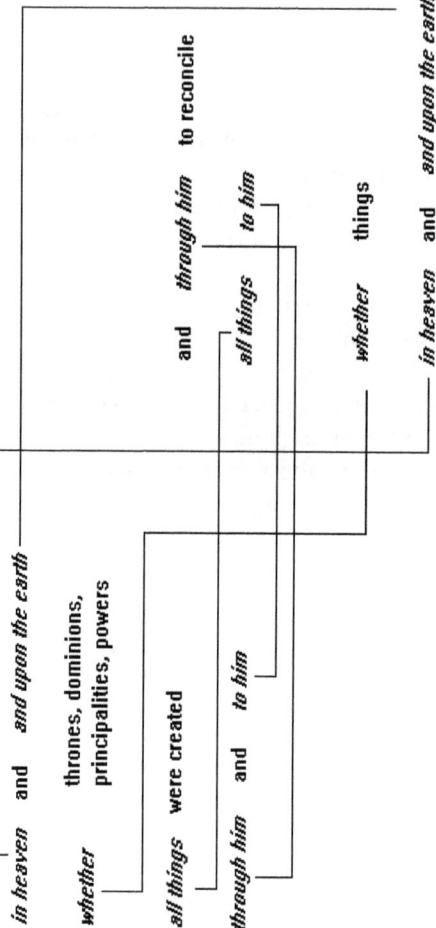

Figure 1

v15-16

who is the image

the firstborn of all creation

for in him were created all things

in heaven and and upon the earth

whether thrones, dominions, principalities, powers

all things were created

through him and to him

v18b-20

who is the beginning

the firstborn from the dead

for in him should all fulness dwell

and through him to reconcile

all things to him

whether things

in heaven and and upon the earth

around the relative pronouns which all relate to the mention of *the Son* in v. 13:

> ...his dear Son: in whom we have... (v. 14) ...who is the image... (vv. 15-18a) ... who is the beginning... (vv. 18b-20)

The second paragraph (vv. 18b-20) uses various expressions from the first paragraph (vv. 15-18a), thereby adding supplementary information to the first paragraph.

The common expressions between the two paragraphs are in italics, and what follows the expression in the second paragraph supplements what follows the expression in the first paragraph. So for example, we read of Christ *who is* the image of God (v. 15a), and *who is* the beginning of creation (v. 18b). Or again, Christ is *the firstborn* of every creature (v. 15b), and *the firstborn* from the dead (v. 18c). Or again, all things were created *in him* (v. 15a), so that *in* (or among) all he might have the pre-eminence (v. 18c), and so that the fulness of God *should eventually* dwell *in him* (v. 19).[1] Or again, all things were created *(by) through him* (v. 16d, cf. Eph 3:9), and so all things are reconciled *through him* (v 20b, cf. Eph 1:5). The work of creation is one of reconciliation.[2]

---

[1] The point here is not that Christ himself is the place where God dwells, though this is true, but rather that the fulness of the Godhead requires Christ to create all things *in him* in order to accommodate a fulness of God. This matches the Father's creation of all things in the beginning as a reflection of his glory. At the end of the millennium, the Son hands over the kingdom to the Father so that at that time the Father may then be 'all spiritual things in all individuals' (1 Cor 15:28).

[2] The Greek prepositions used in Col 1:15-18 are translated in Figure 1 as follows: ἐν αὐτῷ as 'in him' and δι' αὐτοῦ as 'through him'. The KJV (and other translations) uses 'by' for ἐν αὐτω, which is wrong for Colossians 1. This Greek expression occurs some 88 times in the NT and it is overwhelmingly translated as 'in him'. In addition to this consideration, the reproduction of the Greek between the two paragraphs (vv. 15-16 and vv. 18b-20) requires us to read 'in him' for v. 16a as the later clause in v. 19 has 'in him should all fulness dwell' which is locative in sense. It is important to distinguish the sense of δι' αὐτου as 'through him' — but this is not a causal sense, as if to say it is *because of him* something was done, (though this may be generally true). But rather the sense is that of an intermediary through whom something is done, or an instrument through which something is achieved — for example, the Greek is used when describing those who believe through John the Baptist (John 1:7),

3.1 Creatures

The text says that Christ is the image of God and he is therefore the anti-type to Adam (Gen 1:26; 1 Cor 11:7). Adam was 'firstborn' (created first before Eve), and likewise Christ is 'firstborn'. Christ is the 'firstborn' of all creatures, which implies other creatures in the creation. But he is the *firstborn,* and this implies that the other creatures are *like-born* men and women, but second in order. He is 'firstborn' in virtue of being firstborn from the dead,[1] and the other creatures will also be born from the dead, except those who are alive and remain (Rom 8:29; Heb 12:23). Among these he will be pre-eminent (v. 18d), reconciling them to himself (Col 1:20-21).

In the framework of Genesis 2, the creatures were initially the animals created for Adam's companionship (Ps 8:6, 7), but in terms of a new creation, literal animals are not the subject of Colossians 1. Because no help meet was found for Adam among the animals, a special creature was made — a female of the man, *made* from the man. Eve was the last creature to be created (for) and brought to Adam. With this female, the man was to be fruitful and multiply, and thereby gain many companions and helpers in his work. *These* were to be 'his creatures', like-born creatures — other men and women. In the new creation these children typify reconciled *creatures* — new men and women (Col 1:20, 23). These creatures are brought to birth through 'Eve' (the church), with the Word of God (i.e. the seed). This spiritual birth involves suffering, because the children that are so born learn obedience through the things they suffer. Natural childbirth is painful, and this is designed to teach the woman the spiritual truth that the children of God learn obedience through the things that they suffer.

---

when Peter says God did miracles through Jesus (Acts 2:22), when Paul questions whether he gained through any he sent to Corinth (2 Cor 12:17), when Paul describes Christ as an intermediary (Eph 2:18, and other verses making similar points), and these are just typical examples of the twenty verses in the NT which use this construction. In English the semantic fields of 'by' and 'through' overlap: 'by' can imply mediatorship in an action (e.g. the active assertion, 'he did it by getting Jonathan to do it', can become the passive, 'it was done by Jonathan'), but it need not imply such mediatorship; it all depends. The uses of 'by' in the KJV passages that describe the new creation should be taken in the sense of 'through'.

[1] The title 'firstborn' is not necessarily indicative of the process of begettal; it is also a title of *status* (Ps 89:27) and hence, we could translate as 'firstborn of all creation'.

3.2 Things

What are the *things* referred to by Paul? The text talks of *things* as well as *creatures*. The things include thrones, principalities, dominions and powers, and they may be visible or invisible, in heaven or on earth. This aspect of Christ's work as like Adam's lordship over the beasts of the field, as illustrated in his naming of them.

3.2.1 Thrones and Lordships

There are four interpretations of 'principalities and powers' in Col 1:16: civil and religious authorities (viewed concretely or abstractly); angelic orders; demonic powers; and spiritual/social forces at work among people. These are well-trodden paths among commentators. Our proposal is a nuance of the interpretation 'human powers'. Colossians 1:16 refers to the powers (viewed concretely or abstractly) in Paul's **present and future**. Those seen on the earth obviously pertain to Paul's present and those 'in the heavens' are of the future kingdom. We therefore eschew the more common suggestion that the invisible things in the heavens are either demonic powers or angelic orders. Given Paul's expectation of an imminent return of Christ to set up the kingdom, his statement that the powers on earth and in the heavens have been created 'in Christ' is part of that expectation. Paul's use of the language of powers in this way constitutes a criticism of Jewish cosmological fables (Tit 1:14).

On a first look, the text has some ambiguity,

> For in him all things were created, both in the heavens and on the earth, the things visible and the things invisible, whether thrones or lordships or rulers or authorities. Col 1:16 (KJV revised)

This could be saying that some powers are heavenly and some earthly, for example, thrones and lordships might pertain to heaven, while rulers and authorities might relate to earthly powers. Or it could be saying that all the powers listed are both earthly *and* heavenly at the same time depending on your perspective. Or it could be saying that all of these powers might be either heavenly *or* earthly, i.e. there might be heavenly thrones and different earthly thrones, *and so on*. Whatever we say, they 'were created' and this is not about assigning a new status or reconstituting existing powers but, foreseeing Christ, creating them in and around him.

If we examine texts where the terms, 'rulers', 'authorities', 'thrones' and 'lordships' occur separately, biblical and extra-biblical, up to and including the time of the NT writers, the majority of examples will relate to power exercised by human beings. This isn't enough to settle Paul's meaning because 'rulers and authorities' is a collocation that is used elsewhere in the NT and we need to determine whether, as such, it has a specialized use in Paul.

The plural 'thrones' is used in respect of the kings of the earth (Luke 1:52), as well as the twelve (Luke 22:30). There are twenty-four thrones around the throne of God (Dan 7:9; Rev 4:4, 10). The most direct connection with Christ is that of the thrones of the twelve to which Christ appoints his disciples; these can be clearly said to have their authority 'in him'. Paul may be referring to all or some of these kinds of throne; we need to look at other texts to decide this question.

When we look at such texts, there are one or two points which can mislead a reader, but once these are properly analyzed, there is nothing really to overturn the majority reading of 'thrones and lordships' as human powers.

The word 'lordship' is rare in the NT (4x), and it is used of a structure of government (2 Pet 2:10, Jude v. 8). Paul uses a similar four-fold expression of powers in Ephesians using 'lordship',

> …far above all rule and authority and power and <u>lordship</u>, and above every name that is named, <u>not only in this age but also in that which is to come</u>… Eph 1:21 (RSV revised)

Christ has been placed into a position of rule over rulers, authorities and lordships in the age in which Paul lived and with regard to the age to come. The point here for us is that Col 1:16 is not just a statement about Paul's present; it is a prophetic statement about the future. Our proposal is that the pairing of 'this age and the future age' is matched in the pairing of 'on the earth and in the heavens'.

Men and women are baptised *into* Christ, but another way to be *in him* is to be gathered around him. There is a time in the future when all things will be gathered together in Christ,

> That in the administration of the fulness of times he might <u>gather</u> together in one <u>all things</u> in Christ, both which are in the heavens, and which are on earth; *even* in him… Eph 1:10 (KJV revised)

110

The description 'things which are in the heavens' is a way of talking about things then created for the future which will come from heaven and be instantiated on earth, for example, the New Jerusalem will come 'from above' (Gal 4:26). This means that we should read Col 1:16 as (partly) a **prophetic statement** of what has been established in, for and through Christ for the future kingdom on earth – the administration of 'the fulness of times.'

Paul makes a statement about 'the things visible and the things invisible'; the invisible things concern **things to come** rather than angelic orders[1] or demonic powers. Thrones and lordships have been created in Christ for the future because they will be gathered to him at that time. The language of the visible and the invisible is used for the present and the future and indicative of prophetic statements being made about 'things unseen':

> For this slight momentary affliction is preparing for us an eternal weight of glory beyond all comparison, because we look not to the things that are <u>seen</u> but to the things that are <u>unseen</u>; for the things that are <u>seen</u> are transient, but the things that are <u>unseen</u> are eternal. 2 Cor 4:17-18 (RSV)

The example of the unseen things that Paul gives is the resurrection body which was 'in the heavens' (2 Cor 5:1). This is what he was looking for – something 'from heaven' (2 Cor 5:2).[2]

The principle here is expressed by Paul in Romans,

> (As it is written, I have made thee a father of many nations,) before him whom he believed, even God, who quickeneth the dead, <u>and calleth those things which be not as though they were</u>. Rom 4:17 (KJV)

---

[1] *Contra* H. A. Whittaker, "Principalities and Powers" in his *Bible Studies* (Cannock: Biblia, 1987), 375-382; and his *7 Short Epistles*, 11. However, this is not to say that 'thrones' and 'lordships' are terms not used of angelic orders in cosmological statements from Jewish writings from the 1c. BCE – 2c. CE – see in addition *Test. Lev.* 3:8; *Asc. Is.* 7:14-35; 8:18; *1 En.* 61:10 and *2 En.* 20:1.

[2] The point here is twofold: first, the language of 'in the heavens' connects with Colossians; and secondly, the language of 'looking for' is about the future. Hence, it would be a mistake to think that Paul is talking about the unseen eternal properties of the Godhead.

Hence, there is a common connection between the language of seeing and prophecy. Faith is a conviction about things not seen (Heb 11:1) and illustrated in the example of Noah who was warned by God concerning things he as yet could not see (Heb 11:7). The prophets wanted to see the things concerning Christ (Matt 13:17) but only sometimes did they see his day (John 8:56).

We conclude therefore that the future thrones[1] created in Christ are most directly the twelve thrones that pertain to Israel, while the future lordships created in Christ pertain to the Gentiles. This suggestion is supported by the fact that the things in the heavens are 'reconciled' through Christ (v. 20) and reconciliation of Jew and Gentile in Christ is achieved through the cross.

3.2.2 Rulers and Authorities

The traditional topic of principalities and powers goes now under the rubric of 'rulers and authorities'. The collocation occurs as many as ten times in the NT writings, depending on how strict you are in defining the collocation (plural and singular). In order to identify these powers, we can start in Ephesians.

> Unto me, who am less than the least of all saints, is this grace given, that I should preach among the Gentiles the unsearchable riches of Christ; and to make all men see what is the fellowship of the mystery, which from the beginning of the world hath been hid in God, who created (κτίσαντι) all things to the intent that now the manifold wisdom of God might be made known by the church to the rulers and authorities in the heavenly places, according to the eternal purpose which he purposed in Christ Jesus our Lord... Eph 3:8-11 (KJV revised)

This clearly places the rulers and authorities 'in the heavenly places' (ἐν τοῖς ἐπουρανίοις[2]) and gives a role to the church in making the wisdom of God known to them. They are unlikely to be demonic powers or angelic orders (working from heaven or the desert) in a passage concerned with

---

[1] We might say that the twenty-four thrones around the throne were the present thrones.

[2] The adjective here is usually supplied with a spatial noun by translators, e.g. 'places' (KJV); 'realms' (NET). The reason for the spatial noun is the use in Eph 1:20, "set him at his own right hand in the heavenly places". Elsewhere, the adjective has different associated nouns.

preaching to the Gentiles. The problem that commentators have with this passage is with the meaning of 'the heavenly places.'

These places are referred to by Christ when he says, "In my Father's house are many abiding places...I go to prepare a place for you, and if I go and prepare a place for you, I will come again and receive you unto myself" (John 14:2-3). These places (μονή) are where the Father and the Son 'dwell' with believers in their lives on earth, "we will come unto him, and make our abode with him" (John 14:23). Insofar as believers on earth dwell in such places (in a temple, the body of Christ), they dwell with the Father and the Son. Thus, when rulers and authorities engage believers, they do so in the heavenly places.[1]

It might be thought that any rulers and authorities in the heavenly places must be literally in heaven and therefore angelic or demonic. Some commentators connect these powers to the organisation of the angels in the heavens.[2] However, in respect of the new creation, the heavenly places are open to those in Christ,

> And hath raised us up together, and made us sit together in heavenly places in Christ Jesus... Eph 2:6 (KJV) cf. Eph 1:3, 20

We may think of a Christian's place with Christ in the heavenly places in an **ideal sense**; Christians are on earth, but they are also dwell with Christ in the heavenly places because Christ comes and dwells with them – they are part of his body, a temple. This opens up the interpretation that rulers and authorities come to the heavenly places when they engage believers – oppose them. The dichotomy that rulers and authorities are either of heaven (demons, Satan, angels) or of the earth (human government) is therefore false. What we have here in Paul is a concept of the church as the body of Christ, a temple, in which the Father and the Son dwell with believers and from which believers witness to Jew and Gentiles and 'in' which rulers and authorities engage believers. This interpretation explains Paul's comment,

---

[1] A. D. Norris, *Acts and Epistles* (London: Aletheia Books, 1989), 568; Norris presents the critical insight.

[2] Whittaker, "Principalities and Powers", 377; he nevertheless allows that Paul is using "the language of Christian idealism".

...to the intent that now the manifold wisdom of God might be made known <u>by the church</u> to the <u>rulers and authorities in the heavenly places</u> ... Eph 3:10 (KJV)

It is possible to confuse 'the heavenly places' and 'in the heavens'; Paul does not say that God has created all things in the heavenly places but 'on the earth and in the heavens.' The difference is that this creative work is of the visible and invisible and it is the visible authorities on earth that may come to the heavenly places. Moreover, it is worth noting that the mystery of the reconciliation of Jew and Gentile was hidden from rulers and authorities in previous ages. It was the **generation of Paul** who were created by God to receive the revelation of that mystery, the return of Christ, and the establishment of the kingdom.[1]

This interpretation is obviously consistent with the use of the collocation in the plural in Luke 12:11 ("bring you before the rulers and authorities") and Titus 3:1 ("be subject to rulers and authorities"). It is also consistent with Luke 20:20 where we have the singular, "they might deliver him unto the rule and authority of the governor", but this might not be the same collocation.[2] This leaves the other occurrences of the collocation in Ephesians, Colossians and 1 Corinthians to investigate.

A counterargument to the above interpretation is based on Eph 6:12,

Put on the whole armour of God, that ye may be able to stand against the wiles of the devil. For it is <u>not a wrestle against blood and flesh</u>, but against rulers, against authorities, against the world-rulers of this darkness, against the spiritual things of wickedness in the heavenly places. Eph 6:11-12 (KJV revised)

Here it is argued that principalities and powers cannot be human authorities because Paul says, 'it is not a wrestle against blood and flesh'. Following this line of interpretation, one view is that Paul is not talking about human opponents; he is talking about the devil and demonic powers; another view is that Paul is talking about angelic orders.[3] This last

---

[1] *Contra* Whittaker, "Principalities and Powers", 377.

[2] The point to remember here is that the terminology of 'rulers and authorities' is not specific to Judea; its reference will change depending on the setting. If Paul is writing to Ephesus or Colossae, he may refer to either Jewish, Roman or Greek authorities.

[3] Whittaker, "Principalities and Powers", 377.

view is supported by the allusion in 'wrestle' (πάλη, Arndt & Gingrich), which is to Jacob's wrestling with the angel (Gen 32:24, LXX, παλαίω). The contrast offered is pitched at the level of a non-human person, whether the devil, demon or an angel, and the various powers are then seen as diabolic or angelic.

In English, 'flesh and blood' is a well-known idiom.[1] In the Greek New Testament, the same idiom might embrace human nature (1 Cor 15:50) or refer to human beings (Matt 16:17; Gal 1:16). As an idiom for human beings, it carries a particular reference to the *thinking* of the flesh, and it stands in contrast to divine revelation. Jesus says, 'Flesh and blood has not revealed this to you, Simon' (Matt 16:17) and Paul says, 'To reveal his son in me...I conferred not with flesh and blood'. The Greek of Eph 6:12, along with that of Heb 2:14, is 'blood and flesh', and if it is an idiom, it is about the **physical makeup** of the human being; Heb 2:14 is clear in this regard. The wrestling that Christians don't do is physical; instead, their 'standing against' is a metaphorical wrestle against various powers where the wiles of the devil are being encountered.

The contrast that Paul makes in 'not a wrestle against blood and flesh' is not one between human and non-human opponents, but **one between the physical and the mental** – the 'wiles' of the devil.[2] That Paul is talking about *thinking* is further shown by his metaphor of 'darkness' and his reference to 'spiritual things of wickedness' (see below).

The key to Eph 6:12 is the mention of 'the wiles of the devil' because Paul repeats the preposition 'against' (πρὸς) from 'against the wiles of the devil' in 'against rulers, against authorities, against the world-rulers of this darkness, against the spiritual things of wickedness in the heavenly places'. Furthermore, the clause that opens v. 12 begins with ὅτι and this shows that it is explanatory for 'the wiles of the devil'. Paul is saying that 'the wiles of devil' can be seen in the behaviour of various powers and the spiritual things of wickedness.[3]

---

[1] For an introduction to idiom see A. Gibson, *Biblical Semantic Logic* (Oxford: Basil Blackwell, 1981), 110-125.

[2] This explains the allusion to Jacob's wrestling: this had a *physical effect* on Jacob's body – his thigh (Gen 32:25).

[3] Paul mentions armour in vv. 11, 13, and wrestling in v. 12, for which armour would not be used. The mixture of metaphors is quite Hebraic – the reason for vv. 11, 13 uses a different metaphor (v. 12).

115

Ephesians 6:11-12 is about the wiles of various powers that the first century church encountered in their preaching; it is not literally about a devil or demons, nor about angels. The 'wiles' (ἡ μεθοδεία) of the devil uses a word that occurs once elsewhere in Eph 4:14,

> ...so that we may no longer be children, tossed to and fro and carried about with every wind of doctrine, by the cunning of <u>men</u>, by their craftiness in deceitful <u>wiles</u>. Eph 4:14 (RSV)

This puts the thinking of men and particularly their religious doctrine to the foreground, and it allows the suggestion that 'the devil' of Eph 6:11 is a personification of the various kinds of opposition that Paul is encountering and which confront the ecclesias.[1] Paul was saying that their fight was not a physical struggle but a spiritual one against various powers and their ideas.[2]

This is the best sense for 'spiritual things of wickedness in heavenly places.' The term 'spiritual things' (τὰ πνευματικὰ[3]) is used by Paul elsewhere for the spiritual things of the Spirit (1 Cor 2:13; 9:11; 14:1). Those in the heavenly places were those Jews who had infiltrated the church and who manifested the spiritual things of wickedness in their opposition to the gospel.[4]

Ephesians 6:12 has 'world-rulers of this darkness'.[5] The word for 'world-rulers' (τοὺς κοσμοκράτορας) is used variously in Greek texts of spirit beings or gods who control parts of the cosmos, human rulers or kings; in the

---

[1] It is beyond the scope of this chapter to present the case that 'the devil' is a personification of (Roman and Jewish) opposition to the gospel in NT writings; See A. Perry, *Story and Typology* (Sunderland: Willow Publications, 2012), 226-247. The thesis is that the Second Temple idea of 'the devil' is used by the NT church to personify opposition to the gospel.

[2] J. Carter, *The Letter to the Ephesians* (Birmingham: CMPA, 1956), 149.

[3] Translations often opt for 'spiritual hosts' but Paul's usage elsewhere suggests 'things'. The choice of 'hosts' seems to be motivated by the demonic/angelic readings; Whittaker, "Principalities and Powers", 379, has "spiritual ones of evil".

[4] On the counter-reformation of the Jews inside the church see H. A. Whittaker, *Studies in the Acts of the Apostles* (Cannock: Biblia, 1985), 393-399.

[5] The Majority Text has 'world-rulers of the darkness of this age', but the GNT omits 'of this age' and we will follow this shorter text.

singular, it is used of Satan and even the Angel of Death (Arndt & Gingrich). This data, coupled with a reading of 'non-human' for 'not against blood and flesh', leads commentators to posit demonic rulers as its reference in Eph 6:12.

Given this general Greek usage, what use is Paul making when he relates 'world-rulers' to 'this darkness'? He would seem to have something specific in mind because he uses the demonstrative 'this' for the darkness. What does Paul mean by 'this darkness'? Paul's commission to the Gentiles was to deliver them from darkness to light (Acts 26:17-18; cf. 1 Pet 2:9-10), and in his letters, there is an emphasis on the darkness of the Gentiles (e.g. Rom 2:19; 2 Cor 6:14). In Ephesians, he is addressing Gentiles (Eph 2:11; 3:1, 6, 8; 4:17) and the darkness is Gentile thinking (Eph 5:8, 11). The world-rulers of the time were the Romans, and this is the most natural reading of Paul's phrase – they were 'the world-rulers of this darkness'. If we break-up the compound word 'world-ruler', we find Paul using 'world' of the Gentiles in Ephesians (Eph 2:2, 11-12).

There is a thematic connection between Eph 6:12 and Col 1:13, "Who hath delivered us from the power of darkness, and hath translated us into the kingdom of his dear Son" (Col 1:13). This is a quotation of Luke 22:53 which records Jesus referring to the hour of the 'power of darkness' from which he was not delivered. Jesus, however, had delivered Paul and his Gentile converts from the power of darkness. Their transfer to the kingdom of God shows that the power of darkness was itself a kingdom with rulers (the echo is to Abner who translated/delivered the kingdom of Saul to David, 2 Sam 3:10). Our conclusion therefore is that 'this darkness' is the 'power of darkness' embodied in the rule of Rome.

Ephesians 6:12 is a catalogue of various kinds of opposition to the gospel: it refers, in order, to rulers and authorities, in which it agrees with Eph 3:8-11 (see above); it lists the world-rulers of the day (Rome); and it mentions those Jews who were engaged in a counter-reformation inside the church.

The next 'rulers and authorities' text to consider is Col 2:14-17,

> Blotting out the handwriting of ordinances that was against us, which was contrary to us, and took it out of the way, nailing it to his cross.

> Having put off from himself rulers and authorities, he made a shew of them openly, triumphing over them in it.

Let no man therefore judge you in meat, or in drink, or in respect of a holy day, or of the new moon, or of the Sabbath days, which are a shadow of things to come; but the <u>body</u> is of Christ.

Col 2:14-17 (KJV revised)

The list of judgments are typical concerns of Judaizing Christians and Jews – meats, drinks, holy days and the Sabbath.[1] The association of these concerns with 'rulers and authorities' goes to confirm the reading of Jewish rulers and authorities. The context here is clearly Jewish and the most natural reading of 'rulers and authorities' is as a reference to those who took part in the crucifixion of Christ – the relevant tenses are in the past (aorist, perfect).

It might be thought that there is a tension or contradiction between Col 1:20 and 2:15, especially in some translations (e.g. 'spoiled principalities and powers' KJV; 'disarmed the rulers and authorities' NASB). Colossians 1:20 is about reconciliation of the powers through the cross and Col 2:15 is about disarming or spoiling them. The translation issue here is whether to treat the grammatical middle (ἀπεκδυσάμενος) as an active sense ('disarm/spoil') or to retain the middle sense ('put off/divest').

The context supports the middle sense.[2] There is a clothing metaphor here in that Paul says Christ 'divested himself' of rulers and authorities (cf. Col 2:9 – 'you have put off the old man', ἀπεκδύομαι). The related noun (ἀπέκδυσις) occurs in Col 2:11, "putting off the body of flesh". The cross might have seemed a defeat for the nascent Christian movement, but for Paul it was a triumph over the very powers that sought to extinguish the gospel. What was nailed to the cross were the ordinances of the Law, which the Jewish rulers and authorities used against the church ('against us') in the sense that they promoted the Law's necessity and sufficiency.

What we have in Col 2:14-15 are two sentences describing the crucifixion with the actions of the judge and executioners transferred to Christ to

---

[1] Any overview of Second Temple Judaism will demonstrate this generalization.

[2] It is unlikely that Paul is not following his usage in Col 2:9-11, and so 'disarming' seems wrong ('spoiling' just looks idiosyncratic). If these translations were correct, the metaphor of 'disarming' is clearly about what comes before reconciliation in war, but this choice does not sit well with the use of the verb 'to triumph'.

show that he voluntarily submitted to the cross. The echo in nailing handwriting to the cross is to Pilate's handwriting of the title of Christ in his judgement hall which was then put (nailed) on the cross (noted in the parenthesis of John 19:19-22). This title was in effect the legal charge against Christ (Luke 23:2). The echo in 'openly (παρρησίᾳ) triumphing' is to the characteristic of Christ's ministry: "I spoke openly (παρρησίᾳ) to the world" (John 18:12), but the sense of 'triumph' is that of a triumphant procession (θριαμβεύω, Arndt & Gingrich), and this is an allusion to Christ carrying his cross openly to Golgotha (John 19:17).[1]

This latter reading would be consistent with Gal 3:13, "Christ redeemed us from the curse of the law, having become a curse for us -- for it is written, 'Cursed be everyone who hangs on a tree'" (RSV). The curse of the Law was upon the people – the handwriting of ordinances was against them. But Christ took away the power of the Law from the Jewish rulers and authorities.

We might ask why Christ has 'rulers, authorities, thrones, and lordships' in Paul's day, but this is just a consequence of "all authority in heaven and on earth has been given to me" (Matt 28:18) and "the Most-High rules in the kingdom of men" (Dan 4:32). All rule and dominion had been given to the Son, all power and authority, the power to create and the power to destroy, and the final judgement. In all these situations the Lord Jesus Christ had the role and position of king.

3.2.3 In, for, and through Christ
The text says all things were created *in* him, *by* (or *through*) him, and *for* him and each of these prepositions signifies something different:

- Taking the idea of **for** first, this is the creative order of Genesis 2: heaven, earth and then the garden, were created *for* Adam, who was then placed in the garden (Gen 2:8). The beasts of the field were also created *for* him, and so all these things are created *by God*.

- But Adam had a role after all this — he gave order to the beasts of the field by giving them their names. This is the type behind Christ creating thrones, principalities, dominions, and powers,[2] i.e. these things were **through him**.

---

[1] *Contra* Whittaker, "Principalities and Powers", 376. The resurrection made the cross a triumph for Paul.

[2] A study of the expression 'beasts of the...' in the prophets will illustrate this point—it is used to symbolize nations.

- The text also says that such things are created ***in him***, and this detail puts the focus on Christ. Paul preached of the Father that '*in* him we live, and move, and have our being' (Acts 17:28), and this contrasts with the new creation which is '*in* Christ' (Col 2:10).[1]

The idea of 'thrones, principalities, dominions, and powers' is a kingdom orientated idea. Since Paul has already mentioned the kingdom (Col 1:13; cf. 2 Sam 3:10 KJV), this idea is not out of place. All rule and dominion have been given to the Son, all power and authority, the power to create and the power to destroy, and the final judgement. In all these situations the Lord Jesus Christ has the role and position of God, but it is a role and position that has been given to him and it is a role and position that he bears in respect of the things of the new creation. It is a role that he bears, so that he can be seen as the *image* of God, the one in whom God is pleased to dwell with all fulness.[2]

A kingdom has a king, but it also has thrones (e.g. the thrones of the twelve tribes, Matt 19:28), it has principalities or rulers, it has authorities or powers, and there are lordships or dominions. A king creates these for his kingdom and in particular he creates them *when* his kingdom extends over subject peoples. This was true of David and Solomon and the former kingdom of God, and it is unlikely not to be true of the kingdom of Christ. However, the kingdom of God is not yet on earth, for Christ has not yet returned. The thrones, dominions, principalities and powers of the kingdom cannot yet be seen;[3] hence, Colossians talks about invisible things in heaven. The visible things of the kingdom are not yet in place, but there are corresponding invisible things which have been created. This creative work is happening now in the organisation of

---

[1] The expression 'in Christ' (or similar expressions which use the preposition 'in' with a term that refers to Christ), serves the purpose of identifying Christ as the locus for the new creation; it was well pleasing to God that in him all fulness should dwell (Col 1:19).

[2] This status could have been Adam's had he not fell: a status of one who was an image of God. The point here is that we should see in the creation of man a high anthropology as a counterweight to the high Christology advocated by Trinitarians.

[3] There have always been thrones, powers, principalities and dominions, since man began to organise his affairs on earth. Those thrones, powers, principalities and dominions to which Paul refers are those which have been created *in* Christ, since he was given authority over all things.

120

heaven and the administration of the earth that is exercised from heaven.[12]

This function of the king is no different in principle from Adam's exercise of dominion over the animals when he gave them their names. Hence, Paul can say that Christ is above all principality and power, *and every name that is named* (Eph 1:21). Furthermore, as in the days of David, there were those in the kingdom and those outside, so too there are things under him now and things yet to come under him.

Ephesians 1 talks of all things already *put under* the feet of Christ, and Colossians 1 talks of all things having been created by Christ, but 1 Corinthians 15 makes it clear that all things are not subdued unto Christ until the last enemy is destroyed (1 Cor 15:24-28). As with Colossians 1 and Ephesians 1, 1 Corinthians 15 has the same ideas: resurrection, principalities, powers, and might:

> ...Christ the firstfruits; afterward they that are Christ's at his coming. Then cometh the end...when he shall have put down all principality and all power and all might... 1 Cor 15:23-24

Christ was (is) the firstborn of all creation, but here the figure is that of the firstfruits of a harvest. Paul is thinking of the last days when the kingdom is delivered up to the Father. The collocation 'rulers and authorities' is not used, but the same words with 'all'. There is little doubt that this makes the scope universal: all the human rulers and authorities and all the might that stands arraigned against Christ will be put down and then Christ will hand over the kingdom to the Father.

In 1 Corinthians, Paul is thinking of the last days when the kingdom is delivered up to the Father. The principalities, the powers and the might that stand arraigned against Christ before that time will be put down and then Christ will hand over the kingdom to the Father.

---

[1] Joseph is a type of Christ. Pharaoh handed over to him the work of administration of the kingdom saying, 'Only *in* the throne will I be greater than thou' (Gen 41:40); Christ quotes this when he says, 'my Father is greater than I' (John 14:28), and this work will continue until all enemies are subdued (1 Cor 15:28).

[2] Even when the kingdom of God is established on earth, it will be the kingdom *of* heaven - hence Matthew's characteristic phrase.

So there is a prospect in store here: all things *will be* under Christ one day. Nevertheless, Ephesians 1 did talk of Christ as a real head over the church *now* — a head over all *these* things. So there is a distinction to mark here between those things over which Christ is the head now, and those over which he will be in the new age (Heb 2:8), prior to delivering the kingdom over to the Father. It is easier to see Christ's kingdom dominion over principalities and powers as future, while recognising his headship over a body as in the present.

3.3 Body

Christ is the firstborn from the dead so that 'among *all things* he might be pre-eminent' (v. 18d). The pre-eminence of Christ is *as* the head of a body, the church. This emphasis on a 'body' derives from the Genesis account of the creation of Eve. As a matter of anatomy, she was *his* body and by implication he was her head. This is what is meant by Adam's declaration, 'bone of my bones and flesh of my flesh' (Gen 2:23). But Adam also declares that Eve was the mother of all living, and these children are an expression of *her* body. So, Adam would have been head of a much larger body than the 'body' of Eve.

The church is now constituted by those creatures that are like Christ in being prospectively like-born from the dead (Rom 6:4-5). These creatures are an expression of her body. They are those to whom the gospel is preached (Col 1:23).[1] Because of the relationship between Eve and her children, Paul can talk in the same paragraph of both the body of Christ and creatures in a new creation.

The theme of the body of Christ connects up with the theme of the kingdom. This can be seen if we explore the expression 'head over all' from Eph 1:22, which is picked up from 1 Chron 29:11, the model for the Lord's prayer.

This prayer of David is uttered in a celebration of the gifts that the people had brought for the temple building. All the gifts were from God, they were his riches because he possessed all things. These facts surrounding David's prayer are used by Paul to teach about Christ and the temple - 'In whom all the building fitly framed together groweth unto a holy *temple* in the Lord.' (Eph 2:21).

---

[1] In Christ the fulness of God dwells bodily (Col 1:19; 2:9), and the body here is *not* Christ's body, it is Christ's body - the church (Eph 1:23; cf. John 1:16); over which he is head.

And hath put all things under his feet, and gave him to be the <u>head over all</u>[1] things to the church, which is his body... Eph 1:22

Blessed be thou, Lord God of Israel our Father, for ever and ever. Thine, O Lord, is the greatness, and the power, and the glory, and the victory, and the majesty: for <u>all</u> that is in heaven and in the earth is thine; thine is the kingdom, O Lord, and thou art exalted as <u>head above all</u>. 1 Chron 29:10-11

This fact supplies the clue as to why the ideas of a *body* and the ideas of a kingdom — dominion over principalities, powers, thrones, and rulers — come together in the passages we are examining. The temple, or the body, stands at the centre of the arrangements of a kingdom. This was the case under David and Solomon. The connections between Ephesians and 1 Chronicles are set out in Table 1.

Ephesians 1	1 Chronicles 29
Blessed be the God and Father... Eph 1:3	Blessed are you, Lord God of Israel...our Father v. 10
The Father of Glory Eph 1:17	Our Father v. 10
Ye may know...the riches of his glory Eph 3:16	Riches...from you v. 12
Riches of his grace Eph 2:7	
Unsearchable riches Eph 3:8	
Greatness of his power to us Eph 1:19	The greatness, the power...make great to all vv. 11-12
Give unto you... knowledge Eph 1:17	Give strength to all v. 12
Mighty power Eph 1:19	Power and might v. 12
Far above all Eph 1:21	Exalted v. 11
Power and might Eph 1:19	Power and might v. 12
Head over all Eph 1:22	Head over all v. 11
Praise of his glory Eph 1:6, 12	Praise your glorious name v. 13
Strangers and foreigners Eph 2:19	Aliens and pilgrims v. 15

Table 1

---

[1] The expression *head over all* comes in other contexts of military rule: Josh 11:10; Jud 10:18; 11:8.

3.4 Conclusion

The focus of the passage is the resurrection from the dead. Being the firstborn from the dead, Christ is *before* all things. Being the first he has been exalted to a position of mediatorship, so that all creatures and all things are then created by him and consist by him. The church now defines those who are the other creatures of whom Christ is the firstborn (Heb 12:23). In being the firstborn from the dead, *he* is the beginning of the (new) creation of God (Rev 3:14).[1]

The most popular view of Colossians 1 is that the creation is the Genesis creation. The view suffers from a number of objections:

1) The text doesn't mention the 'nuts and bolts' of the Genesis creation, but rather entities like thrones, dominions, principalities and powers.

2) The view doesn't account for the Adamic language — Christ is the 'image of God' and 'firstborn' of all creation; if Christ is a heavenly creator, why should he be compared to Adam?

3) The view doesn't explain the parallelism between 'firstborn of all creation' and 'firstborn from the dead', and how this connects to the 'for' of v. 16, i.e. Paul's argument is that Christ is the firstborn of all creation because *in him* were all things created.

For these reasons, (1) - (3), we reject the common Trinitarian reading that the passage is a hymn to Christ as the Genesis Creator.

4. Hebrews 1:10-12

Hebrews contains two well-known texts for 'proving' that Christ is the creator:

Hath in these last days spoken unto us by *his* son, whom he hath appointed heir of all things, by whom also he made the worlds... Heb 1:2 (KJV)

---

[1] Revelation 1 contains various titles of Christ that re-appear in the letters to the seven churches. In Rev 1:5, the title 'the faithful witness' is followed by the title 'the first-begotten from the dead'. In Rev 3:14, the title 'the faithful and true witness' is followed by the title 'the beginning of the creation of God'. The parallelism confirms that Christ is the beginning of the creation of God in virtue of being firstborn from the dead.

And, Thou, Lord, in the beginning hast laid the foundation of the earth; and the heavens are the works of thine hands... Heb 1:10 (KJV)

Each of these texts requires careful analysis.

4.1 Worlds

In the NT, the principal words translated 'world' are αἰών (*aion*), κόσμος (*kosmos*) and οἰκουμένη (*oikoumene*). The broad meanings of these three words are, respectively, 'age', 'world' and 'habitable earth', but these are rough meanings, and we must pay attention to context when examining particular passages.

The KJV 'worlds' in 'by whom also he made the worlds' translates the Greek word *aion* and this word is translated in a variety of ways but, on its own, as 'age'. The most common translation does not pick out the word on its own but picks out a Greek idiom 'to the *aions* of the *aions*' as 'for ever and ever'. Another idiom is 'to the *aion*' translated as 'for ever'. We are interested in those uses of the word where it occurs on its own rather than as part of an idiomatic expression. On its own it occurs in both plural and singular forms, i.e. there is both an age and there are ages. Let's look at the singular form of the word first.

The meaning of *aion* is 'age'. An age is made of people and events, and everyone has lived in some age or other (Tit 2:12). We might be regarded as rich or poor in our age (1 Tim 6:17), but we must not love our age (2 Tim 4:10). In the NT period there was a transition of ages. One age was coming to an end, and a new age was beginning. But what or who constituted this passing age? Let us set out the evidence first and then draw a conclusion:

1) The age had princes who crucified the Lord of Glory (1 Cor 2:8); the age had princes who presided over darkness (Eph 6:12).

2) The age had a beginning, and holy prophets had been speaking since the age began (Acts 3:21; 15:18), so the age had heard prophets like Moses and Samuel (Acts 3:22, 24).

3) The mystery of the Gospel had been kept secret since the age began (Rom 16:25), and about which the princes of the age knew nothing (1 Cor 2:8).

4) Instead of the wisdom of God (1 Cor 2:6), the age had characteristic *scribal* wisdom (1 Cor 1:20; cf. 1 Cor 3:18); an example of this wisdom concerned food offered to idols (Acts 15:29), and Paul declares that while the age stood, he would not eat food offered to idols (1 Cor 8:13).

5) The age had a god which handled the word of God deceitfully, and as a result the minds of those that did not believe were blinded (2 Cor 4:2-4) - so the age had the word of God, but their minds were blinded to the reading of the Old Testament (2 Cor 3:14) because they did not want to see the end of the Law.

6) Paul's message in Galatians is that Christians were *delivered* from an evil age (Gal 1:4), and Paul goes onto contrast the freedom implied by such deliverance with the bondage of the Law (Galatians 4).

7) Paul had previously been among those who walked according to the spirit of the age and according to the prince of the power of the air (Eph 2:2-3).

8) The age would have an end, being superseded by an age which was to come (Eph 1:21; Heb 6:5).

The age in which the apostles preached the gospel was an age defined by their Jewish circumstances. It was an age made up of their contemporaries. This was their age, but it was an evil age because its leaders sought to retain the Law of Moses and suppress the gospel of Christ. In doing this they distorted the meaning of the Law which was in reality pointing to Christ. The age into which the apostles were born had begun sometime far in the past, because it had seen great prophets like Moses and Samuel, but by their time it was in its last days, and their message was that it would have an end, being superseded by an age to come.

How you define an *age* is a matter of perspective, consequently ages can overlap in time. From our vantage point, we can say that before the Flood was an age, and after the Flood was an age; the Mosaic dispensation was an age; the golden years of David and Solomon were an age; the Babylonian Captivity was an age, *and so on*. What marks out an age is a major event (or series of events) that begins the age and lends character to the age; and then another event (or series of events) happens which ends the age.

The first century believers were aware of the fact that there had been many ages in the purpose of God. The apostle Paul is acutely aware that the gospel was the wisdom of God, and that this had been ordained before the ages had begun and kept hidden from those generations until his day (1 Cor 2:7; Eph 3:9; Col 1:26; 2 Tim 1:9; Tit 1:2). This gospel concerned Christ who had been kept until the end of the ages, before appearing to put away sin (Heb 9:26, RV). Paul was aware of living during times in which the conclusion of these ages was being enacted (1 Cor 10:11). That there are ages to the purpose of God is implied by the use of *aion* in many places. These ages have structure and purpose, and they have largely been under the jurisdiction of the angels. All of these ages had been *made*:

> God...hath in these last days spoken unto us by [his] Son, whom he hath appointed heir of all things, by whom also he <u>made</u> the worlds (*aions*)... Heb 1:1-2 (KJV)

This text should be connected to the following verse,

> Through faith we understand that the worlds (*aions*) were framed by the word of God, so that the things which are seen were not made of things which do appear. Heb 11:3 (KJV)

The point here, though, is slightly different. Firstly, the Greek word translated as *framed* (καταρτίζω) is not the same as that translated as *made* (ποιέω). In Heb 11:3, 'framed' conveys the sense of *perfected* or *made up*, whereas the Greek for *made* in Heb 1:2 is the ordinary Greek for *making something*. Secondly, Heb 11:3 states that the ages were made up by the *word* (ῥῆμα not λόγος as in John 1) of God, but Heb 1:2 says that they were made through the *Son*. This is the difference between the use of language to achieve a purpose and the use of a person as a *intermediary*. Putting the two verses together would suggest that the ages were made up by the word of God but through the Son.

The Hebrews 11 statement occurs at the start of a long recitation of OT saints. This sequence begins with Abel in Heb 11:4, which implies that Heb 11:3 is alluding to the Genesis creation, which was created by the 'and God said' utterances. This invites us to think of God's making the ages in the same vein as we think of his making the literal heavens and the earth, which was by spoken utterances. The utterances are the instrument by which the creation comes about, but the words are not an incidental instrument, as a hammer might be to a nail. In fact, what is created *reflects* the words used in the utterance. If we apply this to the case of the ages, Christ is not really the instrument by which the ages were made up, these are made up by the utterances of God, but the ages are made up in a way that reflects Christ.

How was Christ the conduit of this framing of the ages? The clue lies in the expression, 'so that the things which are seen were not made of things which do appear'. In the various ages of the world there were things to see which were not made of the things of that age around and about and apparent to the naked eye. These things were the things of faith. Some things that the OT worthies saw were as follows:

> Abel saw the sacrifice of Christ (Heb 11:4).

> Abraham saw the resurrection of Christ (Heb 11:19).

> Moses saw the reproach of Christ (Heb 11:26).

They all saw[1] the city of the promises (Heb 11:16), and this city was the bride of Christ (Rev 21:2). This is the point of the chapter: these OT saints saw things which were not made of things that appeared around them. These things that they saw concerned Christ, his work and the kingdom. They were seen with the eye of faith; they saw was not *composed of* the things and events of their times. Much the same point is made by Paul when he says:

> And base things of the world (*kosmos*), and things which are despised, hath God chosen, [yea], and things which are not, to bring to nought things that are... 1 Cor 1:28 (KJV)

The point for us here is that God has **also** chosen belief in the things which are *not*, to bring to nothing the things which are — the things of that *kosmos*. Just as the foolish things of the world are chosen, and the wise do not understand why; and just as the weak things of the world are chosen, and the mighty are at a loss to know why; so too the things that are yet future are chosen, and this shows that the things that are of the present are worth nothing. It is possible for us to have belief in the things that are not, because these have been revealed by the prophets:

> ...the prophets...searching what, or what manner of time, the Spirit of Christ, which was in them, did signify, when it

---

[1] The verb *to see* in Heb 11:3 should be connected to the occurrences in vv. 5, 7, 13, and 27 (although a selection of different Greek verbs is used).

testified before hand the sufferings of Christ, and the glory
that should follow. 1 Pet 1:11 (KJV)[1]

So it is then that God has known the character of all ages since the
beginning of the universe. He has known about Christ and the purpose
of the ages has been 'in Christ Jesus our Lord' (Eph 3:9-11). In fact, we
have seen that the saints of old have also known about Christ, seeing him[2]
in the events of their own lives. This places Christ at the centre of the
angelic ordering of the affairs of those who would be the sons of God.
And it is because of this placement of Christ at the centre of the character of the ages of God — the antediluvian, the patriarchal, and Mosaic
ages — that the author of Hebrews can say that God made up these ages
by his word through Christ; and Christ can say of the Scriptures that they
testified of him (John 5:39). This character of the ages means that the NT
writers can place Christ directly into the middle of many OT situations,
when using the OT to teach the things about Christ.[3]

It is important to distinguish the sense of *through him* — this is not a
causal sense, as if to say it is *because* of him the ages were constituted. But
rather the sense is that of an intermediary through whom something is
done, or an instrument through which something is done. The Greek is
used when describing such things as the betrayal of Christ *through* Judas,
or when describing a journey *through* a place, or entering *through* a gate. In
the case of Christ, we can picture the angels using him as a template for
ordering the ages, and in this sense the ages were drawn up through him.
So it is that we see so many types and patterns of Christ in the Scriptures.
Christ is the archetype and the types of the OT are so constituted as to

---

[1] Perhaps one example of such preaching is that which occurred in the
days of Noah. Christ was preached in those days by Noah, while the ark
was being constructed (1 Pet 3:19). He was preached to those who were
disobedient, identified in Genesis 6 as the sons of God (Gen 6:2-3). Peter
describes these men as 'spirits' because of their possession of the spirit of
God (cf. 1 Tim 4:1; 1 John 4:1). To these spirits, now in the prison of
death (cf. 1 Pet 4:6) in Peter's day, 'Christ' preached the Gospel.
[2] In short, they saw Christ, but Christ was not *there* to be seen.
[3] The use of *heir* in Heb 1:2 alludes to Abraham and Isaac. Of all the
patriarchs, it is Abraham that shows most concern about an heir. He was
the heir to the promises concerning the *land*. This gives us some purchase
on the more abstract idea of *all things* - in Isaac's case it had to do with the
land.

reflect and show him. Each detail is put into place by the angels to correspond to a detail about Christ.[1]

4.2 Heaven and Earth

The text of Heb 1:10-12 is used as a proof text of the pre-existence of Christ because it is said to ascribe the Genesis creation to his hand:[2]

> And, Thou, Lord, in the beginning hast laid the foundation of the earth; and the heavens are the works of thy hands: They shall perish; but thou remainest; and they all shall wax old as doth a garment; And as a vesture shalt thou fold them up, and they shall be changed: but thou art the same, and thy years shall not fail. Heb 1:10-12 (KJV)

This reading is superficial, and an examination of the Psalm from which the quotation is derived reveals the true typological meaning. Furthermore, the orthodox reading betrays a failure to understand the function of the quotation in Hebrews.

4.2.1 Excellency of Christ

The main thrust of Hebrews 1 is a proof of the proposition that Christ has inherited a more excellent name than the angels (v. 4). There are two sub-points being emphasized: firstly, the *excellency of the name*; and secondly, that the name has been *inherited*. However, it is not immediately apparent how the author establishes this conclusion, because he seems to show the *superiority* of the Son in respect of the angels, rather than the *excellency* of his *name*. There is no specific mention of a name inherited by Christ,

---

[1] Of course, the templates were partial ones, as a study of the types of Christ shows, and indeed the testimony of Peter shows that the angels themselves were waiting for the apostolic age in order to look into the things that they had pre-figured in their ordering of the ages.

[2] This reading is common enough; for a treatment by a former Christadelphian, see T. Farrar, "You, Lord, in the Beginning: Hebrews 1:10-12 and Christology", online at www.dianogo.com cited 2020.

unless we regard the use of "God" (vv. 8, 9)[1] or "Lord" (v. 10)[2] to indicate the inherited name of Christ.[3]

It is only when we look at the sources of his quotations that we discover how the author's points concern the *name* of Christ. The argument in Hebrews 1 concerns a name, because it uses OT texts that make points about a name. Two of the Psalms that are used specifically mention the name of "Yahweh", which will be held by the Messiah (Phil 2:9), and declared by him from Zion:

> I will make thy <u>name</u> to be remembered in all generations; therefore, shall the people praise thee for ever and ever. Ps 45:17 (KJV)

> To declare the <u>name</u> of the Lord in Zion, and his praise in Jerusalem... Ps 102:21 (KJV), cf. v. 15

The argument of Hebrews then is derived from OT quotations which refer to Christ in exalted terms in his future kingdom, because at this time the excellency of his name will be declared from Zion.[4]

The first quotation (Heb 1:5) is from Ps 2:7 which affirms Christ's sonship by referring to his resurrection:

---

[1] This is a title rather than a name.

[2] The quotation of Ps 102:12, "And, thou Lord..." applied to Christ does involve the name "Yahweh", and this is why the author inserts the phrase 'And thou Lord' from Ps 102:12 into his quotation from Ps 102:25-27. Failure to see this is the critical mistake made by Farrar (see below).

[3] Inheriting a name is illustrated in the example of Joseph's sons. Jacob says to Joseph that his two sons, Manasseh and Ephraim, were to be his, i.e. Jacob's sons. They were to be as Reuben and Simeon. Joseph was to count his future offspring as his own, but Ephraim and Manasseh were to be called after the *name* of their brethren in their inheritance (Gen 48:5-6).

[4] These quotations are utterances directed towards the Son, but the speaker is not always God the Father. The Father says, "Thou art my Son..." and "Sit on my right hand...", but the speaker of the utterance "...therefore God, thy God, hath anointed thee..." addresses Christ and speaks of the Father in the third person. Similarly, the utterance "And, thou Lord..." is spoken by a prophet to the Messiah.

For to which of the angels said he at any time, 'Thou art my Son, this day have I begotten thee?' And again, 'I will be to him a Father, and he shall be to me a Son?' Heb 1:5 (KJV)

The author of Hebrews establishes Christ's sonship first, because by this device he proves that any name he has is a name by inheritance from his father; a son inherits the name of his father. This affirmation was made at the resurrection (Acts 13:33; Heb 5:5).

The next quotation is set at the time of the return and refers to Christ as the Firstborn:

And when he <u>again</u> brings the Firstborn into the world, he says, 'And let all the angels of God worship him'. Heb 1:6 (NASB revised)[1]

This is the first verse that clearly shows the superiority of the Son to angels, and the worship of the Son is quoted from a psalm[2] that speaks of the future establishment of the reign of the Lord (Ps 97:1, 7). This worship is illustrated in a number of Psalms from this part of the Psalter (e.g. Psalms 95, 96, 98, 99, and 100). In fact, several things will be said at this time, because the author goes on to quote some more utterances from the Old Testament:

... 'Thy throne, O God,[3] is for ever and ever: a sceptre of righteousness is the sceptre of thy kingdom.' Heb 1:8 (KJV)

...therefore God, even thy God, hath anointed thee with the oil of gladness above thy fellows. Heb 1:9 (KJV)

---

[1] The KJV associates the "again" with the previous "again" in v. 5 interpreting the Greek as saying one thing, and then again saying another thing, and then again saying a third thing. The Greek of v. 6 however indicates that "again" should go with the verb "to bring" (because of the presence of the temporal adverb "when") and therefore the NASB is correct.

[2] I adopt the view here that the author is quoting from the Hebrew text of Ps 97:7 rather than the LXX text of Deut 32:43, which has additional distiches to those of the Hebrew text.

[3] Here we follow the majority view of the Greek text, which reads Heb 1:8-9 as a spoken address to the Son. The Greek form is not vocative, but this is not decisive as regards sense. LXX parallel verses which use the same word sequence have been translated as vocative in sense.

These last two quotations are some of the announcements that will be made after the return of Christ. They are taken from Psalm 45 which concerns the time when Christ will be a king (v. 1), anointed with the oil of gladness (cf. Isa 61:1, 3), and adorned ready for his marriage to his bride (vv. 13, 14).

The future aspect of these quotations is further illustrated in the last quotation in Hebrews 1 (v. 13)[1] which is from Ps 110:1, which is all about overcoming enemies and the establishment of the kingdom:

> The Lord said unto my lord, 'Sit on my right hand, until I make thine enemies thy footstool.' Ps 110:1 (KJV)

Saying this at the time of the Second Advent is contrasted with what has not been said "at any time" of the angels.

The opening chapter of Hebrews is focused on the future, and the author confirms this in the next chapter (Heb 2:5), when he says that he *has been* speaking all along of the "world to come"[2] (i.e. in the opening chapter of Hebrews). Failure to see the future aspect of the declarations of Hebrews 1 is part of the common misreading of Heb 1:10-12.

4.2.1 Creation of Heaven and Earth

The largest quotation deployed by the author is from Psalm 102, and it is this quotation that has been misinterpreted to imply the pre-existence of Christ:

> Of old hast thou laid the foundation of the earth: and the heavens are the work of thy hands. They shall perish, but thou shalt endure; yea, all of them shall wax old like a garment; as a vesture shalt thou change them, and they shall be changed: But thou art the same, and thy years shall have no end. Ps 102:25-27 (KJV)

---

[1] Note how this last quotation of the author's argument focuses on *sitting* and this picks up the opening statement of the argument *sat down on the right hand of the majesty on high* (Heb 1:3).

[2] This expression connects with Psalm 102, which was written for a generation "to come" (v. 18).

The quotation in Hebrews 1 is a composite quotation[1] from the Psalm because there is added the extra phrase "...Thou Lord" from v. 12 of the Psalm, "But thou, O Lord, shalt endure for ever...", and so in Hebrews we read:

> And, thou, Lord, in the beginning[2] hast laid the foundation of the earth; and the heavens are the works of thy hands: They shall perish; but thou remainest; and they all shall wax old as doth a garment; And as a vesture shalt thou fold them up, and they shall be changed: but thou art the same, and thy years shall not fail. Heb 1:10-12 (KJV)

This quotation has been thought by some commentators to ascribe the work of the Genesis creation to Christ.[3] However, the language of creation is used to describe other "beginnings" in God's purpose, for

---

[1] Here I eschew the view that the author quotes the LXX text of Ps 102:25-27 (101:25-27), which has the expression, "And thou Lord...". In general, the holy Spirit comments upon its own prior Hebrew Scriptures. As for the common preference for the LXX, it rests on the assumption that the LXX has not been edited to bring it into line with the NT. Furthermore, the *Vaticanus* and *Alexandrinus* principal editions of the LXX have differences with the NT text. Failure to give priority to the Spirit's quotation and modification of the Hebrew (rather than any OG translation) partly explains the mistaken pre-existence reading; (see Farrar, p. 6, who thereby fails to see the "composite quotation" in Heb 1:10-12 from the Psalm).

[2] The Greek expression (κατ' ἀρχάς) is similarly used in Philo *Leg.* 3.92; *Ios.* 1.225; *Pep.* 1.63, 68; *Cnt.* 1.63; and *Fla.* 1.138 to mean 'at the first'; and likewise, in Josephus *Ant.* 1.259; 16.272; 18.3; 19.211; and *War.* 4.460; 5.184.

[3] Some commentators ascribe this utterance to the Messiah who says to the Father that he laid the foundation of the earth. However, this suggestion fits badly with the argument in Hebrews 1 which is centred on things that are *said of the Messiah*. This quotation from Psalm 102 is the largest of the OT texts that the author selects, and it would break the structure of his argument to read it as referring to the Father, especially as the author concludes his reasoning with a quote from Psalm 110 which is an undisputed example of something said to the Messiah. This last quote is tied to the opening quotation of the author's reasoning by the phrase "said he at any time", and this link encloses the whole piece as assertions spoken to Christ.

example, the Flood, the Exodus, and the Gospel.[1] It cannot be assumed that the Genesis creation is the only possible meaning. Literally speaking, the earth and the heavens will not perish,[2] and therefore a 'Genesis' reading seems unlikely.

Another proposal has been that the quotation refers to the creation of Israel, the foundation of that nation viewed as a figurative "heavens and earth". It is argued that these "heavens and earth" were to "perish" in the sense that the Mosaic order and the state were brought to an end in AD70. The difficulty with this view is that it is unclear *how* Christ could be said to be the one who laid the foundations of the Mosaic order. This would require a typological reading of Psalm 102 and/or Heb 1:10-12.

A further interpretation is that the "heavens and the earth" are a new creation, the foundations of which were laid by Christ in his ministry, in the beginning, and which will be realized upon his return. It is further said that *even* these "heavens and earth" will perish, once the millennium has run its course. The problem with this suggestion is that it looks like an *ad hoc* solution; the post-millennial state of affairs is elsewhere not the subject of prophecy. It is difficult to see why the new heavens and earth of the millennium would perish.

4.2.2 Quoting Psalm 102

The presumption in this last suggestion is that the pronoun in "…they shall perish…" (v. 11) refers to the "heavens and earth" of the previous verse (v. 10). If we take the text of Hebrews alone, this may appear to be the only option, but a close reading of Psalm 102 supplies a different reference for what will perish, something other than the "heavens and the earth". Hence, our suggestion is that the author of Hebrews has taken into his text the reference of the "they shall perish" from Psalm 102; he has not created a new reference. In other words, the author of Hebrews

---

[1] The new creation is referred to in Heb 1:2 in the mention there of "all things" (John 1:3-4; Heb 2:8). The Son is the 'heir' of all things (including the most excellent name (v. 4)), and the scope of 'all things' is defined in v. 14 in the reference to the "heirs" of *salvation*. This salvation is grounded in the promises to the patriarchs, because it is these to which the Messiah is an *heir*. Hence, we encounter in the author's exposition a *beginning* and what "the Lord" did in that beginning, for he says, "How shall we escape if we neglect so great salvation; which at the first began to be spoken by the Lord…" (Heb 2:3).

[2] See 1 Chron 16:30, Pss 37:9-11, 115:16, Prov 10:30, Eccl 1:4, Isa 11:19, 45:18, Hab 2:14, Matt 5:5.

expects his readers to understand the whole of Psalm 102 and to use the references *in that Psalm* for the pronouns in his quotation.

Our proposal is that "the Lord" (Jesus) did lay the foundation of the new heavens and earth in his ministry "in the beginning", and that this is spoken to "the Lord" at his return. At that time, when the new heavens and new earth are brought to completion, they will replace an old order which will perish. This old order is identified as the Mosaic order in Hebrews 8. Speaking of the Mosaic system the author of the letter says,

> That which decayeth and waxeth old is ready to vanish away. Heb 8:13

And this is the topic of Heb 1:10-12,

> They shall perish; but thou remainest; and they all shall wax old as doth a garment… Heb 1:11

In contrast, the salvation of the Messiah would be from generation to generation (Isa 51:8; Ps 102:28; Heb 1:14; 2:3).

In Psalm 102 the same transition is outlined, except that the terms of Psalm 102 refer to a "type" rather than the antitype of Hebrews 1. This type revolves around Hezekiah[1] and the foundation of a new earth that God had laid earlier in his reign, overturning the idolatry of Ahaz. During the Assyrian invasion and his sickness, power passed to the political enemies of Hezekiah in Jerusalem. It is against this background that the hope of the psalmist is expressed that these men would perish, and the new earth laid down by Hezekiah would come to fulfilment.

4.2.3 Psalm 102

Psalm 102 is a "Hezekiah psalm", and its language is closely tied to prophecies of the eighth century. At this time Judah was in mortal danger, facing extinction as a nation and deportation to Mesopotamia. Hezekiah was sick and power had transferred to his opponents in Jerusalem who sought a policy of appeasement with Assyria.

The psalm is both a public and a private prayer, for it is addressed both to God and then published for the people. The prayer begins in v. 1 with a first-person address to God. In v. 16 there is a shift to the third person and the psalm addresses an audience describing what "the Lord" will do

---

[1] See G. Booker, *Psalm Studies* (Austin, Texas: Booker Publications, 1988), 592-594.

for Zion. In v. 23 there is a recapitulation of a prayer that has been addressed to God.

4.2.4 Hezekiah's Prayer

The situation of the prayer is one where Zion is under threat from an external enemy and the one who is praying has opponents inside the city who are advocating a policy of appeasement. In addition, the person is sick unto death:

Day of Distress v. 2 (RSV)	A day comparable to the "day of the Lord"
Days consumed in smoke v. 3	Days characterized by the destruction of the cities of Judah, cf. Isa 51:6
My bones are burned as a hearth v. 3	The "bones" are his kinsman who are being "burned" in the land, cf. Job 30:30, Isa 24:6
I am withered like grass vv. 4, 11	This is the refrain describing the state of Jerusalem and Judah in Isa 40:6-8
I am like a vulture of the wilderness and an owl of the waste places v. 6 (RSV)	The wilderness and waste places of Jerusalem Isa 51:3
My "enemies" have access to me and reproach me all day v. 8	These are internal opponents at the Jerusalem court hostile to Hezekiah cf. Isa 51:7
I have been lifted up and cast down v. 10	The king has been replaced during his sickness

Hezekiah is fearful for the state of the nation and his capital city Jerusalem (v. 20), with enemies without and *within* (v. 8). The contrast in the Psalm is between his declining days[1] and the everlasting days of Yahweh. He senses the passing of his generation, he feels the reproach of his political opponents, and so he looks to the next generation, and he writes his words for them — a 'generation to come' and a 'people which shall be created' (Ps 102:18).

Hezekiah laments his sickness and contrasts his plight with the everlasting days of Yahweh. His days are like a shadow, but the Lord endures for ever (vv. 11-12). Nevertheless, he declares to his God that He (Yahweh) will

---

[1] His days were 'like a shadow that declineth' (v. 11), and so the Lord reverses his decline using the shadow of the sun on a sundial as proof.

arise and have mercy upon Zion, because His servants, of whom Hezekiah was one, took pleasure in her stones (v. 14).

At this juncture the Psalm breaks off from recording Hezekiah's prayer and records Hezekiah's own thoughts on the prayer and addresses an audience. Thus v. 16 begins with a confident expression of hope — 'When the Lord shall build up Zion, he shall appear in his glory'. This change of fortune for Zion will come about when the Lord 'appears' in His glory. Hezekiah offers his thoughts on his prayer in vv. 17-22 in a soliloquy.

The immediate fulfilment of Hezekiah's expectations lies in the deliverance of Jerusalem from the invading armies of Sennacherib. Hezekiah is confident that God has 'looked down' and seen the groaning of the prisoner and determined to loosen those appointed to death (by the Assyrian invaders). In this expected deliverance, Hezekiah anticipates that a people will be gathered together and by this process 'created' (vv. 18, 22), and they will praise the Lord in Zion (vv. 18, 21). This 'generation to come' (Ps 78:4; cf. Deut 29:22) are described as the children of Yahweh's servants, who would 'continue', indeed the children of these children would also be established before the Lord; this is a picture of stability and long life. (Ps 102:14, 28).

The prayer and the address to the audience go together, because the soliloquy emerges out of the prayer (v. 17). It is written for a generation to come and the people who would be created out of the coming deliverance. The Psalm concludes with a recapitulation[12] of the prayer and its occasion (v. 23ff). God had weakened Hezekiah and shortened his days, and in response, Hezekiah had said in prayer, 'O my God take me not away in the midst of my days' (v. 24ff, cf. Ps 89:45). Naturally, this review repeats elements of the prayer from vv. 2-15 as well as expanding upon its content. So, we learn again that God is throughout all generations (vv. 12, 24), and that He endures for ever (vv. 12, 26). Indeed, Hebrews 1:10 binds the prayer and the recapitulation together because it quotes from v. 12 (of the prayer) and vv. 25-26 (of the recapitulation), 'And, thou Lord (from v. 12), in the beginning hast laid the foundation of the earth (from v. 25)'.

---

[1] The recapitulative force of Hezekiah's remark is indicated by the change in tense in v. 24, "I said, O my God".

[2] It is possible that the re-capitulation was subsequently added to the Psalm, since Isaiah records that Hezekiah had written similar words when he had recovered from sickness (Isa 38:9-10).

4.2.5 New Heavens and New Earth

While it is natural to take "heavens and earth" to refer to the Genesis creation, these terms can also carry a poetic reference to God's people in the land, Jerusalem, and the temple. Isaiah prophesied of a "new heavens and a new earth" in the context of the restoration of Judah after the invasion of 701 B.C.E.,[1]

> For, behold, I create new heavens and a new earth: and the former shall not be remembered, nor come into mind. But be ye glad and rejoice for ever in that which I create: for, behold, I create Jerusalem a rejoicing, and her people a joy. Isa 65:17-18 (KJV)

The partial interpretation of the figure "new heavens and a new earth" is given in the statement that 'I create Jerusalem a rejoicing'. The most plausible suggestion is that Jerusalem and in particular its temple and priests are the "new heavens" and the "new earth" is the general population and the civic leaders in a restored land. Such a "new heavens" is indicated by Isaiah in other references to Jerusalem and the temple needing to be re-built at this time:

> Our holy and our beautiful house, where our Fathers praised thee, is burned up with fire: and all our pleasant things are laid waste. Wilt thou refrain thyself for these things, O Lord? wilt thou hold thy peace, and afflict us very sore? Isa 64:10-11 (KJV)

> Thus, saith the Lord, 'The heaven is my throne, and the earth is my footstool: where is the house that ye build unto me and where is the place of my rest?' Isa 66:1-2 (KJV)

Isaiah indicates that the work of restoration was not proceeding; but this does not detract from the pleading and encouragement implied in the promise of a "new heavens and a new earth" at this time in Hezekiah's reign. The intention of Yahweh was that righteousness would go forth from Jerusalem (Isa 62:1).

---

[1] We presume here an eighth century reading of Isaiah 40-66, which is contrary to most commentators. For an introduction, see J. Barton Payne, "Eighth Century Israelitish Background of Isaiah 40-66" *WTJ* 29 (1966-1967): 179-190; 30 (1968): 50-58; 185-203.

This (faltering) work of restoration implies that a foundation had been laid for the heavens and the earth. Hence, we read earlier in Isaiah,

> Therefore, thus saith the Lord God, Behold, I have laid in Zion for a foundation a stone, a tried stone, a precious corner stone, a sure foundation: he that believeth shall not make haste. Isa 28:16 (KJV revised)

This text is interpreted in the NT in relation to Christ, but in its primary application it refers to Hezekiah and his faith in Yahweh. Spoken before the siege of Jerusalem has been lifted and before Jerusalem has been delivered, it calls the people to have faith in Hezekiah as God's servant, and to not "make haste" out of the city.

It is this background that informs Hezekiah's thinking in Psalm 102:25-27. He says two things:

1) Firstly, the foundation of the earth was laid "of old"; the expression (לפנים) strictly means "from before" and it is generally translated as an expression of temporal priority (e.g. Deut 2:10; Jud 1:10; Job 17:6). In the context of the Jerusalem siege, Hezekiah is saying that God had *before this crisis* laid the foundation of the earth, and this poetic figure is naturally taken as a reference to Hezekiah's prior reforming reign which was ostensibly the foundation for the future.

2) Secondly, Hezekiah says that the heavens are the work of God's hands;[1] he does not say that the foundation of the heavens has been laid—he is not making the same point as Isa 28:16. However, he is saying that the work of fashioning the heavens belongs to God. In the terms of Isaiah's prophecies, this work has to do with reforming the temple and the priesthood so that righteousness goes forth out of Zion.

These statements are an expression of Hezekiah's confidence in Yahweh: he contrasts work that God has already done (the foundation of the earth) and work he is currently engaged upon (fashioning a new people—the heavens); he contrasts this work with "those who shall perish".

---

[1] This work of constructing the tabernacle was very much the work of God's hands, since he set down the pattern for the tabernacle (Exod 25:9, 40), and he gave the spirit-gifts for its completion (Exod 35:30-35).

140

4.2.6 Garments

The rhetorical flow of the Psalm identifies the "they" of "they shall perish" as the "they that are mad against me" (v. 8). Apart from his own physical health, and apart from the crisis facing the nation, it is about his "enemies" that Hezekiah offers complaint. His expression of confidence in Yahweh is therefore to be contrasted with the future in store for his enemies. The language that he uses to describe them is echoed in Isaiah.

> They shall perish, but thou shalt endure: yea, all of them shall wax old like a garment; as a vesture shalt thou change them, and they shall be changed: Ps 102:26 (KJV)

> Lift up your eyes to the heavens and look upon the earth beneath: for the heavens shall vanish away like smoke, and the earth shall become old like a garment, and its inhabitants shall die in like manner: but my salvation shall be for ever, and my righteousness shall not be abolished. Isa 51:6 (KJV)

> Behold, the Lord God will help me; who is he that shall condemn me? lo, they all shall wax old as a garment; the moth shall eat them up. Isa 50:9 (KJV)[1]

These Isaiah prophecies use some of the language of Psalm 102.[2] The problems that Hezekiah had with his enemies in Jerusalem during the Assyrian siege continued after Jerusalem was delivered. At this time these same enemies advocated policies of treaty and alliance with the surrounding nations as a way of bringing stability to the region in the wake of the power vacuum left behind by the Assyrians. Hence, Hezekiah describes the fate of these enemies in the same terms as Isaiah who saw in them the opponents of Yahweh; Isaiah advocated reliance on Yahweh alone.

---

[1] The echo here goes back to the provision of God during the wilderness. The people were not only fed and watered, but they were also clothed, 'Thy raiment waxed not old upon thee' (Deut 8:4; 29:5; Neh 9:21). This declaration by Isaiah is tantamount to the statement that the provision of God was to be taken away. In other words, a defining act of their redemption from Egypt is reversed in a description of their destruction.
[2] For example, the language of heaven and earth, the figure of the garment waxing old, the theme of what was done 'before', the loosing of the captive, and the everlasting salvation-righteousness of the kingdom age.

Isaiah 50 opens with a rhetorical question about a bill of divorcement. Where were the divorce papers, if God had cast away his people? There were none, even though the people had sold themselves into "slavery" in their efforts to appease the Assyrian Superpower. Now, they were failing to take up arms and re-conquer the land. They had been delivered from Assyria, but they were refusing to take up the task of conquest. Hence, Yahweh was complaining that there was 'no man' to lead the forces out of Jerusalem (Isa 50:2; 52:11; 59:16; 63:1-6).

In this context, the Servant of the Lord meditates about his situation (Isa 50:4-9). He was experiencing considerable dissension inside the city by those in the establishment who favoured diplomatic solutions to the political situation. Nevertheless, they would "wax old as a garment" (Isa 50:9), and so the Servant appeals to those who fear Yahweh that they should follow him.

This appeal is continued in Isaiah 51, 'Hearken to me, ye that follow after righteousness' (Isa 51:1, 4). It would seem that Hezekiah's confidence in God was pilloried and discounted, and his political enemies orchestrated public demonstrations of opposition, during which he (like politicians today) was buffeted and spat on (Isa 50:6-7).[1] In this context, he declares that the earth would 'wax old as a garment' (Isa 51:6). The parallelism of Isa 50:9 and Isa 51:6, namely, '*they* shall wax old' (Isa 50:9) and 'the earth shall wax old' (Isa 51:6), identifies the poetic reference for "the earth"—it is comprised of those who ruled the land.

The same point is being made in Psalm 102. When Hezekiah says, 'Mine enemies reproach me all day, and *they* that are mad against me are sworn against me' (v. 8), this is the language of political opposition. It is these enemies who are metaphorically "the earth" and who would "wax old" as a garment and perish (Ps 102:26).

4.2.7 Hebrews 1 and Psalm 102
The use of Psalm 102 in Hebrews 1 is typological. The words are spoken to the Davidic messiah when he returns to establish the kingdom. At this time, when God brings again the first begotten into the world, it is said that,

---

[1] The messianic focus of Isaiah 50 is the trial of Jesus. It presents Jesus as an obedient son, full of confidence in the Lord God who will justify him in his trial against his adversary (vv. 7-8). His confident assertion is 'who is he that shall condemn me?' (v. 9).

And, Thou, Lord, in the beginning hast laid the foundation
of the earth; and the heavens are the works of thy hands:
They shall perish; but thou remainest; and they all shall wax
old as doth a garment; And as a vesture shalt thou fold them
up,[1] and they shall be changed: but thou art the same, and
thy years shall not fail. Heb 1:10-12 (KJV)

At this time, the "beginning" refers back to the beginning of the Gospel
ministry; it was at this time that the foundation of the new earth was laid.
When the Son returns, those who held sway over the people would perish
and wax old as a garment; the kingdom of the Son would not fail.

This use of Psalm 102 reflects the expectations of the author of
Hebrews. He was living in the "last days" of the Jewish Commonwealth
(v. 2). In these days those who ruled the nation would perish, and the Son
would set up his own rule. Speaking of the Mosaic system, the author
says, 'That which decayeth and waxeth old is ready to vanish away' (Heb
8:13), and 'He taketh away the first, that he may establish the second'
(Heb 10:9). The salvation of the Messiah's age would be from generation
to generation (Isa 51:8; Ps 102:28; Heb 1:14; 2:3).

This ending of the Jewish Commonwealth is described as the *passing away*
of a "heaven and earth" by other NT writers, but it is important to
recognize that the author of Hebrews is not making his point in these
terms; he is not saying that 'heaven and earth' shall perish.

Till heaven and earth pass, one jot or one tittle shall in no
wise pass from the law, till all be fulfilled. Matt 5:18[2]

But the day of the Lord will come...in which the heavens
shall pass away with a great noise, and the elements shall
melt with fervent heat, the earth also and the works that are
in it shall be burned up...Nevertheless we, according to his
promise, look for new heavens and a new earth, in which
dwelleth righteousness. 2 Pet 3:10-13

---

[1] This description of the Messiah's work, 'as a vesture, thou shalt change
them', is chosen because of the way in which his vesture was taken from
him and parted (Ps 22:18). It is therefore *his* work to change their vesture.
The irony is directed against his priestly accusers (cf. Zech 3:4-5), who laid
great store by their own vestures.
[2] See Matt 24:35; Mark 13:31; Luke 16:17; 21:33.

This passage identifies the sequence and the timing of the new heaven and earth: an old heaven and earth passes away, and a new heaven and earth come about in its place. The elements here are the rudiments of the Law of Moses, as is shown by the occurrence of the same Greek word for 'elements' in Gal 4:3, 9, Col 2:8, 20 and Heb 5:12. If we combine the teaching of Heb 1:10-12 with 2 Pet 3:10-13, we add the detail that the foundation of the new earth was laid in the beginning of Jesus' ministry.

4.3 Summary

In Psalm 102, Hezekiah thinks of Yahweh. The use of Psalm 102 in Hebrews is solely messianic, and the thought is not of the Father but of Christ. A fair amount of biblical reading is required to understand Hebrews 1. It is not correct to read 'laid the foundation of the earth' with a modern western cultural perspective, as if the author was describing the planet. The author is using a Psalm which employs figurative language in referring to a heaven and earth, and this language is descriptive of the restoration of Judah under Hezekiah. The interpretation of the author of Hebrews is that this restoration is typical of the kingdom that Jesus will establish on his return. This kingdom will replace a Jewish leadership which will perish.

The letter to the Hebrews is very much a Jewish letter addressing *Jewish* concerns and issues. One such issue concerned the status of Christ, and the author shows that the superiority of Christ derives from his status as a Son who has *inherited* a most excellent name. None of his argument fits well with Trinitarian or pre-existence claims about Christ; indeed, it is difficult to conceive his readers understanding the idea of an incarnation of a pre-existent Son. Instead of this idea, we have seen that the author sets various Psalms in a context of *inheritance* and *delegated* authority. This authority far exceeded anything that had been possessed by the angels.

5. Conclusion

None of the NT 'creation' passages which are used in pre-existence arguments concern the Genesis creation. We have found that they either concern the new creation, the status of the Israelite 'heaven and earth', the kingdom to come, or the ages of God's purpose. In each case a careful consideration of the context supplies the reasons as to why the creation language has been used in respect of Christ.

CHAPTER SEVEN
The Foundation of the World

1. Introduction

There is a group of texts in the NT that mention *the world*, and a sub-group of these passages mention things that happened 'before' the world *began*. These texts are used in pre-existence arguments. For example, John 17 records the high-priestly prayer of Jesus. One verse of this prayer has him saying,

> "And now, O Father, glorify thou me with thine own self with the glory <u>which I had with thee before the world was</u>" John 17:5 (KJV)

This verse appears to speak of glory which the Son was looking forward to *once again* sharing with the Father. If we read this verse with the meanings that these words often have today, then Jesus had glory with the Father before the earth came into existence some four or five billion years ago. On this reading, the verse establishes the pre-existence of Christ beyond any reasonable doubt. This quick strategy applies a meaning to the word 'world' that is perfectly familiar today, but is it correct?

We must apply the meanings intended by the biblical writers. It is all too often assumed that their words must be used in the same way they are used today. When arguing about the pre-existence of Christ, this assumption rears its head at every point. It is so embedded in popular ways of thinking that discussions on this topic often fail to persuade people. In this chapter we will look at the NT understanding of .the world'. This study will help to reinforce the exposition of the previous chapter regarding the question of whether Jesus was the Genesis creator.

2. The Foundation of the World

A foundation usually requires a certain amount of destruction in the preparation of the ground, and then the materials that make up the foundation are laid down. The etymology of the Greek noun   for 'foundation' (καταβολη) suggests something 'cast down' (cf. 2 Cor 4:9; Rev 12:10), because the related verb is made up of the word for 'throw' or 'cast' and a preposition that often conveys the sense of 'down'. Hence, the meaning of the noun is that of a foundation which is laid down (cf. Heb

6:1). In all but one of the places[1] where this Greek word for 'foundation' occurs, it is part of the phrase 'foundation of the world'. The expression 'the foundation of the world' occurs 10 times in two kinds of phrase in the New Testament:

> there are things that pertained <u>before</u> the foundation of the world.

> there are things that have pertained <u>from</u> the foundation of the world.

Common theological commentary placed upon these texts is that the foundation of the world is the Genesis creation of heaven and earth, and that before this event a certain order existed in the divine sphere, for example, the Father and the Son shared glory together (John 17:5). At a certain point in time things were decided, and since that point these decisions have been worked out in the Genesis creation. Let us examine the relevant passages, tackling the 'from' passages first.

3. From the foundation of the World

Our proposal is that *the foundation of the world is the establishment of the Mosaic order*. The Mosaic dispensation was a time of preparation for the Christian dispensation. Those texts which refer to the foundation of this 'world' highlight certain characteristics of that age. Our first example is contained in the comment that Matthew makes about the parables of Jesus. Jesus spoke in parables in keeping with the rule that certain things were to be kept secret during the Mosaic age.

3.1 Matthew 13:35

Jesus uttered words in parables and Matthew observes that this was in order,

> That it might be fulfilled which was spoken by the prophet, saying, I will open my mouth in parables; I will utter things which have been kept secret from the foundation of the world. Matt 13:35 (KJV)

---

[1] The exception is a figure of speech or idiom which has not been carried forward into the English. The author of Hebrews says, "Through faith also Sara herself received strength to conceive seed" (Heb 11:11). This statement literally rendered would be "received strength for a foundation of seed", which is a unique idiom in the NT, (both OT occurrences (Lev 12:2, Num 5:28) of 'conceive seed' use ordinary verbs for 'conceive').

146

The marginal reference in the KJV points us to the Psalm which Matthew quotes:

> I will open my mouth in a parable: I will utter dark sayings of old: which we have heard and known, and our fathers have told us. We will not hide [them] from their children, shewing to the generation to come the praises of the Lord, and his strength, and his wonderful works that he hath done. For he established a testimony in Jacob, and appointed a law in Israel, which he commanded our fathers, that they should make them known to their children. Ps 78:2-5 (KJV)

The Psalm talks of 'dark sayings of old' and the expression 'dark sayings' has been interpreted with the word 'secrets' in Matthew's paraphrase, while the expression 'of old' has become 'from the foundation of the world'. The Psalm gives us the meaning of Matthew's statement. The 'sayings' are enshrined in a law and testimony given to the people but hidden from the fathers. Jesus heard these sayings and was not hiding them from 'the generation to come',[1] a generation which would be born, and which would tell them to their children, so that they would not rebel like their fathers in the wilderness (vv. 8, 9, 41, 57). The parables and sayings recounted in the Psalm record the many works and wonders that God performed in bringing Israel out of Egypt, in leading them through the wilderness, and in bringing them to the door of the promised land. As a catalogue of miracles, they were to give hope to a future generation, and this was the generation being addressed by Jesus in his parables.

We should think therefore of Jesus in his ministry as at the threshold of the promised land, looking forward to the land, but looking back at the people behind him, hesitant, and full of doubts. His appeal to the nation was that 'the kingdom of God was near', as if to say, 'look over that hill, and you can see it'. He encouraged them to 'enter into the kingdom', and to back up his preaching, he told them what 'the kingdom of God was like', just as the two spies had earlier given good reports of the land.

---

[1] We examined the use of this expression in Chapter Five in connection with our exegesis of Heb 1:10-12 and Psalm 102. We saw there that the expression 'generation to come' is a "children motif" defining the rejection of the Fathers and the preaching of the Gospel to the children who *will* enter the kingdom.

The expression 'foundation of the world' then picks up the time reference implicit in the fact that the sayings were 'of old', and this is further delimited by the Psalm as a time when God 'established (raised up) a testimony in Jacob, and appointed a law in Israel'. This identifies 'the world' as the nation and its foundation under Moses.

The apostle Paul mentions the mystery kept secret since 'the world' began:

> Now to him that is able to establish you according to my gospel... according to the revelation of the mystery, which hath been kept secret since the world began... Rom 16:25 (KJV)

> Howbeit we speak wisdom among them that are perfect: yet not the wisdom of this world, nor of the princes of this world, that come to nought: But we speak the wisdom of God in a mystery, [even] the hidden [wisdom], which God ordained before the world unto our glory: Which none of the princes of this world knew: for had they known [it], they would not have crucified the Lord of glory. 1 Cor 2:6-8 (KJV)

What this passage shows is that the princes *of the world* did not 'know' Christ and as a result they crucified him. This identifies what Paul understood by 'world' here — the nation of the Jews. Paul claims that God had hidden the wisdom of the Gospel, ordaining before the 'world' that it should be revealed by the apostles.

3.2 Matthew 25:34

If the sayings about the kingdom have been kept secret from the foundation of the world, we should not be surprised to read also that the kingdom has been prepared from the foundation of the world.

> Then shall the King say unto them on his right hand, Come, ye blessed of my Father, inherit the kingdom prepared for you from the foundation of the world... Matt 25:34 (KJV)

How was the kingdom prepared from the foundation of the world? There are several clues to the answer.

The underlying type is again that of the entry to the land and the people's refusal to take their inheritance. This is why Jesus says 'inherit' the kingdom - he has in mind the promises about the land made to the

148

patriarchs. In the same discourse, Jesus describes the separation of the sheep on his right hand from the goats on the left hand, and this is an allusion to Ps 95:7,

> For he [is] our God; and we [are] the people of his pasture, and the sheep of his hand. Today if ye will hear his voice...
> Ps 95:7 (KJV)

Here the people are the 'sheep of his (right) hand', and it is their response to the king's invitation to 'come' to the temple,[1] for the Psalm has had the people say 'Let us *come* before his presence' (v. 2) and 'O *come* let us worship' (v. 6). These sheep therefore come[2] to the kingdom; they 'enter' it — for it was a kingdom prepared for them. The Psalm illustrates this preparation, for it describes the people's acknowledgement that the sea and the land were made by the Lord, by his hands, i.e. it was his 'work' (Ps 95:5, 9). Such preparation reflects a divine pattern of preparing a garden and placing the man in that garden.[3]

However, it is apparent from the Psalm that not everyone heeds the call to worship before the Lord, because at the same time a warning goes out for the people not to harden their hearts as in the day of provocation and temptation. This is an allusion to the waters of Massah and Meribah, at which the people had exclaimed that they wanted to return to Egypt.

The warning in the Psalm is apposite because the desire to 'return' is the natural contrast to the call to 'come'. The wilderness journey was a leading (Rom 8:15) of the people to the land, but they continually looked back to Egypt. Consequently, the Psalm is not just about the murmuring at Massah and Meribah; it also alludes to the refusal by the people to enter the land, which was also a desire to return to Egypt (Num 14:3). At that time God declared they would 'not enter into my rest' (Ps 95:11).

---

[1] The appeal of the Psalm is about 'coming' to a temple, whereas the warning of the Psalm is about 'returning' to Egypt and not entering the land. It might be thought that the warning was inappropriate, however, the land was a sanctuary (Exod 15:17) in which the nation were to be a kingdom of priests to the nations.

[2] That is, 'come' in Matt 25:34 picks up 'come' of Psalm 95 as part of the allusion.

[3] Typology is a scalable architecture in language, i.e. aspects of a type can be observed at different scales. For example, the typology of heaven and earth is scalable in the sense that differently sized areas function as types of heaven and earth.

Jesus mentions two prepared places — a kingdom for the sheep and everlasting fire prepared for the devil and his angels, i.e. the goats (Matt 25:41).[1] In the Psalm, likewise, the people 'saw' God's prepared work (Ps 95:9). At Massah and Meribah they saw the water from the rock (Exod 17:6), and at Kadesh the people received the report of what the spies 'saw' in the land (Num 13:17ff cf. v. 27, 14:23, Deut 1:25, Heb 3:7). In both cases what was seen was the work of God, and in the case of the land, it was a land prepared by God, flowing with milk and honey.[2]

> Behold, I send an Angel before thee, to keep thee in the
> way, and to bring thee into the place which I have prepared.
> Exod 23:20 (KJV); cf. 15:17, and see Gen 41:32-34

We might not think that the land was prepared and ready for them; it was not like an empty house waiting to be occupied. The nation had work[5] to do in clearing the land of the Canaanites. Once this had been done, they would then have to function as a kingdom of priests under God towards the nations. Israel were God's firstborn son (Hos 11:1, Deut 1:31). They were a created man (Num 14:15), and a nation designed to be priests for the other nations (Exod 19:5). Their sanctuary was to be the land of Israel, a tabernacle in the midst of the nations. Like Adam, they were brought to this Garden of Eden. It was a good (i.e. very good) land full of fruit, evoking images of paradise. However, they refused to enter into

---

[1] This mention of the devil and his angels is an allusion to the rebellion of Korah, which concerned the establishment of a rival tabernacle to that of Moses (Num 16:24). This allusion fits in with Jesus' prophecy because a characteristic of that rebellion was a refusal to "come" to the tabernacle of God (Num 16:4, 9, 12, 14), and indeed the rebels argued that Moses had failed to bring the people to the land (v. 14). A characteristic of this rebellion was the use of fire, both in the false worship of the rebels, and in the mode of their destruction. Hence, the punishment is one of everlasting fire.

[2] Compare the theme of 'seeing' (a city afar off) in Hebrews 11.

[3] The antitype to this preparation is also reflected in Jesus' words, 'I go to prepare a place for you' (John 14:2), but Jesus' focus is on the temple rather than the land.

[4] Another example of preparation is David's preparation of a place for the ark of God (1 Chron 15:1-3).

[5] The fact that after the fall Adam had work to do, should lead us to expect Israel to play a part, and not have it all ready for them. They did not see their work, or they balked at it, and so they chose to return to Egypt.

150

God's 'rest'. As a result, God again proposed making a second man, a second nation from the loins of Moses (Num 14:12).[1] This did not happen, but instead of the Fathers, it was the next generation, the children, that inherited the land under Joshua. This inheritance was not completed, for the Canaanites were not completely destroyed from the land.

We can now answer the question: why was the kingdom *prepared from the foundation of the world?* The expression looks back to the time when the kingdom was first offered to the nation: it was prepared at the time of the foundation of the nation, but they refused to enter the land. Nevertheless, there still remains the same rest for the people of God - it is still prepared for them (Heb 4:9), as we shall see in our next example.

3.3 Hebrews 4:3

The author of Hebrews deploys a comparison in Hebrews 4 between the Genesis creation and Exodus.

> For we which have believed do enter into rest, as he said, As
> I have sworn in my wrath, if they shall enter into my rest:
> although the works were finished from the foundation of
> the world. Heb 4:3 (KJV)

He refers to the rest that God took after the six days of creation, and then he comments, 'And in this place *again*, If they shall enter into my rest' (vv. 4-5). The 'again' signals a second time of rest for God from His works; it shows that God had been working for a second time. This time was the period of Israel's formation and exodus from Egypt. This was a period of many works all directed to establishing Israel in the land.

We might ask why this period in God's purpose should be described using the language of the Genesis creation. This is the wrong question, because the concepts of the Genesis creation have been repeatedly used to describe beginnings and endings in God's purpose, thereby showing that God's purpose remains the same — *to create an image of God.*

The argument is that they did not enter the land because of unbelief (v. 6), and therefore the rest still remains to be realized for the people of God (v. 9). He applies the opportunity of entering God's rest to the

---

[1] In a Psalm recalling the refusal to enter the land, the psalmist exhorts the people to think of God as their 'maker', picking up the theme of nation-making (Ps 95:6).

151

church. The same Gospel that was preached to the tribes in the wilderness was preached to the church, who were likewise a creation of God,[1] and they should take heed that they did not fall (like Adam, and like Israel).

The language describing the exodus is modelled on the language of the Genesis creation. This can lead commentators to suggest that the foundation of the world in the texts we are examining is the foundation of the Genesis heaven and earth. However, this is a mistake because the Genesis terminology is being reused in an exodus context, and it is this that constitutes the foundation of the world. Our next example is the sharpest text for this disagreement over 'the foundation of the world'.

3.4 Luke 11:50

The two prophets that Jesus mentions are Abel (Gen 4:10) and Zacharias (2 Chron 24:19-22).

> That the blood of all the prophets, which was shed from the foundation of the world, may be required of this generation… Luke 11:50 (KJV)

The argument is put that with Abel being mentioned, the foundation of the world must be the foundation of the Genesis heaven and earth. However, Jesus has just made the point that it was the Jewish Fathers that killed the prophets (Luke 11:47-48), and it is certain that Cain, who killed Abel, is not one of the Jewish Fathers.[2]

This difficulty gives rise to the suggestion that Jesus' remark is a literary figure of speech, rather than an historical observation. These two are chosen because they are the first and last martyrs in the Jewish OT, (the Jewish OT ended with 2 Chronicles). Indeed Jesus quotes Zacharias' last words:

> …The Lord look upon it and require it. 2 Chron 24:22 (KJV)

> …That the blood of all the prophets…may be required of this generation. Luke 11:50 (KJV)

---

[1] The author refers to the church as 'creatures' (Heb 4:13), 'naked', and 'opened unto the eyes' of God, alluding to the fall of Adam and Eve, who were naked with their eyes open and subsequently found by God.

[2] Although in a different sense, the Jews were of their father, the devil, who was a murderer from the beginning.

Therefore the expression 'from the blood of Abel unto the blood of Zacharias' is a figure of speech referring to the OT Scriptures, rather than the historical events of their killings. This Jewish perspective identifies 'the World' as the nation, rather than the physical heavens and earth.[1] This Law was the 'foundation' of the nation comprising the covenant with God at Sinai, and his requirements for the nation. It is this law and its requirements on sacrifice that lie behind our next text on what took place after the foundation of the world.

3.5 Hebrews 9:26

Hebrews contrasts the Law of Moses and its sacrifices with the sacrifice and priesthood of Christ.

> For then must he often have suffered since the foundation of the world: but now once in the end of the world hath he appeared to put away sin by the sacrifice of himself. Heb 9:26 (KJV)

Jesus was a priest after the order of Melchizedek and not after the Levitical order (Heb 7:11). Salvation was not possible through the Levitical priesthood, which offered sacrifices for sins on a daily basis (Heb 7:27). The blood of bulls and goats could not take away sins (Heb 10:4). So a better sacrifice was necessary. This sacrifice was not presented by Christ in an earthly tabernacle, but in a heavenly temple (Heb 9:24). Neither was this sacrifice offered repeatedly every year as on the Mosaic Day of Atonement (Heb 9:25). Had this been required,

> ...then must he often have suffered since the foundation of the world: but now once in the end of the world hath he appeared to put away   sin by the sacrifice of himself. Heb 9:26-27 (KJV)

Christ would have had to suffer repeatedly in order to match the pattern of the High Priest entering the Holy of Holies once a year. But Christ's sacrifice was offered once, appropriately, at the *end of the world*, i.e. the end of the Mosaic world. The various sacrifices of the Law of Moses typify aspects of Christ's work. Our next 'foundation of the world' text is based on the sacrifice of the Passover lamb.

---

[1] Abel's death may have been several hundred years after creation.

3.6 Revelation 13:8

It is easy to overlook the central role of the Passover lamb in the exodus; but as far as sacrifices go, the Passover lamb is used in the description of Christ's sacrifice, and therefore the type should have a high measure of importance.

> And all that dwell upon the earth shall worship him, whose names are not written in the book of life of the Lamb slain from the foundation of the world. Rev 13:8 (KJV)

The blood of the Passover lamb was placed on the lintels and posts of the Israelite houses:

> For the Lord will pass through to smite the Egyptians; and when he seeth the blood upon the lintel, and on the two side posts, the Lord will pass over the door, and will not suffer the destroyer to come in unto your houses to smite [you]. Exod 12:23 (KJV)

Since the sacrifice of Jesus is the means through which the new creation is made, this would also be true of the type — the exodus was also a creation made through a sacrifice - that sacrifice was 'Christ' in type. The importance of the Passover sacrifice, as a sacrifice standing at the beginning of things, is shown by the Apocalypse, where Christ is spoken of as the 'lamb' slain from the foundation of the world.

3.7 Revelation 17:8

Revelation mentions a book of life written up since the foundation of the world:

> The beast that thou sawest was, and is not; and shall ascend out of the bottomless pit, and go into perdition: and they that dwell on the earth shall wonder, whose names were not written in the book of life from the foundation of the world, when they behold the beast that was, and is not, and yet is. Rev 17:8 (KJV)

Seeing such a consistent interpretation of the expression, 'the foundation of the world', it should come as no surprise to find a reference to the book of life in the days of Moses:

> Yet now, if thou wilt forgive their sin--; and if not, blot me, I pray thee, out of thy book which thou hast written. And the

Lord said to Moses, 'Whoever hath sinned against me, him will I blot out of my book'. Exod 32:32-33 (KJV)

Moses knows of a book 'of life' which has been written by the Lord. He offered to be blotted out of this book so that his people might live, but this proposal was refused.[1] Let us now explore this idea.

4. Before the foundation of the World—John 17:5

What was before the foundation of the world? If the foundation of the world is the foundation of the nation under Moses, what can we learn about the time-period before this event? In John 17:24 we read of the Father loving Christ *before the foundation of the world*.[2] Similarly, in Ephesians 1:4 we read of the apostles and saints chosen by God *before the foundation of the world*. We do not need to read the notion of pre-existence into either of these passages, because they are explained by the concept of foreknowledge:

> Who verily was foreordained before the foundation of the world, but was manifest in these last times for you, Who by him do believe in God, that raised him up from the dead, and gave him glory; that your faith and hope might be in God. 1 Pet 1:20-21 (KJV)

The point here establishes the superiority of Christ and the independence that the apostles and saints have in Christ, *independence, that is, from the Law* (1 Pet 1:18). This is why God introduces the idea (Rom 8:28-30) of His foreknowledge and pre-destination. It establishes that believers are not grounded in the Mosaic system, but in a new way based on prior promises. He does not introduce the idea to make a point about His decisions before the creation of the Genesis heaven and earth. The pre-destination of Gentile believers (and the book of life) is encapsulated in

---

[1] One suggestion about the book of life is this: this book was set down at the time of the patriarchal promises. This is the time when the purpose of God first focuses on the *descendants* of the Seed, their number and their inheritance. Rather than think of the book of life as a book written before the Genesis creation (as church theologians might propose), think of the book of life as a product of the patriarchal promises (the covenant document).

[2] In the OT the notion of 'foundations' is mostly applied to the building of the temple, but it is used in connection with the founding of nations (Exod 9:18, Ezek 30:4, cf. Deut 32:22, Isa 16:7), and it is also applied to Israel (Pss 82:5, 102:25-26) when they are viewed as an 'earth'.

the patriarchal promises about Abraham's descendants, both Jew and 'Gentile' (Eph 1:4).[1]

Paul makes a similar point about the ages. Promises were made before the (Mosaic) age began (2 Tim 1:9, Tit 1:9) These promises concerned *eternal life* — hence Jesus prays, 'this is *eternal life* that they may know thee the only true God' (John 17:3). The promise is the one which God made to Abraham at Moriah, for Paul stresses that it was in this promise that *God cannot lie* (cf. Heb 6:13ff). This is the promise which states that *in Christ Jesus all the nations of the world should be blessed* (Gen 22:18). Thus Paul comments that this mystery has been made known to all nations, and he comments that *we* Gentiles have been called according to the grace, a grace that was given to us **in** Christ Jesus (the seed of the Abrahamic covenant) before the world began.

Paul's focus is on a particular point before the world began — namely, the hope of eternal life demonstrated in the events surrounding the Father and the Son making a sacrifice on Moriah. Appropriately, the promises are not according to works as in the Law and the world associated with that Law, but the promise is 'of grace' — given by God.

Jesus prayed,

> And now, O Father, glorify thou me with thine own self with the glory which I had with thee before the world was. John 17:5 (KJV)

What did he mean? Did he literally share glory with the Father before the world began? Perhaps the first expression to examine is 'glorify thou me with thine own self" The stress here lies in the words *with thine own self*, but what does Jesus mean by the word 'glorify'? In John 17:1, Jesus opens his prayer by asking God to glorify him so that he might in turn glorify his father. This request is repeated in John 17:5. He is asking to be glorified so that his father would be *thereby* glorified. Jesus is not asking to be

---

[1] In English we might turn this around and say, 'to what is God's knowledge to the fore'? The theological proposal is that it is afore time and space; it is, as it were, in eternity. The Biblical answer is more pointed, this knowledge of God is afore the foundation of the world and demonstrated in the patriarchal promises.

glorified *by being placed alongside* God in heaven; rather he is asking to be glorified *along with*[1] the Father.

What is the glorification? The immediate context suggests that it is Christ's death *and* his resurrection (John 11:4, 12:28-32, 13:32, Acts 3:11-14). We are presented then with the idea that Christ viewed his imminent death and resurrection as a glorification which *he had already had* with the Father *before the world began*. The thought is not therefore one of exaltation to a heavenly position formerly occupied, but it is the thought of a crucifixion, death and resurrection previously shared. How can this have been? The answer is that such an experience *with a father* occurred in type before the world began (cf. Gen 45:13).

To discover the typical basis of Jesus' remark, we need to study the concept of 'thine own self"; the expression occurs only three times in the KJV. It translates a common Greek word (σεαυτῷ) which is usually translated 'thyself". However, the expression 'thine own self' adds a stress that is not present in an ordinary use of 'thyself". This stress comes from Christ using the personal pronoun 'thou'. He does not simply say, 'Glorify me with thyself'. He says, 'Thou glorify me with thyself". This stress is quarried from the following quotation:

> Remember Abraham, Isaac, and Israel, thy servants, to whom thou swarest by thine own self, and saidst unto them, I will multiply your seed as the stars of heaven, and all this land that I have spoken of will I give unto your seed, and they shall inherit [it] for ever. Exod 32:13 (KJV)

We will see in the next chapter that the 'world' in John is the nation as constituted under the Mosaic covenant (e.g. John 1:10, 7:1-8, 18:20), and we have seen that the glory Jesus seeks is the glory entailed by his death and resurrection. What we find *before* this world are the covenants of promise. These covenants of promise are sworn by God, but one in particular is sworn by his own name. Hebrews refers particularly to this covenant:

> For when God made promise to Abraham, because he could swear by no greater, he sware by himself... Heb 6:13 (KJV)

---

[1] The Greek preposition is παρὰ with dative, other examples are Matt 22:25; John 1:39; 4:40; and Acts 9:43.

And this promise comes *just after* Abraham had offered up his only son and received him back to life again in a figure or type (Heb 11:19).

> And said, By myself have I sworn, saith the Lord, for because thou hast done this thing, and hast not withheld thy son, thine only [son]: That in blessing I will bless thee, and in multiplying I will multiply thy seed as the stars of the heaven, and as the sand which [is] upon the sea shore; and thy seed shall possess the gate of his enemies; And in thy seed shall all the nations of the earth be blessed; because thou hast obeyed my voice. Gen 22:16-18 (KJV)

Jesus' appeal to the Father is based on this event. Abraham and Isaac, a father and son, went together to make this sacrifice. And so it is with Jesus and *his father*, for both had set their faces towards Jerusalem (the same Mount Moriah) to make this sacrifice. Abraham lifted up his eyes and *saw* (cf. John 8:56; Heb 11:13) Mount Moriah *afar off* (Gen 22:4). Abraham believed God and it was accounted to him for righteousness; he was a righteous father who loved his son Isaac. In this he foreshadowed the Righteous Father who loved his son before the foundation of the world (John 17:24-25).[1]

The glory that Christ had with the Father was before this foundation and enshrined in the patriarchal promises. Christ had this glory when, typed as Isaac, he went with his father to Mount Moriah. Because Isaac typed Christ in this walk, Christ can speak of this incident as glory which *he* had with His father. In this sense enacted types are like television programmes which actually show the future events.

---

[1] Abraham's function as a type of the Father is alluded to in the text that describes the only begotten son as 'in the bosom of the Father' (John 1:18). The parable of the Rich Man and Lazarus supplies one clue to the interpretation of this word picture. In that parable, it is Lazarus (symbolizing those with faith), who is in the *bosom of Abraham*, and not the Rich Man, who (with his 'five' brethren) symbolizes the Jews and their Law. As Jesus demonstrated in John 8, Abraham was not the father of those Jews who did not have faith in him. In John 1, the contrast is in the same vein - a contrast between the Law of Moses and grace and truth (v. 17). Hence John states that the only begotten son *was* in the bosom of the Father. Abraham's beloved son was Isaac, and he was the son of the free woman. Those who are in the bosom of the Father are those who are born of Sarah and not of the bondwoman (who was wrongly placed into the bosom of Abraham (Gen 16:5; Gal 4:24)).

His death and his resurrection were his glory *and* the glory of the Father. The superiority of Christ over the world rests in his antecedent and superior sacrifice. The glory of Christ rested in his death on the cross and then his resurrection. This glory he had with the Father before the world began.

5. Conclusion

Studying the topic of the 'foundation of the world' provides the background to one of the main pre-existence texts, 'And now, O Father, glorify thou me with thine own self with the glory which I had with thee before the world was'. The foundation of the world is the foundation of the nation of Israel under Moses, and this is shown by a careful consideration of all the texts where this expression occurs. The glory that the Son had with the Father before *this* world began was a glory that he had in type on Mount Moriah.

CHAPTER EIGHT
The Incarnation (1)

1. Introduction
In this chapter we will begin our inquiry into the topic of the incarnation.[1] The main text used for affirming the incarnation is John 1:1, 14. Other popular texts are Philippians 2:5-9, Rom 8:3, Gal 4:4 and Heb 2:14. We will examine the prologue of John (John 1:1-18) in the next chapter, while here we will look at Rom 8:3, Gal 4:4, Phil 2:5-9 and Heb 2:14.

These incarnation texts divide into three types, so we can divide up our subject matter on this basis:

1) Rom 8:3 and Gal 4:4 are seen by orthodox commentaries as *third party* descriptions of the incarnation, which make the Father the agent of the incarnation, i.e. God *sent* his son.

2) Phil 2:5-9 and Heb 2:14, on the other hand, are interpreted as describing God the Son taking *intentional decisions* about becoming human.

3) John 1:1, 14 is different to the above two texts in that the agency of the Father and the decision-making of the Son is absent. Rather, it is said that we have a matter-of-fact description of the incarnation.

The incarnation is a foundation-stone of popular orthodox Christianity. As a doctrine it is regarded as a touchstone of a confessing Christian. If a person denies the full deity of Christ, he is regarded as a heretic, as many orthodox Christian books on 'cults and isms' illustrate (e.g. by J. Oswald-Sanders and M. C. Burrell) and as the traditional creeds affirm.[2] There are surprisingly few passages in the NT which can be used to describe an incarnation process; however, the subject has a major bearing on what it means to be a Christian.

---

[1] For an introduction to the doctrine of the incarnation see S. T. Davis, D. Kendall and G. O'Collins, eds., *The Incarnation* (Oxford: Oxford University Press, 2002).

[2] The Christadelphians are regarded as heretics by orthodox Christian churches. Christadelphians regard orthodox Christians either as apostate or as misguided, depending on how severe they are in their judgment.

2. The Origins of the Doctrine of the Incarnation

In 1980, J. D. G. Dunn published a study into the origins of the doctrine of the incarnation called *Christology in the Making*. His first conclusion was that "we have found nothing in pre-Christian Judaism or the wider religious thought of the Hellenistic world which provides sufficient explanation of the origin of the doctrine of the incarnation, no way of speaking about God, the gods, or intermediary beings which so far as we can tell would have given birth to this doctrine apart from Christianity".[1] We can agree with this conclusion; what Dunn then seeks to do is establish the origin of the doctrine of the incarnation in the text of John's gospel rather than in Paul; we do not have to agree with this argument.

Our concern is not with the origins of the doctrine of the incarnation, since that rather begs the question from our point of view; the history of the first century church therefore lies outside our remit. For example, Dunn's dating of the Johannine corpus can be challenged[2] and the dating of the Gospel of John can easily be brought before AD70. If we did this, we would completely overturn Dunn's historical reconstruction. However, what is of interest to us is whether the raw data itself carries an incarnation meaning. If modern day churches interpret the text wrongly, any mistakes in church history and dating merely compound the error. Consequently, we can put aside the various ideas about the origin of this doctrine (our hypothesis would be that its origins lie in the sub-Apostolic era and the work of the Apologists.)

3. Romans 8:3

Romans 8:3 is a traditional proof-text of the incarnation. This is supported by three features of the text, 'having sent'; 'his *own* son' and 'in the likeness of sinful flesh'.

> For what the Law could not do, weak as it was through the flesh, God *did*: sending his own son in the likeness of sinful flesh and as *an offering* for sin, he condemned sin in the flesh... Rom 8:3 (NASB)

The incarnational reading of Rom 8:3 is simple: The Son was in heaven and then sent to earth. Is this correct? Taking Second Temple texts as our database, we could compare the sending of God's son with the sending of a prophet; the sending of an angel; the sending of an exalted patriarch; the

---

[1] Dunn, *Christology in the Making*, 253.

[2] This is partly the goal of J. A. T Robinson, *The Priority of John* (London: SCM Press, 1985).

sending of a divine hypostasis; or more generally, with God's action in the world. Each of these possible comparisons emerge from Jewish cosmology.

The verb for 'sending' is πέμπω. It is Paul's only use of the verb in Romans, but he uses it elsewhere 14x. It's a common enough verb for sending persons (e.g. 1 Cor 4:17) or things (e.g. Acts 11:29). Here it is an aorist participle (πέμψας) which indicates the action of sending comes before the related action of 'condemned'. This much is clear in the English translation as well.

Is Paul's statement about sending God's son like the historical narrative descriptions of the sending of a prophet or leader? Sometimes prophets are sent on specific tasks like delivering a message (2 Chron 25:15); otherwise they are just 'sent' at the beginning of their ministry (Hag 1:12). Jeremiah, who was formed in the womb, and known beforehand in the purpose of God, and ordained to be a prophet, was still 'sent' to the nations when the time came for his ministry to begin (Jer 1:5-8). Or again, Moses and Aaron were 'sent' to the Egyptians:

> And he said, Certainly I will be with thee; and this shall be a token unto thee, that I have <u>sent</u> thee: When thou hast brought forth the people out of Egypt, ye shall serve God upon this mountain. Exod 3:12 (KJV)

> He <u>sent</u> Moses his servant; and Aaron whom he had chosen. Ps 105:26 (KJV)

These examples of God sending someone aren't exact parallels to Rom 8:3, because Paul's qualifies God sending his son to be 'in the likeness of sinful flesh'. Prophets and leaders are sent in a historical narrative and we are given contextual information about their task or ministry. Paul is abstractly describing an event in history, the sending of God's son as a sin-offering and how that relates to the problem of sin and death.

The fact that Jesus was sent as a prophet or a deliver does not mean that this is Paul's point in Rom 8:3. Jesus' Parable of the Wicked Husbandmen is a case in point (Matt 20; Luke 21). God sent prophets to his vineyard and the people slew them; in the end God sent his son. The sending of the son is not described differently to the servants (ἀποστέλλω, πέμπω) and so the parable offers no framework for any inference of pre-existence. Hebrews presupposes a similar framework in making a comparison between God's speaking through prophets in former times but now

163

through a son (Heb 1:1-2). Again, Rom 8:3 is different to the sending of servants and then a son in the parable because it is the sending of an offering for sin. .

Similarly, Paul isn't alluding to the prophecy of a 'prophet like unto Moses' (Deut 18:15; John 1:21; 6:14; 7:40-41; Acts 3:22; 7:37). The verb 'to send' is not used, it is 'raise up'. However, the prophecy does say that the prophet would be raised up "from the midst of thee, of thy brethren", which is like Paul's emphasis on God's son being sent in the likeness of sinful flesh.

Furthermore, there isn't an allusion to the 'anointed' (messianic) deliverer of Isa 61:1 who claims to be sent by Yahweh to preach good tidings,

> The Spirit of the Lord God is upon me; because the Lord hath anointed me to preach good tidings unto the meek; he hath <u>sent</u> me to bind up the broken-hearted, to proclaim liberty to the captives, and the opening of the prison to them that are bound… Isa 61:1 (KJV)

Jesus appeals to this prophecy (Luke 4:16-21), but again this isn't about Jesus being an offering for sin. Jesus certainly has a notion of being sent by God (e.g. Matt 12:34; Mark9:37) but this doesn't mean that it is this understanding that underlies Paul's point.

Equally, Rom 8:3 is not like the sending of an angel.

> He cast upon them the fierceness of his anger, wrath, and indignation, and trouble, by <u>sending</u> evil angels among them. Ps 78:49 (KJV)

> And the man that stood among the myrtle trees answered and said, 'These are they whom the Lord hath <u>sent</u> to walk to and fro through the earth'. Zech 1:10 (KJV)

The classic example is that of Gabriel who was sent from standing in the presence of the Lord to Zacharias to tell him about the upcoming birth of John (Luke 1:19), again Gabriel was sent 'from God' to Mary (Luke 1:26). There are plenty of other examples of angels being sent, but angels are part of a scriptural cosmology in which they have a place in heaven. These uses of the verb 'to send' in connection with angels are not comparable to Rom 8:3 because there is no pre-existing cosmology for the Son. We are dealing with a first and unique sending of God's son.

God sent his own son and this statement goes against an incarnational reading because that would present two divine beings in heaven, the one being sent by the other. Such a cosmology would be unprecedented in Jewish thinking and so it is an implausible reading for Paul. Instead, we should think of the model of God sending a sacrifice.

The sending that Paul alludes to is the providing of the sacrificial ram on Mt. Moriah. The stress on 'his *own* son' (τὸν ἑαυτοῦ υἱὸν) is an echo here of 'thine only son' and the typology of Abraham sacrificing Isaac (Gen 22:16; Rom 8:32). The typology of 'sending' in Rom 8:3 therefore militates against a more literal reading of sending someone from heaven because it is about providing a ram as an offering (the ram was not literally in heaven).

4. Galatians 4:4

When the time had fully come, God sent forth (ἐξαποστέλλω) his son, born of woman and born under the Law (Gal 4:4; cf. Rom 8:3). Does this mean that the Son was in heaven and sent from heaven? Does this imply that the Son became incarnate in a man born of woman? If these are not valid inferences, why does Paul want to say that Jesus was born of woman? We would not describe one of our children with the words: *he/she was born of woman* (but compare English literature). So, does Paul use this language to describe an incarnation process? Is he using this language to emphasize the humanity of a heavenly being, as Trinitarians advocate?

The language of God *sending forth* is used of angels (e.g. Gen 24:40; Acts 12:11) and human messengers (e.g. Moses, Exod 3:12ff; Ps 105:26; Mic 6:4). God has sent a myriad of prophets down the ages.[1] For God to *send* someone says nothing about the origin or point of departure for the one who is sent; rather it is the heavenly origin of the commission that matters. Thus, in the parable of the dishonest stewards, the Son is the last agent to be sent by the Father. Here Paul makes the point that last of all, or in the fulness of times, God sent out his son (cf. Mark 12:6). If the Son was sent from heaven, we ought to equally argue that the previous agents (the prophets) were also sent from heaven.

It might be thought that 'sending forth' is just the same idea as 'to send' (e.g. John 1:6, ἀποστέλλω; John 5:23, πέμπω), but there is a nuance in Paul's choice of verb that connects up with the story of the exodus. Moses was

---

[1] See Jud 6:8; 2 Chron 36:15; Jer 1:7; Ezek 2:3; Obad v. 1; Hag 1:12; Mal 3:1; John 1:6 and Acts 22:21.

sent forth to bring Israel out of Egypt (Exod 3:12, LXX, ἐξαποστέλλω; cf. Ps 105:26; Mic 6:4). Paul is presenting Jesus as a **new Moses** in his use of this verb and he is doing so because he is presenting Jesus as having been made 'under the Law' sent forth to redeem those under the Law (Gal 3:23; 4:4).

Paul makes the point that in the fulness of time[1] God sent forth his son. This is not about there being a point in the purpose of God for the sending of a Son (a common proposal); it is about there being a point in the purpose of God **for the ending of the Law**. This is shown by Paul's reasoning: Jews were under Law until a time appointed of the Father (Gal 4:2). The time for the Law to end had come and so God had sent his son (Christ was the end of the Law to everyone that believed (Rom 10:4)). We might speculate as to why the Law was to end at this time, but Paul offers no reason on this score. This is consistent with Luke,

> The Law and the Prophets *were* until John: since that time the kingdom of God is preached, and every man presseth into it. Lk 16:16 (KJV)

If we ask *when* did God send forth his son, the verb and the type suggests that he was sent forth at his **baptism** (on which see Chapter Nine). Moses was sent forth from Midian to Egypt and the encounter on Sinai at the burning bush doesn't present itself as a type of Jesus' birth. Equally, prophets are sent to the people, whether we have a commission recorded or not, as grown men. The rare use of the verb, ἐξαποστέλλω, doesn't suggest the common idea of 'sent in the purpose of God' (as John the Baptist, John 1:6, ἀποστέλλω),[2] but 'sent forth' and this verb is quoting the sending forth of Moses to redeem the people – an act of God in respect of a grown man. Hence, this typology cannot support an incarnational reading relating to Jesus' birth.

---

[1] There is an echo of the exodus in that it happened at the end of an assigned period of time (Gen 15:13; Exod 12:40; Gal 3:17).

[2] The verb is used of Moses in Deut 34:10-11, "There has not arisen a prophet since in Israel like Moses, whom the Lord knew face to face, none like him for all the signs and wonders which the Lord sent him to do". It is this statement that Jesus echoes in declaring John the Baptist to 'have arisen' and be 'greater' among those born of women (Matt 11:11; Luke 7:28); Jesus also echoes this statement in his declaration about himself that only the son knows the Father (Matt 11:27; Luke 10:22).

Paul adds a second reason for why God has a son, and this is that believers might receive an adoption as sons. This explains why the Law was not ended by someone who was a prophet or a leader, once again acting under the influence of the angels.

But when the fulness of the time was come,

> (A) God sent forth his <u>son</u>, made of a woman,
>> (B) made under <u>Law</u>, that those under <u>Law</u>, might be redeemed
> (A') that we might receive the adoption of <u>sons</u>.

(Gal 4:4)

There is a small chiastic structure here which points up the association of Jesus being a son and believers' adoption as sons. Their sonship is parallel to Jesus' sonship, but their 'sonship' is not metaphorical; it is an adoption as sons.

Within the purpose that God has with Israel, 'the adoption' is placed alongside the Law as a structural event:

> ...who are Israelites; to whom pertaineth <u>the adoption</u>, and the glory, and the covenants, and the giving of the Law, and the service of God, and the promises. Rom 9:4 (KJV)

This 'adoption' is, in turn, defined by Paul,

> And not only this, but also, we ourselves, having the first fruits of the Spirit, even we ourselves groan within ourselves, waiting eagerly for our <u>adoption</u> as sons, the redemption of our body. Rom 8:23 (NASB)

The adoption as sons is a description of the future redemption of the body, i.e. the resurrected status of believers.

Why does Paul use the expression 'made of woman'? The Greek word translated 'made of' (γίνομαι) is not the more specific word for giving birth, which he uses in respect of Abraham's sons (Gal 4:13, γεννάω). Nor is it the adjective used in Matt 11:11, "among those born of women" (ἐν γεννητοῖς γυναικῶν). But rather it is the more general word for *becoming,* (literally, the Greek is *being out of a woman being under law*). Typology supplies the reason for Paul's choice of language.

The scriptural background to Paul's statement is the promise about the seed of **the woman** (Gen 3:15). The original promise to Eve was that she would give birth to a seed that would bruise the head of the Serpent. Paul is certainly familiar with the typological significance of the Serpent in Eden (Rom 16:20; 2 Cor 11:3) and the role of Christ in relation to the Serpent. Moreover, there had been a long line of 'barren' women who had given birth to a son in God-guided circumstances — women such as Sarah, Rachael, Jochebed and Hannah. This is another typology that Paul is drawing upon in his emphasis that the Son was made of a woman. Further, we cannot exclude an echo of Isa 7:14 and its prophecy of a young woman conceiving a child that was to be called 'Immanuel'.

There is a comparison to be made between Gal 4:4-5 and Gal 3:13-14,

> ...<u>made</u> (γίνομαι) of a woman, <u>made</u> (γίνομαι) under Law to redeem (ἐξαγοράζω)...that we might receive...the spirit of his son... Gal 4:4-5

> ...redeemed us (ἐξαγοράζω)...<u>being made</u> (γίνομαι) a curse for us...that we might receive the promise of the Spirit... Gal 3:13-14

One of the purposes for which God had a son was to redeem and to give the Spirit, which is clarified to involve a spirit of adoption, i.e. a spirit of adopted sonship (Rom 8:15, 23; Eph 1:5).

Enclosed within this teaching about sonship, Paul includes redemption from the Law. The contrast he develops is one between bondage under the Law (Gal 4:3, 9, 24-25) and the freedom of sonship (Gal 5:1). This metaphor of 'bondage' harks back to Egypt and it further explains why Paul chooses the verb 'to send forth' for Jesus. It is more than just a comparison with Moses; it is also a comparison between the bondage from which Moses was sent forth to redeem the children of Israel and the bondage of the Law from which Jesus was sent forth to redeem those who believe in him. Failure to see this typology underpins the misreading of God sending forth his son from heaven to become incarnate in Jesus Christ.

Incarnation is implausible here because the scriptural idiom of God 'sending forth' would not, for a Jew, imply pre-existence. Such an idiom is one way of describing how God relates to the world: he *sent forth* Moses to redeem the people (e.g. Exod 3:12 Judg 6:8 (LXX, ἐξαποστέλλω)). There is an *historical argument* here about what would be a plausible development in Paul's thought-world for his readers. The combination of the ideas of a personal incarnation, a pre-earthly existence, and being a son (let alone being *of* the Godhead) would be exceptionally new as well as radical within Judaism regardless of what flavour we chose to highlight as a background. So, for example, if we were to consider texts about Wisdom existing with God in the beginning and being sent forth (e.g. Prov 8:22; Wisd 9:10, ἐξαποστέλλω), we don't have the ingredients of sonship (Wisdom is female) or a personal **transforming**[1] incarnation in such traditions.

5. Philippians 2:6-7

We have examined Rom 8:3 and Gal 4:4, and we must now turn to examine another two key texts — Philippians 2 and Hebrews 2.

> Who, being in the form of God, thought it not robbery to be equal with God: But made himself of no reputation, and took upon him the form of a servant, [and] was made in the likeness of men: And being found in fashion as a man, he humbled himself, and became obedient to death, even the death of the cross. Phil 2:6-8 (KJV revised[2])

Philippians 2 is a key pre-existence text; it appears to say that Christ was in the form of God, but that he made himself of no reputation and took upon himself the form of a servant, which amounted to being made in the likeness of men; and being a man he submitted to death. This seems to speak of the Son taking decisions about his human nature, and it therefore seems to imply that he must have pre-existed in some way in order to make these decisions.[3]

---

[1] This is the point of difference with Wisdom traditions. Wisdom comes to the earth and lives among men, but she is Wisdom *in* those men (as Torah, Bar 3:37-4:1; or as Wisdom, Sir 24:10).

[2] I follow the KJV in this quotation except for the clause which reads in the KJV, 'thought it not robbery to be equal with God', which I have replaced with the NIV equivalent, 'did not consider equality with God something to be grasped', which is the more common choice of translators. We will see however that the KJV is correct.

[3] Christ was made — this is the testimony of Hebrews 2 — but he was made by God the Father (vv. 7, 9, 10). It was not a question of God the Son deciding to become human, and then assuming human nature

The background to Philippians 2 is sometimes taken to be just the Genesis creation,[1] and this is what we have found with other 'pre-existence' passages. However, this is only one context and the main background is Isaiah. Philippians 2 compares Christ and the Servant, but just as Adam was *formed* from the dust of the ground (Gen 2:7), so too the Servant was *formed* from the womb (Isa 49:5). Genesis is involved as a background to Philippians because it is a background in Isaiah. The *forming* of both Israel/Jacob and the Servant in Isaiah (Isa 43:1, 7, 21; 44:2, 21) is a counterargument to those who would *form gods* (Isa 43:10; 44:10). There are several allusions which can be listed:

1) Like the Servant he was in the form of God, a man with dominion over the people.

Paul is not talking here of Christ as the *image* of God, instead he deploys a related idea with a rare NT word,[2] which the KJV translates as 'form'. He is not therefore making the same point as that which he makes in Colossians 1, where he states that Christ is the image of the invisible God which takes us directly back to Genesis. What does he mean?

The expression 'being in the form of God' uses a Greek present participle which means that Christ was in the form of God *when* he considered equality. The Greek construction does not suggest that Christ was *once* in the form of God, and then at some later time considered equality.

In Philippians 2, Paul is describing an attitude of Christ Jesus when he was on the earth. He is not describing the state of mind of a heavenly being. Why would a heavenly being, or even God the Son, think about equality with God the Father, and why would the thoughts of such a heavenly being be an example for us? The force of Paul's point lies in the fact that Christ displayed humility *as one of us*.

It follows that whatever 'form of God' means, it is certain that it describes Christ *as he was on the earth*. Philippians 2 cannot be used to describe an incarnation process, at best it could only be used to support a

---

himself, neither was it a question of allowing himself to become human through the *work* of God the Father.

[1] Dunn, Christology in the Making, 114-121 argues that Philippians 2 is part of the 'Adam Christology' of the early church, a theology in which Christ is evaluated as Adam.

[2] The Greek occurs elsewhere only in Mark 16:12.

view that Christ was 'fully God' while on earth, and that Christ considered equality at that time.

The expression *form of God* does not describe the essential *nature* of Christ, and this is shown by the parallel expression *form of a servant* (or slave), which uses the same Greek word for 'form'. This can be seen because 'form of God' stands in contrast to 'form of servant' and this latter phrase describes Christ as the Suffering Servant of Isaiah.

Christ took on the role of that servant; he did not take on the role of a servant of men *per se*, although he was at times their servant (Matt 20:28, John 13:4-5), but he *did* take on the role of Yahweh's Servant, (cf. the same Greek word for 'slave' is used in Isa 49:3, 5 (LXX) to describe the Servant of the Lord).

This allusion to Isaiah supplies a reason for the use of the word 'form' in the expressions 'form of servant' and 'form of God'. Of all parts of the Scriptures, the concept of *forming* is most frequently found in Isaiah 40-66 (for Israel/Jacob and the king), and it is found with regard to the action of *forming something* — *the forming of a servant* (e.g. Isa 49:5, 53:2).

The use of 'form' in 'form of God' is new, but it is built upon a contrast with 'form of a servant' and it refers to what could be 'seen' in Christ.

2) He did not think it robbery[1] to be equal with God.

This is the KJV rendering. The thoughts that Christ had about equality with God were about grasping or seizing equality as an **act** of robbery, they were not about retaining or keeping equality. This is not the majority view of translators, but it is allowed by the Greek. The majority view is

---

[1] Most translations opt for variations of 'something to be grasped' (e.g. NASB, RSV, NET, NIV); the KJV translates in terms of an 'act' — 'robbery'. The lexicographical exercise is all about gathering examples of usage from other Greek texts and classifying different senses for the word in their contexts. This has been done by various scholars. However, by way of a conclusion, Arndt and Gingrich observe that the translation can only be made on "an understanding of Paul's thought in general" rather than lexicography. W. F. Arndt and F. W. Gingrich, *A Greek-English Lexicon of the New Testament and Other Early Christian Literature* (Cambridge: Cambridge University Press, 1957), 108. Paul's typological reasoning in the passage will supply a basis for choosing among the lexicographical options.

that Christ considered equality a **thing** to be grasped, although one or two go another way (e.g. NRSV 'did not regard equality with God as something to be exploited'). Had Christ been God the Son in heaven, he might have thought equality was a thing to be kept and then chosen not to keep such equality, but the sense of the Greek is that of taking hold of equality in an act of robbery, and if Christ were God the Son, he would not need to think about seizing equality, he would have it by right, as the creeds assert.

Commentators usually compare Christ to Adam and say that Adam had grasped at being 'like God' even though he was already (!) in the image and likeness of God. Equality with the angels was Adam's concern, but he sought this state in the wrong way. Jesus, however, did not think that equality with God was a thing to be grasped.

This compares Adam before the Fall whereas Paul's typology is actually with Adam **after the fall**. We know from the Gospel that this equality is to be given to the children of the resurrection: they are to be *equal unto the angels* (Luke 20:35-36). It is this equality that Christ did not consider to be robbery, i.e. he thought that he could be given access to the Tree of Life and live forever if only God would change his purpose.

Comparing Jesus and Adam before the Fall suffers from two fatal problems. The first is that Eve *gives* the fruit to Adam; there is no grasping or seizing on Adam's part. The second problem is that while Adam was in the image and likeness of God, this is not the typological basis for 'being in the form of God' (see above). These two objections support the conclusion that the equality that Christ considered does not have a typological basis in Adam seeking to be like God in knowing good and evil.

The second point in the story where we can compare the equality Christ considered is in the *living forever* **like** the 'us'[1] in the narrative:

> Then the Lord God said, 'Behold, the man has become <u>like one of us</u>, knowing good and evil; and now, lest he put forth his hand and take also of the tree of life, and eat, and <u>live forever</u>' — therefore the Lord God sent him forth from the

---

[1] It is beyond our scope to establish that it is the divine council of angels referenced by the 'us'; see F. M. Cross, *Canaanite Myth and Hebrew Epic* (Cambridge: Harvard University Press, 1973), 186-190.

garden of Eden, to till the ground from which he was taken.
Gen 3:22-23 (RSV)

The equality here is about living forever,[1] and seeing Christ consider such equality nicely fits the flow of Paul's argument which is about, instead, being obedient unto death. There is also an intertextual link that explains Paul's choice of verb in '**taking** the form of a servant' (v. 7). This 'taking' is the alternative to what was considered by God when he thought Adam might "put forth his hand and **take** also of the tree of life".

There is a further (and deciding) point to make: v. 22 is **actually a consideration about equality**—a record of thinking about equality on the part of God. We have no description of such thinking on the part of Adam (it is implied for Eve). The typological basis for Christ thinking about equality therefore is **not Adam's thinking but that of God**.

There is, of course, a comparison to be made between Christ's obedience and Adam's disobedience. We should not throw the baby out with the bathwater. This contrast is carried by 'obedient' in v. 8, but the substance of each act (obedience and disobedience) is different. Adam ate of the fruit of the tree, but Christ was obedient unto death.[2]

The KJV has "thought it not[3] robbery to be equal with God" but 'robbery' is not the only possibility.[4] C. F. D. Moule, suggests 'act of snatching;'[5] but this can be nuanced by choosing a phrase such as 'act of seizure', and we could, if we wanted, drop the phrase in favour of

---

[1] Dunn, *Christology in the Making*, 116, while making the wrong Adamic connections, nevertheless usefully observes, "As these parallels indicate we are here in the contrast familiar to Greek thought between God/the gods as possessing incorruption, immortality, and man as corruptible, subject to death."

[2] The linkage between 'equality' and 'living forever' is made in Luke 20:36, "For they cannot die anymore, because they are equal to angels and are sons of God, being sons of the resurrection." We might speculate about whether Paul knew this Jesus' tradition.

[3] The negation goes with the noun in the Greek, although many translations put it with the verb. The choice depends partly on whether we see an idiom here in the text and partly on natural English.

[4] This is discussed by Wright as the classic reading of the Latin Fathers.

[5] C. F. D. Moule, "Further Reflexions on Philippians 2:5-11" in *Apostolic History and the Gospel* (eds. W. Ward Gasque and Ralph P. Martin; Exeter: Paternoster Press, 1970), 264-276 (266).

'snatching' or 'seizure'. This means that Christ thought that an equality with God, one not already possessed,[1] would not be robbery/seizing/snatching.

N. Mullen comments,

> The suffix *-mos* is found a total of 217 times in the New Testament, as the ending of 52 different words. Of these usages the vast majority are *indisputably* active in meaning (that is, they refer to an *action,* like "robbery") and not passive (referring to something which is acted upon, like "a thing to be grasped").[2]

Mullen's analysis is supported by a grammatical/lexical breakdown of *ma/-mos* noun endings;[3] and Moule likewise distinguishes ἁρπαγμός and ἅρπαγμα[4] for the same reason as Mullen.

If we now ask how 'robbery' or 'seizure', as acts, have a typological basis in the account of the Fall, we find that a 'seizure' is the sense we should read in Gen 3:22, "lest he put forth his hand and **take** (seize) also of the tree of life". The Hebrew verb is very common and 'seize' is one of the senses listed in Hebrew lexicons. The nuance that the word has is determined by context.

Is the situation envisaged by Gen 3:22 a kind of seizure or snatching, or even a stealing? The 'putting forth of the hand' doesn't make this certain but it is consistent with this reading (cf. Exod 7:5). However, one of the elements for robbery is the presence of guards, and the placing of a **guard** to the Tree of Life ('to guard the way to the tree of life', Gen 3:24) betrays the thinking of God – that to take of the tree would be robbery and that there might be force used to take of the tree.

So, Christ considered equality. When was this point in time? The moment was in the garden on the Mount of Olives when he could have called

---

[1] Paul here opposes the claim of the Jews which was that Jesus claimed equality with God (John 5:18).

[2] N. Mullen, "Philippians 2:6-11 – A Study in History and Exposition 2. *Harpagmos*: 'Robbery' or 'Something to be Grasped'?" *The Testimony* 56 (1986): 25-29 (27).

[3] F. Blass and A. Debrunner, *A Greek Grammar of the New Testament* (Chicago: University of Chicago Press, 1961), 109 n. 1 and 2.

[4] Moule, "Further Reflexions on Philippians 2:5-11", 266

upon twelve legions of angels to rescue him from the temple guards (Matt 26:53).

3) Made himself of no reputation.

The KJV translation is initially unhelpful[1] here, since the other uses of the underlying Greek verb are concerned with *ineffectiveness or emptiness*. For example, faith would be *void or empty* if the promises were inherited through the Law (Rom 4:14); or again, the cross of Christ might be made of *no effect* (1 Cor 1:17); or Paul's boasting might be of *no effect* (2 Cor 9:3). The corresponding noun is usually translated 'vanity' with the sense of vanity of effort.

So, at what point did Christ make himself of no effect, at what point did he not plead his reputation? He was ineffective on the Mount of Olives, but during his trial he offered no defence, he pleaded no cause, and he allowed himself to be convicted. At all times, he was able to call on as many as twelve legions of angels to his aid and had not his father given his son into the hand of the authorities, they would have had no power over him. As a sheep to the shearers, he was led to the slaughter, the lamb of the world.

It was in this work of salvation that he was the Suffering Servant, and so in this work he took on the role of the Servant of the Lord, even though he was in the form of God. At just this point he might have been tempted to ask for equality with God, (he did ask for the cup to be removed). But such equality was for after the grave in the resurrection. And so, he submitted to the *death of a slave* under the Roman hand.

Other versions translate the Greek as 'emptied himself' and this links with Isa 53:12 which reads, 'he *poured out* his soul unto death'. It was in this process that Christ took on and fulfilled the work of the righteous servant who bore the sins of many.

4) Made in the likeness of men.

The KJV reads, '**and** was made in the likeness of men', which can read as if there is some connection between Christ making himself of no reputation and being made in the likeness of men. It can read as if he became a man after making himself of no reputation, but the conjunction

---

[1] It has the advantage though of chiming in with the context which is about *status* and *esteem*, and this is a theme throughout Philippians.

is absent in the Greek. In fact, this clause can equally go with the following clause rather than the preceding, which would give the reading, 'Being made in the likeness of men, and being found in fashion as man, he humbled himself'. The two aorist participles here naturally fit together and are connected by a conjunction; as such they form preliminary clauses to the main verb 'he humbled' in the main clause. [1]

If we concentrate on vv. 6-7, we can see that Paul's thought begins and ends with the same kind of expression: 'who *being in the form of God*...taking the *form of a servant*'. This is the first argument: Christ was in the form of God, but he took on the form of a servant. The second starts with the fact that Christ was made in the likeness of men, and this was the work of God the Father.

Christ was *made* in the likeness of men (cf. Heb 2:7), and the allusion is again to the Suffering Servant who was made by God. The fundamental fact is that Christ was begotten by God, made by him. The fiction proposed by Trinitarians is an eternal begettal, but the Lord formed Christ from the womb to be *his* servant to bring Jacob again to him (Isa 42:1, 44:2, 49:5). The use of the word 'likeness' is significant, and Paul is alluding to Gen 5:3, where we read, Adam begat a son in his own *likeness*. Christ was in the likeness of men, although in the form of God. The emphasis is that Christ partook of our human nature (cf. Rom 1:23), when, as the son of God, we might have expected him to have divine nature.

The phrase 'being found in fashion as man' is unusual and with 'made in the likeness of men' gives us a double emphasis that Jesus was a man.[2] The Greek word for 'being found' is an aorist passive participle, which suggests that Christ was found *by others* to be in fashion as a man, rather than Christ found *himself* to be a man. When was Christ 'found out' in this way? Jesus was stripped during his scourging and 'found' to be a man and this is Paul's euphemism for this part of Christ's sufferings Hence, Paul

---

[1] The RSV has 'being born in the likeness of men' but *birth* is not part of the meaning of the Greek verb. This is a deponent verb with a broad range of meanings that cluster around the concept of *what something or someone is or becomes*. As a deponent verb, it is middle in form but active in sense.

[2] This is ironic for a passage used by Trinitarians to establish the incarnation.

immediately follows on with the thought that - he humbled himself on the cross and submitted to death.[1]

There is a connection here with Genesis. Adam also discovered something about himself - he found himself to be *naked*. Though he was the image of God, yet in his grasping at equality, he found himself to be *man*. And so it was with Christ, he was in the form of God, but knew himself to be man. There is an ironical echo of the Serpent's words — he had said to Adam and Eve, 'ye shall be **as** Gods', but instead they became *as* men are today. Likewise, even though Christ was in the form of God, he was in fashion **as** a man.

The idea of a 'form of God' invites us also to think of those occasions when Moses saw the 'similitude of the Lord' (Num 12:8). The Angel of the Presence was this similitude, and a parallel between Christ and this angel is not out of place, as we saw with John 1. So, the expression 'form of God' is inviting us to see Christ as the archetypical 'similitude of the Lord', (he that hath seen me hath seen the Father). The idea of someone being a similitude is similar to the idea that Adam was in the likeness of God. This idea is one of manifestation, and both the Angel of the Lord and Adam were designed to manifest God.[2]

5) Obedient unto death.

The point of this emphasis is that Christ, knowing that he was a man, was thereby ready to be obedient unto death, and to follow the course of a human life through to death. As a result, he was resurrected and highly exalted by God. The contrast with Adam could not be more pointed — he was *dis*obedient unto death (cf. Rom 5:12), Christ was *obedient* unto death.

---

[1] *Contra* Marshall, "Incarnational Christology in the New Testament", referring to Dunn, "In particular, his interpretation does not do justice to the force of the recapitulatory phrase 'and being found in form as a man' (Phil 2:8) which is very odd if it refers to a person who had never been anything else but a man; again the contrast clearly expressed between 'being in the form of God' and 'becoming in the form of men'

[2] An analogy drawn from modern society could be television. Watching a television, we see similitudes of people such as newscasters or actors. In talking about such *individuals*, we refer to them through the similitude. So it is that we might point to the television and say of a newscaster, 'he has just said there has been a murder'. Our *pointing* shows that we are referring to the individual through the *similitude*.

6) God hath highly exalted him.

And so God exalted him. This is the constant refrain of the NT — the exaltation of Christ by God the Father. But it is a refrain that fits very badly with the Trinitarian notion that Christ was in fact the incarnation of God the Son. Why would God the Father choose to exalt a co-equal being?

The fact that Christ was exalted to be *lord* of all things reflects the intentions of the Genesis creation, and the mention of his exaltation at this point confirms our approach to the passage. We have suggested that the expression 'form of God' has to do with *lordship*. Because Christ did not grasp at equality with God, while having a position of *lordship on earth*, God has highly exalted him so that he has lordship over all things, both in heaven and on earth. The touchstone of Adam's lordship was his *naming* of the animals. So it is that the Scripture expresses Christ's lordship in terms of naming: He has been given a name above every name (Eph 2:21).

6. Hebrews 2:14

As with Philippians 2, we have to pay attention to the phrases of this passage:

> Since then the children are partakers of flesh and blood, he also himself likewise took part of the same...Wherefore in all things it behoved him to be made like unto his brethren... Heb 2:14, 17 (KJV)

The emphasis of the Trinitarian argument is on the phrases 'he also himself likewise took part of the same' and 'it behoved him to be made like unto his brethren'. The Greek verb underlying 'took part' (μετέσχεν) can be used to describe intentional action, for example when it is used to describe our *partaking* of the bread and wine. On the other hand, it is also used to describe how Christ took part in the tribe of Judah (Heb 7:13), and this is a comment on his genealogy.

There is no ambiguity about the expression 'behoved him', since this conveys the idea of obligation. But the expression 'made like' does not necessarily match the Greek (ὁμοιωθῆναι), which does not have to carry information about *making*. A common use of the Greek is in the familiar phrase, 'the kingdom of heaven is *like*' (e.g. Matt 13:24; 18:23; 22:2; Mark 4:30; cf. Matt 6:8; 7:24; 11:16; Luke 13:18, 20). Insofar as Christ knew he was a man, he recognised an obligation to *be like*[1] his brethren in all things, but not to be *made* like his brethren in all things.

Did then Christ choose to take part in flesh and blood? What does the OT say? The author makes several quotations from the OT, and there are several allusions as well, which we ought to examine. If we do this, we shall see that a pre-existence reading of Hebrews 2 is foreign to the text. The phrases which lend themselves to a pre-existence view are in fact chosen to place Christ into the middle of OT typical scenarios. In this way we are being taught to read the OT with Christ in mind, and we are being shown how Christ fulfils the prophecies of the OT as well.

The language of Hebrews 2 is unusual, and this is displayed in 'word for word' versions like the KJV. Why should the text say, 'he took not on angels' and 'he took on the seed of Abraham' (v. 16)? What is special about 'taking' here? Why should the Devil be mentioned? Why should a power of death be mentioned? Why use the expression 'the children'? How did children have a fear of death? Why is it important to mention that these *children* have been given to Christ? Why are not men and women mentioned instead?

The way that the language is cast suggests a type. A first clue to the type is in the quotation 'Behold I and the children which God hath given me' (Heb 2:13). This comes from Isa 8:18, but the source for the Isaiah quotation is Genesis 33,[2] 'The children which God hath graciously given thy servant' (Gen 33:5). These are the words spoken by Jacob to Esau in their encounter at the brook Jabbok.

The children had been given to Jacob, but not to Esau, who "*lifted up his eyes* and saw...the children; and said, 'Who are those to thee?'" (Gen 33:5, KJV mg.). Jacob answers that they are his children given to him from the Lord (Gen 29:31; 30:22). Esau's question is echoed by Jerusalem, for she is told: 'Lift up your eyes...and behold all these...then shalt thou say, who hath begotten me these, seeing I have lost my children and am desolate...' (Isa 49:18f). And this connection between Jerusalem and Esau is why Isaiah 8 quotes Jacob. These children ought to have been a sign to Esau (cf. Isa 8:18), and especially the placement of Joseph as 'the seed'

---

[1] The NRSV translates in this sense with, 'Therefore he had to become like his brothers and sisters in every respect'.

[2] The immediate context of the Isaiah 8 quote (v. 17) mentions the house of *Jacob*. Other allusions to the Jacob and Esau story in this chapter are 'face', 'children' and 'hunger'.

presented to him last, but it does not seem to have had its effect on him. It will be different for Jerusalem in the future when she sees her children born as it were in a day.[1]

The backdrop to this encounter began many years previously with the deception of Isaac. In this deception Jacob put on goats' skins, thus symbolizing 'being made flesh' (Gen 27:16). This was done by *the woman*, who favoured Jacob, indicating that Jacob was the seed of the woman in her eyes. Hence Hebrews comments, 'as the children are partakers of flesh and blood, he (Jesus) also himself likewise *partook* (RV) of the same (flesh and blood)'. That Jacob *would* 'take hold' of this flesh, which *was* the seed of Abraham, was prophesied by his birth: he *took hold* of Esau's (red earth) heel. Hence Paul says that Christ *took hold* of the seed of Abraham (Heb 2:16).

In this way Jacob became subject to the wrath of Esau and to a threat of death, and a chain of events were put in motion that would lead to Jacob marrying a (Gentile) woman and getting children. He fled from Esau (Gen 27:43) and came to the 'children' of the east (Gen 29:1 mg.) at Padanaram, and Laban the *Syrian* recognised him as 'my bone and my flesh' (Gen 29:14). In this state of 'being flesh' with Laban,[2] he became a 'servant' (Gen 29:18) and served Laban for his wives and children. Jacob was 'of one flesh' with his children, which he had *gotten* from the Lord (Gen 29:31; 30:22), and he remained in Padan-aram in fear of Esau his 'lord'. Eventually, he left Laban for his homeland.

Jacob and his children were fearful of Esau and consequently had been in bondage to Laban. There was a need for Jacob to deliver his children: 'to deliver them who through fear of death were their entire lifetime subject to bondage' (Heb 2:15). That there was a real fear is shown by the comment that Jacob was greatly distressed at the prospect of seeing Esau,

---

[1] Jacob understood the significance of these events, because he alludes to them in his encounter with Joseph many years later. Like Esau he beholds Joseph's children and says, 'Who are these?' (Gen 48:8). Joseph's reply is similarly an echo of Jacob's earlier reply to Esau, 'They are my sons, whom *God hath given me* in this place' (Gen 48:9). And in like manner, a blessing follows the enquiry and answer: as Jacob blessed Esau earlier, so too he now blesses Ephraim and Manasseh. The typology is the same: children have been begotten to the seed of the woman in a Gentile land, and they are presented to a man in need of redemption as *his own* children.
[2] This signals that Laban has taken the role of Esau in the typology of Jacob's life.

and this fear would undoubtedly have been communicated through the whole family. (Gen 32:7). Jacob had been given 'all things' (Gen 33:11 KJV mg.; Heb 2:8), but there was now a need to deliver the children and bring his many sons unto glory (Gen 32:22; Heb 2:10) — to the 'land of promise'.

Paul comments that Christ did not take hold of angels, but Jacob was a man who did take hold of an angel. This bout of wrestling was a parable of his life, showing that he had kicked against their purpose all his life. But in his failure to prevail, Jacob realises that the angels guide his life, and that his arm is and can only be an arm of flesh, therefore although he stops wrestling, he continues to 'take hold' of (the) angel(s) until he is blessed. This blessing signals a new beginning in his life for he is given a new name. Jacob is called a 'prince of God' and one who had power with God (Gen 32:28).

Unlike Jacob, Christ did not wrestle with angels, he did not take on angels, and he did not go against their guidance and guarding of his life. Both he and Jacob had to suffer for 'the mother (of all living)' (Gen 3:20, 32:11) and the children. So both he and Christ crossed the brook Jabbok alone before the rest of the family to wait for Esau. Taking the role of a servant Jacob prostrates himself before Esau. He makes himself of no reputation. He goes forward, as it were, to taste death for the family. This was the reversal of the true situation: Jacob was the lord of the family, but for a time he recognises Esau as his lord. In a figure he falls down to the ground, prefiguring his own death and the death of Christ. Through this act Esau is reconciled to Jacob and the children with him. He makes of no effect (καταργέω) the intentions of Esau, who had the power of death over him (Gen 27:41).

The blessing Jacob offers Esau shows his awareness of his priestly role (Heb 2:17).[1] And here he prefigures Jesus as one able to make reconciliation for the sins of the people. This reconciliation is the reconciliation of brethren, and with Christ it will be the same: he will be reconciled to those who once killed him as they look upon him and mourn.

7. Manifestation or Incarnation?
The title of this section is not necessarily constraining; we do not have to choose between these two alternatives; we could affirm either or both depending on where the argument leads. This said, we will need a clear

---

[1] The present is deliberately called a 'covering' (Gen 32:20).

view of our two principal terms and some easy point of contrast to evaluate. Immediately we lay down this desirable first step, we come up against the limits of our language in talking about God.

If we ask the innocent question, 'Where is the person of God?', we might well answer that he is in heaven. We might go on and say that God is also everywhere by his Spirit, but despite the limits of our language, to say that God is in heaven is uncontroversial and understood. In Trinitarian doctrine, if we asked, 'Where is the person of the Son?' at any time during Jesus' earthly life, then our answer would be that the person of the Son was Jesus, the Son was incarnate in Jesus. The Son was not in heaven but on earth in the person of Jesus Christ. It does not matter if we feel our language is breaking down in stating these things; whether we are being metaphorical or literal, the answer to our 'Where?' question is that the Son was incarnate in Jesus.

The concept of manifestation gives a different answer to the 'Where?' question. The Son is not incarnate in Jesus; rather, Jesus *just is* the Son. Further, Jesus manifests the Father, who remains in heaven, rather than any Son (a 'heavenly' Father, rather than a 'heavenly' Son). At all times, and in all ways, God is in heaven during Jesus' life. A person may manifest *another* person, but not if they are that person. If there is a human body in the equation, then a person will not be manifested in another person if they are incarnate *as* that person. Of course, in Trinitarian terms, the Son could be incarnate in Jesus while at the same time manifesting the Father; hence, the notions of 'incarnation' and 'manifestation' are not logically opposed alternatives.

The idea of 'manifestation' is used in 1 John 1:2,

> For the life was <u>manifested</u> (φανερόω), and we have seen it, and bear witness, and shew unto you that eternal life, which was with the Father, and was <u>manifested</u> (φανερόω) unto us... 1 John 1:2 (KJV)

Manifestation is about 'showing' something or someone:

> And I knew him not: but that he should be made <u>manifest</u> (φανερόω) to Israel, therefore am I come baptizing with water. John 1:31; cf. 2:11, (KJV)

> But now the righteousness of God without the law is <u>manifested</u> (φανερόω), being witnessed by the law and the prophets... Rom 3:21 (KJV)

182

And by common confession great is the mystery of godliness: He who was revealed in the flesh, Was vindicated in the Spirit, Beheld by angels, Proclaimed among the nations, Believed on in the world, Taken up in glory. 1 Tim 3:16 (NASB)

For then must he often have suffered since the foundation of the world: but now once in the end of the world hath he appeared (φανερόω) to put away sin by the sacrifice of himself. Heb 9:26 (KJV)

Who verily was foreordained before the foundation of the world, but was manifest (φανερόω) in these last times for you... 1 Pet 1:20 (KJV)

And ye know that he was manifested (φανερόω) to take away our sins; and in him is no sin...He that committeth sin is of the devil; for the devil sinneth from the beginning. For this purpose the Son of God was manifested (φανερόω), that he might destroy the works of the devil. 1 John 3:5, 8; cf. 4:5 (KJV)

What these texts show is that 'manifestation' is the leading idea in relation to Jesus, whether this be God the Father being manifested in Jesus or Jesus being foreordained in the Scriptures and then being manifested to Israel.

8. Conclusion
Whereas church beliefs about the return of Christ and the establishment of the kingdom are much more varied, the central place given by the churches to the doctrine of the incarnation has remained secure. This doctrine is central to their doctrine of the atonement and to their acts of worship. We have argued so far that the doctrine is not *biblically* based.

We have seen that the background to Philippians 2 is Genesis and the events surrounding Adam and his fall. What happened back then *accounts for* Paul's choice of language. This language is determined by the possibility of Adam becoming equal with God and living forever. And so it might be, for Adam was a 'type of him who was to come' (Rom 5:14); he was first and Christ was second (1 Cor 15:45). The comparison between Christ and Adam is not dependent on any particular time-scale — a pre-existence and then an incarnation.

The Trinitarian proposals about Philippians 2 reverse the intentions of the passage. The Trinitarian proposes that the passage is about *beginnings* — it is about the start of the Lord's life — his incarnation. However, we have seen it is about the *end* of his life, it is about his trial, his death and his resurrection.

Had *Philippians* been written in a later century, then we might indeed have supposed it was about beginnings, since heavenly-redeemer myths were common in the second century CE But for a letter composed in the mid-Fifties (or Sixties) CE, the background would be Jewish, and by far the most developed thoughts about Christ in the NT involve the many types from the OT, and in particular the types based on Adam. The natural reading for Paul's readers would have been an OT one and not the kind of speculation suggested by theologians of the third century onwards.

The Hebrews 2 'incarnation' text is speaking of reconciliation, and OT examples of reconciliation are being used to describe Christ's work of reconciliation. Two principal OT events of reconciliation come to mind. One between Esau and Jacob, the other between Joseph and his brethren. We have seen how the language relates to Jacob and Esau, and by this we have shown *why* the language is chosen. It is not a choice that has to do with a heavenly being becoming incarnate.

Equally, the Galatians and Romans 'sending' texts do not present the sending of an individual from the throne-room of heaven, but the natural idiom of the Scriptures for sending a prophet or a deliverer to the people.

Because the types of the OT point forward to the work of Christ, it is possible to lay passages from the NT as templates upon OT events and see how such stories relate to Christ. By doing this we can see a number of types in one NT passage (the Hebrews passage also relates to the exodus). In the next chapter, we will examine the main 'incarnation' text – John 1.

CHAPTER NINE
The Incarnation (2)

1. Introduction

In this chapter we will look at the chief witness for the doctrine of the incarnation, the prologue of John (John 1:1-18) The task before us is to investigate "all things were made through him/it" (John 1:3) and "the world was made through him/it" (John 1:10). We must also look into the meaning of the title 'the Word' and what it means to affirm that the Word 'was with/toward God' and 'was God' (John 1:1), and we need to answer the question of how and when "the word became flesh" (John 1:14). Over and above these specific questions, we should endeavour to get an understanding of the whole prologue as it relates to the question of pre-existence. When we have done this, we will have completed our consideration of the prologue of John, even though there will be much more to be said.

Theorizing against a background which assumes that Johannine writings are later than Pauline ones, Dunn locates the significant development in Christian thinking about an 'incarnation' in John's prologue and avers, "as the first century of the Christian era drew to a close we find a concept of Christ's real pre-existence beginning to emerge, but only with the Fourth Gospel can we speak of a full blown conception of Christ's personal pre-existence and a clear doctrine of incarnation".[1] We might well ask whether instead this development began in the sub-Apostolic era with an **interpretation** of John 1 informed by contemporary thinking about *the Logos of God*, but this historical question is beyond our scope.

Dunn's analysis is useful in that he opposes scholarship that locates the significant origin of the doctrine of the incarnation in other texts like Rom 8:3, Gal 4:4, Phil 2:5-7 or Heb 2:14 (which we discussed in the last chapter). Rather, he locates its key genesis in John 1:1-18. Of all the texts in the NT that might be pulled into an argument about 'incarnation', John 1:1-18 is undoubtedly the most important for the frequency of its use; it is

---

[1] Dunn, *Christology in the Making*, 258. See I. H. Marshall's reply, "Incarnational Christology in the New Testament" in Donald Guthrie's festschrift *Christ the Lord: Studies in Christology Presented to Donald Guthrie* (ed. H. H. Rowdon; Leicester: Intervarsity Press, 1982), 1-16.

the strongest text for such a doctrine.[1] If there is a plausible interpretation of John 1:1-18 suggested by the Jewish Scriptures that is not incarnational, then this will be significant for our understanding of Jesus and show that the sub-Apostolic church and the Apologists went wrong in their exegesis,[2] a mistake since followed by all subsequent orthodox commentators.

There are plenty of debated issues surrounding the prologue which will not concern us. These include the authorship and origin of the prologue. Some scholars have seen a separate source in the prologue, perhaps a hymn, incorporated by the author and added to later by others.[3] Conservative scholars have argued for the unity and single authorship of the prologue and Gospel and pointed to the lack of agreement among those who have posited a source.[4] This is our position.

Another area of debate has been the background for John's idea of *the Logos*.[5] Proposals have included Gnosticism,[1] the Hermetic writings,[2] the

---

[1] B. Lindars, *John* (Sheffield: Sheffield Academic Press, 1990), 74, "The crucial point in the Prologue is v. 14: 'And the word became flesh'. This is the first clear statement of the incarnation, which became a fundamental doctrine of Christianity". Lindars makes much the same point as Marshall, ibid., 1.

[2] See J. N. Sanders, *The Fourth Gospel in the Early Church* (Cambridge: Cambridge University Press, 1943), 12ff, and Ignatius' *Letter to the Magnesians* and *Letter to the Ephesians*, and the *Letter to Diognetus*. We can only compare the Apostolic Fathers' declarative statements about 'the Word' as we don't have their intra-scriptural and typological exegesis of John 1. If the NT writers engage in intra-scriptural and typological exegesis of the Hebrew Scriptures (which they do with the Spirit), and we copy their approach, we might well ask why it is that we have no sub-Apostolic writings in this vein with which to draw contrasts and comparisons. The citations are usefully collected in J. C. Elowsky and T. C. Oden, *John 1-10 4a Ancient Commentary on Scripture* (Downer Grove: IVP Academic, 2007).

[3] These are reviewed in critical commentaries; see R. E. Brown, *The Gospel According to John I-XII* (Anchor Bible 29; New York: Doubleday, 1966), 18-23.

[4] Barrett, *The Gospel According to St. John*, 13-17, 125-126.

[5] See C. A. Evans, *Word and Glory: On the Exegetical and Theological Background of John's Prologue* (JSNTS 89; Sheffield: Sheffield Academic Press, 1993). This is a discussion of all the major proposals in the field. For an introduction see R. N. Longenecker, *The Christology of Early Jewish*

Memra of the Aramaic Bible,[3] Philo,[4] and Wisdom traditions in Second Temple writings including the Jewish scriptures.[5] Of these proposals, a Wisdom traditions background is currently the most popular. Certainly, there are parallels to be set up between the prologue and other writings. We would discount parallels with later Gnostic and Hermetic writings because the direction of influence travels from John to those writings. As for John's co-text, we would argue that the presentation of Jesus as 'the Word' begins in v. 1. This means that this verse doesn't give us either a linguistic or attributive hypostatization nor a personification. All of these can be found in relation to 'the Word', the Torah, 'God's Memra', and Wisdom in Second-Temple writings. John may have known of such traditions, but he isn't using them when he presents **Jesus** as 'the Word' simply because he is dealing with Jesus. His doctrine of Jesus as 'the Word' is **unique revelation**.

Rather than discuss these contextualisation proposals, we will put aside the question of the relationship of the prologue to its cultural environment and just consider the intertextual links it has within the Hebrew Scriptures. On our method, the pecking order of what is relevant to the interpretation of John 1 starts with the Johannine writings, then includes other NT writings, followed by those writings held to be authoritative Scripture (now the OT); only after this, should the cultural environment be included.

In sum, there are nine questions about John 1:1-18 to answer:

- What is the beginning?
- What/Who is 'the Word' in v. 1?
- How is the Word involved in the making of 'all things' (John 1:3)?

Christianity (Grand Rapids: Baker Book House, 1981), 144-147, and then Dunn, *Christology in the Making*, 213-250.

[1] R. Bultmann, *The Gospel of John* (Oxford: Basil Blackwell, 1971), 13-17; P. Perkins, *Gnosticism and the New Testament* (Minneapolis: Fortress Press, 1993), chap.8.

[2] C. H. Dodd, *The Interpretation of the Fourth Gospel* (Cambridge: Cambridge University Press, 1953), 10-53.

[3] P. Borgen, "Observations on the Targumic Character of the Prologue of John" *NTS* 16 (1970): 288-295.

[4] A. F. Segal, *Two Powers in Heaven: Early Rabbinic Reports about Christianity and Gnosticism* (Repr.; Waco, TX: Baylor University Press, 2012), 159-181.

[5] Dunn, *Christology in the Making*, 163-212.

- What does 'the world was made through him' mean?
- How is v. 14 related to v. 1?
- What does 'the word became flesh' mean (John 1:14)?
- How and when did the word of God become flesh?
- How is Jesus before John the Baptist?
- What is the original text of v. 18?

We can take them in sequence, but first we will discuss the structure of the prologue.

2. The Structure of John's Prologue

How do we know that the Gospel of John has a 'prologue'? What do we mean by the word 'prologue'? The opening verses of the first chapter are made up of 'summary statements' about Jesus as 'the Word', John the Baptist as a witness, the Word as the true Light, and lastly a description of the reality of Jesus the Word among his disciples (vv. 14-18). These statements appear to come to an end in v. 18, and from v. 19 onwards the apostle John begins *narrating* the 'testimony' of John the Baptist. It is this switch from more abstract statements to the concrete detail of a testimonial record at v. 19 which marks out John 1:1-18 as a 'prologue'.

The extent of the prologue and its structure are debated.[1] It is important to see how the prologue of John is structured. The strongest structural connection made by commentators is between v. 1. and v. 14. In effect, this turns John 1:2-13 into a kind of parenthesis.[2] Commentators assert that we have the same Word in v. 1 and in v. 14 and they connect these two verses together in a kind of **sequence**—in the beginning was the Word *and then* the Word was made/became flesh. The bedrock of the doctrine of the incarnation is this sequence and this concentration on v. 1 and v. 14. Another reason for this structural analysis is the seemingly

[1] For example, P. Lamarche, "The Prologue of John" in *The Interpretation of John* (ed. J. Ashton; 2nd ed.; Edinburgh: T&T Clark, 1997), 47-65 (55-57); M. Coloe, "The Structure of the Johannine Prologue and Genesis 1" *Australian Biblical Review* 45 (1997): 40-55.

[2] Carter, *The Gospel of John*, 14; Carter presents the traditional Christadelphian approach to John 1, working with a Genesis beginning and a personification reading of v. 1. Whittaker, *Studies in the Gospels*, 45-54, presents a new creation reading of v. 1 and with Carter retains a birth reading of v. 14. For a critique of Whittaker, see J. Adey, " 'In the Beginning' of John 1:1: A New View Examined" (Unpublished paper supplied by the author). We follow Whittaker on v. 1 but present a baptism reading of v. 14.

pointless repetition in v. 2, 'the same was in the beginning with God' which is then given a purpose in introducing the parenthesis.

The second strongest structural proposal is a **chiastic analysis**.[1] These identify the main thread of the prologue as a new creation of men and women in Christ and locate the centre of the prologue somewhere inside vv. 10-13.[2] We don't intend to argue against chiastic analyses, although they seem to rely on the analyst rather more than the text. Our interest is just to present the case for **a three-paragraph parallel structure**.[3]

We can start with v. 2 and v. 7., and translating the Greek consistently, the purpose of this repetition becomes clear:

The same[4] was in the beginning with God. John 1:2

The same came for a witness, to bear witness of the Light... John 1:7

Both uses of 'the same' occur in the same *position* in the development of thought in each paragraph,[5] and the purpose is to stress two different and contrasting roles:

---

[1] R. A. Culpepper, "The Pivot of John's Prologue" *NTS* 27 (1980): 1-31.

[2] Some commentators have chosen other verses as the central part of the prologue. E. Käsemann, "The Structure and Purpose of the Prologue to John's Gospel" in *New Testament Questions of Today* (London: SCM Press, 1969), 138-167 (152), says that v. 12 is the "culmination" of the prologue; Culpepper, "The Pivot of John's Prologue", 16, proposes v. 12b to be the pivot of a chiastic structure; and Lamarche, "The Prologue of John", 55, claims that vv. 10-13 are the centre of a chiasm. Each of these commentators criticize alternative chiastic proposals in the course of advocating their own analysis.

[3] Many commentators divide the second paragraph at v. 9 and see vv. 6-8 and vv. 9-13 as separate paragraphs.

[4] This is just the ordinary Greek for 'he' or 'this one'; hence, the KJV of v. 15 has 'this was he'.

[5] The same expression occurs in the third paragraph, also in its second sentence, "*The same* was he of whom I spake..." (John 1:15). This shows that each paragraph is concerned to correctly identify Jesus distinctly from John. The gospel writer is clearly picking up John the Baptist's *stress* on Jesus' identity, and using the same Greek word (in vv. 2, 6 and 15) to make this link.

189

'*This one* was in the beginning' v. 2.

'*This one* came for a witness' v. 7.

There was a need for this stress, since part of the aim in John 1 is to define both John the Baptist and Jesus and their relationship to one another. In defining these roles, John the Baptist's words of witness are repeated *no less than three times*. This priority is reflected in v. 2: it is Jesus, 'this one', who was in the beginning with/toward God, and *not* John the Baptist. This second verse is not then an incomprehensible repetition, but part of the text's contrast between Jesus and John the Baptist, a contrast made repeatedly.[1]

The prologue consists of three parallel paragraphs, see Figure 1.[2] These paragraphs are collections of sentences grouped according to their focus. The first paragraph (vv. 1-5) is concerned with the relationship between the Word and the new creation of life in him which is the light of men. The second paragraph (vv. 6-13) is a contrast between the true Light and John and their respective ministries. The last paragraph (vv. 14-18) explains how we have 'the Word' and it reveals his identity as Jesus Christ, the only begotten son. There are points in each paragraph which 'hold' each of them together as coherent wholes.

The first two paragraphs introduce two different individuals — the Word (v. 1) and John the Baptist (v. 6), and then the third paragraph explains how what we have just read has been made possible with the proposition that the word[3] became flesh (v. 14). The connection between the first two paragraphs is the concept of light and what is not received (καταλαμβάνω, v. 5) by some, or that which is received by others (vv. 11-12, παραλαμβάνω). The third paragraph explains that the word became flesh and experienced by John and the disciples so that his fulness was received

---

[1] John the Baptist was present at the beginning of the ministry as was Jesus, but the contrast between John and Jesus is about who was 'toward' God. It was Jesus who was 'toward' God in the beginning rather than John.

[2] For a three-paragraph approach see M. Endo, *Creation and Christology: A study on the Johannine Prologue in the Light of Early Jewish Creation Accounts* (Tübingen: Mohr-Siebeck, 2002), 195-205; Endo rejects other structural proposals.

[3] We have tried to capitalize where we see either a title for Jesus or a linguistic hypostatization; we use lower-case where we see a reference to the ordinary word of God.

(v. 16, λαμβάνω) by those who believed.[1] This paragraph then identifies 'the Word' as Jesus Christ.

The second paragraph is about John's witness to the true Light and the power of the ministry of the true Light. Jesus is both the Word and the true Light, and we need to see that John integrates these two identities in vv. 6-13. We can see the unity in the third paragraph in the way that John has tied v. 14 to v. 18 with common expressions. He begins the paragraph using expressions such as 'only begotten' and 'of the Father'; and he rounds off the paragraph by repeating these expressions in v. 18.[2] Over and above this, we can see that this third paragraph has a focus upon what followed from the word becoming flesh.

The third paragraph begins with 'the word became flesh', and then mentions John's witness again,[3] like vv. 6-7, i.e. the same sequence of thought is followed. This shows that the third paragraph is not continuing a temporal progressive sequence of events from v. 1 but **giving an explanation** of what has already been stated in the previous two paragraphs albeit in different terms. The contrast between Jesus and John is set out by the first two paragraphs and restated in a different way in the third paragraph. We have then the Word and the true Light identified and further detail about what believers receive from Christ. There are other connections that criss-cross across the three paragraphs (see Figure 1).

We don't have a sequence in time from v. 1 to v. 14 but rather **a description of the same beginning**. The usual reading of v. 1 is the Genesis beginning and v. 14 is the birth of Jesus.[4] We will argue that v. 1 is the beginning of the new creation (the ministry of Jesus) and that v. 14 is the same time and a description of the baptism of Jesus. With John 1:19-34 being the testimonial record of John the Baptist from the time of Jesus' baptism and the beginning of his ministry, we have a start to John's

---

[1] The λαμβάνω verbs are translated differently because they carry different nuances, but we translate them the same here to bring out this thread across the three paragraphs.

[2] Accordingly, we would not begin the third paragraph at v. 15 which is done by some scholars; see Coloe, "The Structure of the Johannine Prologue and Genesis 1", 43.

[3] Coloe, in "The Structure of the Johannine Prologue and Genesis 1", 41, notes that the "major problem" with the progressive sequential reading of the prologue is the double mention of the witness of John the Baptist.

[4] Texts which connect v. 14 to the infancy stories of Matthew and Luke: for example, the apocryphal *Epistle to the Apostles*, 3 (c. late 2c. CE).

Gospel similar to the other Gospels. Because v.14a is the causal explanation of vv. 1-13, and vv. 14b-18, the sequence doesn't flow from v. 1 to v. 14, but rather **the reverse**: vv. 14-18 relates vv. 1-13 to the experience of the disciples. This means, in turn, that we should mark a distinction between 'the Word' of v. 1, which refers to Jesus, and 'the word' of v. 14, which is *what* became flesh (see below).

Figure 1

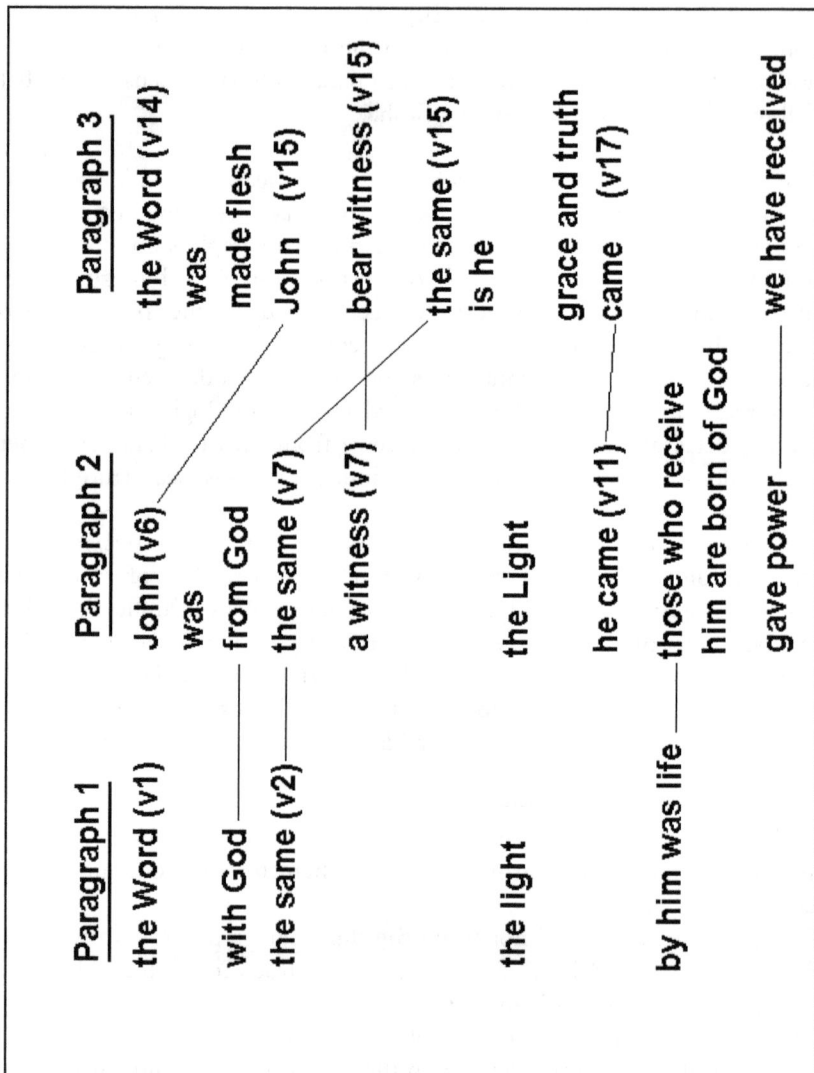

The above three-paragraph structure is, to be fair, a pedestrian analysis. Chiastic structures are more elaborate and rely on the reader taking an abstract and generalising approach to the text rather than just correlating the repetition of textual material. Chiasms that rely on a reader's own descriptions of a verse are inherently weak. Chiastic structures often suggest v. 12 as the centre of the prologue. In our structure, the key verse is v. 14 and the proposition that the word became flesh (the traditional view). This is because it is the third paragraph that *supplies* the identity of 'the Word' and makes his ministry personal ("us", "we"). John moves from abstract third-party description to **first person description** of both himself and the disciples.

Of the three paragraphs, v. 14 begins with a conjunction (καὶ). Up until this point, the use of this conjunction has been for sub-sentential clauses (with the possible exception of vv. 4-5, depending on how the Greek is read). This καὶ in v. 14 is a conjunction of result or consequence,[1] "And so" – it explains and concludes what has gone before: "And so the word became flesh and dwelt among **us** and **we** beheld". Vv. 14-18 explains and concludes what has gone before by making it personal. This personal dimension shows that the conjunction is not part of any abstract sequence, "In the beginning was the Word...*and* the Word was made flesh". Rather, 'the word becoming flesh and dwelling among us and we beheld...' matches a shared Christian experience to the reality John has been more abstractly describing in the third person in vv. 1-5, 6-13. This shift to a personal dimension also explains the position of the third paragraph. Having introduced the real-world character of John the Baptist in v. 6, John has prepared his readers to include themselves ("us", "we") in the story. They entered the story at the baptism of Jesus as they were drawn to follow Jesus, and this is what we read about in the next part of the Gospel (John 1:19-51).

3. In the Beginning

John's Gospel was written sometime after the preaching of the apostles began in Acts 2. If we picture John at his table, writing the gospel, of

---

[1] The καὶ in v. 16 is epexegetical, "even grace for grace". See the Friberg and Danker lexicons for a general description of the flexibility of the conjunction and all the ways in which it could be used in the NT, including 'And so...'. For the LXX, see the LEH lexicon which also notes the 'And so...' possible usage. It is the reader's sense of the passage that determines the role of the conjunction.

what beginning is he thinking? Is it, as some say,[1] some timeless beginning beyond the aeons of time — before the Big Bang? Was it the Genesis beginning (Gen 1:1)?[2] Was it the exodus beginning (Exod 12:2; Hos 9:10)? Was it the birth of Christ (Matt 1:1)? Was it the event of Pentecost (Acts 11:15)?[3] Was it the baptism of Jesus and the beginning of his ministry (Mark 1:1)? The allusion[4] to Genesis is unmistakeable but the reason for it (along with other allusions) is to draw a typological comparison between Jesus, the Word, the new creation and the Genesis creation.[5] So, we favour the above 'beginning of the ministry' interpretation on the basis of the following evidence:[6]

---

[1] For example, J. Jeremias, "The Revealing Word" in *The Central Message of the New Testament* (London: SCM Press, 1965), 71-90 (79).

[2] The term 'beginning' does refer to the Genesis beginning in the NT, (e.g. Matt 19:4 (RV), 8; 24:21 (RV); Mark 10:6; 13:19; John 8:44), where it is part of the expression 'from the beginning', but the 'beginning' here might be anything between the creation of Genesis 1 and the murder of Abel. All commentators see a reference to the Genesis beginning in John 1 (e.g. Barrett, *The Gospel According to St. John*, 126-127); it is just that some see a *primary* reference to the beginning of the ministry of Jesus.

[3] The first visit of Paul to Macedonia is the 'beginning of the gospel' there (Phil 4:15). When he departed, he took gifts, and these, as previously in another much earlier beginning, rose as a sweet smell, a sacrifice well pleasing to God (Gen 8:21).

[4] The Greek of John 1:1 *quotes* the Hebrew of Gen 1:1, as suggested by the LXX — which like the NT has the form Ἐν ἀρχῇ. (Genesis and John are the only two Biblical books which **open** in this way and this is the decisive point). But the evidence we list shows that the expression's value is transformed by its use in John 1 so that it refers to a *new* beginning in which there was the Word.

[5] F. F. Bruce, *The Gospel of John* (Grand Rapids: Eerdmans, 1994), 28-29, "In Gen 1:1 'In the beginning' introduces the story of the old creation; here it introduces the story of the new creation." Bruce, however, thinks that it is the same Word that is the agent of both creations, whereas we mark a distinction between the word of God in Genesis and the Word of John 1:1 because "the word became flesh". Commentators may see both beginnings in John 1:1 and sit on the fence as to which if either is the chosen sense, for example, E. C. Hoskyns and F. N. Davey, *The Fourth Gospel* (2nd ed (rev).; London: Faber & Faber, 1957), 140-141.

[6] The evidence is data for the following conclusion: John and other writers of the early church have a strong conception of 'the beginning' vis-à-vis Jesus' ministry.

1) This opening is *retrospective* (John is writing years after the beginning of the ministry), for in the rest of the Gospel he mostly describes a beginning which is about the ministry of Christ (John 2:11; 6:64; 8:25; 15:27; 16:4), a beginning signalled by the baptism of Christ.[1] [2]

2) And so in 1 John[3] we read,

> That which was <u>from the beginning</u>,[4] which we have heard, which we have seen with our eyes, which we have looked upon, and our hands have handled, of the Word of Life..." 1 John 1:1 (KJV); cf. 2:7, 3:11[5]

This is the beginning, which is the beginning of the gospel of Jesus Christ, the Son of God (Mark 1:1). It involved the disciples and it contrasts with the Genesis beginning, because from this beginning, a man

---

[1] The expression 'the beginning' does not refer to a particular day or week, but rather it is that undefined period of time which the apostles thought of as 'the beginning' of the Gospel. See Whittaker, *Studies in the Gospels*, 45-49, for the list of evidence although he overstates the case.

[2] This is a traditional Anabaptist interpretation. See, *The Racovian Catechism* (Amsterdam: 1652), p. 31 for 'the beginning of the Gospel' reading of v. 1 and p. 44 for 'the new creation' reading of v. 3. [Available @ Early English Books Online.]

[3] For a discussion of the relation between 1 John and the Gospel see W. E. Sproston, "Witnesses to what was ἀπ' ἀρχῆς: 1 John's Contribution to our Knowledge of Tradition in the Fourth Gospel" in *The Johannine Writings* (ed. S. E. Porter & C. A. Evans; Sheffield: Sheffield Academic Press, 1995), 138-160 (especially 151). Our comparison of the Johannine writings does not depend on any thesis of common authorship.

[4] The expression 'from the beginning' (1 John 1:1) is taken from Proverbs 8:23 but this is an allusion. The allusion of itself does not establish a time frame for 'the beginning', because it could be a comparison between two timeframes: a comparison between the Genesis beginning and the gospel beginning. Handling and seeing clearly invokes a physical reference for the expression 'the Word of Life' and therefore this is a title for Jesus.

[5] Notice here that John is quoting from Isa 64:4: he quarries the following concepts *in order* from the Isaiah text — *from the beginning, hearing,* and *seeing* — "For since the beginning of the world [men] have not heard, nor perceived by the ear, neither hath the eye seen, O God, besides thee, [what] he hath prepared for him that waiteth for him". John is pointing to a man who did wait for God and who had been seen and heard by them (the apostles) 'from the beginning'.

had been seen and heard - a man who was the Word of Life and the embodiment of the wisdom of God.

3) Both John and Mark start their Gospels with the word 'beginning'.[1] Both omit the birth stories and focus directly on the beginning of the ministry of the gospel. Both first describe the ministry of John and then the start of the ministry of Christ, which *began* when he was about thirty years old (Luke 3:23).[2]

4) Luke confirms the view of an end and a beginning at this time,

> The Law and the Prophets were until John: since that time the kingdom of God is preached, and every man presseth into it. Luke 16:16 (KJV); cf. Acts 1:22

The expression 'enter (presseth) into [the kingdom of God]' is unusual, but it is carefully chosen to connect up with the concept of *entry into God's rest* or entry into the land of promise (Heb 3:11, 18). This was the thrust of the preaching of Christ: the kingdom of God was near; in type it was as if they were at Kadesh-Barnea, near to the promised land; the appeal was 'to enter', but they refused and once again they vexed his holy Spirit.[3]

5) Luke is the Gospel writer who was concerned to stress that he had enquired of those "who *from the beginning* were eyewitnesses and ministers of the word" (Luke 1:2).

6) Even Matthew is not without his concept of a 'beginning' as he opens his Gospel with a 'genealogy' or 'the beginnings' (γένεσις) of Jesus Christ. All three Synoptics open their Gospels with Jesus. Would John be an exception and open with Genesis?[4]

7) The apostles clearly had a conviction that the preaching of the word began at a certain point in time:

---

[1] The difference is 'In the beginning' versus 'The beginning'. Barrett, *The Gospel According to St John*, 127, regards a link between John 1:1 and Mark 1:1 as "probable".

[2] The Greek for 'began' here (ἀρχόμενος) is unusual, indicating that Christ 'made a beginning' when he was thirty years old.

[3] Entry into the tabernacle and entry into the congregation of the Lord are parallel kinds of entry; these are types of the kingdom of heaven.

[4] S. Irving, *Studies in John's Gospel* (Nottingham: Dawn Publications, 2015), 12-13.

...all the time that the Lord Jesus went in and out among us, beginning from the baptism of John, unto that same day that he was taken up from us... Acts 1:21-22 (KJV)

The word which [God] sent unto the children of Israel, preaching peace by Jesus Christ...That word, [I say], ye know, which was published throughout all Judea, and began from Galilee, after the baptism which John preached... Acts 10:36-37 (KJV)[1]

How shall we escape, if we neglect so great salvation; which at the first began to be spoken by the Lord, and was conformed unto us by them that heard [him]... Heb 2:3; cf. John 19:39 (KJV)

8) Jesus was the 'beginner' and finisher of the Christian faith (Heb 12:2, KJV mg.).

Looking through the NT, there is obviously a prevalent consciousness of a new beginning[2] in the purpose of God marked by the baptism and then the ministry of Jesus. Contextually, John 1:6-13, 14-18, and then the testimonial record of John the Baptist (John 1:19ff), are about that beginning. The question is whether John 1:1-5 also specifies that beginning. The argument that it does rests on the intra-scriptural reasoning below which exegetes 'was toward God', 'was God' and 'all things came through [the Word]'.[3]

---

[1] Compare (but contrast) Heb 6:1, (KJV mg.), which reads, 'the word of the beginning of Christ'

[2] Note carefully the *historical* argument: as time passes the length of a beginning stretches. A few years after the death of Christ, the apostles look upon the start of Christ's ministry as 'the beginning'; some several thousand years on, the 'beginning' for us becomes the era of the apostolic church.

[3] The nature of typology is such that the information we have on the anti-type enlarges our knowledge about the type. As a result, we can profitably place the major beginnings of God's purpose (Creation, Flood, Exodus, and the Gospel) in parallel columns. Various parts of the Scripture will be *mainly* about one beginning or another, but this does not exclude our use of later parts of Scripture to teach about earlier events. So it's perfectly possible to think of passages about the new creation and ask how that

197

We can consider **three objections** (or alternatives) to our reading. First, the beginning is the Genesis beginning pure and simple. As in the OT and other Second-Temple writings, the word of God is presented with the language of agency; it was with God, even facing towards God as God's agent, and in action it was God. All things have been created through it (v. 3) and in particular new life (v. 3c-4a). New life has been created through belief in God's word since the Fall and the promise of God that there would be a seed of the woman who would deal a mortal blow to the head of the Serpent. And so in John's day this light of the proto gospel was shining in the darkness (v. 5). The whole of vv. 1-5 is a prologue in itself, a summary of salvation-history. In v. 6 we get the new beginning of the gospel with the announcement of John the Baptist. In v. 14, this Word of God that has been active throughout history in creating new life in men and women became flesh in the person of Jesus Christ.

There are other 'Genesis' readings of vv. 1-5, 14, but the above can be taken as representative of the genre and we present it as the strongest[1] form of that interpretation, albeit as a summary. The difficulties with it are as follows: presentations of the interpretation lack intra-textual exegesis; the exegete supplies the sense of 'with/towards God', 'was God'. The interpretation also relies on Second-Temple writings and their presentation of the Word and Wisdom of God to strengthen its case. And lastly, it doesn't account for the repetition in v. 2 which sets up a comparison between the Word and John the Baptist in v. 7, a comparison that requires the Word and John the Baptist to be contemporaneous.

The second objection affirms that the beginning is before the baptism of Christ, it is the time before the bestowal of the Spirit and Jesus' commencement of his ministry. It is before Jesus is declared to be the Son of God. The beginning is John the Baptist's ministry. Jesus is properly only 'the Word' at this time. He is 'with God' and receiving the word from God and about to present himself to John the Baptist. . He is called 'the Word' rather than 'the Son of God' – because the baptismal declaration hasn't happened. In this immediately prior stage he is ready to be like Moses, i.e. 'God' to the people. After his baptism and the declaration of his sonship, the use of the title 'the Word' falls away for he is now manifested as 'the Son' in the rest of the Gospel.

---

information is to be placed into the context of the Genesis or Exodus beginning.

[1] You could say that this interpretation is the backwards application of the new creation interpretation to Genesis, i.e. typology in reverse. Hence, it comes over as plausible.

The above reading is close to ours since there is overlap between John the Baptist's ministry and that of Christ. Both prophets are a beginning in their own way; some of the texts we have cited above better fit the beginning that is John the Baptist's ministry rather than that of Christ. However, we can't *localise* the significance of 'the Word' to John the Baptist's ministry as the Genesis typology is wholly general. Moreover, the generality of the new creation in v. 3 requires a beginning that is tied to 'the Word'. Ironically, this second alternative is actually a way of preferring John the Baptist over Jesus, an error which the prologue combats.

Thirdly, it could be said that the beginning is the resurrection of Christ (Acts 13:33), a beginning that signals the start of the new creation that is the resurrection to new life for all. After his resurrection, Christ has divine nature and is God's Word, interceding with God for the disciples and being 'God' for his disciples. Vv. 2-5 are a general statement about this new creation and the church. Vv. 6-13 goes back and narrates the beginning of John's ministry and compares it with Jesus' ministry. V. 14 presumes the death and resurrection of Jesus and describes Jesus' resurrection appearances and the ascension period of forty days as the Word becoming flesh. This is why they beheld his glory; it was as of the only begotten from the dead as per Psalm 2:7 and Acts 13:33.

This reading founders on the comparison that the prologue makes between the Word and John the Baptist in vv. 2, 7, and 15. This comparison is dovetailed into the narrative at three points and only makes sense if the Word and John the Baptist are contemporaneous figures. We should distinguish the beginning of Jesus' ministry from the beginning that is Jesus' resurrection from the dead (Rev 3:14; Col 1:18).[1]

4. Identifying the Word

Jesus is 'the Word' (i.e. the referent of the expression) in John 1:1 and the subject matter dealt with is *not* the Genesis creation. If we were going to develop a doctrine of incarnation, we might note that John's prologue apparently mentions the incarnation of 'the Word' (*logos*) rather than that of the Son (John 1:14). The way for commentators to get around this difference is to take 'the Word' to be a title for the Son, i.e. to say that

---

[1] John doesn't use the expression 'new creation' anywhere in his writings; this is a Pauline term (2 Cor 5:17; Gal 6:15). We can use Paul's terminology for John 1:1-5 because it is about 'life in him', i.e. life in Christ.

John transforms traditions about 'the Word' by identifying 'the Word' to be the Son. We don't offer an incarnation reading of v. 14. The title 'the Word' refers to Jesus the man in John 1:1 for the following reasons:

1) The statement, 'the Word was *with* God', uses a stative verb (εἰμί) with a transitive preposition (πρός). A stative verb will usually override the dynamic sense of the transitive preposition which is why translations usually have 'was with God'.[1] In this case, however, the *state* indicated is one of being *towards* God. This in turn implies a person *being* an intermediary or intercessor facing toward God.

We will look at some examples:

(i) Exod 4:16

> σὺ δὲ αὐτῷ ἔσῃ τὰ πρὸς τὸν θεόν
> but you shall be to him the things pertaining to God. (NETS)

The NETS version is a quite literal translation of the Greek. And it has conveyed the preposition πρός as 'pertaining to'. As with John 1:1, we have the stative verb 'to be' with the preposition 'to, towards'. The text says that Moses would be priestly things towards God for Aaron.

(ii) Deut 31:27

παραπικραίνοντες ἦτε τὰ πρὸς τὸν θεόν
you are being fractious concerning the things of God (NETS)

Here NETS has translated the preposition πρός, the verb 'to be', and a participle, rendering the preposition as 'concerning...of'.

There are 29 verses in the Greek Bible and the NT that show a collocation of the verb 'to be' and the Greek preposition πρός.[2] Most translations have differing English prepositions for πρός depending on the sense of what is being said in the text. For example, Jdt 13:6 is about a bedpost which 'was above' Holofernes' head (ὃς ἦν πρὸς κεφαλῆς

---

[1] D. B. Wallace, *Greek Grammar Beyond the Basics* (Grand Rapids: Zondervan, 1996), 358-360.

[2] We are excluding from our consideration the use of πρός and πρὸς τὸν θεόν with active verbs where these is a sense of 'to/towards God', for example, 'return to God' (Hos 5:14), 'cry to God' Ps 56:3). For an analysis of the dynamic nature of the relationship indicated by πρὸς, see E. L. Miller, "The Logos was God" *EQ* 53.2 (1981): 65-77.

Ολοφέρνου); Gen 31:2 is about Laban's attitude toward Jacob not being as before (καὶ ἰδοὺ οὐκ ἦν πρὸς αὐτὸν ὡς ἐχθές). Where we have two or more people in a situation in a text, we might have 'with you', 'with each other', or 'with one another' for πρός (e.g. Mark 14:49; Luke 9:41; 23:41).

So, while it is clear that ἦν πρὸς τὸν θεόν is about a state of being, we require exegetical reasoning to choose its sense. Is it a sense of 'being alongside' or 'being in the company of' as in 'was with God' or is it more about being 'towards God?' The choice of 'with God' is usually given a Wisdom background for ὁ λόγος (Prov 8:20). The choice of 'towards God' can be given an intermediary[1] background in a typology of 'Moses and Aaron'. A quotation of the Hebrew of Exod 4:16 which is "you will be to him for towards God" (תהיה לו לאלהים) is certainly possible. We will argue further below that we do have a 'Moses and Aaron' typology in John 1:1-2, 6-7. We should not lose sight of the intermediary pattern generally implied in πρὸς τὸν θεόν.

2) The statement, 'the Word was God', makes a predication of the Word which suggests that the Word is a person. This use of 'God' here at the beginning of the gospel matches Thomas' confession, 'My Lord and my God' at the end of the gospel which is wholly addressed to Jesus (i.e. we have an *inclusio*).

(a) What Thomas saw in Jesus was the Father and Jesus acknowledges this in his response to Thomas. Jesus alludes to 'He who has *seen* me has *seen* the Father' (John 14:9) in his acknowledgment to Thomas that 'you have *seen* me' (John 20:29), a statement that goes beyond the literal seeing of the resurrected Jesus. This is the **first reason** why Jesus 'was God'—he manifested/declared the Father (John 1:18).

(b) John's reasoning is that 'in (or by) him (the Word) was life; and the life was the light of men' (John 1:4) and this coheres with the description of Jesus as 'the Word of Life' (1 John 1:1). The clearer identification of Jesus in 1 John 1:1 should control our identification of him in John 1:1—the Word of

---

[1] The main intermediary in the OT is the high priest and his actions are πρὸς τὸν θεόν (See Exod 18:19, LXX; 2 Cor 3:4; Heb 2:17; 5:1; 1 John 1:1-2; 3:21; Rev 12:5; 13:6). The Greek is consistent and is particularly clear in Hebrews where we read, 'a merciful and faithful high priest in things pertaining *to God*' (Heb 2:17). The use of the expression helps us see the priestly role of Rev 12:5 in being 'caught up *unto God*', and the false priesthood implicit in the 'blasphemy *against God*' of Rev 13:6.

Life is the Word. This relationship of Jesus to the creation of new life, i.e. a new creation is the **second reason** why he 'was God' (v. 1).[1]

3) The common demonstrative expression, 'the same' (John 1:2), is often used of persons. It is used of John the Baptist (John 1:7), and it is used elsewhere of Christ (e.g. John 1:15, 30, 33, 34; cf. Ps 102:27; John 7:18; Heb 1:12; 13:8). It is the use of the demonstrative in John 1:7 that is important here because vv. 2 and 7 are in a contrasting relationship: Jesus, the same, was with/toward God in the beginning, but John the Baptist, the same, came for a witness. This contrasting relationship between vv. 2 and 7 establishes Jesus as the referent of 'the Word' in v. 1.

What we have between vv. 2 and 7 is a 'Moses and Aaron' typology applied to Jesus and the John the Baptist in which John the Baptist speaks out for Jesus in the same way that Aaron spoke out for Moses. The typology is struck with John's emphasis on identity: 'this one was towards God…this one came for a witness'. The demonstrative pronouns are picking up the personal pronouns in Exod 4:16,

It will be that <u>he, even he,</u> will be to you
for a mouth

וְהָיָה הוּא יִהְיֶה־לְּךָ לְפֶה

<u>You, you</u> will be to him towards God

וְאַתָּה תִּהְיֶה־לּוֹ לֵאלֹהִים

Of the all the arguments for identifying Jesus as the referent of 'the Word' in v. 1, this typology explains why v. 2 would pick up 'towards God' from v. 1 to emphasize, rather than 'was God'.

4) Jesus is elsewhere referred to as 'the Word of God' (Rev 19:13; cf. Wisd 18:15, which is a counterargument), which invites the view that Jesus is 'the Word' of John 1:1, especially if we regard the Book of Revelation and the Gospel of John as written by the same person under inspiration. We

---

[1] New Testament scholars from time to time consider the question of whether the NT calls Jesus 'God' but seldom do they ask this question in relation to the new creation; see D, A. Fennema, "John 1:18: 'God the Only Son'" *NTS* 31 (1985): 124-135 (124).

should note however that GJohn doesn't use the expression 'the Word of God' for a reason.

5) John 1:1 does not use the name 'Jesus' but this does not mean that Jesus is not the referent of 'the Word'. Various names and titles can be used to refer to the same person (this is co-referentiality[1]) and there is a reason why John uses 'the Word' for Jesus instead of his name. This title depicts Jesus as the voice of God's word, the powerful word of the new creation; this teaching would be lost if John had used the name 'Jesus'.

In view of (1)-(5), we reject the views, a) that 'the Word' is used in v. 1 as or for a linguistic or attributive hypostatization; b) that 'the Word' is a heavenly being; and c) that 'the Word' is pre-existent. Rather, Jesus is the one who gives effect to God's word and is that very ongoing 'Word of Life'. Jesus had the words of eternal life (John 6:62, 68); these words were given to him by his Father (John 12:44-50); and so, the word of God abode in him (John 5:38). To repeat, the intertext of 1 John 1:1-3 is particularly clear:

> That which was from the beginning, which we have heard, which we have seen with our eyes, which we have looked upon, and our hands have handled, of <u>the Word of Life</u>; (For the life was manifested, and we have seen it, and bear witness, and shew unto you that eternal life, which was with the Father, and was manifested unto us;) That which we have seen and heard declare we unto you, that ye also may have fellowship with us: and truly our fellowship is with the Father, and with his son Jesus Christ. 1 John 1:1-3 (KJV)

The exegetical steps in these verses mirror the prologue of John. First, we have the mention of the 'Word of Life' which is shorthand for 'the Word...in him was life' from John 1:1,4. The neuter relative pronoun, 'That which...' treats the 'Word of Life' abstractly, but this was heard, seen and handled, and these are witness statements pertaining to the Word of Life as a person. Secondly, the 'For (καί) the life was manifested' of v. 2 mirrors the 'And so (καί)' of John 1:14, "And so the word became flesh". It is explanatory, which is why the KJV has translated the conjunction as 'For'. Thirdly, the personal dimension of vv. 1-3 ('we', 'us') matches the personal dimension in John 1:14 ('we', 'us'). John tells us that they beheld the glory of the word made flesh, just as the Word of Life was heard, seen and handled. Fourthly, it is the manifest Word of Life that

---

[1] For example, 'Elizabeth Windsor is over ninety' has less information than 'The Queen of England is over eighty' although the name and title are co-referential at the time of writing.

203

is towards the Father (πρὸς τὸν πατέρα) and this tells us that it is Jesus who was towards God (πρὸς τὸν θεόν). Lastly, the fellowship mentioned in 1 John picks up the "dwelt among us" of John 1:14.

In sum: the *sense* of the title 'the Word' in v. 1 is that of the spoken word of God and what is said, but the *reference* of 'the Word' is Jesus and this is because the word became flesh. The language of John 1 is too personal for any other reading: The Word was towards (with) God and was God.

There are **three objections** to the above reading. First, there is the problem of the rarity of this title. Jesus never claimed the title in his 'I am' statements. Why isn't it used more often in John or the NT? Surely this means that 'the Word' in v. 1 is a linguistic hypostatization of God's word as conceptualized in the OT which then becomes flesh in v. 14. As such, the significance of the title falls away after the incarnation and this explains its non-use. Secondly, the personal pronouns and demonstrative in vv. 2-4 agree in gender with ὁ λόγος, but it is up to the translator whether these should be 'him', 'it' or 'the same' depending on what/who they take to be the referent of ὁ λόγος.

However, we would argue that the title is an integral part of a specific Genesis creation typology and this is why it is not used elsewhere (see the next section). Hence, in both Jesus' ministry and the ministry of the apostles it is the word *as God's word* that is emphasized; Jesus is not presented as 'the Word'. For example,

> And they were all amazed, and spake among themselves, saying, 'What a word *is* this! For with authority and power he commandeth the unclean spirits, and they come out'. Luke 4:36 (KJV)

> If he called them gods, unto whom the <u>word of God came</u>, and the scripture cannot be broken; Say ye of him, whom the Father hath sanctified, and sent into the world, Thou blasphemest; because I said, I am the Son of God? John 10:35-36 (KJV)

> Now ye are <u>clean</u> through the <u>word</u> which I have spoken unto you. John 15:3 (KJV)

> I have given them <u>thy word</u>; and the world hath hated them, because they are not of the world, even as I am not of the world. John 17:4 (KJV)

And when the Gentiles heard this, they were glad, and glorified the word of the Lord: and as many as were ordained to eternal life believed. Acts 13:48 (KJV)

The word of God remains God's word in the mouth of Jesus and the apostles; it is a word that cleanses the soul; and belief of the word leads to eternal life.

As regards the second objection, the case for identifying the referent of ὁ λόγος as Jesus does not rest on the pronouns in vv. 3-4; translations differ as to 'it' and 'him'. Our case rests on the linkage between the demonstrative 'This one' in vv. 2, 7 which is properly a contrast between two individuals. There is also a further point: the third person masculine pronoun in v. 10, 'knew him not' requires a masculine antecedent and this is ultimately ὁ λόγος.

The third objection misreads vv. 1-5. It is argued that 'the Word' in v. 1 cannot be Jesus because he did not create all things at the beginning of his ministry (v. 3). Instead, 'the Word' must be a reference to God's word and its role in the Genesis creation and throughout history until it became flesh in Jesus, only in this case does it make sense to affirm that "all things were made through it/him".

This objection overlooks the significance of the perfect tense in "that which has been made was life in him" (ὃ γέγονεν ἐν αὐτῷ ζωὴ ἦν, v. 3c-4a). This shows the temporal perspective of the narrator: he is looking back on what has been created and this is "life in him". This means that the aorist tense of v. 3 (ἐγένετο) is a **statement of fact** by the narrator. There is no sense of creation all happening at once at the beginning of the ministry.

5. The Word of God
No title of Christ is more associated with the idea of pre-existence, but surprisingly it's not a very common title of Christ.[1] John 1, which speaks of 'the Word' in the beginning and 'the word became/was made flesh', is

---

[1] The exact form of words (ὁ λόγος τοῦ θεοῦ) are definitely applied to Jesus in Rev 19:13, but elsewhere (Heb 4:12 and 1 John 2:14) it is not certain that they refer to Christ. The shorter phrase 'the Word' may be applied to Christ in Luke 1:2. The title 'the Word of Life' (τοῦ λόγου τῆς ζωῆς) is used of Jesus in 1 John 1:2.

the main passage for the doctrine of the pre-existence of Christ.[1] But what *does* the title itself mean (in addition to it referring to Jesus in v. 1)?

The lexicons give the meaning of 'word' (Gk: λόγος, *logos*; Heb: דבר, *dabar*) as: the word or that by which the inward thought is expressed, or the inward thought itself (*logos*, L&S); speech, discourse, saying, word, as the sum of that which is spoken, or saying, utterance, words, or a matter or thing about which one speaks (*dabar*, BDB[2]). There isn't a complete match between the semantic fields of *logos* and *dabar*.[3] The English translation will vary depending on the assessment of **what is being said**. So, for instance, *logos* may be translated as 'word, matter, thing, subject, statement, assertion, declaration, or more specifically as reason, motive, message, account, etc'. (BAGD). We can infer from this lexical data that the sense of *logos*/*dabar* is fundamentally **about language** (words and what is said with words), but there is also figurative usage as well.

In studies of Jewish cosmology the category of 'hypostasis' (roughly speaking, for our purposes, an entity) is important, but the category is vexed as a result of confusion between 'linguistic' hypostatization and 'attributive' hypostatization.[4] L. W. Hurtado has argued that proposals in this area are "neither very clear nor compelling".[5] An attributive hypostatization is one where an attribute of the deity, like his word or his wisdom, is spoken of as a real agent acting in the world. A linguistic hypostatization is one where the attributes of the deity are presented in a *narrative* as agents without any implication as to their actual existence in reality.

The suggestion that *the Logos* is the thought or the reason of God can be found in Greek philosophy, particularly Stoic philosophy, and also in Jewish literature of the inter-testamental period, of which the Jewish

---

[1] Dunn claims, "Here, beyond dispute, the Word is pre-existent, and Christ is the pre-existent Word incarnate", *Christology in the Making*, 239. We will see that it is easy enough to dispute Dunn's confidence.

[2] F. Brown, S. R. Driver and C. A. Briggs, *A Hebrew and English Lexicon of the Old Testament* (Oxford: Oxford University Press, 1907).

[3] Abbott-Smith matches *logos* chiefly with *dabar*.

[4] See C. A. Gieschen *Angelomorphic Christology* (Leiden: E. J. Brill, 1998), 36-45, for a methodological discussion of 'hypostasis' terminology.

[5] L. W. Hurtado, *One God, One Lord*, (2nd. Ed.; London: Continuum, 1998), 37.

philosopher, Philo (c. 20 – 50 CE), is the main example.[1] Philo has an elaborate philosophical understanding of the Word, which appears to be an attributive hypostatization, for example,[2]

> But the divine Word which is above these does not come into any visible appearance, inasmuch as it is not like to any of the things that come under the external senses, but is itself an image of God, the most ancient of all the objects of intellect in the whole world, and that which is placed in the closest proximity to the only truly existing God, without any partition or distance being interposed between them... *Fug.* 1.101

> Why is it that he speaks as if of some other god, saying that he made man after the image of God, and not that he made him after his own image? Very appropriately and without any falsehood was this oracular sentence uttered by God, for no mortal thing could have been formed on the similitude of the supreme Father of the universe, but only after the pattern of the second deity (*ton deuteron theon*), who is the Word of the supreme Being; since it is fitting that the rational soul of man should bear before it the type of the divine Word; since in his first Word God is superior to the most rational possible nature. But he who is superior to the Word holds his rank in a better and most singular pre-eminence, and how could the creature possibly exhibit a likeness of him in himself? *Quaest.* 2:62

Philo took ideas from Greek philosophy and shaped these in accordance with his understanding of the Jewish religion. He married the idea of *the Logos*, which he found in philosophy, to his view of 'the Word of God' which he found in the Old Testament. He develops the idea so that it becomes a quite sophisticated philosophy of the way that God relates to the world. It is a matter of scholarly dispute as to whether Philo actually thought of *the Logos* as a heavenly being, or whether he uses the language

---

[1] Depending on the school of philosophy, *the Logos* idea will be different. For Heraclitus (c. 500 BCE) *the Logos* was the principle of reason in nature. Stoics distinguished between *logos* as thought and *logos* as expression of thought.

[2] Texts are from C. D. Yonge, ed., *The Works of Philo* (New York: Hendrickson, 1993).

of an intermediary in heaven as a *way of talking* about God.[1] But that it was a mainstay in Philo's thought is generally accepted; he makes over 1300 (Kittel) references to *the Logos*.

Scholars are divided as to whether Jewish writings use the one or the other type of hypostatization (or both); and different judgments might be offered for different texts. In the Wisdom of Solomon, Wisdom likewise appears as an attributive hypostatization,

> Give me Wisdom, that sitteth by thy throne; and reject me not from among thy children...O send her out of thy holy heavens, and from the throne of thy glory, that being present she may labour with me, that I may know what is pleasing unto thee. Wisd 9:4, 10 (KJA); cf. 18:15

Whether this example is an attributive hypostatizations is not something we need to settle; it seems that the more elaborate the writer's description of the Word or Wisdom in terms of an agent of God acting in the world, the more plausible is the judgment that the writer saw the Word or Wisdom as a hypostasized attribute of the deity. In contrast, the Hebrew Scriptures lack any metaphysics for attributive hypostatization, nor are they given 'voice and face' and personified;[2] rather we have brief linguistic hypostatization of divine attributes.

Whether the apostle John is indebted to philosophy is doubtful,[3] if only because in Greek and Jewish thought, the idea of *the Logos* is part of a

---

[1] See Dunn, *Christology in the Making*, 220-230. This issue is introduced by K. Schenck, *A Brief Guide to Philo* (Louisville: WJK Press, 2005), 43-44; it is further discussed as a "fourth sphere of ambiguity" in Philo's thought in R. Radice, "Philo's Theology and Theory of Creation" in *The Cambridge Companion to Philo* (ed. A. Kamesar; Cambridge: Cambridge University Press, 2009), 124-145 (128-129).

[2] On the relative distinction between hypostatization and personification, see J. Paxson, *The Poetics of Personification* (Cambridge: Cambridge University Press, 1994), chap. 2.

[3] For a discussion see R. V. Peltier, ' Christology in the Prologue of John: A Rejection of Philo of Alexandria's Logos Philosophy' (M.Th. Thesis, Univ. of South Africa, 2019) [Online]. See also, T. Gaston, 'Why Three? An Exploration of the origins of the doctrine of the Trinity with reference to Platonism and Gnosticism' (DPhil Thesis, Oxford University, 2013), 110, "The Semitic character of the gospel makes it unlikely that John's Logos is an allusion to the Stoic or Platonic Logos, and there are more than sufficient Jewish precedents..." [Online.]

cosmology, whereas John's Gospel only has a couple of verses that use the title 'the Word' and there is nothing philosophical in the context.

The contrast with John 1 could not be greater. The statements he makes boil down to *the Word was in the beginning, the Word was toward (with) God, the Word was God,* and *the word became flesh.* In addition, there are statements made of the Word which don't involve the title and rely on pronouns (e.g. vv. 3, 8, 10). The explicit statement (v. 1) is important, but compared to non-Biblical sources, it is rather isolated. Consequently, scholars have placed John's prologue in a context which will enlarge what it means. The lack of information in John has motivated scholars to look elsewhere for the meaning of the title. And, to be fair, they are also trying to understand *the Logos* Christology of the 2c. church by rooting it in John. They are not satisfied with what the lexicons suggest for *logos/dabar* which would be that 'the Word' would be what God says and/or God's spoken word(s), whether literally or figuratively presented. Scholars today are doing the same thing as the Church Fathers from the sub-Apostolic period onwards.

Is any Second-Temple or Greco-Roman cultural context the correct place for the prologue of John's Gospel? Was John aware of other ideas? Is NT Scripture opposing these ideas by way of redrawing them or is it a development of these ideas?[1] The early Church Fathers, and in particular the Apologists, lived in a Greco-Roman and Jewish cultural context when they developed the idea of the pre-existence of the Word. Were they right to use those contexts of ideas?

We know that the NT writings use the OT, so it would seem best to look at the OT first for the background to John's prologue. If v. 1 is not a reference to Jesus, two scriptural backgrounds have been commonly put forward in order to explain the 'personal' aspect of the verse. The first is the personification of Wisdom in Proverbs (e.g. Prov 8:22ff). Second Temple writings develop Proverbs and associate the wisdom of God, the Torah and the word of God (e.g. Wisd 7:12; 9:1-4; 18:14-16; 1 Enoch 42:2; Sirach 1:1; 24:6-8; 42:15). The suggestion is made that 'the Word' is another way of referring to the Wisdom of God in Second Temple Judaism.[2]

---

[1] This is speculative because the points of contact with opposing literature are so slight. We could use John 1 to oppose contemporary views, but it is another question whether this is an intention of the author. Nevertheless, scholarly views of John 1 put it into one cultural context or another.

[2] This is a familiar commentary position; see G. R. Beasley-Murray, *John* (WBC36; Waco: Word, 1991), 6-10, "The employment of *the Logos*

The three main points of contact between Proverbs and John 1 are that Wisdom is with God in the beginning (Prov 8:22, 27, 30); it is with Wisdom that the Lord creates heaven and earth (Prov 3:19); and there is an identity between the Word and Wisdom (Prov 9:1). The main problems with this proposal are that Wisdom is before any Genesis beginning; it is presented with various female figures;[1] John doesn't use the term for 'wisdom' in the prologue; and while Proverbs might give us a textual basis for 'toward (with) God' it doesn't do so particularly for 'was God'.[2] Second-Temple concerns with regard to Wisdom are cosmological whereas the prologue's concerns with the Word are about life and light – soteriology and revelation. The prologue is about Jesus as the Word rather than about the Word as conceived in Second-Temple writings (or Greek philosophy for that matter). The only sense indicated by the text is that supplied by Genesis and later scriptural commentary on Genesis.

The second background lies in the OT hypostatizations[3] of 'the word of God' (e.g. Pss 107:20; 147:15, 18; Isa 9:8; 45:23; 55:11; Hos 6:5).[4] These texts are clear *linguistic* hypostatizations rather than *attributive* hypostatizations because they are brief, incidental, and not part of any

---

concept in the prologue to the Fourth Gospel is the supreme example within Christian history of the communication of the gospel in terms understood and appreciated by the nations" (10). On the contrary, it is an example of intra-scriptural and typological reasoning.

[1] This problem was recognised early, for example in Philo; see R. M. Grant, *Jesus after the Gospels* (London: SCM Press, 1990), 32-33.

[2] This view is detailed in M. Scott, *Sophia and the Johannine Jesus* (JSNT 71; Sheffield: Sheffield Academic Press, 1992). Scott observes, 88, "It has long been recognised that the Gospel of John contains elements of a Wisdom Christology, even though no word of the σοφία/σοφός family appears in the text."—a telling remark.

[3] They are not 'personifications' because God's word lacks its own voice and face.

[4] Scholars have pointed to a Second-Temple background for 'the Word' in *the Memra* of the Jewish Aramaic Targums. This concept is extensive in these translation-paraphrases of the Hebrew Scriptures. However, if the Hebrew Scriptures are what the Spirit quotes, and we can explain John 1 just in scriptural terms, we don't need to hypothesize that John had knowledge of Targumic paraphrases. See M. McNamara, "Logos of the Fourth Gospel and Memra of the Palestinian Targum (Ex 12:42)" *ExpT* 79 (1967-68): 115-117, details the weaknesses of the comparison, not least of which is the metonymical use of 'Memra of the Lord' for 'Lord', a use which John does not deploy with logos.

210

cosmology relating to the attributes of God, and they use physical verbs with the more abstract *dabar*. Hypostatization involves speaking of non-corporeal things in corporeal ways. So, for example, Ps 107:20 and Isa 55:11,

> He sent his Word, and healed them, and delivered *them* from their destructions. Ps 107:20 (KJV); cf. 147:15, 18

> So shall my Word be that goeth forth out of my mouth: it shall not return unto me void, but it shall accomplish that which I please, and it shall prosper in the thing whereto I sent it. Isa 55:11[1] (KJV); cf. 9:8; 45:23

These examples are easily understood. A king may utter his word and that word may be carried out by servants; his commanders may report back what has happened on the battlefield and in this sense the king's word has not returned to him empty. In each case, the hypostatization is not very developed. These two examples are different to Ps 33:6, 9 which is often listed alongside them because that text juxtaposes 'word' and 'breath of his mouth' in a parallelism,

> By the word of the Lord were the heavens made; and all the host of them by the breath of his mouth...For he spake, and it was done; he commanded, and it stood fast. Ps 33:6, 9 (KJV)

This example is not a linguistic hypostatization because the utterance of God is in and of itself powerful to effect what God's commands. It should be clear that what we have in John 1 is much more developed than these OT examples.

Linguistic hypostatization of the word of God is found in the NT. For example,

> And the Word of God increased; and the number of the disciples multiplied in Jerusalem greatly; and a great company of the priests were obedient to the faith. Acts 6:7 (KJV)

> But the Word of God grew and multiplied. Acts 12:24 (KJV)

---

[1] This text underlies John's language of Jesus being sent forth; see J. V. Dahms, "Isaiah 55:11 and the Gospel of John" *EQ* 53.2 (1981): 78-88.

So mightily grew the Word of God and prevailed. Acts 19:20 (KJV)

These are clear hypostatizations and in keeping with the examples of hypostatization we noted above in the OT, although somewhat more developed. The examples also show that rather than being a late Gospel, John could be dated early in the apostolic ministry. John's 'the word became flesh and dwelt among us' has a parallel in Luke's understanding of the Word of God increasing amongst the early Christians as they grew in number.[1]

It isn't a natural idiom to say that the Word of God grew and multiplied although we can see how this worked out on the ground; it is more of a natural idiom to 'send a word by someone',

> The word which God sent unto the children of Israel, preaching peace by Jesus Christ: (he is Lord of all:) That word, I say, ye know, which was published throughout all Judaea, and began from Galilee, after the baptism which John preached... Acts 10:36-37 (KJV)

This text is interesting because it corroborates John 1:1, 14 in that God sent his word by Jesus Christ and that word began from Galilee. A beginning, the baptism of John and the word of God are the ingredients of John's prologue (even if Luke's terminology is different). John's way of stating Luke's 'God sent his word by Jesus' is 'the word became flesh'. The question is whether this then the personal language of John 1:1.

How hypostatization is cashed out in real terms is an important exegetical task. For example, Heb 4:12,

> For the Word of God is living and active and sharper than any two-edged sword and piercing as far as the division of soul and spirit, of both joints and marrow, and able to judge the thoughts and intentions of the heart. Heb 4:12 (NASB)

If the word of God is in the hearts and minds of faithful believers who are preaching the gospel, we can see how this hypostatization works; how

---

[1] There is a comparison here to be made between the word becoming flesh in the person of Jesus and dwelling amongst the disciples and the word becoming flesh in the early Christians and growing as they multiplied – this is all about the bestowal of the Spirit.

the word is living and active. The general point is that with OT and NT examples alike, we can discern what is going on with the figurative use of language in linguistic hypostatizations.

It is because John 1:14 follows John 1:1 that commentators reject a reference to Jesus for v. 1 and the verse is read as a linguistic or attributive hypostatization. It is thought that Jesus appears on the scene in v. 14. However, when we instead read the prologue in terms of three parallel paragraphs, and vv. 14-18 as explanatory for what has been described in the first two paragraphs, the requirement to read v. 1 in terms of a hypostatization falls away.

In addition to this consideration, the examples of linguistic hypostatization in both the OT and NT are not close parallels to John 1:1, where we need a sense and a reference for 'the Word' that will sustain 'toward (with) God' and 'was God' as predicates, both of which seem **more personal** and suggest a personification akin to Wisdom. This is even more so if we think the first predicate should be 'was toward God' or if we note that there isn't an OT text where the Word is said to be with God (it might be with the people or an individual; e.g. 2 Kgs 3:12; Jer 27:18). What we find ourselves doing when we treat 'the Word' of John 1:1 as a linguistic hypostatization is that we *say to ourselves* that this is like the agency of the word of God in the OT, but 'towards (with) God' isn't about agency, and 'was God' relies on *our seeing* the agent as 'God in action'.

Linguistic hypostatization or personification readings of John 1:1 go hand in hand with the Genesis reading of 'the beginning' of that verse. We might well ask why John 1:1-5 should be about such a beginning when the other three Gospels start with the beginning that is John the Baptist and Jesus. Or, we might ask how such a reading is relevant to the rest of John's Gospel.

When we read 'the beginning' as the beginning of the ministry of Jesus, a reference to Jesus under the title 'the Word' is required by the association of Jesus with the new creation elsewhere (1 Cor 8:6; Col 1:20; Eph 3:9). In the terminology of Hebrews, and to bring out the connection with John 1:1, "Jesus is the beginner (ἀρχηγός) and finisher of our faith" (Heb 12:2).

If John 1:1 is not a linguistic hypostatization of 'the word', there is no momentum for treating John 1:14 in this way and we can utilise the more common literal meaning of *logos/dabar* for understanding 'the word became flesh'. The way that the word of God is conceived of as words

213

spoken and what is said by God—this is the only picture that informs the reader of how to think of a man as 'the Word'. The only realities on the ground are the person of Jesus and the word of God; devices of linguistic hypostatization and literary personification are irrelevant to the metaphysics of the new creation.

In sum: The Hebrew Scriptures do not know of a being called 'the Word'. What we do have in these Scriptures is an *occasional* linguistic hypostatization of the word of God. Such hypostatization is rare; generally, the word of God or the word of the Lord is that prophetic word that comes to a prophet (218x, e.g. 1 Kgs 12:22; Isa 38:4), or it is God's direct utterance, and in both cases it is what is said. The temptation is to extemporize and elaborate on this basic sense and to get to something more substantial for an incarnation.

The *hypostatizations* of the word of God in the OT picture how God acts in a figurative way.[1] It is enough for God to speak his will, and his purpose is accomplished. Indeed, the word of God tells us of the wisdom of God. Is the word of God then *equivalent* to his reason, his purpose, his wisdom or even the power of God? The problem here is a lack of analysis on our part. We are blurring the distinction between 'the word of God' understood as made up of *spoken words* and then *what* this 'word' expresses, which is only *sometimes*,[2] say, the purpose(s) of God.

Now, if we take Jesus to be the reference of 'the Word' in v. 1, the motivation for personification or hypostatization readings is removed. The focus of exegesis shifts to v. 14 and the common usage of *dabar* can be invoked as John's OT background for that verse. Here we don't have the title, 'the Word', referring to Jesus, but simply 'the word' and this is because Jesus is the *realisation* that is 'the word become flesh'.

We have noted that the standard Hebrew lexicons show that the noun *dabar* is used to refer to **spoken words** as well as **what is said**. These are the main uses of *dabar* in the OT and such usage should be distinguished from any further analysis that we might undertake of such usage into speech acts and the content of those acts.

---

[1] Had the Word of God been part of the Godhead, or a divine being, these OT texts would have been less attribute-like in their configuration of the word of God.

[2] In addition to statements of purpose, the word of God contains expressions of desire, wishes, statements of facts, musings, expressions of hope, exclamations, reports of falsehoods, *and so on.*

We can illustrate this analytical framework below:

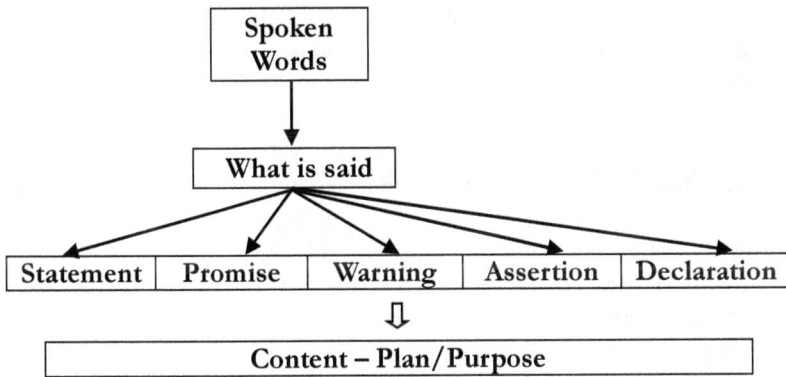

```
                    ┌─────────────┐
                    │   Spoken    │
                    │   Words     │
                    └─────────────┘
                           │
                           ▼
                    ┌─────────────┐
                    │ What is said │
                    └─────────────┘

┌───────────┬──────────┬──────────┬───────────┬─────────────┐
│ Statement │ Promise  │ Warning  │ Assertion │ Declaration │
└───────────┴──────────┴──────────┴───────────┴─────────────┘
                           ⇩
┌──────────────────────────────────────────────────────────┐
│                 Content – Plan/Purpose                      │
└──────────────────────────────────────────────────────────┘
```

Most usage of *dabar* covers the top two levels of the diagram. Hence, we read, 'my word...goes forth out of my mouth' (Isa 55:11), 'the words of my mouth' (Hos 6:5), as well as 'and brought the king word' (1 Kgs 22:9), 'Hear the word of the Lord' (Isa1:10) and 'The word of our God shall stand for ever (Isa 40:8).

We can distinguish the act of speaking from the kind of speech act.[1] In Genesis 1 God speaks and he commands, and what is important to John's typology is the act of speaking rather than the speech act of commanding. To be clear, the related verb *diber* and the verb *amar*[2] are used for the act of speaking but the mere act of speaking should be distinguished from the classification of the various speech acts (promise, warning, etc) and the further characterization of the content of those acts. The noun *dabar* is used for what is spoken and what is said. We might suppose that Jesus is the fulfilment of what was spoken and what was said, but this is not the meaning of 'the word became flesh'.

The concept of *what God says* is more abstract than, say, the concept of the expression of a purpose because the word 'purpose' further characterizes the *content* of what God has said. So, we cannot gloss John 1:1, 14 with something like, 'the purpose of God became flesh in the

---

[1] See J. R. Searle, *Speech Acts* (Cambridge: Cambridge University Press, 1969); R. S. Briggs, *Words in Action: Speech Act Theory and Biblical Interpretation* (Sheffield: Continuum, 2001). For an application to John 1, see G. Jackman, *The Word Became Flesh* (Pub. By the Author, 2016).

[2] This is extensively used in 'God said' reporting such as that which we find in Genesis 1.

person of Christ' even if this might be good theology. We would need intertextual links with expressions of God's purpose. Rather, what we have available in the OT background of *dabar* is God speaking words and saying things directly or speaking through the prophets. We should consider whether there is a specific situation serving as a type or precedent for John 1:1, 14.

Philo, of course, goes beyond this analysis, to consider *the Logos* as God's Reason in terms of a **divine attribute** (a faculty) and he considers all that God says as a reflection of that attribute. So, what God says, and the various speech acts he utters—these are all expressions of his Reason. This further analysis is not reflected in the OT, but we find it in Greco-Roman culture and Hellenistic Judaism. To take an analogy: the word of the king may be uttered from the throne or delivered through spokespersons but such a word is different from any aspect to do with his human nature, whether we think of mental faculties, dispositions, abilities, powers, personhood, or intellectual qualities.[1] However, what we need for a doctrine of incarnation is something from the latter list of properties. The difficulty for our doctrine is that such properties remain with the Father even when the Son is 'the Word'.

With *dabar/diber* as our background, we should distinguish texts that report God speaking or have God talking about his speaking and those texts in which prophets claim to be or are said to be speaking the word of the Lord. Prophets are representative and delegated speakers on behalf of God.[2] The phrases, 'word of God', 'word of the Lord' and 'the word' are most often used of the message delivered by OT prophets to the people (John 10:35; cf. Acts 17:13; 2 Cor 4:2). Both individual examples of prophecy (e.g. 1 Kgs 12:22; 1 Chron 17:3), and the whole message (enshrined in Scripture) of God to man is described as 'the word' (e.g. Ps 119:9, 105). This dual application of the language is found in the NT, with Jesus' parables and sayings described as 'the word' (e.g. Mark 8:32; 9:10), along with his whole message (e.g. Mark 2:2; 4:33).

Should our paradigm for John 1:1, 14 be God speaking directly or should we think of the word of God through the prophets? If we take first as our model God speaking, what example of his speaking could John be

---

[1] The list is taken from a general introduction to the Philosophy of Mind; see A. Kenny, *The Metaphysics of Mind* (Oxford: Oxford University Press, 1989).

[2] See N. Wolterstorff, *Divine Discourse* (Cambridge: Cambridge University Press, 1995), chap. 2.

using as a type? In reviewing OT usage of *dabar/diber*, we should be guided by the allusion in John 1 to Genesis 1 ("In the beginning"). There we have a series of 'And God said' utterances, which are then picked up in Psalm 33 and generalized as 'the word of the Lord' (*dabar*). We can think of Jesus as comparable to God's utterances because God's word was the instrument of creation in Genesis and Jesus is God's agent in the new creation.

This typology works for v. 1 and is explained by v. 14, 'And so the word became (ἐγένετο) flesh'. This statement is about what Jesus became and what it was about Jesus that was **ongoing**, namely, that he was now 'the Word'—he spoke the word of God, he had the authority so to speak and act. This explains any typology in v. 1 – why we can compare Jesus as the Word of the new creation to the 'And God said' utterances of the Genesis creation.[1] No doubt God spoke directly in sending his son and in sending the Spirit at his baptism; no doubt also Jesus is the fulfilment in the flesh of all that the prophets had foretold; but these two aspects do not explain the *ongoing nature* of Jesus being 'the Word'. Instead of (or in place of) the word that God has uttered either himself or through the prophets, there is now the only begotten son, Jesus Christ (Heb 1:1-2).

When choosing the nuance for 'the word' in v. 14 from the OT we should be guided by the typology of Genesis 1. We can say therefore that what was a spoken word for the Genesis creation is now (has become) flesh for the new creation.

What are the **objections** to this analysis of 'the Word'? First, it is said that no one from the sub-Apostolic or Apologist eras has offered this analysis and they are closer to John in time and more likely to have got him right. Secondly, the analysis is too sophisticated for the average person to have understood and so it is unlikely to represent John's meaning. Thirdly, the audience's background knowledge would have consisted of either a Greek idea of *the Logos* or a Second-Temple idea of the hypostasized Word/Wisdom of God; John must therefore be using one or both of these ideas. How do we address these objections?

The assumption with which the Fathers are read is that they represent legitimate Christian thinking. If instead we take on board the warnings of the apostles that false teachers were present (and would arise) in the church (2 Cor 11:13, 26; Gal 2:4; 2 Pet 2:1; 1 John 4:1), we cannot just

---

[1] The comparison with the 'And God said' utterances is certain, but we don't have to regard this as typological; we could treat it as literal.

simply think those now venerated as the Fathers are right; they could be false teachers on all sorts of issues. Moreover, while the church today may identify an orthodox strand of doctrine in the 2c. CE, as historians we should just recognize the variety of Christian doctrine and sects in that period.

The writings that we have from the early church Fathers have declarative statements about John 1 which are consistent with incarnational readings; we don't have sustained exegetical intra-scriptural reasoning using typology. Rather, their exegesis is of the surface text of John informed by cultural understanding of the terminology (Irenaeus, *Against Heresies* is a good example).

Further, where they cite opponents' views on Christ, it is not the citation of opposing exegesis, but more their opponents' own declarative statements. Comparing the Fathers' declarative polemics with exegesis that covers textual issues, grammar, literary structure, and typological interpretation is like comparing apples and pears. The absence of this kind of written material does not mean that exegesis wasn't practised; it is just that we don't have that evidence.
Tradition is important in the church as is the veneration of the Fathers. However, the only method for determining the truth of a scriptural matter is through reasoned intra-scriptural exegesis. The historically driven exegesis that modern commentators offer in support of incarnational readings isn't the correct method for getting to the bottom of the matter.

The second objection above was that sophisticated exegesis is unlikely to represent John's meaning because he wrote for the average person. It's an easy rhetorical point to make, but John's writing did not exist in a vacuum. We have no way of knowing what teaching surrounded the reading of John, especially in the repeated reading of Scripture over the years. Simple exegesis can develop over time into the sophisticated.

There is a binary assumption in the objection: either John wrote a sophisticated piece of theology or a simple and straightforward one. But there is no reason why we should accept this binary choice as writing can have both simple and sophisticated aspects depending on what nuanced meanings a reader perceives. We see this today in the difference between devotional and scholarly use of John.

The third objection is that we need to go to Jewish traditions or Greek philosophy to understand John. If we generously assume a knowledge of Greek philosophy on the part of John's audience, does this mean John is bound to use that knowledge? We might be sceptical that many would have known Greek philosophy, but we can equally presume that they would have had scriptural knowledge. In any event, John can use and rely on any background knowledge, including scriptural knowledge, and exactly what area of his audience's knowledge he is relying on is **determined by his text**.

The linguistic hypostatization and personification of the Word and Wisdom in Scripture was developed by Jewish writers. John's prologue is of an ilk with those writers. We can see this if we put John into parallel columns with those writings – there *is* comparable language (although the case is overstated). The reason, however, is that both John and other Second-Temple authors are developing Scripture. John is doing so with respect to the word of God and Jesus; Second-Temple writers are doing so with respect to God, the Word and Wisdom and with cosmological overtones.

6. The Word of the New Creation

The reference to 'a beginning', and things which are made[1] in such a beginning, clearly echoes the Genesis 1 creation. The intention in vv. 1-3 is to place Jesus as the Word in a position parallel to what God says: the '...and God said...' utterances (Gen 1:3ff). The parallel involves the idea of doing something by an *agent* compared to doing something by some *instrument*. The original creation was created by God the Father *by* the angels by his delivery of fiats or commands (cf. Ezek 37:4-5, 9; John 20:22; Heb 11:3). For the work of the new creation, Christ holds the position of 'the word of God', and the angels would be under his feet. Hence, the new creation is being created by God the Father, *by* the Word, *by* angels,[2] who are sent forth to minister unto those who would be heirs of salvation.

This is **new revelation** in John: that *a person* could be in the place of God's spoken word and *be* 'the Word'. When we think of Christ as 'the

---

[1] The Greek is ἐγένετο, and it occurs in vv. 3, 6, 10, 14 and 17. It is like a refrain in the narrative reinforcing the topic of creation, albeit of various entities - *all things* (v. 3), *John* (v. 6), *the World* (v. 10), *the word* (v. 14), and *grace and truth* (v. 17). However, it is important to note that this verb isn't the Greek for 'create' (κτίζω) or 'make' (ποιέω); rather, it is verb used to describe what comes to pass, particularly in history. It is an open question why John 1 doesn't use more create/make vocabulary.

[2] I do not exclude here the work of the apostles who were sent forth and were directed by the holy Spirit in their *creative* work, but my point primarily concerns angels.

Word', we think of him as the creative word or voice[1] of God the Father, and what is created is meant to be a mirror of him. This is how it was in Genesis: "God said, 'Let there be'...and there was...it was so". What was created was the substance of what was said. With the new creation, what is created is *Christ in us* (Gal 4:19); we are an image of Christ who is both the Word of our creation (1 Pet 1:23) and the God whose image we bear (John 20:28; Rom 8:29; 2 Cor 3:18; Col 3:10).[2]

In Genesis, words are spoken, and these produce an effect. In GJohn, the Word is said to be *with/toward* God and also said to *be God*. The ideas of being 'with/toward God' as well as 'was God' are extra details not found in Genesis. It is important to see that these details are an *addition*, because the text has fused teaching from Genesis and Exodus. The overtone behind the Greek of 'with God' is intercession and priesthood, and this is why we prefer to render the phrase as 'the Word was *toward* God'. Because the Word is a *person*, intercession is not a strange idea.

The mention of the Word *as* toward God and also *as* God (was God) has been a matter of controversy. Some see in this text a mention of a plurality in the Godhead; others see an affirmation of Christ's essential deity. However, this dual aspect of Christ as 'toward God and God' is based on Moses who was a man 'toward God and God' (Exod 4:16 (MT); 7:1; 18:1; cf. Exod 4:31, and see Zech 12:8 for a similar reason justifying the application of the title 'God' to the house of David).[3]

---

[1] Compare and contrast Ignatius, *Letter to the Magnesians* 8:2, "there is one God, the Almighty, who has manifested himself by Jesus Christ his son, who is his Word, not spoken, but essential. For he is not the voice of an articulate utterance, but a substance begotten by divine power, who has in all things pleased him that sent him."

[2] This makes the effect of what is said by God a mirror of what he has said: if he says, 'let there be light', then the light mirrors and points to what he has said. This may be the divine basis for a correspondence theory of truth, when we consider that *language* originates with *God*. If this is so, philosophy of language gets it the wrong way around: the problem is not how language can correspond to reality, but how reality corresponds to language - the language is *first*.

[3] Notice that Zechariah juxtaposes the application of 'as God' and 'as the Angel of the Lord' in his description of the house of David. This shows the crucial role of the Angel of the Lord in an understanding the establishment of the kingdom and therefore the work of the Messiah.

The Mosaic typology is forged by John's use of the same idea of 'toward God' found in Exod 4:16 and 18:19,

> ...and the Word was <u>toward</u> God... John 1:1 (KJV revised)

> ...the Word of Life...<u>toward</u> the Father and... manifested to us... 1 John 1:1-2 (KJV revised); cf. 2 Cor 3:4

> And he shall be thy spokesman unto the people: and he shall be, even he shall be to thee instead of a mouth, and thou shalt be to him <u>towards</u> God. Exod 4:16 (KJV revised)

> ...be thou for the people <u>to God-ward</u>, that thou mayest bring the causes unto God... Exod 18:19 (KJV)

The type is also forged by the position of Moses as 'God': "...thou shalt be to him towards/for God..." (Exod 4:16; cf. Exod 4:31). This idea is not found in Genesis 1,[1] but it is packed into the text of John 1 from Exodus 4 and 18. This should not surprise us, as it is a characteristic of Scripture that texts often carry allusions to many places. A mediator can create, deliver the commands of God, and bring order to chaos, as did Moses. Accordingly, we conclude that John is not asserting that Jesus is in his essential nature God, but that he is 'God' ('god') in relation to the disciples (his 'Aaron'), or the 'God' in whose image Thomas wanted to be created (John 20:22, 28). In short, Jesus was 'God' in respect of the new creation.[2]

7. All Things

Does John 1 refer to the Genesis beginning? Is 'the Word' the maker of this creation? Or does John 1 refer to a new creation? And is 'the Word' the maker of this creation? To settle these questions, we must look at the usage of the expression 'all things' in the NT.

The apostles understood their age to be radically new, and they used creation language to describe their work and experience. It was a creation of *creatures* — a creation of a new man in each believer. James pinpoints

---

[1] The idea of intercession is however implicit in Adam's role of dominion over creation.

[2] The use of the Greek definite article in 'was toward God' but its absence in 'was God' supports this attributive reading. Jesus was the Word of Yahweh in respect of Yahweh's new creation but god in respect of that new creation.

God the Father as the Creator in this creation (Jms 1:18), but this does not exclude the possibility that God the Father was carrying out his creative work *by* Jesus, his Word. And in fact we shall see that Jesus is involved, because it is a creation of new men and women in him (2 Cor 5:17; Gal 6:15; Eph 2:10; 4:24; Col 3:10; Jms 1:18; 1 Pet 1:23).[1]

This is how it was in Genesis. Partnership is not a foreign idea to the Genesis creation. All the things of the Genesis creation were created by God through his word and through the angels. This relationship is seen in the expression 'let us make' (Gen 1:26). This relationship between God and the angels in heaven is reflected on the earth when man is brought into partnership with God. His work is to be one of ordering and governing creation (lordship) and this is a *kind of creative work*. The partnership is reflected *again*, when the woman is given unto the man as a helpmeet in the creative work of bearing children to the honour and glory of God. This principle is found also in the making of the sanctuary, where there is partnership in creative work (Heb 8:5) between the Angel of the Lord and Moses.[2] And the Levites are again explicitly 'given'[3] to the priests to be helpmeets in this sanctuary.[4]

One of the tests for good doctrine is that it is based on clear statements of Scripture. There is no clear scriptural statement of Trinitarian doctrine. Had the doctrine been true, it would have been reasonable to expect a statement to the effect that God is one in three,[5] instead we only get affirmations of the singleness of God. A general statement about God and the creation of all things is this:

---

[1] It is worth distinguishing Jesus' new creation of men and women in him from his creation of powers which are *of the world* (Col 1:16). Jesus has old creation authority and new creation authority.

[2] Moses made things on the earth; Christ's role in making things extends to heaven.

[3] Hence in John 17, the disciples are repeatedly referred to as the ones that have been *given* to Christ, the man, the priest.

[4] We read that God builds *all things* (Heb 3:4) and is the architect (1 Cor 3:10). We read also that Christ *builds* the church — this is a creative work of reconciliation, and we read that Paul builds the church also laying foundations, so creative work is proceeding in a co-operative partnership.

[5] After all what is special about the third and fourth centuries CE — why did we (supposedly) have to wait until then to get the right expression of the doctrine of God? Is it credible to suggest that the apostles were *too thick* to understand such a doctrine?

> ...there is but one God, the Father, <u>of whom</u> are all things,
> and we in him; and one Lord Jesus Christ, <u>through whom</u>
> are all things, and we <u>through him</u>. 1 Cor 8:6 (KJV revised)

This text establishes the fundamental relationship: all things are *of* the one God, the Father, but *through* the one Lord, Jesus Christ. Some have argued that Paul is modifying the Shema here,[1] but this is unlikely for a devout Jew. Instead, we should see that the singleness of God, the Father is affirmed alongside an affirmation about Jesus' lordship.[2]

Paul uses the expression 'all things' and his point is about the new creation, not the Genesis creation, because it talks of the *things* including people alive in Paul's day — (the 'we' in him) - *of God through Christ*. The idea of *reconciliation* connects people with the concept of *all things*, as is shown by the following parallelism between the creation of powers and the reconciliation of Jews and Gentiles:

> ...through him were all things created... [whether] ...in the heavens... [or]...in earth... Col 1:16cb (KJV revised)

> ...by him... [were]...all things [reconciled]... whether...in earth...or...in the heavens... Col 1:20bc (KJV revised)

The reconciliation of things *under* heaven, that is, things in the earth, was achieved through the gospel, and Paul's ministry to the Gentiles (Col 1:23), but how was it accomplished for things in the heavens? The contrast between heaven and earth here is also illustrated in Ephesians:

> That in the dispensation of the fulness of times he might
> gather together in one all things in Christ, both which are in
> the heavens, and which are on earth; even in him... Eph 1:10
> (KJV revised); cf. John 11:52

In Ephesians 1, the expression 'the heavens' embraces those who will come (the future comes from the heavens). These will be gathered to Christ along with those of the present (Eph 2:15). This reading makes it easier to see how things are reconciled in the heavens and on the earth. In

---

[1] For example, R. J. Bauckham, *Jesus and the God of Israel* (Milton Keynes: Paternoster, 2008), 100, 101, says 1 Cor 8.6 is a "remarkable rewriting of the Shema'...this unprecedented reformulation of the Shema'."

[2] On which see T. Gaston and A. Perry, "Christological Monotheism: 1 Cor 8:6 and the Shema" *HBT* 39 (2017): 176-196.

a dispensation called 'the fulness of times', all things are gathered together in Christ. The type is clearly the gathering of the animals to Noah by God in the ark (Gen 6:20), but the type also goes back to the gathering of the animals to Adam by God (Gen 2:19).

God was in Christ reconciling the world to himself, making peace through the blood of the cross, and *by* Christ he was reconciling all things unto himself (2 Cor 5:18; Heb 2:17). Paul is not teaching universalism here, since all things are not reconciled as a *fait accompli*. Paul goes on to say that the Gospel was preached to every creature and *those to whom* Paul was writing *had been* reconciled. This shows that the character of the work of creation has to do with the position and status of men and women (Eph 2:10).

The relationship between Christ and God is clear, but elsewhere the 'for' and the 'by' are predicated of God alone:

> For it became him, for whom are all things, and by whom are all things... Heb 2:10 (KJV)

But the stress on people is still found, because the text goes on referring now to Christ:

> ...for whom are all...by whom are all...both he... and they...are all of one [flesh?] ... Heb 2:10-11(KJV)

And again, in this next text, the expression 'all things' is tied to a mention of people:

> For God hath concluded them all in unbelief, that he might have mercy on all...For of him, and through him, and to him, are all things: to whom be glory for ever. Rms 11:32-36 (KJV); cf. 1 Cor 11:2

The expressions *to him* and *for him* are conveying the point that those who receive God's mercy ascribe *to* him the glory and they are *for* him as a belonging. We set out a summary of early church teaching on 'all things', how the concept embraces the new creation of men and women in Christ and Christ's authority over the world, in Tables 1 and 2.

Of all the things that are through Christ, it is this connection between *things* and *people* that is made by John, but we need to translate the Greek differently to many versions. The RV mg. it right:

...All things were made through him; and without him there was not anything made. That which hath been made (ὃ γέγονεν ἐν αὐτῷ) was life in him; and the life was the light of men... John 1:3-4 (RV mg. revised)

B. M. Metzger comments on the punctuation of the Greek of these two verses as follows,

> A majority of the committee was impressed by the consensus of ante-Nicene writers (orthodox and heretical alike) who took ὃ γέγονεν with what follows. When however in the fourth century Arians and the Macedonian heretics began to appeal to the passage to prove that the Holy Spirit is to be regarded as one of the created things, orthodox writers preferred to take ὃ γέγονεν with the preceding sentence, thus removing the possibility of heretical usage of the passage.[1]

Athanasius (4c.), Irenaeus (2c.), Clement of Alexandria (2c.), Origen (3c.), and Tertullian (2c.), all quote John 1:3 without the phrase "that which was made" at the end of the verse giving, "that which was made was life in him".

The first five verses of John concern Jesus and his relationship to the *things* of the new creation. The claim of John is the same as that of Paul — all things were made from God *through* Jesus; or, in other words, all things were made (by God) by Christ. This approach is confirmed by the phrase '*without* him there was not anything made' (John 1:3), which implies partnership. (We would say today, of a colleague, '*without* him I would not have got the job done').[2]

---

[1] B. M. Metzger, *A Textual Commentary on the Greek New Testament* (London: United Bible Societies, 1971), 195, who cites in support the analysis of K. Aland "Eine Untersuchung zu Johannes 1, 3-4. Über die Bedeutung eines Punktes" *ZNW* 59 (1968): 174-209. Metzger demurred from the majority view. Hoskyns and Davey, *The Fourth Gospel*, 142-143, agrees with the GNT committee view that the RV mg. translation is more natural, it respects the rhythmical balance of the sentences, and is used by all orthodox and Gnostic writers before 350 CE except for Alexander. See also P. Comfort, *Early Manuscripts and Modern Translations* (Cambridge: Tyndale Press, 1990), 104-5, for a discussion.

[2] The emphasis here is on 'without him' rather than 'not anything made'. Commentators may argue that the scope of what was made is broader

All Things	
For of him, and through him, and to him are all things Rom 11:36, Heb 2:10	Here we have the three main prepositions: *out of, to,* and *through* the Father are all things.
Through him to reconcile all things unto himself Col 1:20, 2 Cor 5:18	God does the reconciling through Christ
Whom he hath appointed heir of all things Heb 1:2	Here the Father has gathered together things and the Son is the rightful heir.
All things...for him Col 1:16	All things given for the Son.
All things are delivered unto me of my Father Matt 11:27, John 17:7	The Father is passing down to his son his inheritance.
The Father loveth the Son and giveth all things into his hand John 3:35, 13:3	Again, the Father has things ready made to give to the Son.
For he hath put all things under his feet 1 Cor 15:27	The Father does the putting.
Head over all things, to the church Eph 1:22	This is the headship of the church.
Subdue all things unto himself Phil 3:21	This has an element of opposition.
Among all things he might have the pre-eminence Col 1:18	This includes principalities and powers.

Table 1

than 'life in him' because *nothing* has been made without him. See P. Borgen, "Creation, Logos and the Son: Observations on John 1:1-18 and 5:17-18" *Ex Auditu* 3 (1987): 88-97, (95).

All things	
The Father, of whom are all things, and we in him... Jesus Christ, through whom are all things, and we through him 1 Cor 8:6	A statement of partnership.
Who created all things through Jesus Christ Eph 3:9	
All things were made through him, and without him was not anything made John 1:3	
For in him were all things created Col 1:16	
All things that the Father hath are mine: therefore I said that he shall take of mine, and shall shew it unto you John 16:5, 1 Cor 2:10	All things are given to believers through the holy Spirit.
How shall he not with him also freely give us all things Rom 8:32, 1 Cor 3:21	
In him all things consist Col 1:17, Heb 1:3	Christ as sustainer.
Old things are passed away, behold all things are become new 2 Cor 5:17, Rev 21:4	Relationship between old and new things.

Table 2

A similar stress on partnership is seen regarding man and woman: 'neither is the man *without* the woman, neither the woman *without* the man' (1 Cor 11:11). Christ is **not** therefore presented as the Creator *sui generis* (that is, as uniquely the creator), but as one **with** whom the new creation was taking place (Rom 8:32). Hence, John will go on and state, "But as many as received him, to them he gave power to become the children of God, even to them that believe on his name, which were born, not of blood, nor of the will of the flesh, nor of the will of man, but of God" (John 1:12-13). The theme of the new creation is present throughout John's prologue.

This partnership in the new creation is a reflection of the cooperation between the Father and the angels in the original creation: '...Let *us* make man in our image...' (Gen 1:26).[1] And so of Christ it is written, '...for to *make* in himself of twain one new man so making peace...' (Eph 2:15).[2] Here we read that Christ is our peace, having abolished in his flesh the enmity in order to make in himself one new man by reconciling both Jew and Gentile unto God. Nevertheless, in Col 1:19-20, we read that *God* makes peace through the blood of his cross, and by Christ, reconciling all things unto himself, in the body of his flesh. So both God the Father and his son are involved with this work.

The 'life' made through Jesus (the Word) is characterized as being 'light':

> ...that which hath been made was <u>life</u> (ζωή) in him; and the life was the light of men... John 1:3-4(RV and RV mg.)

It is the 'in him' and John's use of 'life' that provides the key. Individuals have the water of life and the light in themselves (John 4:14; 11:10), but John is saying first that such lives are 'in Christ' (to use Paul's phraseology). This is all about spiritual life, as the metaphor of 'light' shows; it is not about the physical life of the Genesis creation.

> I am the vine, ye are the branches: he that abideth <u>in me</u>, and I in him, the same bringeth forth much fruit: for without me ye can do nothing. John 15:5 (KJV); cf. 6:56; 14:20; 15:2, 4, 6, 7; 16:33

---

[1] The male and the female are, together, *man*.
[2] See also John 5:17; 1 Cor 12:6; Eph 1:11; Phil 1:6; 3:21.

> But these are written, that ye might believe that Jesus is the
> Christ, the Son of God; and that believing ye might have <u>life</u>
> through his name. John 20:31 (KJV); cf. 5:39; 6:27; 12:25

The allusion in John 1:4 is to the making of Eve, the mother of all living. The LXX has the same interpretation and has Adam giving his wife the name 'Life' (ζωή, Gen 3:20). Therefore, John is saying that that which was built through Jesus 'in him' was 'Eve' (cf. 1 John 4:9).[1] The typology of Eve is that she represents the church, the bride of Christ. Hence, John changes his tense from the past to the present to say that the light is shining (Matt 5:14) but the darkness has not comprehended it (John 1:5).

Our Genesis perspective on John 1:1-5 is reinforced by the mention of darkness, because light requires darkness (Isa 6:9-10). This darkness was the state of the world at the time that the true Light came into the world (John 1:9; 12:35), and it persisted after his ascension, for the believers subsequently shone as lights in the darkness. This is what we would expect from Genesis 1, because in the beginning when God created the heavens and the earth, the earth was without form and empty, and darkness covered the face of the deep. The world of John's day was then a place of *darkness*.[2] Such darkness is as much the work of God as the subsequent introduction of order.

The fact of this darkness should not be dismissed in our thinking, for it is part of the pattern of creative redemption and new creation *through* a destruction of the old creation. When creations in God's purpose are destroyed, they return to darkness. If the people are darkened, then the creation of that people, which was initiated in light (!), has ended. Hence, the Gospel of John introduces us to a dark world into which the Light comes, and in which light subsequently shone.[3]

In Genesis, we are taught that God the Father created all things in heaven and earth and the sea (Acts 14:15; 17:24; Rev 4:11; 10:6). We also see that all things were placed under Adam (Gen 1:26; Ps 8:6). Adam was like Noah, given *all things* to eat (vegetable/animal, Gen 1:29; 9:3). He was also given dominion over all the beasts of the field (not the beasts of the

---

[1] The concept of life is important in the NT — believers rise from the dead to new life (Col 2:12-13).

[2] It is also what we would expect at the time of the exodus: the plague of darkness still saw Israel with lights, thus indicating that they were lights in that darkness (Exod 10:23).

[3] Pharaoh (Egypt) had his heart hardened, and destruction followed, with the emergence of the new creation of Israel.

earth), having had them first presented as companions (Gen 2:19; Ps 8:6-7).[1] Finally, he was given Eve.[2] We have then the following:

> All things *created* to fill heaven, earth and sea.
> All things placed *under* a man, ordered *by* him.
> All foodstuffs given *to* a man to eat.
> All creatures given to a man for dominion.

The idea of *all* in Genesis embraces *things*, including vegetation, and creatures, including animals; and we cannot exclude Eve from the domain of the idea either, because she was a work of God's hand, given to the man. This kind of usage of 'all things' can be found in the inter-testamental literature

Psalm 8 is an exposition of Genesis 2, and it acts as a filter for the NT usage of "all things". The NT employs the concept of 'all' from Psalm 8, and through this passage, the creation of Genesis 2 is brought into the NT as a backdrop to the apostolic age and a new creation. Thinking of both the First and the Last Adam, we read:

> For thou hast made him a little lower than the angels, and hast crowned him with glory and honour. thou madest him to have dominion over the works of thy hands; thou hast put all [things] under his feet: all sheep and oxen, yea, and the beasts of the field; the fowl of the air, and the fish of the sea, [and whatsoever] passeth through the paths of the seas. Ps 8:5-8 (KJV)

If[3] the idea of a new creation is valid, we should expect to find the expression 'all things' in connection with a new creation in the NT (and

---

[1] Dominion and companionship is implicit in Genesis 2, because Adam was given the beasts of the field to see *what names he would give them*.

[2] It is usually assumed that when Eve was created, she was the sole intended companion. This overlooks the fact that, as the mother of all life, Eve would have given birth to a large community of companions.

[3] We should not assume that the concept of a new creation is valid, it requires proof. This can be found in the reproduction of 'creation language' in the NT and the application of this language to the work of God at that time. A word study on the word 'new' helps here, see for example, the 'new commandment' given at the beginning (e.g. John 13:34; 2 John v. 5) and compare Adam's commandment; or the new covenant and compare Noah's covenant (e.g. Heb 12:24); or the new man (e.g. Eph

the OT). But if we do, we should be on the lookout not only for the idea of 'all', but also for the mention of creatures as well as a mention of the counterpart to Eve — the bride of Christ. Besides the idea of creation, we should be on the lookout for the idea of a man who is placed over the creation and *by (through)* whom the creation is ordered. We should also bear in mind that all things were given *to* the man, so the idea of *giving* should also feature prominently. All these elements should figure in something that was going on in the time of the apostles. When we go looking, we find all these ideas in both John and Paul.

It might be objected that we shouldn't use Paul to interpret John. We should instead take the 'grace and truth' that 'came' (ἐγένετο) through (διά) Jesus Christ (v. 17) to be solely the 'things' that 'came' (ἐγένετο) through (διά) the Word (v. 3). This is a relevant observation to make, however, the two things of grace and truth are only part of what comes through Jesus the Word. As indicative of the new covenant (in contrast to the Law of Moses), they are what brings about life in Christ (vv. 3c-4a).

8. The Light of the World
The light that is Eve is different to 'the Light' of John 1:7ff, and translations choose upper-case because they see a title 'the Light' in vv. 7-8, a title for Jesus, the Word, based on the fact that his life was the life and light of men. The subject of John 1:4-5 and John 1:7 is *light*, but the referent is different.[1] Identities are carried by individuals and often encapsulated in titles. Jewish traditions associated life and light with the wisdom of God in the Law. We now have the identity of Jesus as 'the Light' or 'the true Light' (John 1:9). The exegetical task is to distinguish what details cluster around this identity.

> The same came for a witness, to bear witness of the Light,
> that all might believe through him (δι' αὐτοῦ). He was not

4:24) or new creature (e.g. 2 Cor 5:17). The new heavens and new earth are yet future for when the man and the woman come together (Rev 21:1-2).

[1] Israel were to be the 'light' to the nations, and the Angel of the Presence stands to Israel as Christ stands to the renewal of Israel. This is shown by the fact that Israel had light when Egypt was in darkness (Exod 10:23); it is shown by the fact the Angel of the Lord gave them light, but Egypt darkness (Exod 13:21); it is shown by the fact they would have appeared as a train led by the Light in the wilderness; and it is also shown by the fact the candlestick represents Israel.

that one (ἐκεῖνος), the Light (τὸ φῶς), but he was sent to bear witness of the Light. John 1:7-8 (KJV revised)

John the Baptist is positioned here as a witness to 'the *true* Light', who was Jesus. The use of 'true' marks out Jesus in a way that the light of his bride is not marked, for Eve is the glory of the man (1 Cor 11:7). Jesus is the true Light and we need to determine the underlying type. John the Baptist was a lamp with light (John 5:34-36) but Jesus was the true Light.

Typology is like saying we have a paradigm; we are saying that Jesus is the archetype for any typological 'Light'. Other examples of this use of 'true' which involve typology include 'true riches' (Luke 16:11), 'true bread' (John 6:32), 'true vine' (John 15:1), 'true tabernacle' (Heb 8:2), 'figures of the true' (Heb 9:24) and 'true witness' (Rev 3:14[1]).

> In the beginning was the Word (ὁ λόγος)...This one (οὗτος) was ...towards God...This one (οὗτος) came for a witness...he was not that one (ἐκεῖνος), the Light... vv. 1-2, 7-8 (KJV revised)

We have translated the 'far' demonstrative ἐκεῖνος in v. 8 because it is pointing forward to 'the Light' (τὸ φῶς) in contradistinction to the 'near' demonstrative, 'this one' (οὗτος) in v. 7, which is pointing backwards to the one whose name was John (Ἰωάννης) in v. 6. However, a representative group of translations of v. 8 shows different approaches to the demonstrative.

> οὐκ ἦν ἐκεῖνος τὸ φῶς
>
> He was not that Light (KJV)
>
> He was not the Light (NASB)
>
> He himself was not the light (NET)
>
> That one was not the Light (YLT)

The most common choice among translators is that of the NASB which doesn't carry across the demonstrative. Translations often leave out the ἐκεῖνος but we should try and carry it across into English. The next most common choice is to translate the demonstrative as an emphasis giving

---

[1] Here the true witness is contrasted with the typical witness in the heavens of the rainbow (Ps 89:37) — all covenants require a witness.

'He himself [John the Baptist] was not the Light' (NET), which is possible. The YLT choice, 'That one [John the Baptist] was not the Light', looks implausible because John doesn't have ἐκεῖνος in the first position as was the case with οὗτος in v. 7, 'This one came...', and moreover, it would be more natural to repeat οὗτος if John the Baptist was the intended reference. On the other hand, we cannot know for certain what the reasons are for the word order; it could be that the negation is being stressed and ἐκεῖνος is in its position for that reason.

The KJV couples the demonstrative with 'Light' but stops short of making it appositional. The translation you choose is a matter of how you read the flow of John's prologue, but the position of ἐκεῖνος in v. 8 looks appositional.[1] Having used the near demonstrative οὗτος in v. 7 to refer to John the Baptist, it would be natural to use the far demonstrative ἐκεῖνος to refer to the Light.

> He was <u>the true Light</u>—the one who lightens every man—
> coming into the world. John 1:9 (NASB revised)

The syntactical issue with this verse is whether 'coming into the world' attaches to 'every man' or 'the true Light' as we translate the verse. Commentators are divided. Our choice is much more likely in view of the fact that John the Baptist's message revolved around there being one who was coming (Acts 19:4), and elsewhere in GJohn it is the Light that comes (John 3:19; 12:46).

The concept of 'the world' (κόσμος) here is a **societal concept**; it is about a world of people, a social environment; it is not a Genesis concept like 'the heavens and the earth' or 'the created environment'. The most common interpretation of 'the world' in John is 'the people', 'humanity' or 'humankind'. So, D. Guthrie is typical, "the world comes to stand for the whole order of existence into which men are born".[2] This approach is taken regardless of how a commentator translates v. 9.

---

[1] G. B. Winer, *A Treatise on the Grammar of New Testament Greek* (2nd ed.; Ed. W. F. Moulton; Edinburgh: T & T Clark, 1877), "That words in apposition, standing as they do on the same level with the nouns to which they are joined, agree with them in case, is a well-known rule: there is no such agreement in gender or number" (665).

[2] D. Guthrie, *New Testament Theology* (Leicester: InterVarsity Press, 1981), 130-135 (131).

Guthrie is not quite right; it is the *sense* of the word that is always about people, but the *reference* of the word can vary . The **focus** can be this or that group of people, depending on where a person is metaphorically standing and who is in their line of vision. We can see a 'them and us' usage of the term in, for example,

> Now if the fall of them be the riches of the world, and the diminishing of them the riches of the Gentiles; how much more their fulness? ... For if the casting away of them be the reconciling of the world, what shall the receiving of them be, but life from the dead? Rom 11:12, 15 (KJV)

This is a simple 'Jew-Gentile' contrast in which only the Gentiles are 'the world'. Again, Gentile converts are 'aliens from the commonwealth of Israel' and 'without God in the world' (Eph 2:12), but when they are baptised, they are graffed into Israel (Rom 11:17); the contrast here is between Israel and the world. Again, there is a sense in which believers 'come out of the world' when they choose to follow Christ (1 John 2:15-17; 3:1, 13, 17; 4:5; 5:4; John 17:6, 9, 14, 16). In short, 'the world' is not so much 'the people' as those outside of the individual and outside of the group in which the individual is a member. In this kind of speech, the reference of 'the world' is not humankind but those who are not of you and your group.

Exactly who is the focus of a use of 'the world' in GJohn can be determined from the context. There may be a more general reference to all of humankind or there may be a focus on a specific group. A Jew living in Judea or Galilee in the 1c. might think of the world that was presence of Rome, or the world that was the Hellenistic environment in which he lived, or the world that was his own people, its Temple and Law, or even just the people out there around him on the street and in the community.

The term for 'the world', κόσμος (*kosmos*), is prominent in GJohn (78x) in comparison to the Synoptics (15x) and we should note when different speakers use the word (Jesus, the Pharisees, the Samaritans, the narrator). Jesus uses κόσμος frequently to refer to those he is among and who are not 'of him', particularly those who are against him, i.e. those who are religious leaders among the people. For each of its uses in GJohn, we can ascertain the **scope** of κόσμος from the context.

Jesus' own sense of his mission was that he was sent to the lost sheep of the house of Israel and this sets the primary focus of his uses of 'the

234

world': he doesn't use the term for all of humankind but for his own people who were either for or against him – the society to which he came, whether the people on the streets or those who were vocal in their opposition.

John, as the voice of the narrator, follows Jesus' own usage of 'the world'. Hence, he writes that the true Light, coming to the world, came to his own home (v. 11). However, these people did not receive him, because they did not know him.

> The true Light ...was <u>coming</u> to (εἰς) the world...he <u>came</u> to (εἰς) his own home (εἰς τὰ ἴδια[1]), and his own people (οἱ ἴδιοι) received him not. John 1:9-11 (RSV)

This summary statement defines the focus of 'the world' in GJohn. Jesus' perspective is towards those around him and this limits the focus of 'the world'. The problem for modern readers is that they have a different and larger understanding of the scope of the term: we might think of the whole world, the Western world, the world order, the third world, a world in need of salvation, *and so on*. We have a tradition of reading John for our own times and our own sense of 'the world'.

The scope of 'the world' is a *crux interpretum* for John 1:10 and the wider understanding of the term is why it is read as a pre-existence text. But the scope of κόσμος in GJohn should be interpreted in terms Jesus' sense of those who not 'of him' among whom he ministered.[2]

There are two other texts that talk about the *existence* of 'the world'—John 17:5, 24. Along with John 1:10, these texts give us, 'the world was made through him', 'before the world was' and 'before the foundation of the world'. All three texts mutually define the scope and nuance of κόσμος for Jesus and the narrator of GJohn.

John 17 is a prayer of Jesus to his father in which he uses κόσμος 18x to refer to God's people. The following points delimit its scope:

a) Scripturally, the 'foundation' of the world (John 17:24) was the Law and the Mosaic covenant. This is clear from

---

[1] This idiom is consistently translated in the LXX as 'to home' (Est 5:10; 6:12; 3 Macc 6:27, 37; 7:8); see also John 16:32, 19:27; and Acts 21:6.

[2] We can usefully contrast 1 John 2:2, 5:19 where we have a concept of 'the whole world'.

Matt 13:35 and its quotation of Ps 78:2-5. Here the 'foundation' is the 'establishment' from 'of old' of the Law in Israel. This identifies 'the world' as the nation and its foundation under Moses. Paul uses a similar concept of 'the world' and the mystery of the gospel that the princes of the world did not understand (Rom 16:25; 1 Cor 2:6-8).

b) Hebrews contrasts the Law of Moses and its sacrifices with the sacrifice and priesthood of Christ. Jesus was a priest after the order of Melchizedek and not after the Levitical order (Heb 7:11). Had he been a Levitical priest, Christ would have had to suffer repeatedly in order to match the pattern of the High Priest entering the Holy of Holies once a year, a practice that had happened since the 'foundation of the world'. But Christ's sacrifice was offered once, appropriately, at the 'end of the world', i.e. the end of the Mosaic order (Heb 9:26-27).

c) The glory that Christ had with the Father 'before the world was' (John 17:5) is a glory he had before the foundation of the nation under Moses. Christ viewed his imminent death and resurrection as a glorification which *he had already had* with the Father *before the world was*. Such an experience *with a father* occurred in type before the world began. Abraham and Isaac, a father and son, went together to make a sacrifice. And so it is with Jesus and *his father*, for both had set their faces towards Jerusalem (the same Mount Moriah) to make a sacrifice. Abraham lifted up his eyes and *saw* (cf. John 8:56; Heb 11:13) Mount Moriah *afar off* (Gen 22:4). Abraham believed that God would raise his son from the dead (Heb 11:17-19) and it was accounted to him for righteousness; he was a righteous father who loved his son Isaac. In this he foreshadowed the Righteous Father who loved the Son before the foundation of the world (John 17:24-25). Jesus saw in the resurrection of Isaac his own resurrection. Abraham's sacrifice of Isaac was accounted to him for righteousness (Rom 4:3), and in this 'sacrifice' Jesus sees himself in God's mind and he sees God's love for him.[1]

---

[1] Jesus calls his father, 'the only true God' which picks up on God being true to his promise to Abraham about a seed that he would send; hence 'and Jesus Christ whom you have sent' (John 17:3).

236

Jesus saw the people around him as 'the world' and it is with this scope that we should understand the 'in/out' language of his prayer. The world is the outside of an inside/outside relation; the world is the other side of a boundary. Jesus was not 'of the world' whereas his opponents were 'of the world' (John 8:23). Hence, his disciples and followers are 'in the world' but not 'of the world' (John 17:11, 13, 14, 16; cf. 13:1; 15:19), because they had been taken 'out of' the world (John 17:6, 15). This language is a description of the covenant people but without any recognition of their covenant status. They had   a true foundation and a beginning under Moses, but they **had become** 'the world'. The people were now like Egypt and those who responded in faith were like the children of Israel of old 'coming out' of Egypt. (John 8:33, 36; cf. 2 Cor 6:16-17).

This usage of 'the world' for the people of Israel is consistent for Jesus, and we can suppose that the narrator understands Jesus' conception of 'the world'. Jesus' negative characterization of Israel, the people and its religious leaders, is reflected in the narrator's comments in John 1:9-10; 3:16-17, 19; 13:1; and 21:25.

We can group the usage of κόσμος in the following way:

1) The world *hated* Jesus because he testified that its deeds were evil (John 7:7; 15:18), but not everyone hated him because many wanted him to heal them (particularly those of Galilee). Jesus also says that the world hated him because he had done works *among them* (John 15:24). This tells us that 'the world' is comprised of those who were jealous of his works. So, for example, the Jews wanted to stone him for his works (John 10:31-32); these were those of Jerusalem and Judea who were against him (John 7:1). Jesus goes onto say that their hatred was a fulfilment of prophecies in *their law* (John 15:24; from Ps 35:19; 69:4), which clearly identifies the scope of 'the world' to be particularly his religious opponents. The world would rejoice and be glad at his death and this describes the gladness of those of the temple who plotted to kill Jesus (John 16:20; Luke 22:5; Mark 14:11).

2) Jesus uses the expression, 'the prince of this world' (John 12:31; 14:30; 16:11), when referring to his imminent arrest and crucifixion. This was about to happen ('now') and it was a prince of *this* world he was talking about. As he neared the time of his arrest, he warns his disciples that the prince of the world was coming but would have nothing on him. The word for 'prince' is the ordinary word for 'ruler', and in GJohn it is used for religious authorities (John 3:1; 7:26, 48; 12:42), and the singular expression 'prince of this world' would pick out Caiaphas the High Priest (John 11:49, 51). Jesus' trial before the High Priest (John 18) was

ostensibly for his judgement but Jesus' reverses this perception by saying that his trial would be for the judgement of 'this world'. He prophesies that 'the prince of this world' would be 'cast out' and this picks up on the fear of being put out of the synagogue which the Jews were doing to followers of Jesus (9:22; 12:42). Jesus was saying that the High Priest would be cast out of the kingdom (John 6:37; see Matt 8:12; Luke 13:28).[1]

3) Jesus says that he was *sent* to the world (John 8:26; 10:36). The most famous verse in GJohn is, "God so loved the world that he gave his only begotten son...For God sent not his Son into the world to condemn the world, but that the world through him might be saved" (John 3:16-17). The purpose of Jesus coming into the world was to save the world (John 12:47). Readers today apply these texts to themselves and therefore the whole world, but Matthew records Jesus saying that he was *sent* to the lost sheep of the house of Israel (Matt 15:24). Jesus says that just as he had been sent to the world, he had sent his disciples (John 17:18); Luke records this mission to "every city and place" that Jesus had already visited in the land (Luke 10:1).

On the other hand, the purpose in Jesus coming into 'the world' was also judgment: "For judgment I am come into this world, that they which see not might see; and that they which see might be made blind." (John 9:39; 18:37). Here Jesus quotes Isa 6:9-10, "Go, and tell this people, 'Hear ye indeed, but understand not; and see ye indeed, but perceive not.'" The world could not receive 'the Spirit of Truth' because it could not 'see' him as prophesied by Isaiah (John 14:17; cf. 8:26). The application of this prophecy is to Israel and so the scope of 'the world' here and in John 3:16-17 is narrow. The reason why these texts are timeless and relevant to us is that Jesus is configuring the people of Israel, and particularly those who opposed him, as 'the world'.

4) The world was in 'darkness' and this is explicitly stated and implied by Jesus being the Light of the World (John 1:9-10; 8:12; 9:5). The darkness evokes both the Genesis creation and the light that Israel had while Egypt was in darkness, except that now the people of Israel were in darkness (i.e. like Egypt and like the darkness over the deep). The darkness is a state of non-belief in Christ (John 12:46). This 'darkness' was 'of men' whose deeds were evil (John 3:19); it was to this world that Jesus came as the

---

[1] It is beyond our scope to discuss Jewish mythology surrounding Satan and the Devil; our position is that Jesus is applying such terminology to the Jewish authorities.

Light of the World (John 8:12; 9:5; 11:9). He taught openly in the world, in synagogue and temple, wherever the Jews congregated (John 18:20).

5) Jesus uses 'the world' to characterize Israel negatively, but some of the other individuals recorded in GJohn will have used 'the world' without this characterization; we might say that these others had a 'normal' usage of κόσμος for 'the people'. The Pharisees express at one point that 'the world is gone after him' (John 12:19) and this is clearly just a reference to the people. Similarly, Jesus' family urge him to show himself openly to the world by which they mean particularly Judea (John 7:3-4). The Samaritans declare that 'Jesus is the saviour of the world' (John 4:42), but Jesus has just said to the Samaritan woman that "Salvation is out of (ἐκ) the Jews" (John 4:22). Those Samaritans who had faith would have had a concept of the world that embraced them, i.e. it would be larger in scope.

6) The disciples and the people may have understood Jesus' nuanced usage of 'the world' or they may have used κόσμος in a normal way. There was an expectation among the people that a prophet would *come* into the world (John 6:14), but Jesus' followers express the stronger belief that the Christ, or the Son of God, was to *come* into the world (John 11:27). Both beliefs are part of the scriptural heritage of Israel, i.e. prophets and the Messiah were 'of Israel' (Deut 18:15; Dan 9:25-26). Judas queries why Jesus will not manifest himself to the world (John 14:22), and perhaps he would have no understanding of Jesus' teaching about 'the world'. John the Baptist, on the other hand, understands Jesus' mission as the lamb of God.

7) We can expect Jesus' teaching about 'the world' to carry his negative characterization of Israel as he warns his disciples; we can certainly see this nuanced understanding of 'the world' in his prayer to his father in John 17. When he talks to others, they no doubt understand him on their own terms. As readers we can read him either way in such situations. So, to Pilate he says that his kingdom was not of this world, otherwise his servants would fight, but he further localises 'the world' when he says that his kingdom is 'not from here'; i.e. his kingdom would not begin from that Jerusalem (John 18:36; cf. Luke 4:9).

The above groupings, (1)-(7), on the usage of κόσμος, show that Jesus' had a consistent view of Israel and those who opposed him as 'the world'. We can see the more normal concept of 'the world' on the lips of the Pharisees and Samaritans, the people and perhaps the disciples. Jesus however nuances this societal concept of 'the world' in negative ways when applying it to his own people. John has followed this usage in his narrative commentary, and it is to this 'world' that Jesus came as 'the Light'.

> But as many as received him, to them he gave the right to become children of God, even to those who believe in his name... John 1:12 (NASB)

Those that did receive him, he gave power to become the 'children (τέκνον) of God' (John 1:12; 11:52). The echo here is to the 'children of Israel' and their collective identity as God's firstborn son (Exod 4:22-23)—Jesus, who was sent to the lost sheep of the house of Israel, made those who believed in him members of the *true* Israel.[1] This typology is an exodus/wilderness one based on the Angel of the Lord who led the nation from Egypt.[2]

The introduction of John the Baptist as 'a man sent' (John 1:6) echoes the description of Moses 'the man' sent from God (Exod 3:14; 11:3, Num 12:3). This in turn means that the type behind 'the true Light' of John 1 is the Angel of the Lord to whom Moses was a witness.[3] John confirms this when he records Jesus' words, "I am the Light of the World; he that *follows* me shall not walk in darkness but have the light of life" (John 8:12). The

---

[1] On this, see Kyunga Ra, *New Exodus in John* (London: Apostolos Publishing, 2018), 46.

[2] Light is a common OT metaphor and we could attempt to construct a typology based on the Servant of the Lord (Isa 42:6, 'light to the Gentiles') or the Arm of the Lord (Isa 60:1) since these are messianic prophecies. See S. R. Davis 'Jesus is Light: The Meaning of Light in the Gospel of John' (MA Thesis; Reformed Theological Seminary; 2018), 49-50, [Online]. We might also construct a typology contrasting Jesus as the true Light with the Law of Moses where we think of light as illumination for life. However, John's narrative seems to require a typology of leadership and presence rather than one centred on the Law. See P. Borgen, "Logos was the True Light: Contributions to the Interpretation of the True Light", *Nov. T.* 14/2 (1972): 115-130 (123-125), for a Law based typology.

[3] There is Genesis typology in John's prologue but there is also exodus/wilderness typology, particularly from v. 6 onwards. See Evans, *Word and Glory*, 77-83, who cites other commentaries; see Whittaker. *Studies in the Gospels*, 45-55, who sets out the exodus typology in detail. We should distinguish the wilderness journey from the deliverance from Egypt in our typological interpretation.

allusion here is to the Israelites *following* the pillar of fire at night through the wilderness (Exod 13:21; cf. Isa 9:2; 42:6; 60:1).[1]

The Angel of the Lord gave Israel light during the plague of darkness, Exod 10:23, '...all the children of Israel *had light* in their dwellings ...' (cf. Esth 8:16).[2] The Angel of the Lord had appeared as a light first to Moses at the bush (Acts 7:30, 35), and then after the plague of darkness to Israel when taking them out of Egypt, he stood as a pillar of fire to protect the nation at the Red Sea (Exod 14:19-20; Num 14:14). He then led Israel through the wilderness, again as a pillar of fire and a cloud (cf. Exod 40:38; Num 9:15; Deut 1:33). John presents the Angel of the Lord in the exodus as a type of Jesus.[3]

> He was in the world, and the world was made <u>through him</u> (δι᾽ αὐτοῦ), and the world did not know <u>him</u> (αὐτὸν[4]). John 1:10 (NASB)

Commentators take this to be a pre-existence verse, but we have noted that the concept of 'the world' for John is societal (that of the Jews), so it is not about the Genesis creation. An insight into the work of the Angel of the Lord is provided by the remark made to Moses, 'I will *make* of thee a great nation' (Exod 32:10 (quoting Gen 12:2); Num 14:12). This remark shows the angel's own perspective upon his exodus work — it concerned *making a people*.[5] He had delivered the people from the destroying angel, brought the children of Israel out of Egypt and delivered them again at the Red Sea, and the Israelites had responded by making *false gods* whom they claimed had brought them out of Egypt (Exod 32:4). The Angel of the Lord's response to this was a proposal that he make of Moses a great nation, and he would have destroyed the people. This shows us how he

---

[1] Carter, *The Gospel of John*, 103-105.

[2] Hence, we read that light comes into the world and that men should not live in darkness (John 3:19; 12:46).

[3] Classic studies of typology have made this connection; see A. M. Hodgkin, *Christ in All the Scriptures* (London: Pickering & Inglis, 1922), 16.

[4] The definite masculine pronouns in vv. 10-11 are commonly taken to pick up on ὁ λόγος. See P. Borgen, "Logos was the True Light: Contributions to the Interpretation of the True Light", 122; H. Alford, *The Greek Testament* (4 vols; London: Rivingtons, 1859), 1:645, makes a similar point about the third person masculine pronoun in v. 10.

[5] Other verses which mention the *making activity* of the Angel of the Lord are Exod 4:11; 14:21; 15:25; 24:8; and 1 Sam 12:6. Certain Psalms also describe the creative activity of the angel, e.g. Pss 95:6; 100:3.

viewed his work for God; he viewed his work as one of *making a nation*. Moses' intercession saved the people on that day.

The allusions in John's prologue then direct our attention to the exodus and the work of the Angel of the Lord. This work was a *creative* work in which a 'world' was made, and this 'world' was the **nation**. Such a work was a continuation of the promises to Abraham, Isaac, and Jacob, for God through the Angel of the Lord had likewise declared to Abraham that he would *make* of him a great nation (Gen 12:2).

Other elements of vv. 6-13 fit this OT typology.[1] For example,

(1) Moses had asked the Angel of the Lord for his *name*, and the *name* of the Lord was placed in the angel (Exod 23:21), and so John comments of the Jews of his day that some 'believed on his (Christ's) *name*' (John 1:12).

(2) Again, Christ came to 'his own (people)', and the belonging of a people is an emphasis we find in Exodus – "And I will take you *to me* for a people, and I will be to you a God: and ye shall know that I [am] the Lord your God, who bringeth you out from under the burdens of the Egyptians" (Exod 6:7; 1 Chron 17:21; Ps 78:52). When the people rejected the Angel of the Lord, God's representative, and fashioned golden calves, the Levites remained faithful and they were rewarded with the office of priesthood — they became the 'sons' of God (Exod 32:29, RSV). Similarly, in John's day, those who believed on the name of Christ, were given power to become children of God (John 1:12).[2]

(3) The word became flesh and tabernacled with the disciples (John 1:14ab), just as the Angel of the Lord had tabernacled with Israel and manifested the presence of Yahweh (Exod 33:14-17; 40:34; Isa 63:9). The word (*dabar*) of Moses was fulfilled in Jesus (Exod 33:17). The nation had beheld the glory of the Angel of the Presence reflected in the face of Moses (Exod 33:18; 34:29-30) and likewise, the disciples beheld the glory of Christ (John 1:14c).[3] Jesus was full of grace and truth (John 1:14e) just

---

[1] See M. Hooker, "The Johannine Prologue and the Messianic Secret" *NTS* 21 (1974): 40-58 (43-44); A. T. Hanson, "John 1:14-18 and Exodus 34" *NTS* 23 (1976): 90-101.

[2] This is ironic because it was the priests and Levites who came out to challenge John the Baptist in John 1.

[3] Another example where Christ is equated with the Angel of the Lord is found in 2 Cor 4:17 — 'Now the Lord is that Spirit'. This is an identity in typology, because Paul is inviting us to see the Angel of the Lord who

as the name that the Angel of the Lord proclaimed was "abundant in goodness and truth" (Exod 34:6[1]).

(4) Instead of the grace of the Law the disciples had received the grace of a new covenant, for the Law was given through Moses but grace and truth came through Jesus Christ who was the Light (John 1:16-17). The disciples had received 'grace for grace' and the type here lies in Moses' statement, "if I have found grace in thy sight, shew me now thy way, that I may know thee, that I may find grace in thy sight" (Exod 33:13). Moses has grace but seeks another grace based on a knowledge of God's way.

(5) No man had ever *seen* God (John 1:18a), as the Angel of the Lord had said to Moses, "You cannot *see* my face, for no man can see me and live!" (Exod 33:20). The Angel then *proclaimed* the name of the Lord (Exod 34:5). Moses carried Israel in his bosom as a father and complained about the burden (Num 11:12); Jesus was in the bosom of the Father (John 1:18c) and he *explained* him (John 1:18d).

Abraham's function as a type of the Father is alluded to in the text that describes the only begotten son as 'in the bosom of the Father' (John 1:18). The Parable of the Rich Man and Lazarus supplies one clue to the interpretation of this word picture. In that parable, it is Lazarus (symbolizing those with faith), who is in the *bosom of Abraham*, and not the Rich Man, who (with his 'five' brethren) symbolizes the Jews and their Law. As Jesus demonstrates in John 8, Abraham is not the father of those Jews who do not have faith in him. In John 1, the contrast is in the same vein - a contrast between the Law of Moses and grace and truth (v. 17). Hence John states that the only begotten son *was* in the bosom of the Father. Abraham's beloved son was Isaac, and he was the son of the free woman. Those who are in the bosom of the Father are those who are born of Sarah and not of the bondwoman (who was wrongly placed into the bosom of Abraham (Gen 16:5; Gal 4:24)). This typology is set out in the table below:

---

revealed God to Moses on Sinai *as* Christ. Believers are like Moses beholding with open face the glory of the Lord (Exod 33:23). And this glorious Light is reflected upon them as their faces shine as lights to the world. In this way, their image is changed by the Lord the Spirit (2 Cor 3:18). This light that they are given is a ministry of righteousness, and this is made with great plainness of speech, and without the use of a veil, which Moses used whenever he communicated the words of the Lord to the people (Exod 34:32-35).

[1] John is modifying 'goodness' with 'grace' from Exod 33:13.

John 1	Exodus
A man sent v. 6	I will send thee Exod 3:10
Whose name was John v. 6	I know thee by name Exod 34:12, 17
To bear witness of the Light v. 7	Moses' testimony to the Angel of the Lord
Lighteth every man v. 9	Pillar of Fire
Many received him not, but some received him vv. 11-12	Some murmured but not Levi
Believe on his name v. 12	Levi was faithful
Become sons of God v. 12	Adoption of Levi as the priestly tribe Exod 32:29 (RSV)
Dwelt among us v. 14	Go thou amongst us Exod 34:9 My presence shall go with you Exod 33:14
And the word became flesh and tabernacled v. 14	Angel of the Presence in the tabernacle Exod 40:34
We beheld his glory v. 14	Show me thy glory Exod 33:18 Moses' face shone Exod 34:29

This deployment of typology is like Paul's use of 'the rock' (1 Cor 10:1-5). The people journeyed through the wilderness with a rock, and Paul comments that this rock was Christ. So, they journeyed with Christ through the desert. But the rock that was struck was a literal rock, and the water was provided by the Angel of the Lord who led them through the wilderness. He sustained them by day with manna (also Christ) and water. So, Christ went with them and sustained them, if only they had eyes to see the doctrine being taught in their midst. Christ was there *in type*, as Paul says, the exodus/wilderness journey was a type, and the things that happened to the Israelites were types.

In the narrative story of Genesis-Exodus, the Light of the World is the Angel of the Lord; he brought Israel out of Egypt. His work was the making of Abraham's people (his seed), fulfilling the promise in Genesis 17 that Abraham would be the father of a multitude (Gen 17:2, 7). The reason why John's prologue has both Genesis and then Exodus typology presenting the reality of Jesus and the new creation is to tie that reality into God's purpose with the earth since creation.

The Jews were blinded in their reading of their Scriptures because they did not see Christ in its pages (2 Cor 3:14). The glory that shone on Moses' face was the glory of the Angel of the Lord and this glory was a glory depicting the glory of the name of the Lord (Exod 33:19). Moses covered up this glory, at the request of the people. In this act the people illustrated that they could not look to the end of the Law, which was Christ (2 Cor 3:13; Rom 10:4). Instead of beholding this glory with Moses, it was veiled from them in type and figure. Once it is realized that John sees Jesus in the role of the Angel of the Lord acting as the voice of God there is no basis for affirming pre-existence. Jesus is present in OT history only in an *ideal* sense but that isn't an existence.

There is an association of light and the baptism of Christ in Justin Martyr and the Diatessaron and others.[1] In Justin's *Dialogue with Trypho the Jew*, 88, he records that when Jesus entered the water, "a fire was kindled in the Jordan". In Ephrem's commentary on the Diatessaron IV.5, we read, "And when he had seen, from the bright light upon the water and by the voice from heaven…". And this is supported in other witnesses to the Diatessaron.   Epiphanius (4c. CE) reports that the Ebionites used a 'Hebrew Gospel' in which it was stated that "immediately a great light shone around the place". The mention of a light also found its way into two Latin manuscripts prior to the Vulgate, "a great light shone about from the water" and "a big light shone from the water". This tradition also seems to be reflected in the Sibylline Oracles 7. 81-84 (3c. CE), which interestingly use the title of 'the Word' for Christ,

> As the Father begot you, the Word, so I have dispatched a
> bird, a word which is swift reporter of words, sprinkling
> with holy waters your baptism, through which you were
> revealed out of fire. *Sib. Or.* 7. 81-84 (OTP[2])

With such a diverse and early set of witnesses[3] to this extra-canonical tradition about Jesus' baptism, it is interesting to note both the prologue's

---

[1] The evidence is set out in W. L. Peterson, *Tatian's Diatessaron: Its Creation, Dissemination, Significance, & History in Scholarship* (Leiden: E. J. Brill, 1994), 14-21. [Online].

[2] J. H., Charlesworth, ed., *The Old Testament Pseudepigrapha* (2 vols; New York: Doubleday, 1983-1985).

[3] J. R. Edwards, *The Hebrew Gospel and the Development of the Synoptic Tradition* (Grand Rapids: Eerdmans, 2009), 71, notes "the tradition of a light/fire at Jesus' baptism is very old and pervasive in early Christian tradition".

mention of 'the Light', its context of John the Baptist's ministry, and the 'baptism' reading of 'And so the word became flesh' (see below).

9. The world was made through him

In modern parlance, the expression 'the making of the world' means the creation of the earth, but we saw in the last chapter that in GJohn 'the world' is a societal concept. Jesus was then *in that world* circumscribed as the world of his own nation rather than among the peoples of the whole world.[1]

The identity of Jesus as 'the true Light' (v. 9) is placed alongside his previous identity as 'the Word', which was introduced to us in v. 1. The identification of the Word and the true Light as Jesus is made explicit in vv. 14-18 (v. 17). This is shown in two ways. First, as we have already indicated, we should note John's consistent use of the far demonstrative ἐκεῖνος,

> In the beginning was the Word (ὁ λόγος)...This one (οὗτος) was in the beginning...This one (οὗτος) came for a witness...he was not that one (ἐκεῖνος), the Light...the only begotten son, that one (ἐκεῖνος) has explained him. vv. 1-2, 7-8, 18 (KJV revised[2])

There is a chain of reference in the demonstratives, secured in v. 18 with the description, 'the only begotten son'. The 'only begotten' is identified as 'the word made flesh' in v. 14; and he is in turn identified in v. 15 as the one to whom John the Baptist bore witness, whom we have seen was the true Light.

Secondly, we should note the way John introduces the name 'Jesus Christ', as part of a refrain in the prologue of ἐγένετο + διά, which we will translate consistently with 'came' and 'through',

---

[1] The idea that Israel should be taken as 'the World' is unusual by today's standards of socio-political commentary. On this approach, see J. W. Pryor, "Jesus and Israel in the Fourth Gospel – John 1:11" *Nov. T.* 32/3 (1990): 201-218. That the nation of Israel should be regarded as equivalent to a creation is based on links between Exodus and Genesis 1 and 2, on which see A. Perry, *Beginnings and Endings* (2nd ed. Rev. 3; Sunderland: Willow Publications, 2018).

[2] The textual issue here is whether 'son' is original with 'the only begotten'; we discuss this below in the Appendix.

All things came <u>through</u> him...the world came <u>through</u> him...grace and truth came <u>through</u> Jesus Christ...

...πάντα δι' αὐτοῦ ἐγένετο... ὁ κόσμος δι' αὐτοῦ ἐγένετο... ἡ χάρις καὶ ἡ ἀλήθεια διὰ Ἰησοῦ Χριστοῦ ἐγένετο

This second structure identifies Jesus Christ as 'the Word'. The δια is distinctively used of Jesus. This preposition is used of agency: someone does something *through* someone else. Thus, God sent his son into the world so that the world might be saved *through* him (John 3:16-17); or again, God did signs and wonders *through* Christ (Acts 2:22). For this reason, when John states in v. 7 "that all men might believe through him", we should take the 'him' as Christ and not John the Baptist. Accordingly, John 1:10 is not affirming that Jesus is the Genesis creator, but rather that the world that was the nation was made *through him*.[1]

What we see in these two structures is John identifying the reference of 'the Word' and 'the true Light' as Jesus Christ. The Genesis and Exodus types we have so far traced in the prologue have revolved around these identities. We now need to consider v. 10 and its typology.

He was in the world, and the world was made <u>through him</u> (δι' αὐτοῦ), and the world did not know <u>him</u> (αὐτὸν). John 1:10 (NASB)

Here we see Jesus but not configured as 'the Light'. We know this because we have the masculine pronoun (αὐτὸν) rather than a neuter one which would link with 'the Light' (τὸ φῶς); instead, the masculine pronoun links with the masculine demonstrative 'that one' (ἐκεῖνος) in v. 8 and then ultimately back to the masculine noun 'the Word' (ὁ λόγος) of v. 1, who we know from the two syntactic patterns we described above is Jesus Christ, the only begotten son.

In terms of Jesus being both the Word and the Light, the world was made through him in type. We noted in the last chapter that in one sense the nation was made *by* the Angel of the Lord in the events narrated in Exodus. This is a 'making by x' and God 'making *through* x'. The Angel of the Lord as a type of the true Light.

However, it is the Word that is the reference of the masculine pronoun in v. 10. The typology that we are looking at is one where Jesus as 'the Word'

---

[1] This is clearer in the RSV than the KJV which has 'made by him'.

is the one through whom the nation came or was made: the nation was made through the word of God.

What we have in v. 10 is a reference to the word of God through Moses and Aaron. God directs Moses through his word and Moses uses the word of God to deliver the people. Thus, we can see in the extended conversation between Yahweh and Moses at the burning bush Moses' concern for his voice in the signs that Moses was to perform to Pharaoh; the inadequacy of his own voice; and the provision of the voice and mouth of Aaron. God promises that he would be both Moses and Aaron's mouth and it is through what would therefore be the word of God that Israel were delivered.

> Then Moses said to the Lord, "Please, Lord, I have never been eloquent, neither recently nor in time past, nor since Thou hast spoken to Thy servant; for I am slow of speech and slow of tongue." And the Lord said to him, "Who has made man's mouth? Or who makes him dumb or deaf, or seeing or blind? Is it not I, the Lord? Now then go, and I, even I, will be with your mouth, and teach you what you are to say." But he said, "Please, Lord, now send the message by whomever Thou wilt." Then the anger of the Lord burned against Moses, and He said, "Is there not your brother Aaron the Levite? I know that he speaks fluently. And moreover, behold, he is coming out to meet you; when he sees you, he will be glad in his heart. And you are to speak to him and put the words in his mouth; and I, even I, will be with your mouth and his mouth, and I will teach you what you are to do. Moreover, he shall speak for you to the people; and it shall come about that he shall be as a mouth for you, and you shall be as God to him." Exod 4:10-16 (NASB)

Typology is characteristic of GJohn. Jesus is placed into the middle of typological situations. By placing him into the middle of such situations, it can appear on the surface as if Jesus had some manner of existence before his birth but perceiving the typology in the narrative prevents such a reading. The basic mistake that commentators make with the Gospel of John, when they argue for the pre-existence of Christ, is to misconstrue or miss altogether the typological language.[1] The perception of typology is a reader-response to the text; some will not see a type where others do see

---

[1] In doing this they copy the Jews, who also did not understand who Jesus was; *the world knew him not.*

one. Further, types may lose their hold on a reader – they once saw a type and then they no longer see one. Types may be present in one verse but not the next; readers can extend a type too far. It's easy to get types wrong.[1]

An objection can be put forward against this typology. Early exegesis in the Apostolic Fathers of 'the world' in John is not related to Israel. For example, take the *Epistle to Diognetus*,

> For God has loved <u>mankind</u>, on whose account he made the world, to whom he rendered subject all the things that are in it, to whom he gave reason and understanding, to whom alone he imparted the privilege of looking upwards to himself, whom he formed after his own image, to whom he <u>sent his only-begotten Son</u>, to whom he has promised a kingdom in heaven, and will give it to those who have loved him. *Ep. Diog.* 10.2

This text is using John 3:16 in its reference to God's love of mankind and his sending of an only begotten son. It reads 'the world' in GJohn as 'mankind'. The author of the *Epistle to Diognetus* is perhaps the earliest exponent of what is the common commentary position of reading 'humankind' for 'the world'. This objection is sweeping in its scope. It rejects the 'Israel' interpretation of 'the world' for GJohn and the Exodus typology of Moses and Aaron being the 'Word of God' delivering the people.

We have already argued the case for a focus on Jesus' own people for 'the world' in GJohn. We can make two additional points. Commentators intuitively sense that a text such as John 3:16 has a general application. If in that text 'the world' applies to all men and women, so too it must in John 1:10.[2] This overlooks how the focus of 'the world' is dependent on the perspective of the speaker or the narrator. God's love for Israel is

---

[1] In earlier editions and drafts of this book we have argued for a Passover Lamb typology in v. 10 because John mentions Jesus as 'the Lamb of God' and the nation was delivered from the destroying angel through the blood of the Passover Lamb. We have also argued for a typology based on the sacrifice of Isaac because that foreshadows God's provision of a lamb and the nation came through Isaac's death and resurrection on Moriah.

[2] P. Borgen, "Creation, Logos and the Son: Observations on John 1:1-18 and 5:17-18" *Ex Auditu* 3 (1987): 88-97, (93), attempts to circumvent this issue by asserting that Israel represents the world.

well-attested in the Prophets (e.g. Jer 31:3; Ezek 16:8); they are the nation whom God chose to marry. It was to Israel that Jesus was sent. But, as the gospel is taken to the Gentiles by the apostles, the scope of John 3:16 naturally widens and comes to have a universal application.

Our conclusion therefore is that Jesus as the 'the Word' is brought forward from v. 1 into v. 10 in a typology of God being the mouth of Moses and Aaron.

10. Only Begotten

We have been reading v. 14 in terms of the 'only begotten' which has been the traditional reading for the underlying compound adjective (μονογενής). The question is whether μονογενής carries a begettal overtone in a specialized context like that of the prologue (or GJohn) and/or whether it carries such an overtone more generally in contexts where there is a claim about having an only son, daughter or child. This question is pertinent because μονογενής suggests an etymology (μόνος/γένος) and a meaning of 'one/only' and 'kind/kindred'. However, "Etymology is not, and does not profess to be, a guide to the semantic value of words in their current usage, and such value has to be determined from the current usage and not from the derivation."[1] Lexicons are a guide to etymology and summarize usage but there has been disagreement over this word and we need to review the arguments.

Lexical lists for γένος include meanings such as 'race, nation, stock, birth, descendants' as well as 'kind, sort, class' (BAGD). So, for example, the following list of translations for γένος shows that 'only-begotten' or 'only-born' is not an implausible possible meaning for μονογενής when used of an individual child.

> 'Behold, they are one people (γένος)…' Gen 11:6 (RSV)
> '…a Syro-Phoenician by birth (γένος)…' Mark 7:26 (RSV)
> '…gathered to his kindred (γένος)' Gen 25:17 (RSV)
> '…him and his offspring (γένος)…' Jer 43:31 (RSV)
> 'This kind (γένος) cannot be driven out…' Mark 9:29 (RSV)
> 'You are a chosen race (γένος)' 1 Pet 2:9 (RSV)

The variety here is typical for γένος and it illustrates how usage and context is key for ascertaining the nuance. Lexicons that include 'only begotten' in their lists of meanings for μονογενής include, for the New

---

[1] J. Barr, *The Semantics of Biblical Language* (Oxford: Oxford University Press, 1961), 107.

Testament, Friberg, BAGD, and Abbott-Smith; for Classical Greek, the short intermediate Liddell & Scott; and for the LXX, Lust, Eynikel and Hauspie. One lexicon that doesn't include this meaning for μονογενής is Moulton & Milligan.[1]

There are examples of attributive occurrences of μονογενής which can be read with or without 'begotten' (Jud 11:34; Tob 6:11; *Pss. Sol.* 18:4; Luke 7:12). There are examples of substantive uses of μονογενής, where there is no son/daughter/child word, which could be read as 'only begotten' (Tob 3:15; 8:17; 25:16; Luke 9:38). There are examples of substantive uses of μονογενής which have different meanings (LXX Ps 21:21 'my only life'; 34:17 'my only one'; Wisd 7:22 'one only'; *T.Ben* 9:2 'only begotten prophet'; *1 Clem.* 25:2 'one of its kind'). Two examples from the Apostolic Fathers that use GJohn and would be 'only begotten son' if this is correct for GJohn are *Mart. Pol.* 20:2 and *Diogn.* 10:2. It is perhaps obvious that sentences that can be read as affirming that such and such is an only son could also be read as affirming that such and such is an only begotten son.

The word μονογενής on its own carries no implication[2] as to son or daughter and translators will add a son/daughter/child word to give 'only [begotten] son/ daughter/child' based on the surrounding context (narrowly or widely drawn). It is however often used with separate son/daughter/child words and in other ways where children are not the subject. Given the above range of examples where 'begotten' is possible, we cannot rule out the historical roots of the word (μόνος/γένος) still being in play.

The question is whether John uses μονογενής to convey 'only begotten'. Some translations translate the compound adjective without an overtone of 'begettal' (e.g. 'one and only', NET; 'only Son' RSV). The term occurs in John 1:14, 18, 3:16, 18 and 1 John 4:9 in the Johannine writings. The word for 'son' is used with the adjective in John 3:16, 18 and 1 John 4:9

---

[1] J. H. Moulton & G. Milligan, *The Vocabulary of the Greek Testament* (London: Hodder & Stoughton, 1930). Moulton & Milligan don't just miss out this nuance; they deny its possibility and propose what they think an 'only-begotten' Greek form would have been had they been able to cite an example. D. Moody, "God's Only Son: The Translation of John 3:16 in the Revised Standard Version" *JBL* 72/4 (1953): 213-219, also notes Thayer as not listing 'only begotten' and the revised (1940) larger edition of Liddell & Scott (213). Moody's paper is cited by later scholars as having settled the question against 'only-begotten'.

[2] *Contra* Fennema, "John 1:18: 'God the Only Son'", 127.

but not in John 1:14 and it is disputed whether 'son' occurs in John 1:18 (see Appendix). Elsewhere the adjective is used without the word for 'son' in Heb 11:17 but it is used in context with son in Luke 7:12 and 9:38 and 'daughter' in Luke 8:42.

If we turn more specifically to GJohn, the question which the word poses when it is on its own is whether it carries a filial sense (i.e. whether we can infer a son/daughter/child word). This is an important issue because we can't just say that the word means 'only' – we need to complete the adjective and answer 'only what?' We can therefore dismiss 'one and only' (NET) because it leaves hanging in the air the question of 'one and only what?' The RSV's 'only Son' chooses a filial sense for the adjective in a sentence without 'son/daughter' language and in a broader context which refers only to children (v. 12). The choice is presumably based on John 3:16, 18 but this usage is distant and attributive. What is happening here is that translators see that a substantive use of the adjective needs completing but are unwilling to take that completion from the etymological resources of the word itself, i.e. just from μονογενής.

The argument for a 'begettal' overtone in v. 14 is the distant relationship of the adjective to the verb for 'to beget', γεννάω, and the presence of γεννάω in John 1:13, "born...of God". This is a decisive argument in favour of 'only begotten' for John 1:14, 18, but the overtone also fits with the emphasis in v. 14 on '*from* the Father'.[1] This is part of what distinguishes Jesus from John the Baptist and it is what distinguishes Jesus from those who are metaphorically born of God – Jesus is the *only begotten* of God. An overtone of 'begettal' is also required in John 3 because of the use of γεννάω in Jesus' conversation with Nicodemus (John 3:5) which sets the context for John's commentary in vv. 16, 18. And, moreover, γεννάω is also present in the context of 1 John 4:9 (7) which suggests that 'only begotten' is the way to complete the adjective in that verse.[2]

It is because Jesus' distinctive origins are a question (he is 'of God', John 3:16, 18; 1 John 4:9) that John's μονογενής is 'only begotten'. The Nicene

---

[1] *Contra* Fennema, "John 1:18: 'God the Only Son'", 126-127; he says that 'only-begotten' is a "misconception" citing the influence of the Vulgate on the KJV and later English versions. On the other hand, as we argue, maybe the knowledge of the possibilities of the Greek on the part of Jerome is superior to that of Fennema.

[2] It is ironic that translators add 'son' which is absent but ignore γένος which is present in the background. Eliminating an overtone of 'begettal' helps commentators like Fennema argue for θεός in John 1:18.

and Post-Nicene Church Fathers recognised this reading of John in their stress upon the begettal of the Son in its Trinitarian theology. So, for instance, the 4c. CE Vulgate recognises this reading of GJohn in that it uses *unigenitus* ('only begotten') for John 1:14, 18; 3:16, 18; 1 John 4:9 and Heb 11:17, and *unicus* ('only') in Luke 7:12; 8:42 and 9:38. Jerome was revising earlier Latin manuscripts which had used only *unicus* in all the verses. This is the second decisive argument in favour of 'only-begotten' - the knowledge of the possibilities of the Greek as used in GJohn on the part of the Fathers.

The repeated refrain 'the only begotten' (μονογενῆ) of vv. 14, 18 is an allusion to the episode of Abraham and Isaac on Mount Moriah. This is suggested by John the Baptist's description of Jesus as 'The Lamb of God' (John 1:29, 36).

> And Abraham said, 'My son, God will provide himself a lamb for a burnt offering.' So they went both of them together. Gen 22:8 (KJV)

> And he said, 'Lay not thine hand upon the lad, neither do thou anything unto him: for now I know that thou fearest God, seeing thou hast not withheld thy son, thine only[1] from me'. Gen 22:12 (KJV revised)

> By faith Abraham, when he was tried, offered up Isaac: and he that had received the promises offered up his only begotten (μονογενῆ)...Accounting that God was able to raise him up, even from the dead; from whence also he received him in a figure. Heb 11:17-19 (KJV revised)

> Behold the Lamb of God, which taketh away the sin of the world. John 1:29-36, 3:17 (KJV)

Hebrews identifies the sacrifice of Isaac as a 'figure' (παραβολῇ), whereas we have used the notion of typology. Hebrews also emphasizes that feature of the episode which describes Isaac as 'only begotten'. John uses the same word twice in his prologue to describe Jesus and this secures Jesus' identity as the anti-type to Isaac. On Moriah, God provided a ram rather than a lamb (Gen 22:13), and with Abraham's promise to Isaac that God would provide a lamb, the reader is told that there will be a lamb 'of

---

[1] The Hebrew is 'thine only' which is picked up in 'only begotten' without 'son' in John 1:14.

God', which is precisely what John records with the Baptist's declaration, 'Look, the lamb of God!'. The 'Look!' here is picking up Abraham's name for the place of sacrifice which carries the meaning, 'The Lord will see' and 'of God' is picking up 'God '+'provide' (Gen 22:14).[1] Finally, we have in this typology an explanation of why we have 'from the Father' in John 1:14. Abraham had said that God would *provide* a lamb and so this has to come *from* the Father. John's juxtaposition of 'only begotten' and 'from the Father' interprets Abraham's statement about a lamb in terms of an only begotten one.

Although in his prologue John presents the 'sacrifice and resurrection' of Isaac as a type of Jesus, the Lamb of God, through whom the children of God are born, we could also identify the Passover Lamb as a similar type through which, in this case, the nation was delivered. Since Christ was a Passover Lamb (1 Cor 5:7),[2] we might think that it is this typology that John draws upon. However, though Jewish traditions associated the two sacrifices, we should keep them distinct when tracing types in NT writings.

John the Baptist's declaration associates the lamb with sin, The Passover lamb teaches that a lamb will deliver the people. The Isaac typology teaches that the nation that was of Abraham, Isaac and Jacob had been made through a figurative death and resurrection,[3] and this in turn is a type of a people that would be made through Jesus' death and resurrection. Jewish commentary associates both sacrifices with the forgiveness of sin.[4] And if we look elsewhere and ask what is *through*

---

[1] The verb involved is the ordinary verb for seeing' but it is used metaphorically in the account when Abraham answers Isaac's question about the missing sacrifice Abraham says to Isaac "God will see to it that there is a lamb" (Gen 22:8). English translations usually render the verb as 'The Lord will provide'. With Isaac being an only son, and 'giving' being such a feature of the story, we have an explanation of John 3:17, "he gave his only-begotten son".

[2] On the links made between the two sacrifices, see C. Shaker, 'The Lamb of God Title in John's Gospel: Background, Exegesis and Major Themes' (MA Thesis; Seton Hall University; [Online]).

[3] Interestingly, there are echoes of the Moriah episode in Jesus' Gethsemane experience as the Father and the Son approached the time of the crucifixion; see Shaker, 'The Lamb of God Title in John's Gospel: Background, Exegesis and Major Themes', 13-14.

[4] Shaker, 'The Lamb of God Title in John's Gospel: Background, Exegesis and Major Themes', 8-11.

Christ, we have texts such as: Rom 5:9, believers are justified by his blood and thereby 'saved' through him (cf. Col 1:20).[1]

Finally, it is worth noting here a connection with the baptism of Jesus and Moriah. The Angel of the Lord called unto Abraham "out of heaven" and, in the same way, at the baptism of Jesus there was a voice "out of heaven" (Gen 22:11; Matt 3:17; Mark 1:11). In both cases the voice is about a son: 'my...son' and 'thy son'. Interestingly, the LXX paraphrases the Hebrew as 'your beloved son' which is the term used at Christ's baptism.

An objection to the foregoing typology is that Isaac wasn't Abraham's only-begotten son, there was Ishmael – so Isaac isn't a suitable type for Jesus being the only-begotten son of God. Isaac was Abraham's 'only' (יחיד) son (Gen 22:2), and yet Ishmael was also his son by Hagar. How so? The objection proves too much. Hebrews shows that Isaac being the 'only' son of Abraham is a type of Christ. How Jesus was 'only' like Isaac is in his divine begettal. Isaac was a miraculous son of promise (whereas Hagar was not and of the flesh). What John is doing is pulling together Isaac's 'only' status and his miraculous birth with the compound adjective μονογενής. We discuss this typology further in the next chapter and in the Appendix.

Our conclusion, based on the foregoing, is that the correct sense for μονογενής is 'only-begotten'.

11. And so the word became flesh
We have said that some commentators see a *sequence* in the flow of the prologue from v. 1 to v. 14, rather than a separate third paragraph beginning at v. 14. This is why they are led to say that v. 2 to v. 13 is a single parenthesis:

> In the beginning was the Word...<u>and</u> the Word was made/became flesh and tabernacled (KJV 'dwelt') amongst us... John 1:1, 14 (KJV revised)

---

[1] The Akedah (the Abraham and Isaac Moriah episode) is important to NT writers. It is the typology present in John 17:5, another classic pre-existence text. More importantly, the promise to Abraham at Moriah was that all the families of the world would be blessed, and this is an essential part of the gospel message (Acts 3:26-26).

This sequence is interpreted as saying that there was a 'time' before the Word was made or became flesh.[1] And so it is argued that the Word *existed* before being made flesh. This view envisages that the person of the Word or the attributive[2] hypostasis that was the Word existed in heaven before the birth of God's only begotten son. Exactly who or what the Word was is open to debate and this is why here we list the choices of 'person' and 'attributive hypostasis'. Stoic or Greek philosophy, or Philo, or Second Temple writings, or even the Targums may be invoked to shed light on the text and assist the commentator in his/her choice.

The problem is that while the OT has some literary personification and linguistic hypostatization, the overwhelming use of *dabar* (and *logos* in the LXX) is for the words spoken and what is said. The distinctions are straightforward: God speaks, and he may perform various speech acts which then have substantive content. Some Second Temple writers, however, treat God's word as a divine attribute and thus personify and/or hypostasize his word. In doing this, they are developing and applying Scripture for their readers.

The question is whether this is just their way of talking about God or whether they regard the divine attribute as having a substantive reality. They may go further and treat the divine attribute in more personal terms, which again presents us with the decision as to whether this is the language of personification or the depiction of a personal being called the Word. These distinctions are illustrated in the diagram below which is a ladder of ascent towards a metaphysical commitment for *dabar/logos*,

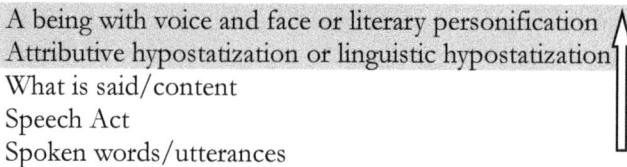

A being with voice and face or literary personification
Attributive hypostatization or linguistic hypostatization
What is said/content
Speech Act
Spoken words/utterances

---

[1] So, Ignatius, *Letter to the Ephesians* 7:2, "But our Physician is the only true God, the unbegotten and unapproachable, the Lord of all, the Father and Begetter of the only begotten Son. We have also as a Physician the Lord our God, Jesus the Christ, the only begotten Son and Word, before time began, but who afterwards became also man, of Mary the virgin. For the Word was made flesh." *Letter to the Magnesians* 6:1, "He, being begotten by the Father before the beginning of time, was God the Word, the only begotten Son, and remains the same for ever".

[2] In traditional Biblical unitarian exegesis, it is just the Word of God that pre-exists, presented in John 1 with a linguistic hypostatization.

The concept of incarnation requires a being or a hypostasis or a person to be incarnated. So, to read John 1:14 in an incarnational way requires us to read v. 1 as referring to a divine being, a person, or a hypostasis called 'the Word'. We can make the difference clear if we ask, where is the Word? If the Word is a personal being or a hypostasis, after v. 14, the Word is on earth and not in heaven. If instead we have a reference to making someone the voice of God in v. 14, the question makes no sense.

God speaks and this is a speech act with content; it may be an expression of his purpose or plan; it may be a command or a promise. It may be good theology to affirm that the purpose or plan of God became flesh in Christ, or that in Christ, all the promises of God are fulfilled, but this doesn't mean that this is the point of John 1:14. We have seen that the Word was towards God and was God, and these are things we would say of a *person*. The underlying typology of these predicates is that of Moses' role and position towards God and with Aaron as God. The point of John 1:14 then is about a person, a begotten son, and what it is for that person to be 'the Word'.

Jesus is 'the Word' because it was given to him to be God's word in respect of the new creation. This is a **wholly general identity** for Jesus and one which explains why Jesus is called 'the Word' in v. 1. God did indeed speak to send Gabriel, and that word became flesh, but this is a particular event and doesn't account for the ongoing significance of the title 'the Word'; also, the prophecies about the Christ in the word of God through the prophets no doubt were fulfilled in and by Jesus but this fact doesn't account for the dynamic aspect of Jesus then being God's word in the work of new creation.

The use of Genesis 1 in John 1 is well known; 'In the beginning' is an obvious allusion, but the reference to 'all things', 'the light', and 'darkness' are confirming pointers to the reader that s/he should look for a Genesis background to the prologue. In "And so the Word was made/became flesh", we have the same past tense form of the verb 'to become' (ἐγένετο) that is used in the LXX for the 'was' statements of Genesis 1: 'and there **was** light' (v. 3); '**was** the evening', '**was** the morning' (vv. 5, 8, 11, 19, 23); 'it **was** so' (vv. 6, 9, 11, 14-15, 20, 24, 29-30). The LXX is giving a literal translation of the Perfect form of the Hebrew verb 'to be/become' and it is unexceptionable. The KJV translation of John 1:14, however, is interpretative in giving "And the Word **was made** flesh". It would be better to follow the Genesis 1 paradigm and render the Greek as "the word became flesh" (NASB, RSV).[1]

This form of the past tense of the verb 'to become' is variously translated. In John 1 we have it as "There **was** a man sent from God" (v. 6); this is like the Hebraic "And it came to pass" (e.g. Gen 6:1; 27:1; Jud 1:14; 2 Chron 34:19). We also have it in "**were made** by him" (v. 3); "**was made** by him" (v. 10); and "grace and truth **came** by Jesus Christ" (v. 17). We can see that the aorist form of the verb 'to become' is treated flexibly by translators. The normal Greek verbs for 'to make' (ποιέω) or 'to come' (ἔρχομαι) are not in vv. 3, 10 or 17; just the simple verb 'to become'. It is our reading assumption as translators/interpreters if we render v. 14 as "And the Word **was made** flesh", but it is better rendered as "And so the word became flesh".

The use of the verb 'to become' in Genesis 1 is to state what happens or comes about—it marks a change. We noted above that there is an 'it was so' refrain in Genesis 1, and this is part of the pattern, "And God said...and it was so". God spoke to the effect that such and such should happen or come about, and it was so. Following this pattern, when we read that *the word became flesh*, we don't have the coming about of light or the separation of the waters or a storm or a plague, we just have flesh instead of the word. The reality of a man being 'the Word' consists in his words being the word of God. The difference between Jesus as 'the Word' and a prophet speaking the word of God lies in Jesus *being* 'the Word' of the new creation.

Putting the first chapter of GJohn to one side, the use of the word *logos* everywhere else in the Gospel is for what is said or spoken, a saying or a word (35x, e.g. John 2:22; 10:35).[2] There is no text elsewhere in John's Gospel which uses *logos* for something abstract, a personification or hypostatization, or for a heavenly individual. If we were to extend our search to include all the occurrences of *logos* in the NT, we would come to the same conclusion; the only individual anywhere called 'the Word' is Jesus, but the word *logos* is really all about the message of the gospel.

.

---

[1] Similarly, it would be wrong to translate v. 14 as "And the word **was** flesh"—a simple statement of fact, because this loses the sense of 'becoming' in the verb and fails to reflect Genesis.

[2] For a study of the thematic links between the prologue and the rest of John see S. R. Valentine, "The Johannine Prologue—A Microcosm of the Gospel" *EQ* 68:3 (1996): 291-304.

Calling Jesus 'the Word' is rare in the NT;[1] the phrases, 'word of God', 'word of the Lord' and 'the word' are most often used of the message delivered by OT prophets to the people (e.g. John 10:35; cf. Acts 17:13; 2 Cor 4:2) or for the message being preached by Jesus and the apostles. And more broadly, taking the OT into consideration as our background for John 1:14, both individual examples of prophecy (e.g. 1 Kgs 12:22; 1 Chron 17:3), and the whole message of God to man (enshrined in the Jewish Scriptures) is described as 'the word' (e.g. Ps 119:9, 105). The words that Jesus spoke were the word of God and they were life. The reason why 'the Word' is rare is because this is part of John's Genesis typology.

The exchange in John 10:35-36 is instructive here because it uses the same form of the verb as John 1:14,

> If he called them gods, to whom the word of God came (ὁ λόγος τοῦ θεοῦ ἐγένετο)..., Say ye of him, whom the Father hath sanctified, and sent into the world, 'Thou blasphemest'. because I said, I am the Son of God? John 10:35-36 (KJV revised)

The comparison to be made is that it is a short step from 'to whom...came the word' to 'the word became'. There is here a reason for 'was God' in John 1:14, namely, there is a precedent in those to whom the word of God came were called gods.

12. The Baptism of Christ

We should not concede that there is a sequence in time from v. 1 to v. 14 (the default reading[2]). Instead of seeing a sequence from a beginning (v. 1) to a later event (v. 14) — the Word becoming flesh, we should see that the event referenced in John 1:14 is **the baptism of Christ**, which is at the beginning of his ministry. What are the arguments for this reading? [3]

---

[1] Hooker, "The Johannine Prologue and the Messianic Secret", 52-58, argues that *the Logos* is absent from GJohn, but it is replaced by the notion of Christ's glory which is hidden from the Jews lest they believe (John 12:40).

[2] This is the critical mistake made by scholars; see Marshall, "Incarnational Christology in the New Testament", 1-4, for a good example of how the mistake is not even perceived.

[3] See F. Watson, "Is John's Christology Adoptionist?" in *The Glory of Christ in the New Testament* (eds. L. D. Hurst and N. T. Wright; Oxford: Oxford University Press, 1984), 113-124, "...the union of *the Logos* or Son of God

1) The concept of 'the word of God' is about God speaking, with things happening as a result, or it is about his speaking through the prophets and expressing his mind. We should use this background rather than any development of the idea of *the Logos* in Second Temple or later writings in terms of an attributive hypostasis.

> a) So, we should eschew metaphysical elaborations such as saying that the attribute of the deity that is the Word is a faculty like the 'Reason' of God, or a dispositional capacity like his 'Wisdom'. The scriptural model for speaking the word of God uses the language of 'the Spirit'. Nevertheless, being 'the Word' is more than just being an inspired prophet.

> b) Equally, if the concept of 'the word of God' is about what God says, we should forgo specifying the specific *content* of any speech, by saying that it is the 'plan' or the 'purpose' of God. We have seen that the Genesis typology of v. 1 suggests that the 'the Word' would be someone speaking as God.

> c) Finally, we cannot treat the 'the word of God' in terms of a written body such as the Torah or the Prophets. Being 'the Word' in John 1 is altogether more dynamic.

2) In general terms, we should ask *when* does a person become a prophet—when do they receive the Spirit of prophecy? The answer is at some point as an adult. The speaking of God's word is associated with the inspiration of the Spirit,

> The Spirit of the Lord spake by me, and his word was in my tongue. 2 Sam 23:2 (KJV)

> For the prophecy came not in old time by the will of man: but holy men of God spake as they were moved by the holy Spirit. 2 Pet 1:21 (KJV revised)

---

with Jesus of Nazareth took place in the descent of the Spirit at his Baptism" (113). Watson cites precedents for his view in the work of A. Loisy and R. H. Fuller. Watson's arguments are historical and centred in the sub-Apostolic period; we present exegetical arguments.

From this it follows that the word of God would have become flesh in the person of Jesus at his baptism when he received the Spirit.

> And Jesus, when he was baptized, went up straightway out of the water: and, lo, the heavens were opened unto him, and he saw the Spirit of God descending like a dove, and lighting upon him. And lo a voice from heaven, saying, 'This is my beloved Son, in whom I am well pleased'. Matt 3:16-17 (KJV)

This is the beginning of Christ's ministry, that is, the time when he was to begin preaching the word of God to the people. The baptism of Christ is not therefore about the Son becoming incarnate (Jesus was the son of God from his birth), nor is it about a man being adopted by God to be his son; rather, it is about Jesus becoming and then being 'the Word'.[1]

> In many and various ways God spoke of old to our Fathers by the prophets; but in these last days he has spoken to us by a son... Heb 1:1-2 (RSV revised)

The Genesis typology of 'the beginning' in v. 1 requires another beginning for the corresponding word of God. That beginning is the ministry of Jesus. It follows that the word became flesh, i.e. flesh came to stand in place[2] of God's word in Genesis at the baptism of Christ.

3) The baptism of Christ was accompanied by a theophanic display with the heavens opened and the Spirit descending like a dove[3] and a voice declaring Jesus to be God's son. The 'upon him' of the Spirit (Matt 3:16; Luke 3:22) picks up the common motif of the Spirit being 'upon' an individual, which in turn is associated with the word of God:

> My spirit that is upon thee, and <u>my words</u> which I have put in thy mouth, shall not depart out of thy mouth, nor out of the mouth of

---

[1] Orthodox commentators haven't sufficiently addressed the point that while a birth may be appropriate for the incarnation of a son, a baptism of the Spirit is appropriate for the 'incarnation' of the word of God.

[2] This is a substitutional interpretation of 'became flesh' rather than an incarnational and objectual interpretation. On this analogy see S. Haack, *Philosophy of Logics* (Cambridge: Cambridge University Press, 1978), 42-43.

[3] The dove here is a sign of the prophet Jonah marking out Jesus' mission to die on behalf of the people.

thy seed, nor out of the mouth of thy seed's seed, saith the Lord, from henceforth and for ever. Isa 59:21 (KJV)

This biblical pattern suggests that the word of God would become flesh through a bestowal of the Spirit.

4) The use of 'only begotten' is usually taken to imply that John is focused on Jesus' birth. But,

a) The reason for 'only begotten' here is to signal Jesus as the anti-type to Isaac rather than to support the mention of the event of his birth; the reason for 'the Father' (rather than 'God' as elsewhere with 'only begotten') is to draw in Abraham as the father to Isaac and a type of the Father (like John 17:1, 5).

b) The glory that was beheld by the disciples was ultimately[1] the glory of Jesus' death and resurrection which is presented with Isaac typology in John 17:1, 5.

c) 'Only begotten' is about status and need not be part of a focus on a person's birth (e.g. Luke 7:12; 8:42; 9:38).

d) In v. 13 there is an allusion to the virgin birth in that the birth of believers is not 'of man' but 'of God'.[2] This sets a begettal context for v. 14, where the term μονογενής is best translated as 'only begotten'.

e) The LXX renders the 'only one' (יחיד, Gen 22:2, 12, 16) that was Isaac as the 'beloved' (ἀγαπητός). God's declaration that Jesus was his beloved son, made at his baptism, implies Isaac typology.[3]

f) Ps 2:7 and "Today, I have begotten you" is spoken at Jesus' baptism in the Western text of Luke 3:22 and in the Hebrew

---

[1] T. F. Glasson *Moses in the Fourth Gospel* (London: SCM Press, 1963), 65-73 argues correctly that they beheld Christ's glory throughout the ministry, but ultimately in his death and resurrection.

[2] With Hoskyns and Davey, *The Fourth Gospel*, 164, and against Watson, "Is John's Christology Adoptionist?", 113.

[3] Beasley-Murray, *John*, 14.

Gospel.[1] John's use of 'only begotten' may be the scriptural equivalent to this interpretative tradition.

Certainly, 'became flesh' and 'only begotten' might be words used in a description of the birth of Christ and in a context (v. 13) where there has been a mention of spiritual birth. However, we cannot assume that the flesh is not *already* present to become the Word; this *crux interpretum* must be argued rather than taken for granted (see below).

5) John records that the disciples saw that Jesus was 'full' (πλήρης) of grace and truth. This idea is particularly associated with the possession of the Spirit: "And Jesus being full (πλήρης) of the holy Spirit returned from Jordan" (Luke 4:1; see also Acts 6:3, 5, 8, "full of grace and power"). Equally, the disciples received of Christ's 'fulness' (John 1:16) which is best interpreted as a reference to the gifts of the Spirit (Eph 1:23; 4:8-13).

6) The next verse (v. 15) continues with the words of John the Baptist from the time of Jesus' baptism (vv. 27, 30). John only came to know Jesus' true identity after he had seen the descent of the dove (v. 34), and it was then that he was able to declare that Jesus was the one who was preferred before him.

> John bare witness of him, and <u>cried</u>,[2] saying, 'This was he of whom I spake, he that cometh after me is preferred before me: for he was before me'. John 1:15 (KJV); cf. vv. 27, 30

The connection between v. 14 and v. 15 ('bare witness of *him*') doesn't suggest a thirty-year gap between the birth of Christ and the ministry of John the Baptist.

7) GJohn goes on in v. 19ff to include John's witness statements,

> And <u>this is the record</u> (μαρτυρία, 'witness') of John, when the Jews sent priests and Levites from Jerusalem to ask him, Who art thou? John 1:19 (KJV)

The introduction to the witness statements, 'this is the record (μαρτυρία)', connects to John 1:7, 'This one came for a witness (μαρτυρία)' but it also

---

[1] Edwards, *The Hebrew Gospel and the Development of the Synoptic Tradition*, 70-71.
[2] The verb (κράζω, 'cry out') is characteristic of John as 'The voice of one crying in the wilderness' (John 1:23).

introduces a break into the text and closes the prologue if we take the prologue to comprise vv. 1-18. John has described the two ministries of John the Baptist and Jesus in vv. 1-18 and now he incorporates the personal testimony of the Baptist's words in his gospel. The difference between vv. 1-18 and v. 19ff is that the prologue is more abstract description of events, while the Baptist's record is a more concrete narrative.[1] For example, John's denial 'I am not the Christ' (v. 20) reflects the more abstract denial in John 1:7, 'He was not that Light'. In short, John 1 is all about the two ministries and there is no room here for a reference to the birth of Christ.

8) The introduction of John the Baptist in v. 6 is obviously not the time of the birth of Christ. The description in vv. 6-18 describes the Baptist's ministry in contrast to that of Christ, but most of the description is of Christ's ministry of light. It is chronologically out of place to take v. 14 as a throwback reference to the birth of Christ.

9) The statement "tabernacled amongst us" could refer to the time immediately after Jesus' baptism or the whole ministry as in "all the time that the Lord Jesus went in and out amongst us" (Acts 1:21). More importantly, though, the "we" and "us" aspect in v. 14 draws in the disciples' experience and this began at the baptism of Christ after which they followed him when he called each of them.

For these reasons, (1)-(9), we take 'the word became flesh' to be a description of part of what happened at the baptism of Christ in the descent of the holy Spirit. It is in this episode that Jesus became 'the Word'.[2]

F. Watson argues for a baptismal reading of v. 14 but with different conception of *the Logos* to that which we have laid out in this chapter. He avers, "If Jesus' birth as the moment of divine incarnation is as important for John as is usually thought, it is strange that he completely ignores it and appears to know nothing of the beliefs held in other parts of the early church."[3] He also thinks that the evangelist's documentation of John's witness to the descent of the Spirit (John 1:32-34) signifies his view that it

---

[1] If we take the prologue to comprise vv. 1-5, vv. 6-18 begins the story and starts off somewhat abstractly before becoming more concrete; it is just that v. 19 closes that description and begins the Baptist's record.
[2] This is not to deny that in childhood Jesus grew in the Spirit.
[3] Watson, "Is John's Christology Adoptionist?", 114, 121.

was at the baptism of Jesus that "divinity and humanity became one".[1] The parallel to which he appeals is with the descent from heaven of the Son of Man and the bread from heaven (John 3:13; 6:33). On this basis he argues that John held an Adoptionist Christology, i.e. the Son, or Christ, or the Word, became human at the baptism of Jesus:

> "Johannine Christology rests on the presupposition that, before the descent of the Spirit, Jesus of Nazareth is an ordinary man, born of human parents. But with the descent of the Spirit, his human mind is set aside, and the divine Logos or Son, enters and becomes united with his human body."[2]

Watson's paper is brief and programmatic and in a different logical space to our treatment. He presumes an attributive hypostasis view of *the Logos*. We have discussed this earlier in this chapter. The new consideration for us is his 'descent' comparison. The problem with his descent parallels though is that they are from different discourses. The descent language of John 3 and 6 is part of two typological comparisons rather than any cosmology. The descent of the Spirit at Jesus' baptism was a literal theophanic display and indicative of a bestowal.

We should mention **two kinds of objection** to our exegesis of John 1:14. First, there is the historical point that this interpretation of v. 14 has not been the traditional church reading since the sub-Apostolic era and therefore it is likely to be false. The counterpoint to this argument is that the above interpretation is more compatible with an Adoptionist Christology which was deemed heretical by the Fathers; in short, nuanced varieties of our view have antiquity, but in heresies that fell away.

So, J. Daniélou comments, "Heterodox literature, both Ebionite and Gnostic...sees in the Baptism the descent of the Godhead on the man Jesus" and "The Baptism episode clearly occupied a position of exceptional importance in the early days of Jewish Christianity. But the whole body of heterodox authors, Ebionites as well as Gnostics, Cerinthus as well as Carpocrates, drew from it heterodox conclusions, namely that this was the moment of the descent of the Holy Spirit into the man Jesus...It is easy to see why from then onwards the tradition of

---

[1] Watson, "Is John's Christology Adoptionist?", 121.
[2] Watson, "Is John's Christology Adoptionist?", 123.

the Great Church tended to play down the Baptism in favour of the Gospel of the Infancy, and to bring out the divine aspect of the latter."[1]

It is beyond our scope to discuss detail here, orthodox or heterodox; our point is simply that heterodox writings, insofar as we have them, offer comparable theology to a baptism reading of John 1:14 and so our approach has antiquity.[2]

Watson's discussion is in terms of Adoptionist and Docetic Christology rather than intra-textual and typological exegesis. He believes that v. 14 is Adoptionist, i.e. that the divine *Logos* descended and became incarnate in the man Jesus of Nazareth at his baptism. This obviously depends on a certain view of *the Logos*, but exegetically we can immediately note that the motif of 'descent' is absent from v. 14. Our counterargument against Adoptionist and Docetic reading of John 1 would first off simply be the infancy story of Matthew and Luke: Jesus was literally the Son of God. This matters no less than the bestowal of the Spirit and the word becoming flesh. The problem that both the Fathers and the heretics have alike is that they are working with a cultural conception of *the Logos*. This is the prior mistake before any exegesis they offer on the birth stories or John 1.

The second objection is exegetical, and it affirms that the more plausible interpretation of 'became flesh' is that is describes **the birth of Jesus**. This is the traditional reading (since the early Church Fathers) and often

---

[1] J. Daniélou, *The Theology of Jewish Christianity* (London: Darton, Longman and Todd, 1964), 224, 230-231. So, for example, Daniélou notes that the Orphites held that the descent of the Word took place at Jesus' baptism, (213).

[2] On Cerinthus see Irenaeus, *Against Heresies* 1.26.1; On Carpocrates and the Ebionites, see *Against Heresies*, 1.26.2. On Gnostic interpretation, see the Nag Hammadi literature, for example, the *Testimony of Truth* 9, 30, 19-30, "But the Son of Man [came] forth from Imperishability, [being] alien to defilement. He came [to the] world by Jordan river, and immediately the Jordan [turned] back. And John bore witness to the [descent] of Jesus. For it is he who saw the [power] which came down upon the Jordan river; for he knew that the dominion of carnal procreation had come to an end." Another example: Theodotus of Byzantium (late 2c. CE), an Adoptionist, believed that "At his baptism in the Jordan he received the Christ from above", R. M. Grant, *Heresy and Criticism* (Louisville: WJK Press, 1993), 72.

coupled with talk of an incarnation. The following exegetical points can be made in support of the Fathers:

a) The context of v. 13 mentions spiritual birth; it also mentions the flesh.

b) The immediate comment in v. 14 is of 'the only begotten'.

c) Origin is important in v. 14 because the only begotten is *from* the Father.

d) A Johannine concern is that Jesus Christ 'came in the flesh' (1 John 4:2; 2 John 1:7).

e) Paul says that Jesus "was of the seed of David according to the flesh" (Rom 1:3), linking 'flesh' to matters of origin.

f) Paul says, "God sent his son in the likeness of sinful flesh" (Rom 8:3), again connecting flesh to the coming of God's son.

This is a fair list of exegetical points. If 'became flesh' is a description of the birth of Jesus, then this section of this chapter and all references that we have made to the baptism of Christ vis-à-vis the prologue need to be excised. A 'birth reading' of 'became flesh' is perfectly compatible with a new creation reading of the prologue simply because it is a brief mention: John immediately moves onto the experience of the disciples vis-à-vis the ministry of Jesus: "we beheld his glory'. However, we should ask ourselves whether our acceptance of the birth reading is due more to habit and familiarity than exegesis.

It is unusual to read that the word became flesh, and this is why 'plausibility' judgements about what 'became flesh' means don't work. Discussing the exegetical points above, we can say,

a) The context uses the metaphor of birth for believers, and 'born of God' in v. 13 is clearly connected to a man being 'born again/from above' and 'born of water and of the spirit' (John 3:3-5). But this teaching about spiritual birth suggests Jesus' baptism was a being 'born of water and of the Spirit'. The context of v. 13 is more supportive of a baptismal reading of 'the word became flesh'.

b) The context (v. 13) leads with 'will of the flesh' which sets the tone for 'flesh' in 'became flesh'. This usage for 'flesh' just looks like a denotation for the human being rather anything about human nature.[1] So, we can't infer that 'became flesh' means that the Word was made *of* flesh.[2] We have an *event* of becoming (or replacement).

c) The strongest exegetical point in favour of the birth reading is the conjunction of 'became flesh' with 'only begotten'. We can't prove that 'only begotten' exegetes 'became flesh'; we can only claim that the association is suggestive of a meaning for the more difficult 'became flesh'. On the other hand, John's first point is about glory and this is the glory that the disciples beheld at Cana (John 2:11) and throughout the life of Jesus. It is the glory that is associated with 'only begotten from the Father' and this is the glory of the death and resurrection of Christ which was pre-figured in Abraham and Isaac on Moriah (John 17:5).

d) The statement 'became flesh' isn't combating the heresy that bombarded the early church, viz. that Christ had *not* come in the flesh (1 John 4:1-3; 2 John v. 7). That heresy is about the messiah rather than the word of God.

e) Equally, as 'son' and 'seed' are not used in the statement 'the word became flesh', the Pauline texts are not relevant. Instead, we propose that what was spirit and life ('the word') became flesh at the time of the bestowal of the Spirit. The use of 'flesh' implies this contrast and it reflects the meaning in Acts 2:17, "I will pour out of my Spirit upon all flesh", i.e. all human beings.

Which is correct? The baptism or the birth reading of 'became flesh'? The key question is when would've the word become flesh.

13. The Tabernacling of the Word
As well as the Genesis beginning, John alludes to the exodus beginning. The exodus/wilderness beginning is relevant because the word was made/became flesh and *tabernacled* (pitched a tent) amongst the disciples. The allusion to the tabernacle requires us to see v. 14 in an exodus light. Israel were redeemed from Egypt and given new life, but they rebelled, and some rejected their salvation. It was then that the tribe of Levi was

---

[1] *Contra* Whittaker, *Studies in the Gospels*, 47.

[2] Hebrews says that Christ Jesus was faithful to him that 'made him' (Heb 3:2, KJV mg.).

selected out from among them because of their faithfulness. It was after this, and Moses' intercession, that the Lord agreed to go among them as they journeyed to conquer the land. A tabernacle was built, and the Angel of the Presence typologically became flesh,[1] when he dwelt in the goat-haired tabernacle among the children of Israel.

With God's word becoming flesh through the baptism of the Spirit, we have the idea of *presence* — the presence of God and the voice of God. This perspective on Jesus stresses links with the Angel of the Presence. During the exodus period, the Angel of the Presence was the voice of God (e.g. Exod 3:18; 5:2; 15:26; 19:5; 23:21) and the manifestation of God;[2] in NT times this was Christ.

Can the title, 'the Word', describe the presence of God? The answer lies in the distinctive use of 'the Oracle' or 'the Word' to describe the Holy of Holies in Solomon's temple. The Hebrew word for 'the Oracle' (דבר/דביר) is unique to the Holy of Holies and means 'word'. This was a *place* where God chose to dwell, and a *place* from which God chose to speak. It was the same with Christ:

> Destroy this temple, and in three days I[3] will raise it up' John 2:19[4]

> Behold the tabernacle of God is with men... Rev 21:2

Jesus was a temple of God's presence, and his cleansing of the temple is meant as an object lesson of the fact that God was *in Christ*. He was the new Bethel, the house of God to which angels would ascend and descend (Gen 28:17; John 1:51). Around this place Solomon constructed 'ribs' or 'chambers', and the use of this word goes back to Genesis 2 when we are told that Eve was constructed out of the 'rib' (same word) of Adam. This

---

[1] Paul has plenty to say about 'the flesh' as unregenerate human nature. The question is whether this sense fits John 1:14 or whether we should regard that sense as an overtone in v. 14.

[2] The Greek order in John 1:1c is 'God was the Word', and this fits in with the idea of God being manifest or *present* in a person.

[3] This 'I' here is an example of God speaking through Christ, as a prophet declares the words of God.

[4] As Hebrews states, the flesh of Christ was the *veil* (Heb 10:20) enclosing the place of God's presence. This veil was done away with when Christ destroyed the flesh in his death.

is the body around the Holy of Holies — of one spirit with the Holy of Holies (cf. Col 2:9).

This concept of the *place* of God's presence is another key to John 1. This place was made flesh. The use of the title 'the Word' points to a connection with the first temple, as well as going back to the tabernacle and Genesis.[1] [2]

So it is that we can often interpret a stretch of language like that of the prologue of John as embracing many things. This is the nature of typology and meaning in the Scriptures — it is multi-faceted and multi-layered. Ingredients of meaning are drawn from all over the Scriptures to make up a basis for reflection upon the things of God.

14. Before John the Baptist

There is some evidence to support the view that the people (and their leaders) were confused over John the Baptist and Jesus, as to exactly who was the Messiah. Today, we have no doubt, but it is worthwhile trying to think ourselves into the first century frame of mind, and ask ourselves: *What is the relationship between these two prophets, who is the greater?* Imagine we are talking with a disciple of John the Baptist. What would we think if he made the following points?

1) John was pre-announced by an angel, just like Jesus (Luke 1:13). He was declared to be a 'great' prophet (Luke 1:15).

2) John's childhood is described in terms very similar to that of Jesus, and these terms are picked up from the type of Samuel (Luke 2:80; 3:52; cf. 1 Sam 3:19).

3) John came first, and *he* baptized Jesus (Matt 3:13), so was he greater?

4) His style was that of Elijah (Matt 11:14), who was the great prophet of the OT, while Jesus' style fitted Elisha.

---

[1] It is worth pointing out that the ideas of a place where God dwelt, his actual presence, and the voice of God are all ingredients of the Garden of Eden. This is a parallelism we cannot explore at this point.

[2] Hence, in Genesis 1, there is not only what God says, but also 'the Spirit of God hovering over creation' (Gen 1:2).

5) The Law and the Prophets were until John, who therefore represented the beginning of a new phase in God's purpose (Matt 11:13).

6) John's ministry had a great impact (Luke 1:16; 3:3), he preached about things of which we have no record (Luke 3:18).

7) Many were baptized by John, and they were not re-baptized by Jesus' disciples (Luke 7:29).

8) John's message was much like the message of Jesus. He preached repentance and baptism for the remission of sins. He inveighed against any confidence in the Jews' natural lineage from Abraham (Luke 3:8).

9) The people wondered whether he was the Christ (Mark 1:4; Luke 3:15).

10) Jesus said that no prophet born of woman was greater than John, and the people thought of him as *that prophet* (Matt 21:26; Mark 11:32; cf. Deut 18:15).

11) The people thought that Jesus might have been a resurrected *John the Baptist* (Matt 14:2; 16:14).

12) John had his own band of disciples, whom he taught as a master (Luke 5:33; 11:1; Acts 19:1).

These points show that there was a clear need to state the relationship between John and Jesus and establish Jesus as the Messiah. This was a burning requirement in the presentation of the gospel, because all the people venerated John as a prophet.[1]

The opening chapter of John's Gospel therefore emphasizes the priority of Jesus over John the Baptist:[2]

---

[1] Dating the Gospel of John is another subject, but this would be one argument for an early date in the late thirties or early forties CE.

[2] This requirement is fulfilled in various ways, for example, although we read 'there was a man...whose name was John' (v. 6), this mention of John's *name* contrasts with the role given to Christ's *name* - 'to them he gave power...even to them that believe on his name' (v. 12).

...for he was before me...he it is, who coming after me is preferred before me...After me cometh a man which is pre-ferred before me: for he was before me. John 1:15, 27, 30 (KJV)

It is possible to mistake this emphasis by inferring that Christ was 'before' John in time, as if to say that he was a pre-existent being in heaven. But to understand John's message, we need to look at its OT background. Are there any OT types behind John's testimony?

John's testimony (John 1:30) was 'after me cometh a man which is preferred before me: for he was before me' (KJV). The Greek uses two different words for 'before' here (ἔμπροσθέν and πρῶτός), which mean, roughly, 'before in place' and 'first' respectively. Furthermore, the Greek for 'preferred' is literally 'became' (γέγονεν), and the Greek for 'man' (ἀνὴρ) is very often used when referring to a husband. A literal rendering of John's testimony therefore could just as well be, 'after me cometh a husband, who has become before me, for he was first of me'. In addition to this John states that he was not worthy to unloose the Messiah's shoe latches (John 1:27).[1]

A main stress in John's testimony is a 'before...after' relationship—he says that the one coming after himself had become before him. This use of 'after' is often used in contexts denoting genealogical relationships.[2] It is reasonable to suggest that Jesus was 'after' John in the sense that he was after him in descent - a younger cousin. But John's testimony is that Jesus 'became before him'. How so?

Jacob was a man who came 'after' Esau (Gen 25:26), and later he 'became before him', when he sold his birthright to Jacob. Esau was a man of the earth, earthy — typical of the first Adam. Jacob, however, was typical of the second man. The privileges of the firstborn were sought by him. These included among other things, wealth and the family inheritance; the duties of priesthood, and responsibility to act as redeemer to the name of

---

[1] The KJV has 'preferred' because it is trying to make sense of two Greek words in combination — the Greek word for 'become' and the Greek word meaning 'before' in a spatial sense. My construction is neutral in using 'after me cometh a husband, who has become before me, for he was first of me', however, I am not averse to 'preferred' since the typology is one that involves position in a family structure.

[2] See Gen 17:6-10, Deut 1:8, Josh 22:27, Ruth 4:4, 1 Kgs 3:12, 2 Chron 1:12, Ecc 4:16, Isa 43:10, Acts 7:45.

a dead brother. So, this is one example of someone being 'after' and then becoming 'before'. Turning to the story of Ruth there is another example of the first giving way to the second:

- Naomi needed a redeemer (Ruth 4:14) to raise up the name of the dead (Ruth 4:5) according to the law. Jesus was a redeemer who was willing to raise up the name of the dead.

- Boaz was a kinsman but there was a 'nearer' kinsman before him; he was 'after' that kinsman (Ruth 4:4). John and Jesus were kinsmen. John was before Jesus who was 'after' him.

- The nearer kinsman was unwilling to be a husband, but after him there was a husband — Boaz. John was not the redeemer or the bridegroom, he was (part of) the lover of the bridegroom (John 3:29); Jesus was the husband.

- The nearer kinsman relinquished his right and transferred his rights to Boaz by taking off his shoe, he made Boaz *first* kinsman in this transaction. John the Baptist pronounced himself unworthy to untie Messiah's shoe latches and declared that he must decrease; and he pointed to Christ.

In both these cases there is a common pattern of the second man[1] becoming the first man. This pattern is reflected in Paul's words that Christ was a 'second' man. Both cases also illustrate how the second man was 'first *of me*', to use John the Baptist's own words: Jacob was first *of* Esau, and Boaz was first *of* his near kinsman.

John is not saying Christ was before him in time, but rather alluding to that OT pattern of a first man giving way to a second man, where the 'first' man has a part in the handover to the second man.[2][3]

15. And the Word was God
How are we to think of the statement, 'the Word was God'? The normal proposal is that this implies that Christ is fully God. This verse is used as a

---

[1] There are a number of 'second man' types in the OT.
[2] The stress on 'before me' contrasts with Malachi 'Behold I send my messenger *before thy face*' (Mal 3:1).
[3] This places John's testimony in v. 15 at Jesus' baptism which supports our 'baptism of Jesus' interpretation of v. 14.

'proof-text' in the doctrine of the Trinity.[1] A counter proposal is that the Greek should be translated by 'the Word was *a* God', because the definite article is absent in the Greek. Such a counter proposal is not decisive, because a noun like 'θεὸς' ('God') may be used without an article before the verb 'to be'.[2] Still, the absence of a definite article does indicate that we do not have an absolute identity in 'the Word was God'.

Another proposal is that the statement means, 'the Word was divine'. The problem with this proposal is that 'divine' is descriptive of nature, and a different (but related) Greek word is translated 'divine', viz. 'θεῖος'. This word is found in the NT in Acts 17:29 and 2 Peter 1:3. Wouldn't John have used this word if he had meant to convey a point about the divinity of Christ?

We can reject the above suggestions for the understanding of the predicate 'was God'. Another mistake we can reject is to say that the predicate ascribes a title, 'God', to Jesus. There is nothing in the passage that would suggest that giving names and/or titles is part of its subject-matter. This suggestion is too formal and trivial; it suggests that John is saying Jesus bore the title, 'God'. Rather, we should look for something more substantial in the context; something to which v. 1 can be related.

The word *theos* occurs in the expressions, 'was toward/with God' and 'was God'. The first predicate (as it is used) conveys the ideas of intercession and priesthood between man and God the Father. The second predicate conveys some sort of identity between *logos* and *theos*. It is a mistake to simply assume that the reference of 'God' is the same in the two expressions 'was toward/with God' and 'was God'. The first predicate (...*was toward/with*...) conveys a two-way relation that allows us to identify two referents for the associated terms. The second predicate is different, consisting of '*x* was God', and we should not infer that John is asserting an absolute identity.

The first reason for exercising caution here is John's previous assertion that the Word was towards God and what this implies for the referents of the terms involved. A second reason consists in the fact that John may not be using *theos* as a referring term in '...was God'. The mere occurrence of *theos* does not carry the implication that it is used as a referring term. It may be a fundamental part of a predicate, rather than a term slotted into a

---

[1] One (misguided) motivation for adopting a linguistic hypostatization interpretation of 'the Word' in v. 1 is to counter Trinitarian readings.
[2] For example, see John 1:50; 10:24; 19:21; 1 John 4:8.

predicate. This is suggested by the fact that John drops the article in 'was God', whereas it had been present in 'was toward God'. What John is predicating is a relative identity with respect to some aspect of God. As Dunn comments, "Philo demonstrates that a distinction between *ho theos* and *theos* such as we find in John 1:1b-c, would be deliberate by the author and significant for the Greek reader". [1]

The main reason for affirming that Jesus 'was God' is his **role** and **function**. The context (v. 3) presents Jesus as one *through* whom 'all things were made', which is a reference to the new creation. From one perspective (that of the old creation) Jesus is God's word in respect of the new creation. From another perspective, that of the creatures of this new creation, Jesus is the God in whose image they are created. This reading is confirmed by the reader's sense of what is missing. In quoting Gen 1:1, 'In the beginning...' the reader expects the next word to be 'God' but it is missing from the quotation. John places the word at the end of his sentence and the reader is brought to see that 'the Word' has this role of God *as a creator* because Genesis had gone on to state 'God created'. An expectation that John will go on and describe a creation is engendered by what he quotes and how he transforms the language elements of Gen 1:1.

In addition to Jesus being the God of the new creation, Thomas' confession (John 20:28) carries another dimension of meaning. Jesus' response was

> Thomas, because thou hast <u>seen me,</u> thou hast believed: blessed *are* they that have not seen, and *yet* have believed. John 20:29 (KJV)

Jesus' words allude[2] to his earlier statement, "He that hath seen me hath seen the Father" (John 14:9). The disciples had asked Jesus, "Show us the Father" and this reply was designed to tell them that in seeing Jesus they were seeing the Father. The episode reflects the closing words of the prologue,

---

[1] Dunn, *Christology in the Making*, 241; see grammatical discussion in D. B. Wallace, *Greek Grammar Beyond the Basics*, 266-269.

[2] The allusion introduces another layer to the meaning of the episode with Thomas; he wanted to literally see the physical living Jesus before he believed. When he did so, his belief was expressed in a way that shows that was now seeing Jesus for who he was, and in John's terms from the prologue, Jesus 'was God'. The literary structure here is that of an *inclusio*.

275

No man hath seen God at any time; the only begotten son,
which is in the bosom of the Father, he hath explained *him*.
John 1:18 (KJV revised)

Here John states that no man had seen God, and he further identifies him
as the Father; but the Son had explained him. The declarations of Jesus
about his father were part and parcel of what he was showing his disciples
each day about the Father in his own life. This is also one of the ways in
which Jesus was God as the opening verse of the prologue states. In fact,
v. 18 represents an *inclusio* with v. 1 because, as 'the Word', or God's
mouth, Jesus *explained* God in words and showed him in deeds.

16. My Lord and My God

Why does Thomas call Jesus 'My Lord and My God'? Why does he use
two titles, 'Lord' and 'God' rather than one? Why does he combine the
titles in this distinctive twofold affirmation? These are questions which we
can only answer by examining the *conversational context* of his utterance, and
by *perceiving* the allusions in that context. These allusions take us back to
the Genesis creation, and through this device they teach us that Thomas'
remark presupposes the new creation and venerates Jesus as one in whom
he could **see** the Father.[1]

It is easy to overlook the fact that Thomas' remark is part of a conversation, and a conversation charged with emotion. It is not part of a *theological*
treatise and it is not just an ordinary exchange. Jesus' conversations always
allude to the OT Scriptures, and those with whom he talked also show an
awareness of the Scriptures; their remarks being often recorded to
illustrate insights of faith. In addition, the biblical writers have recorded
the conversations in such a way (with details of time and place), so as to
bring out the significance of the things that are said in the conversational
exchange. The conversation between Jesus and Thomas illustrates all these
points.

The main allusion is in John 20:20, "...he breathed on [them] and said
unto them, 'Receive ye the holy Spirit' ", which connects up with Gen 2:7,
"...breathed into his nostrils the breath of life" (e.g. see KJV mg.; cf. Isa
42:5). Such an allusion introduces to a reader the theme of creation, and

---

[1] Another expositional strategy for explaining why Christ is called 'God'
would be one which explained his role as the anointed king of the future
kingdom of God (Ps 45:6, Isa 9:6-7, Heb 1:8). Another would be one
which showed Jesus as the anti-type to the Arm of the Lord (Isa 40:3, 9,
61:6, 64:4).

the disciples are being presented to us as types of Adam. Other creation allusions are not far away: the breathing takes place on the *first day* of the week (John 20:1), but in the evening of that day (John 20:19; Gen 1:5), and the day had begun very early while it was dark (cf. Gen 1:2); this is the language of the creation week (Genesis 1) being brought into John 20.[1]

Thus, the allusion implicit in Christ's breathing[2] on them takes the reader back to the event of Adam becoming a living soul, and this makes Christ the creator of a new man. It is partly because Christ has this *creative* role in respect of the new creation that Thomas calls him '*my* God'. Thomas had been absent at the occasion of the 'breathing' upon the disciples, but eight days later, again on the first day of the week, with the door shut again, Thomas invites Christ to breathe on him by calling Jesus '*my* God' - addressing one with power to *create* (John 1:3-4). But, more precisely, Thomas' possessive '*my* God' is his acknowledgement that he needed to be created in the image *of Christ* as Adam was created in the image of God.

There is a contrast between Gen 1:26 and Gen 2:7. The first text reads 'Let us make man in our image...', but the second text states 'the Lord God formed man'. John's 'breathing' allusion goes back to Genesis 2, but we should not forget the details we have in Genesis 1: the 'Lord God' of Gen 2:7 *who forms* the man is part of the group who says, 'Let *us* make man in *our* image'. Thomas' confession, '*my* God', is recognizing Jesus' as the one in whose image he is created. Paul makes the same point when he says, "And have put on the new man, which is renewed in knowledge after the image of him that created him" (Col 3:10).

The Genesis creation is not the only background to Thomas' remark. The conversational setting is described in language reminiscent of Noah's Flood, and this is because the Flood was a time of destruction and re-creation of life upon the land. The room in which the disciples are gathered is like the ark, for there is the emphasis on the shut door and a separation from the world (Gen 7:16; John 20:19, 26). In the ark, there

---

[1] The woman was deceived first, so she is the first at the tomb and the first to believe. She fell through touching the tree of knowledge and eating of the fruit, but here she resists the temptation to touch.
[2] Christ's birth by the holy Spirit is an analogue to this reception by the disciples of the breath of the holy Spirit.

was everything 'wherein is the *breath of life*' (Gen 7:15; cf. 2:7), and in the enclosed room the disciples received the *breath of life* (John 20:22). [1]

Christ has used the expression 'my God' earlier in the text, (see also Matt 27:46 and Rev 3:12), and his God, he says, was also Mary Magdalene's God, and this God is the Father. Does Thomas have a different God to that of Christ and Mary Magdalene? This question begs the answer, no.

We have been thinking of Adam, but the theme of the creation of the woman also is present in John 20. The incident of 'breathing' upon all the disciples takes place after Christ has showed his 'side' to them. Since it was from Adam's side that Eve was taken, Christ is showing to the disciples that they are also a woman taken from *his* side. They recognise this fact by calling him 'lord', which is a term used between husbands and wives in the Jewish historical traditions (cf. Abraham and Sarah, 1 Pet 3:6). The Gospel writer has set the scene for this use of 'my lord' by Thomas, because he has also recorded the exchange between Mary and Jesus, in which she calls Jesus 'my Lord' and 'Master'.

The disciples are part of the bride of Christ, taken from his side. Indeed, since the woman was taken from the man, and since she was bone of his bone and flesh of his flesh, there is a close identity between the man and the woman. When the woman was formed from Adam's rib, *she* would then have had the breath of life breathed into her so that *she* became a living soul. Thomas had expressed his doubt in terms of the *side* of Jesus, and so his faith is expressed in terms of the *side* of Jesus. Jesus is his lord, from which he needs (in a figure) to be taken. Thomas recognises the creation of both the male and the female when he calls Christ 'my lord' as well as 'my God'.

The breathing upon the disciples takes place *before* the baptism of the holy Spirit in Acts 2. Since this breathing corresponds to the creation of man (and woman) in Genesis, the baptism of the holy Spirit would refer to the next act in the Genesis 2 sequence — the giving of knowledge to Adam (i.e. the word of God). Christ's argument to Mary is that he had not yet ascended to the Father to receive gifts of *knowledge* for men, and it is this

---

[1] Although we may trace these allusions in the context which explain Thomas' address to Christ, it should also be recognised that we have here a common address for the emperor. For example, when Tiridates, king of Armenia, paid a state visit to Nero in 66 CE, he addressed Nero with the words, "I have come to you, my god, to worship you as I do Mithras" *Dio Cassius* 63.5.2.

that Mary accepts (John 14:26; 20:17; Eph 4:8). The purpose of this knowledge was for Adam to fulfil a *priestly*[1] role in the Garden of Eden in respect of Eve and their children. Jesus breathes on the disciples and sends them into the world with an Adamic *commission*. This apostolic-priestly role (1 Pet 2:9) needed knowledge which was to be used in building a temple (Eph 2:20-21).[2]

Passing from death to life is a theme in John 20, and of Jesus who is the resurrection and the life, Isaiah says, 'Lo, this is our God; we have waited for him, and he will save us: this is the lord; we have waited for him, we will be glad and rejoice in his salvation' (Isa 25:8).

Taking John 20:28 as an example of a text used by Trinitarians, what does it prove? It does not prove anything about pre-existence, coequality, or co-eternity among the persons of the Godhead. But then perhaps the text is not meant to be used for these ideas. Indeed, the text shows the separate personhood of the Father and the Son *after* the resurrection of the Son; it indicates that the Son has a God, the Father, (whom Paul calls the one God), and Jesus calls the only true God; it also shows that the *person* of the Son *had been* dead.

17. Conclusion

Dunn observes that "that only in the Fourth Gospel can we speak of a doctrine of the incarnation".[3] If this is the case, the doctrine is unproven. First, Jesus is 'the Word' who was in the beginning; he interceded towards God for the people. He manifested the Father and he is the one through whom new men and women are created and in these two ways he was 'God' (John 1:1). Secondly, the word became flesh with the bestowal of the Spirit at Jesus' baptism, i.e. flesh came to stand in place of the word of God in Genesis. This isn't an incarnation of a pre-existing hypostasis or a

---

[1] The keepership of the garden delivered unto Adam was a priestly role; and this is confirmed by Christ when immediately after breathing on the disciples, he instructs them to remit sins (John 20:23; cf. Exod 23:21). Cain rejected this role when he said of Abel, "Am I my brother's keeper"?

[2] The disciples' dominion over the fish of the sea and the domestic beasts of the field is shown following their creation as a typical man (John 21:1ff). Nevertheless, the cycle of creation followed by a fall is shown by Peter in his going to Galilee and being found 'naked' (John 21:7).

[3] "The doctrine of the incarnation began to emerge when the exalted Christ was spoken of in terms drawn from the Wisdom imagery of pre-Christian Judaism", Dunn, *Christology in the Making*, 259.

person but rather (reversing the tables) it is Jesus becoming the living Word of God in word and deed (John 1:14).

John 1:1, 14 is usually read as a progressive sequence. Instead, the prologue is comprised of three parallel paragraphs which are all about Jesus and his ministry. Their purpose is to differentiate Jesus' person and ministry from that of John the Baptist. The paragraphs do this first more abstractly with mainly Genesis typology (vv. 1-5), then with primarily Exodus typology (vv. 6-13), and finally more concretely, (but still with some typology), with regard to the historical experience of the disciples (vv. 14-18). The key verse is v. 14 and the key statement is 'And so the word became flesh'.

Traditional and more common readings of the prologue, whether Trinitarian or Biblical unitarian, usually treat 'the beginning' of John 1 as the Genesis beginning. There may be a nod to a timeless eternity by Trinitarians. This goes hand in hand with seeing either the **real** (as in Trinitarianism) or the **ideal** (as in Biblical unitarian) pre-existence of 'the Word' in v. 1. However, while using Genesis 1 as a template, 'the beginning' of John 1 is actually the beginning of the gospel and a new creation (Mark 1:1).

John 1 is often aligned with a cultural background and it has been since the sub-Apostolic era. Although we lack typological exegesis of John 1 from the sub-Apostolic and Apologist eras,[1] the declarative statements that we have from those writings show that they interpreted the prologue through the lens of pre-Christian Judaism. This is the basic methodological mistake that explains the emergence of the doctrine of the incarnation. This was their error; it need not be ours. If, instead, we only use the background of the Hebrew Scriptures, typological interpretation and intra-scriptural reasoning will unlock the true meaning. Jesus stands in the place of the word in Genesis as the Word of the new creation of life in him; he is as Moses to John the Baptist's Aaron; he is as the Angel of the Lord leading and guiding the people through the wilderness, tabernacling with the people and making the nation; he is as Isaac with Abraham his father dying and being raised to life on Moriah through whom the nation was born; and he is the grace and truth foreshadowed on Sinai.

---

[1] The point here is that the Church Fathers certainly engaged in typological exegesis of the Old Testament just like the NT writers; what they didn't do for John 1 was show how John was engaged in typological exegesis.

Appendix

There is a well-known textual issue with v. 18 represented in the following four versions,

No man hath seen God at any time; the only begotten son, which is in the bosom of the Father, he hath declared him. (KJV)

No one has ever seen God. The only one, himself God, who is in closest fellowship with the Father, has made God known. (NET)

No man has seen God at any time; the only begotten God, who is in the bosom of the Father, He has explained Him. (NASB)

No one has ever seen God. The only Son, God, who is at the Father's side, has revealed him. (NAB)

Θεὸν οὐδεὶς ἑώρακεν πώποτε· μονογενὴς θεὸς ὁ ὢν εἰς τὸν κόλπον τοῦ πατρὸς ἐκεῖνος ἐξηγήσατο. (GNT)

Θεὸν οὐδεὶς ἑώρακεν πώποτε· ὁ μονογενὴς υἱός, ὁ ὢν εἰς τὸν κόλπον τοῦ πατρός, ἐκεῖνος ἐξηγήσατο. (BYZ)

The two Greek variants represent the overwhelming bulk of manuscripts, versions and Patristic citations. There is a minor variant worth noting which adds an article before μονογενὴς θεὸς. Most older versions align with the KJV; newer translations align with the NET, NAB or NASB with nuanced variations. The KJV follows its Greek Byzantine text in a fairly literal manner. The NAB, NET and NASB follow an Alexandrian text represented in the GNT but differ in how they read μονογενὴς.

How you read μονογενὴς is crucial to the Alexandrian argument, since it has to be read the same way in v. 14. The NAB takes μονογενὴς to imply 'son'; the NET restricts its translation to 'the only one' which looks vacuous if not confusing vis-à-vis Jewish monotheism. The Alexandrian text will fare better if we read μονογενὴς either as 'the only son, God' or 'the only begotten one, God'. The Byzantine text, with its inclusion of υἱός, requires μονογενὴς to be read as 'only begotten' if the compound adjective is to be respected and not treated as just equivalent to μόνος.

The majority of textual critics today favour the Alexandrian reading (GNT); a minority favour the Byzantine reading (BYZ). Earlier generations of NT scholars favoured the Byzantine reading; today, the bias in favour of that reading among such scholars is less pronounced. The text critical argument boils down to how you weigh early manuscripts that go against the consensus of the later manuscripts, i.e. the argument is a Byzantine text versus Alexandrian text contest. The text critical argument is all about the **external evidence** of the manuscripts and text-critical methodology and history, and the New Testament argument is all about the **internal evidence** of Johannine style and thought in a first century context, i.e. whether John would have written 'the only son, God' or 'the only begotten one, God'.

We have no prejudice against the Byzantine text nor a bias in favour of the earlier Alexandrian manuscripts. As an outsider reading the text-critical arguments for and against, the disagreement looks stalemated because of a lack of manuscript evidence and a textual history for the 2c. CE. However, our view is that the internal evidence favours the Byzantine reading and so we think that this is the original text ('only begotten son').

External Evidence

The overwhelming **Manuscript Evidence**[1] (the Western, Byzantine and Caesarean traditions) favours the KJV and 'the only begotten son'. So, for example, the uncial manuscripts, Alexandrinus (A, 5c. CE),[2] Ephraemi Rescriptus[c] (9c. CE correction of C), and the Freer Gospels 7c. CE, W[supp]), among many others, have 'the only begotten son'. This is not to say all Western and Caesarean texts have υἱός, just that it is more strongly represented amongst these texts. The mass of Byzantine manuscripts has υἱός, including all the later Byzantine miniscules.[3]

---

[1] The evidence is conveniently listed in P. R. McReynolds, "John 1:18 in Textual Variation and Translation" in *New Testament Textual Criticism, its Significance for Exegesis* (eds., E. J. Epp and G. D. Fee; Cambridge: Cambridge University Press, 1981), 105-118. P. Comfort, *New Testament Text and Translation Commentary* (Carol Stream: Tyndale House Publishers, 2008), 255-256, also lists the translations that align with each variant, whether in the main text or in the margin.

[2] This manuscript is judged in general to be an Alexandrian text-type, even though in John 1:18 it agrees with the Western, Byzantine and Caesarean text-types; see B. M. Metzger, *The Text of the New Testament* (2nd ed., Oxford: Oxford University Press, 1968), 47.

[3] For a list of the important miniscule manuscripts see B. J. Wright, "Jesus as ΘΕΟΣ: A Textual Examination" in *Revisiting the Corruption of the New*

The Alexandrian tradition of manuscripts favours the NET, NASB and NAB and θεὸς. So, for example, 𝔓66 (3c. CE) and the uncial manuscripts, Sinaiticus* (4c. CE),[1] Vaticanus (4c. CE, B), Ephraemi Rescriptus* (5c. CE, C*), and Codex Regius (8c. CE, L), along with the Diatessaron^{Arab} support μονογενὴς θεὸς. 𝔓75 (3c. CE), Sinaiticus^c (a 6c.-7c. CE 'correction' of Sinaiticus*) and a 9c. CE manuscript 033 have an added article. However, some later secondary manuscripts in the Alexandrian tradition favour υἱός, (T (5c. CE), Υ (8c.-9c. CE), Δ (9c. CE), 892 (9c.-10c. CE), 1241 12c.-13c. CE)) which is significant.

P. R. McReynolds states that the argument in favour of the Alexandrian reading is the earlier date of its uncials and the early date of the Bodmer papyri.[2] P. Comfort comments that the discovery of the Bodmer papyri in the 1950s and 1960s "tipped the balance" in favour of the Alexandrian reading and offered the hypothesis that 'only begotten son' was a change made in the 3c. CE or earlier because it was "more ordinary".[3] Equally, we might counter by saying '(the) only begotten God' was an early change made for doctrinal reasons in Alexandria and the wider church resisted this change.

When we move onto the evidence of the **Versions**, McReynolds summarizes the evidence as, "This versional evidence shows that θεὸς and υἱός are both early readings and both have some geographical spread, although υἱός clearly dominated in the West, while the evidence is more evenly distributed in the East."[4] Significant evidence on the side of θεὸς is the Peshitta, and in favour of υἱός we have the Vulgate. The key point here is that both readings are *early*, a fact supported by the Greek Fathers.

As for the **Greek Fathers**, McReynolds notes that 11 Fathers support μονογενὴς θεὸς across 39 citations but some of these writers also have υἱός. On the other hand, there are 20+ Fathers who cite John 1:18 more than 40+ times with υἱός. McReynolds also claims evidence in the Greek

---

Testament (ed., D. B. Wallace; Grand Rapids: Kregel Publications, 2011), 229-265 (241-242), and see Metzger's evaluation of the miniscules in his *The Text of the New Testament*.

[1] Metzger, *The Text of the New Testament*, 46, classifies Sinaiticus as in general Alexandrian, but it has been corrected in later centuries and it has Western readings; in respect of John 1:18, it is Alexandrian although the opening chapters do have Western readings.

[2] McReynolds, "John 1:18 in Textual Variation and Translation", 105-106.

[3] Comfort, *New Testament Text and Translation Commentary*, 255.

[4] McReynolds, "John 1:18 in Textual Variation and Translation", 107.

Fathers when they use μονογενὴς θεὸς but don't cite the Gospel; he claims that these are allusions to John and are evidence of the θεὸς variant. However, he is unwilling to include references to ὁ μονογενὴς υἱός without citation of John 1:18 because this idea is used in more than one place in John. This rather loads the dice in favour of θεὸς, and we should instead accept the allusive evidence of ὁ μονογενὴς υἱός as embracing all of the Johannine writings including John 1:18 and count it equally against the allusive evidence for μονογενὴς θεὸς. This is especially the case if the allusion uses the exact form of the phrase in John 1:18 as John's use of the idea of 'only begotten son' in John 3:16, 18 and 1 John 4:9 employs different grammatical forms.

On the other hand, it could be argued methodologically that allusions on either side cannot be claimed as evidence for the text without specific citation because we cannot be certain about the reason for the language being used – is it because of John or just a reflection of general dogmatic theology. Notwithstanding this point, statistically, the Greek Fathers favour μονογενὴς υἱός.

The **Latin Fathers** are overwhelmingly in favour of 'only begotten son' with only Hilary using 'only begotten God'. This is consistent with the evidence of the Latin versions.

In sum, from the GNT committee, Metzger gives the Alexandrian reading a {B} second-highest rating from a four-point scale {A}-{D} for assessing a text's likelihood to be original.[1] A. Wikgren from the same committee disagrees and assigns a {D} reading to the Alexandrian reading suggesting it is the result of a transcriptional error.[2] The judgment of textual critics has been mixed over the years but the majority today favour μονογενὴς θεὸς. The principal reason seems to be the evidential weight they give to the Alexandrian text type and its early manuscripts. However, the ubiquity of μονογενὴς υἱός in the other textual traditions implies an equal antiquity (supported by the earliest Fathers, e.g. Irenaeus, who supports both readings), and we might therefore suppose that the absence of those text-types among the earliest manuscripts is due to constant preferential use, wear and tear and disposal, whereas the survival of the early Alexandrian Egyptian manuscripts that we have is due to a lack of use and/or happenstance.

---

[1] Metzger, *A Textual Commentary on the Greek New Testament*, 198.
[2] Ibid.

New Testament scholars[1] have been less inclined to follow textual critics for reasons internal to the text. Before we look at internal evidence, we should consider matters of transmission history and historical methodology. Historical hypotheses and historical methodology go together because the question of which text is original depends on how we evaluate eclectic textual methodology versus using a text like the majority Byzantine text.[2]

It is worth saying up-front that the 'textual critics' of the Byzantine period (i.e. the more professional scribes) came to favour μονογενὴς υἱός first in the West and then in the East and they are much closer to the evidence than the critic of the modern period. Furthermore, we should give due weight to the mixed witness of the Alexandrian textual tradition because this shows later correction of the text in favour of υἱός (e.g. Ephraemi Rescriptus[c] (9c. CE correction of C); Υ, Codex Athous Laurae 8c-9c. CE). Of course, it could be countered that this is due to peer pressure from the dominance of the other textual traditions (but then why are they dominant?).

We should also note that both an early date for a manuscript and its being part of a superior textual tradition[3] does not automatically confer greater probability on all of its distinctive readings. The case has to be made for each of its variants. Given that we don't have a textual history for the second century after the autograph for the Alexandrian and Byzantine readings under investigation, hypotheses explaining the readings for and against them being original can be put forward.

The earliest use of the phrase μονογενὴς θεὸς is by the Gnostic Valentinus (c. 170 CE, Irenaeus, *Against Heresies*), but this doesn't mean that it is a

---

[1] For example, older commentaries favour the majority reading: Hoskyns and Davey, *The Fourth Gospel*, 153-154; R. H. Lightfoot, *St. John's Gospel: A Commentary* (Oxford: Oxford University Press, 1956), 90; Barrett, *The Gospel According to St. John*, 141. In favour of the Alexandrian reading, are the more recent commentaries: Lindars, *The Gospel of John*, 98-99; Beasley-Murray, *John*, 2-3; Marsh, *Saint John*, 112.

[2] For a discussion of the issues over the Majority Text versus the Eclectic Text see D. A. Black, ed., *Rethinking New Testament Textual Criticism* (Grand Rapids: Baker House Academic, 2002).

[3] The Alexandrian tradition is regarded as superior and this common opinion is often repeated as if it settles the question of any textual variant, but we should weigh each case on the evidence.

Gnostic invention; he could be alluding to and misusing a copy of the Gospel.[1] If the phrase is not scriptural, its origins are lost in the 2c. CE., but if it is scriptural, we have no historical puzzle to explain. On the other hand, if μονογενὴς θεὸς is scriptural, we have then to explain the origins of μονογενὴς υἱός. Historical guesswork, one way or another, is unavoidable.

The historical hypotheses available to both variants are transcriptional error and/or corruption or benign harmonization. There is obviously some similarity in the uncial letters for θεὸς and υἱός. The shortened forms of the two words (ΦΣ and ΥΣ) have a common letter and an accidental error in transcription could explain the difference among the uncial manuscript traditions if ΥΣ was being used as a *nomina sacra* at the time (if not, then accidental error is harder to envisage).

Neither reading is more difficult in terms of syntax or semantics which might have given rise to scribal emendation. In terms of Johannine usage, the two words in μονογενὴς υἱός are found closely coupled elsewhere in John, and so μονογενὴς θεὸς is more difficult to explain as a scribal change, whereas a scribe might have substituted μονογενὴς υἱός for reasons of internal harmonization or wider consistency with other texts or church formulations. This is the principle of *lectio difficilior*.[2]

The counterpoint to the above *lectio difficilior* argument is to claim μονογενὴς θεὸς as an 'orthodox' corruption of Scripture to affirm the deity of Christ, whereas μονογενὴς υἱός is consistent with Johannine usage.[3] McReynolds states that for any scribe to have intentionally changed υἱός to θεὸς "defies imagination".[4] This rather depends on how imaginative the scholar is in coming up with scenarios vis-à-vis any orthodox corruption of Scripture.

---

[1] Comfort, *New Testament Text and Translation Commentary*, 256.

[2] The rules of Textual Criticism are summarized in K. Aland and B. Aland, *The Text of the New Testament* (Rev ed.; Grand Rapids: Eerdmans, 1989), 280-282; their warning is that they "must not be taken too mechanically" (281).

[3] B. Ehrman, *The Orthodox Corruption of Scripture* (Oxford: Oxford University Press, 1993), 78-82. This is discussed in various essays in Wallace, *Revisiting the Corruption of the New Testament*. Ehrman and Wallace have debated the issue, and this is recorded in B. D. Ehrman and D. B. Wallace "The Textual Reliability of the New Testament" in *The Reliability of the New Testament* (ed., R. B. Stewart; Minneapolis: Fortress Press, 2011), 13-60.

[4] McReynolds, "John 1:18 in Textual Variation and Translation", 114.

In terms of which reading more easily gives rise to another, we would say that the minor variant ὁ μονογενής (which has a witness in the Diatessaron^cur) would explain both ὁ μονογενὴς υἱός and ὁ μονογενὴς θεὸς as competing natural expansions. This in turn would allow us to explain the non-articular μονογενὴς θεὸς, because ὁ μονογενὴς θεὸς could be construed adjectivally as 'the only begotten God' and less Johannine, whereas μονογενὴς θεὸς could be construed appositionally and be more in keeping with Johannine usage in John 1:1, 14.[1]

As for the two major variants, μονογενὴς θεὸς and ὁ μονογενὴς υἱός, neither naturally give rise to the other directly. The earliest church Fathers knew both readings, so any early manuscripts which favour 'only begotten God' are not decisive. Nothing can turn on minority readings from early manuscripts when the early church Fathers are split. Furthermore, the Byzantine tradition, being less congenial to Trinitarianism, adds to its claim to originality.

If the traditions are not explicable in terms of accidental changes to the early 2c. CE manuscripts, theologically motivated change is the next hypothesis. In the context of Alexandria in Egypt in the 2c. CE is θεὸς a likely or possible theologically motivated corruption? This is the claim of B. D. Ehrman in his book *The Orthodox Corruption of Scripture*. The variant was created and supported by Gnostic and orthodox writers to affirm a High Christology against Adoptionists (albeit a different High Christology in each case).[2] Ehrman is correcting J. W. Burgon's thesis which was that the corruption originated with Valentinus.[3]

If [ὁ] μονογενὴς θεὸς is original, why would scribes change it in Egypt or elsewhere? There isn't an obvious theological motivation for such a change. The appositional reading is understandable in terms of John's prologue and in keeping with later Arian and Trinitarian Christology. If it was changed accidentally, why didn't the original (which would still be extant in other copies) re-assert itself? This leaves the better hypothesis which is that such a change was intentional and benign and designed to harmonize the text with Johannine usage.

We have then the two best historical hypotheses for the two major variants: one was a theological corruption while the other was a benign

---

[1] Comfort, *New Testament Text and Translation Commentary*, 256.

[2] Ehrman, *The Orthodox Corruption of Scripture*, 82.

[3] J. W. Burgon, *The Causes of the Corruption of the Traditional Text of the Holy Gospels* (London: Geo. Bell & Sons, 1896), 215-218.

harmonization. In the absence of historical data, no decision can be made between the two. We have a stalemate.[1] We have to consider internal evidence. Here the question is: What do we think John would have written?

Internal Evidence[2]

The adjectival interpretation of μονογενὴς θεός is 'only begotten God' and it rests on the normal rule that adjectives that agree in number, gender and case modify their nouns. The appositional interpretation is 'only begotten one (or son), God' and this is said to reflect John 1:1, 14. We will evaluate both understandings of μονογενὴς θεός along with μονογενὴς υἱός. Internal considerations from both sides brought to bear include (in no particular order),

(1) John 3:16, 18 and 1 John 4:9 have 'only begotten son' (albeit with different Greek forms). So, μονογενὴς υἱός is in keeping with Johannine phraseology.[3] This point can be made stronger. John 3:16, 18 are about "believing in him" and "in the name of the [only begotten son of God]". These are elements of the prologue (John 1:12) and the argument is that for John, 'belief in the name' is about the name of the son rather than 'God'. The counter to this is to claim that scribes have harmonized John 1:18 to bring it into line with Johannine usage elsewhere, and so the phrase need not be original, but John 1:18 is not just about *usage*; it is part of a *theology* of belief in the name of the son.

(2) V. 18 and μονογενὴς θεός is an appropriate *inclusio* with vv. 1 and 14: 'was God' in v. 1 matches 'God' in v. 18; 'explaining' the Father is a natural function of the Word; further, being 'with/towards' God could have the same import as the figure, 'in the bosom of the Father'. This literary argument overstates its case and is more the construct of the literary critic. If John was recapping v. 1 in v. 18, he would have had 'the only begotten one (or son), the Word'. Further, facing towards God is about being an intermediary which is not a plausible sense for the figure of being in the Father's bosom. Nevertheless, this argument shows that

---

[1] On the other hand, suppose the error was accidental in one manuscript in John's first batch of five copies of the Gospel and it went to Egypt, while the other copies were sent by John to other destinations. Which if any of the five copies could claim to be the autograph?

[2] Internal evidence is a series of checksums on the integrity of the text.

[3] Lightfoot, *St. John's Gospel: A Commentary*, 90; Bultmann, *The Gospel of John*, 82; Barrett, *The Gospel According to St. John*, 141; Hoskyns and Davey, *The Fourth Gospel*, 154.

we cannot claim it is completely contrary to Johannine theology to have 'the only begotten one (or son), God' in v. 18, unless we also jettison 'and was God' in v. 1.

(3) John 1:14 has '*from* the Father' which implies a begettal sense for μονογενής in v. 14 and therefore v. 18. We can't go with ideas of 'only one' or 'unique'. So, it is more likely that μονογενὴς υἱός is original because υἱός is specifying what is naturally '*from* the Father'. On the other hand, v. 14 did not use υἱός, so why couldn't it be the case that v. 18 has 'God' from v. 1 in apposition, giving 'only begotten one (or son), God'?

(4) John only relates attributive uses of μονογενής + υἱός to θεός (John 3:16, 18 and 1 John 4:9). With πατήρ in v. 18, Johannine usage suggests we would not have an attributive use of μονογενής + υἱός. This argument fails because it is evident that the attributive use of μονογενής + υἱός in v. 18 relates to the θεὸς in 'No man has seen God'; the πατήρ clause is an *additional* relation.[1]

(5) The variant μονογενὴς θεὸς introduces an awkwardness, "No man has seen God at any time...the only begotten one (or son), God...he has explained him". An only begotten son being seen by men and explaining God is not difficult, but how does God declare God? It might be countered that this awkwardness exists with v. 1 if it exists for v. 18, since the Word was both with God and was God. In both cases, the difficulty is removed by understanding the different sense in which the Word was God compared to the Father. But this reply concedes the point: it inadvertently suggests that v. 18 should be using the title 'the Word' for "has explained him" rather than 'God'.[2]

(6) Vv. 14-18 is a concluding paragraph that relates vv. 1-13 to the experience of the disciples, describing in more concrete terms the ministry of Jesus and John the Baptist's witness. The name 'Jesus Christ' and the Law are mentioned for the first time (v. 17), and the giving of power (v. 12) is mirrored in the receiving of fulness (v. 16). A first use of υἱός in v. 18 better fits this pattern of the paragraph. It is only in v. 17-18 we get given the identity of the Word and the true Light. If v. 18 had θεός it wouldn't be giving us anything more by way of identification than v. 1.[3]

---

[1] *Contra* Fennema, "John 1.18: 'God the only Son'", 127.
[2] *Contra* Fennema, "John 1.18: 'God the only Son'", 127-128.
[3] *Contra* Fennema, "John 1.18: 'God the only Son'", 127-128.

(7) Hebrews 11:17 uses μονογενής substantively of Isaac in an explanation of a typology of death and resurrection (Heb 11:19). This is support for reading substantive uses of μονογενής elsewhere as indicative of an Isaac typology if there are other reasons in the context for such a reading. Of the 9x uses in the NT, only John 1:14 and Heb 11:17 do not have an accompanying 'son/daughter/child' word (Luke 9:38 has 'son' in the previous clause). We have seen above that there are indications in the prologue that John 1:10, 14, 18 is using an Isaac typology. This argument is not about Johannine usage, but a deeper reason for υἱός based on Isaac typology being a father/son typology. However, the counterargument is that this Isaac typology only requires a coupling of πατήρ/μονογενής and not υἱός.[1] We might concede this point, but equally it goes to show that θεός is not original because such a juxtaposition is not part of an Isaac typology. The argument would support the minor variant ὁ μονογενής as original.

(8) In v. 14, υἱός is not used because μονογενής on its reflects the emphasis of 'thine only' in Gen 22:2, 12 and it complements 'from the Father' in explaining how God *provided* the lamb (Gen 22:8).[2] In v. 18, no such emphasis is needed because Abraham ('the Father') has now *received* Isaac, his son (Gen 22:13), back from the dead, a fact typed by the son now being 'in the bosom of the Father'.[3] Hence, where we have Isaac typology, we can expect υἱός and so it is original to v. 18.[4]

On the other hand, it could be said that whereas John elsewhere couples 'Father' and 'Son', he doesn't couple 'only begotten son' and 'Father', he couples 'only begotten son' and 'God'.[5] However, even if the 'bosom'

---

[1] Fennema, "John 1.18: 'God the only Son'", 126, makes this point although not in the context of developing an Isaac typology.

[2] Josephus, *Ant.* 1.222 follows the Hebrew and describes Isaac as Abraham's μονογενής.

[3] Barrett, *The Gospel According to St. John*, 169; Bultmann, *The Gospel of John*, 81, make a similar point without the Isaac typology.

[4] This father/son Isaac typology lies in the background of Jesus' discourse in John 5.

[5] Fennema, "John 1.18: 'God the only Son'", 126. Fennema deploys a standard analytical argument of shifting the unit of analysis. We have argued that 'Father' naturally couples with 'son'. Fennema counter-argues that this doesn't necessarily show that 'Father' naturally couples with 'only begotten son'. However, Fennema fails to see the Isaac typology in μονογενής which is a Father/son typology.

figure did not imply a filial relationship, it does imply a Father *taking care* of his only one,[1] and this notion manifestly goes better with υἱός.

The Isaac typology shows why a translation such as 'the only son' (v. 14, RSV) is wrong for this substantive use of μονογενής; it takes away the explanation of how God *provided* the lamb (i.e. through begettal). For the same reason, 'the only son' would be wrong for v. 18.[2]

In older translations (Pseudepigrapha, LXX, NT, etc.) μονογενής is often given an overtone of begettal, when it modifies a daughter/son/child word. In more modern translations this is not the case. Our argument is that John sets up his 'begettal' use in the prologue because he will be teaching about Jesus' **origin** throughout the Gospel.

(9) The juxtaposition, 'the only begotten one (or son), God' is too developed theologically for John.[3] The status of 'only begotten' in v. 14 is about the humanity of the Son. In v. 1, deity is predicated of 'the Word' and the status of 'only begotten' is absent. This coupling in v. 1 is not out of step with Second Temple thinking about 'the Word' (albeit this is applied to Jesus). To juxtapose 'only begotten one (or son)' and 'God' in v. 18 is too advanced theologically for the 1c. CE (the juxtaposition should be 'with 'the Word'); μονογενὴς θεός is 2c. CE doctrine and a first step towards Nicea.

(10) The reason for 'was God' in v. 1 is to identify Jesus as the 'God' of the new creation (vv. 3-4). Creation is not the focus of v. 18 but rather revelation, and in Johannine theology, this is the function of the Son. The contrast in John 1:17 between Moses and Jesus is continued in v. 18 in several ways. First, 'No man has seen God' echoes the Sinai declaration that 'no man can see me and live' (Exod 33:20). Moses did not see God; he saw only the back of God (Exod 33:20); secondly, Jesus is said, in contrast with Moses, to be the one who was in the bosom of the Father (Moses carried Israel in his bosom; Num 11:12); thirdly, he is the one who has *explained* God. This is the role of being a mouth for God and the allusion is to Exod 4:12-16, where Moses is a mouth for God and Aaron is a mouth for Moses. Explanation is not a pertinent function for the mention of 'God', and so υἱός is original.

---

[1] It is worth noting here that Isaac was Abraham's only son because Ishmael had been sent away and not because he was the child of promise.

[2] *Contra* Fennema, "John 1.18: 'God the only Son'", 127.

[3] Brown, *The Gospel According to John I-XII*, 17.

The balance of the internal considerations (1)-(10) support the conclusion that the Byzantine text has preserved the original text.

CHAPTER TEN
Coming Down from Heaven

1. Introduction

When you think of the Son as being first and foremost a heavenly being, the idea of his coming down from heaven is natural. If we were to ask the hypothetical question, 'What textual evidence would we expect if Christ were indeed a heavenly being?', one kind of evidence we would seek would be statements that he had come from heaven. For example, statements like:

> [That] was the true Light, which lighteth every man that comes into the world. John 1:10, cf. 3:19, 6:14, 9:39, 10:36, 11:27, 12:46, 16:28, 18:37 cf. Heb 10:5

> And no man[1] hath ascended to heaven, but he that came down from heaven, [even] the Son of man who is in heaven. John 3:13, 6:33, 38, 41, 42, 50, 51, 58

> He that cometh from above is above all...he that cometh from heaven is above all. John 3:31

> ...the same works that I do, bear witness of me that the Father hath sent me... John 5:36

> ...I proceeded forth and came from God; neither came I of myself, but he sent me. John 8:42, v. 14, cf. John 7:29, 13:3, 16:27,28, 30, 17:8

Most of these passages come from the Gospel of John. We will look at these texts as examples of the 'coming' argument that Trinitarians use when arguing for the pre-existence of Christ. The passages that deal with Christ coming from heaven are often grouped together on the assumption that they all imply the same point — that he had a literal pre-existence in heaven. However, each statement is different in its essential point, and we need to mark these distinctions.

---

[1] The KJV translates the Greek as 'no man', but it could theoretically be 'no one'. However, since angels have ascended and descended, man is implied. This means that 'he...' in 'he came down' is a reference to a man; a pre-existence view requires a *heavenly being* to have come down.

The verses can be tackled in a sequence, for they are not all making the same point. First there are the verses that speak of the Son *coming out* (e.g. John 13:3) of God; next there are the texts which speak of the Father *sending* the Son (e.g. John 3:17); next there are the verses which speak of the Son *proceeding forth* from the Father (e.g. John 8:42); and finally there are the verses which speak of the Son *coming down* (from above) to earth (e.g. John 3:13, 31), or coming *into* the world (e.g. John 11:27). The distinctions in this sequence are important, because different emphases underlie the choice of language.

- It is one thing to speak of coming *out* from God, where the stress is on *origin*.

- It is another thing to speak of *sending* where the stress is on *prophetic commission*.

- It is one thing to speak of coming *into* the world, where the stress is on the *fulfilled prophecy*.

- And it is another thing to speak of coming *down* from heaven, where the language is *typological*.

It is too easy to slide these passages together, as if they all amount to the same thing - say, an incarnation and personal pre-existence. However, the Gospel of John is not as straightforward as the other gospels in its use of language, and we need to challenge whether this is what it means to *be heavenly* in John's terms. In addition, we need to be sensitive to the typological talk in John and consider when this accounts for a coming from heaven.

2. Coming forth out of God

First, we need to consider Christ's origin, which was a matter of dispute with the Jews. It is when these origins are in dispute that Jesus characteristically affirms that he came forth *out* from God. Thus, the preaching in the temple recorded in John 7 sees Jesus address the Jew's scepticism 'we know this man whence he is' (v. 27) with 'Ye both know me, and ye know whence I am: and I am not come of myself...' (v. 28).[1] Similarly, the dialogue in John 8 is about origin, for the Jews argue that

---

[1] There is an echo here of Moses' disputes with the children of Israel at Sinai about who the true God was, and whether he was sent from God; see remarks below on John 3.

Abraham was their father (John 8:39). In this context, Jesus states 'out of God I came out and am come' (John 8:42), he did not come of himself (as we might expect of a pre-existent heavenly being) but he was sent.

The emphasis to distinguish here lies in the repetition of 'out' which is picking up a stress in the Greek. The intertextual echo is a contrast with the origins of Adam and Eve. Adam was taken *out* from the ground (Gen 2:7; 2:19) and Eve was taken *out* of Adam (Gen 2:21-23). But the main sense in Jesus' language of 'coming out' is a birth metaphor describing his origin. The language of 'coming out' is naturally used of birth and coming *out* of the womb (Gen 38:28-30; Num 12:12; Job 1:21; Ps 22:9; Jer 1:5); and, indeed, of coming *out* of the loins of a man (Exod 1:5).

The prophet Micah personifies Bethlehem as a woman giving birth in these terms:

> But thou, Bethlehem Ephrathah, [though] thou art little among the thousands of Judah, [yet] out of thee shall he come forth to me [that is] to be ruler in Israel; whose goings forth [have been] from of old, from everlasting. Mic 5:2, cf. Matt 2:6

This shows how *coming out* goes with *coming forth* in describing birth. Hence, childbirth is often described as bringing *forth* a child (Matt 1:21, 23, Luke 1:31, Rom 7:4, Jms 1:15); this chimes in with the description of *coming out* of the womb. But it is one thing to describe the Messiah coming forth out of the 'woman', Bethlehem (cf. Ruth 4:11), and coming forth to an expectant father. (And we know the Messiah was born of a virgin through the operation of the holy Spirit (Luke 1:35) and this happened in Bethlehem.) It is another thing for Jesus to describe himself as 'coming forth out from the Father into the world' (John 8:42, 13:3, 16:28, 17:8) because this places God to the foreground rather than his mother Mary. Nevertheless, the language is still birthing language rather than that of any prior personal existence in heaven.

> To this end was I born, and for this cause came I into the world, that I should bear witness unto the truth. John 18:37, cf. the idiom 'born into the world' John 16:21

> But when the fulness of the time was come, God sent forth his son, born of a woman, born under the law... Gal 4:4

Micah says that the Messiah's 'goings forth' had been of old and from everlasting. The allusion here is to the Sun, whose 'going forth' is from one end of heaven to the other (Ps 19:6; Isa 13:10). The figure likens the rule of the Messiah to the rule of the Sun in heaven. His going forth was as prepared as the morning (Hos 6:3) and laid down 'of old' in the Scriptures.[1]

3. Sending Someone

There are many verses in John's Gospel which mention the sending of Jesus. Many of these associate the sending of Jesus with some other aspect of his coming, such as his descent from heaven or his coming forth from God. The pre-existence argument to consider here is that for Jesus to be *sent* by God, he needed to be with God in heaven in order to be sent to the earth.

The main sense relevant to our subject is the *sending* of a prophet by God:[2]

> Behold, I will send my messenger, and he shall prepare the way before me: and the Lord... Mal 3:1, cf. 4:5

> And he said to me, Son of man, I send thee to the children of Israel, to a rebellious nation... Ezek 2:3

> But the Lord said to me, Say not, I [am] a child: for thou shalt go to all that I shall send thee, and whatever I command thee thou shalt speak. Jer 1:7

---

[1] Paul's statement, 'The first man [is] from the earth, earthy: the second man [is] the Lord from heaven.' (1 Cor 15:47), is a contrast between Adam's dust origins and the origin of Christ — the Lord was born *from* above. Paul does not mention birth, but he does mention heaven and being *from* heaven in a context of *coming into existence*. John 3 is helpful here because Jesus uses the concept of birth *from above* (v. 6 KJV mg., cf. v. 31) in a context which makes the same contrast as Paul — between the earthly and the heavenly. It is difficult to resist the inference that Paul is quoting John, and inviting his readers to make a reference to Christ's miraculous birth. Both John and Paul are using Jesus' birth from above to model the new spiritual birth of believers.

[2] See also Exod 3:10, 4:13, Jud 13:8, Pss 43:3, 57:3, 68:9,33, 110:2, Isa 10:6, 19:20, Jer 16:16, 25:15, Am 8:11.

Also I heard the voice of the Lord, saying, 'Whom shall I send, and who will go for us?' Then said I, 'Here [am] I; send me.' Isa 6:8 (KJV)

For a prophet to be sent from God it is required that he be told to go and fulfil a prophetic commission. Since there have been other prophets sent to the world (e.g. John 1:6) there is no need to infer pre-existence for Christ from the language.

4. Coming into the World

It is natural in a Christian culture to think that 'Christ coming into the world' means he was previously 'outside' the world and then 'came into' it, but this is too hasty a conclusion. It tends to assume (in our day) that the Son was outside the space-time structure we call the universe. (It is worth noting that an early church father would probably not have had such a view of being 'outside' the world. He might have thought of heaven in the more local terms of the sky.) What does the Biblical concept of 'outside' the world mean?[1]

'All the world is a stage, and we are but actors upon it' — so the proverb goes, but it highlights an important point: you can either be outside the world in terms of time, or outside the world in terms of space. Jesus Christ came into the world at a certain point in time:

> This is truly that prophet that should come into the world...
> John 6:14

> I believe that thou art the Christ, the Son of God, who was to come into the world. John 11:27

The stress here is on the fulfilment of prophecy. God has declared the end from the beginning in the Scriptures, and we can read of this purpose ahead of the time of its fulfilment. It was the same for the Jews of the first century. They recognised that a Messiah was predicted, and when Jesus came, some of them acknowledged that he was the Messiah. This is the sense of 'into' in 'come into the world'. The Messiah was 'outside' the world before he was born, but he was predicted, and therefore he 'came into' the world. The stress is not on *where* the Messiah came from, i.e. which place he came from, but rather on his arrival according to

---

[1] This is not the same concept as not 'being *of* the world', as we are exploring a *spatial* metaphor.

297

prophecy. This is what an 'arrival' is in practice: if someone is expected and they come, then we speak of their 'arrival'.

This sense of coming in accordance with prophecy is found in Hebrews:

> Then said I, Lo, I come (in the volume of the book it is written of me) to do thy will, O God. Heb 10:7

The explanation of what 'I come' means is supplied in the parenthesis: it means the Messiah was written about in the volume of the book.

5. Coming Down

John 3 and John 6 are the two most frequently used texts in 'coming down' arguments. John 3 is different to John 6 — different, that is, in its allusions. In John 3, the typology is more complex and multi-threaded. The idea in John 6 is of the *miraculous provision* of food, whereas in John 3 it is the ideas of *sending a prophet* into the world and *sending a deliverer* into the world.

5.1 John 6

The fact of Christ coming down from heaven is mentioned some six times in John 6, usually in a statement about Christ as the bread of life. Is there an implication of *personal* pre-existence in these statements? Does such an implication lie in the use of 'I' by Christ, when he says, 'I came down from heaven'? After all, we might say, Christ was the *person* there and then speaking that sentence, so doesn't he mean that he existed previously in heaven?

Let's focus on the 'I': if we use 'I' in everyday language, then the meaning is fairly straightforward. In stage-acting it's slightly different. A Shakespearean actor is not the historical person he portrays, and he will use 'I' *as if* he were the historical character. Is Christ's use of 'I' a simple everyday use, or is it more involved like the actor's usage? Well since Christ is taking on the identity of the wilderness manna, perhaps the 'I' *is* like that of the actor. He says, 'I am the living bread which came down from heaven' (John 6:51). Is this like Christ acting a play in which he invites his audience to see him as that bread?

Role-plays are a kind of type. The lives of many individuals in the OT portray aspects of Christ and his life. The actions of a nation and the actions of angels portray aspects of Christ. Events and objects also typify aspects of Christ. We can look on these *historical facts* as role-plays about Christ. In order to cement the link with such types, Christ uses language that draws the type into his teaching. So it is that we find Christ talking of himself *as if* he was the manna, and hence it is quite proper to read of him saying, 'I came down from heaven'.

The Trinitarian contention is that Christ implies his personal pre-existence in his 'come down' assertions. My argument against this is that the 'I...' as used by Christ is not like the ordinary 'I...' of 'I live in England', but rather it is like the 'I...' used to describe someone's role and function, e.g. in a nativity play we might say of little Johnny who played the angel Gabriel that 'he was the one who came down from heaven'.

The narrative of John 6 rewards closer attention, for Jesus says two distinct things to the Jews. On the one hand, he says that the Father was currently (as he spoke) giving true bread from heaven, as in the wilderness, on a daily basis (John 6:32). Jesus was that bread which was there and then *coming down* from heaven (John 6:33, 50). This idea is not the same as that which says Jesus came down (past tense) from heaven at some one point in time. However, he does also say that he came down (past tense) from heaven (John 6:38, 42), as if to say that at some point in time he came down from heaven. So then, putting ourselves into his listener's shoes, we would hear two things: (a) the true bread has come down from heaven, and (b), the true bread is still coming down from heaven, sent from and by the Father.

Where Christ speaks[1] in the past he makes an explicit comparison with the manna: he says he was the living bread (bread of life) which came down from heaven (John 6:51); and he identifies the wilderness manna as himself with the words, 'he that eateth me, even he shall live by me. This is that bread which came down from heaven' (John 6:58). This *living* bread was now sent to Israel *by* the *living* Father, and it was being sent daily. (Hence we pray, give us our daily bread, always conscious that we travel a wilderness route to the kingdom land). Had the Fathers seen the manna with the eyes of faith, they would not have failed to enter the land. But like father like son, the Jews of Christ's day *murmured* against Christ at his claims (John 6:41). They had a literal and face-value perspective — was not he Joseph's son? And their Fathers in the wilderness also had a face-value perspective on the manna — was not it a rather dull diet?

---

[1] The Greek tense is perfect in John 6:38, 42, meaning 'I have come down from heaven', and aorist in John 6:41, 51, 58, meaning 'I came down from heaven'.

How do we understand 'I came down from heaven'? We suggest it is Christ placing himself into the middle of the OT exodus scenario, as if we might in a play. The bread *was not in* heaven and then sent down, but rather, it appeared on the ground in the morning, sent from heaven. The point is about *giving and origins*. The Jews said that Moses gave the bread, and they said that Jesus was Joseph's son, but the bread was and is given by God from heaven, not by Moses and not by Joseph. What is it about the manna and Christ that allows Christ to assert that he was that bread sent from heaven? In short, it is the means to life given from heaven (cf. John 1:4).

The mistake of the pre-existence view is to introduce a foreign element into the narrative. The dialogue is at the level of type and anti-type, and personal pre-existence is not a feature of the type. To invoke the passage as a basis for a pre-existence view is to go beyond the (Scripture interprets Scripture) typical basis. Existence is just not an issue in the type and neither therefore in the anti-type.

There is no doubt that Christ 'came down' from heaven, but it is all a question of how we understand this fact. In John 6 'come down' amounts to the miraculous provision of the Christ-bread by God.

5.2 John 3

John says that the Son of Man has '...come down from heaven' (John 3:13). Our exposition of his statement will be that if Christ is a prophet or a deliverer sent from God, then it is a natural OT idiom to say that he came down from heaven. In contrast, the pre-existence argument is this: John says (in the same breath) no one has ascended to heaven except Christ, who came down from heaven, and this makes the ascent like the descent; therefore he literally came down from heaven.

The Bible teaches that Christ is a prophet and deliverer by using types. In John 3, one type concerns the Angel of the Lord who *delivered* Israel, and another type concerns Moses through whom the Angel of the Lord worked. It is the use of these types that has dictated the kind of language we find in John 3. The concepts are lifted from Exodus and brought into relief in John's Gospel, in order to depict Christ and his work by making us think of the exodus. If Moses and the Angel of the Lord typify Christ, we would expect to find 'Israel' in John's typology and this is what we shall see — Nicodemus is the backdrop for John 3, and he is typical of Israel.

It is important to observe that the pre-existence text (John 3:13) contains the words of John. It is John who narrates, using the third person, '...*he* came down from heaven'. These *are not* the words of Jesus to Nicodemus,[1] although they reflect Jesus' own words in the first person, 'I came down from heaven' in John 6. The author has placed a narrative commentary at this point, to indicate an exposition of Jesus' exchange with Nicodemus.

Jesus had been talking with Nicodemus of 'earthly things' and Nicodemus had struggled to understand such things. This was preventing Jesus from talking about heavenly things. Earthly things were those things that pertained to the Law, and these were patterns or types of the heavenly things (Heb 8:5; 9:23-24).[2] Jesus had been talking with 'the teacher of Israel', a man schooled in the Law, and holding the pre-eminent position amongst the Pharisees; but he had not yet seen how these earthly things patterned or typed heavenly things.

Earthly things relate to types. Jesus' conversation with Nicodemus had therefore been of types, and he was trying to draw out the spiritual significance of these types. The principal type that Jesus was talking about was the crossing of the Red Sea — 'born of water and of the Spirit' (John 3:5).

It is in this context then that we find the language of 'coming down'. We ought not to abandon the language of typology when we read of Jesus 'coming down', when Jesus himself has just been using this *very same kind of language*. John places his remark at this point (v. 13) to show how Christ could *talk* of heavenly things, and he quotes Deuteronomy 30 against the contemporary Jewish scepticism:[3]

---

[1] I think v. 13 is a bracketed parenthesis of John. Jesus' dialogue with Nicodemus resumes at v. 14 with the words, 'And as Moses lifted up...even so must the Son of Man be lifted up', which are words expecting a future event.

[2] The argument here is that Hebrews uses the expression 'heavenly things' and contrasts these things with a set of patterns. Jesus does not use the language of 'shadow' and 'pattern', but he is making a *contrast* between heavenly things and *earthly things*. The suggestion that the earthly things embrace the things of the law receives confirmation from 2 Cor 5:1 which describes an earthly body as a *tabernacle*. Further, note the anti-Jewish context for those 'who mind earthly things' in Phil 3:19 (cf. Jms 3:15).

[3] John 3 is about knowledge and the authority to teach, and John bases Jesus' knowledge and authority in a descent from heaven. If John is

For this commandment which I command thee this day, it [is] not hid from thee, neither [is] it far off. It [is] not in heaven, that thou shouldest say, 'Who shall ascend for us to heaven, and bring it to us, that we may hear it, and do it?' Neither [is] it beyond the sea, that thou shouldest say, 'Who shall go over the sea for us, and bring it to us, that we may hear it, and do it?' But the word [is] very near to thee, in thy mouth, and in thy heart, that thou mayest do it. Deut 30:14-16

In Deuteronomy 30, death and life (blessing and curse) are set before the people, and the statement of God is that the commandment to love[1] God (v. 16) was not in heaven such that the people would wonder who would ascend into heaven to receive the commandment (v. 12), but the word of the commandment was near to them in their mouth and in their heart (v. 14). It had been given in the Law (Luke 10:26-28). They had been given a revelation of God's will through Moses.[2] The quotation from Deuteronomy is a rebuke to the nation, and John uses this rebuke to oppose Jewish scepticism about Christ and thereby validate Jesus as a prophet like unto Moses. As with Moses, Jesus had received the word of God from heaven.

Paul uses Deuteronomy 30 in a similar way to establish the prophetic nature of *his* ministry (rather than that of Jesus). He uses the Deuteronomy 30 text as a prophecy about those who would doubt whether God had revealed his will to man through Christ.

But the righteousness, which is by faith, speaketh on this wise: Say not in thy heart, 'Who shall ascend into heaven?' (that is, to bring Christ down:) Or, 'Who shall descend into

---

making a pre-existence claim, Jesus would have to have known of that existence, in order for John's argument to work. But on such a reading, what must it have been like for Jesus to have the knowledge that he was indeed a previously existent being in heaven with all that entailed? Such knowledge would critically affect his self-understanding, how would he accept that he was a man? Can you be a man with the knowledge that you were (are or will be) God the Son?

[1] Hence John goes on in his narrative to mention, 'God so *loved* the world'.

[2] This principle of God's dealings with the nation is the same as that expressed in the words, 'Surely the Lord God will do nothing, but he revealeth his secret to his servants the prophets.' (Amos 3:7).

the deep? (that is, to bring Christ again from the dead.)' But what saith it? The word is near thee, [even] in thy mouth, and in thy heart: that is, the word of faith, which we preach; That if thou shalt confess with thy mouth the Lord Jesus, and shalt believe in thy heart that God hath raised him from the dead, thou shalt be saved. Rom 10:6-9

The righteousness of faith, the word of faith, of which Paul spake and preached, was near and in the heart of those who confessed Christ (Rom 10:6-9). The faith that understood that Christ was the end of the Law (Rom 10:4), also understood that Christ had come and did not say that the Christ was yet to come down from heaven (Rom 10:6). Neither did this faith say that Christ was dead in the grave and not raised (Rom 10:7, 1 Cor 15:12-14). This faith *knew* that if a person confessed, (with a word in the *mouth* according to Deut 30:14), the Lord Jesus; and believed in the heart, (the word in the *heart* as per Deut 30:14), that God had *raised* Jesus, and then they would be saved.

Opposed to this faith there would be those who would say that the Messiah had yet to come and that Jesus was still in the grave. This opposition is illustrated in the table below:

Prophecy in Deut 30:12-13	Jewish Position in Romans 10	Christian Answer
Jews would say who will bring the Messiah down	The Christ yet to come(v. 6)	confession by mouth Jesus was the Messiah
Jews would say who will raise the dead	Jesus in the grave (v. 7)	belief in the heart that Jesus was raised

Paul's use of the OT here is similar to John, because the Jews opposed Jesus in the same way. They questioned whether he was the one to come, and so John asserts that Jesus had come down from heaven using language from Deuteronomy 30 to oppose their scepticism. The Jews also doubted that the Messiah could descend into the deep (i.e. the grave) and rise again, and so John remarks that the Son of Man was now in heaven (c. 13c).

Jesus stated to Nicodemus that he could speak of heavenly things, and the Jewish murmur of Deuteronomy 30 suggests that this claim would require ascension to and descent from heaven. Hence, John makes this point about Christ that he had come down from heaven. The *point* in

Deuteronomy and in Romans is of revelation — there was no need to literally send someone to heaven or down into the deep. God had revealed his will in the Law through Moses, and he had revealed the Gospel through Christ and his apostles. The point in John is similar, God had revealed heavenly things to Christ, but to make this point and to *connect* up with Deuteronomy's way of expressing this point, he uses the idea — he had come down from heaven. The key words are 'we speak that we do *know*, and testify that we have *seen*, and ye receive not our witness' (John 3:11, cf. 8:38). This is the language of revelation and vision. The apostle John, Ezekiel, and Daniel are similar examples. It does not necessarily imply that Christ had literally been in heaven in any other way than John, Ezekiel, Daniel, or Moses. These key words point to the prophetic function — Christ had come down from heaven.

After John's remark about Jesus coming down from heaven, Jesus' conversation with Nicodemus continues in v. 14 with the further exodus typology: 'And as Moses lifted up the Serpent in the wilderness, even so must the Son of Man be lifted up'. This type is Jesus' next selection from the wilderness period, having just dealt with the typology of the Red Sea crossing. John's parenthesis thus affirms the resurrection before Jesus' prediction of his death. In focusing first on the significance of the Red Sea and baptism (1 Cor 10:2), Jesus puts Nicodemus' salvation first; he then mentions the work that underpins that salvation using the incident of the brazen serpent.[1] [2]

---

[1] An evangelical Christian of a certain kind will use Rom 10:9-10 as a proof text that *all you need to be saved* is to confess Jesus as Lord and believe in the heart that he has been raised from the dead. But this overlooks the fact that Paul's point is *controlled* by the OT quotation of Deuteronomy 30:12-14. Deuteronomy mentions the *mouth* and the *heart* only, and so Paul fashions his points around the *mouth* (confession) and the *heart* (belief). This *control by the OT quotation* is an example of a perfectly familiar device in general writing. Our attention to the OT basis of the language of the NT prevents a false conclusion being drawn.

[2] Ascent and descent are a feature in another letter of Paul — Ephesians. Jesus had to ascend to heaven and go away so that he might give the disciples the gifts of the holy Spirit (Eph 4:8). But before being able to do this, he had descended into the lower parts of the earth, i.e. die (Eph 4:9, cf. Ps 63:9). We have then another example of the association of ideas between ascension ('far above' is coined as an antithesis to 'lower parts of the earth') and the prior condition of death.

6. Coming from Above

There is yet more in John's use of Deuteronomy, and this comes out when we consider the language of 'coming from above' later in John 3. This language is modelled on Moses receiving the Law on Mt. Sinai, and then descending to give the Law to the people. The stress in John's typology is that Jesus has *come down* and *come from above*,[1] but Moses had ascended and descended the mountain *several* times. Does John have a particular ascent/descent in mind? The links to Exodus suggest that the point in the story at which the type begins is when Moses is at the top[2] of the mountain, having just received the Law.

The type is this: Moses is told by God to descend the mountain, because the people were indulging in idolatry. He then descended to deliver the Law. Likewise, Jesus came down from heaven and preached the Gospel. To those who accepted the Gospel (cf. the Levites acceptance of Moses' testimony), it was life, but to those who rejected the message, it was death.[3] The ascent after the golden calf conflagration was for *atonement* (Exod 32:30). Likewise, for Christ the ascent after his ministry was for presenting the atonement (John 20:17; Heb 9:23, n.b. the mention of 'heavenly things'), and to receive gifts for men (Eph 4:8-10).

The allusions suggesting this typology are these: John says that Christ 'came *down* from' heaven, and not just that he 'came from' heaven - there is a stress on 'down'. He also says later on that Christ was the one who 'cometh from above' (John 3:31), because he is above all. Moses had come *down* from the mount, a position *above* the nation who were at the foot of the mountain, and he came with the *testimony* with authority over all Israel (Exod 31:18, 32:15). Likewise, Christ came from above with a *testimony* (John 3:32). Both Moses and Christ testified concerning what they *heard* and what they had *seen* in 'the body of heaven' (Exod 24:10).

---

[1] No man had ascended up to the mountain top and into the cloud except Moses, and this illustrates that there is only one mediator between God and man. Hence, John says that no man has ascended up to heaven except the Son of Man, referring to his resurrection.

[2] John's point is not that Jesus was on earth and ascended and descended during his ministry. Although, Jesus did ascend and descend during the forty days of ascension, and this is typed by Moses' ascending and descending the mountain.

[3] In Chapter Eight, we saw that the prologue of John reflected the same sequence where the Angel of the Lord comes to the people (his own) but is rejected by most of them.

Moses was confronted by the apostasy of the Golden Calf. The people who had received the Law (Rom 3:2-4) had said, under the influence of a special party of adversaries, that the calf represented the elohim who had brought them out of Egypt (Exod 32:4, 8). The issue was about who was the *true God* (the Aaronic calf or Yahweh), and Moses confronted the people with the testimony of the Law. Likewise, the testimony of Christ was about the true God (John 3:33). The people were given a choice and the Levites sided with Moses; they believed his testimony.

This comparison between Moses and Christ casts Nicodemus in the role of Aaron (a master in Israel who had not understood Israel's passage through the Red Sea as a baptism of the spirit and of water). The comparison also makes Nicodemus representative of the people insofar as they had not received (John 3:11) the basic teaching about God's deliverance of the nation at the Red Sea. This is the underlying type ('earthly thing') in Jesus' conversation with Nicodemus. A paraphrase of the conversation can bring the type into clearer focus:

> There was a man (Adam)...named...a ruler of the Jews (like Aaron) ...he came to Jesus and said of Jesus that God was with him just as God was with Moses (Exod 3 *passim*). Jesus knowing what was in man, however, teaches this latter day Aaron, and illustrates the typical significance of the crossing of the Red Sea...unless a man is born from above he cannot enter into the kingdom of God (enter the land)...this is the birth of water and the spirit which took place at the Red Sea when they were baptised to Moses in the cloud and in the sea (1 Cor 10:2-4)...that which is born only in Egypt of the flesh is of Egypt, but that which is born of the spirit is spirit. As at creation when the spirit hovered over the waters (Gen 1:2, Deut 32:11), so too in a new creation the spirit (KJV - wind) blows where it wills...as shown at the Red Sea when a wind (Exod 14:21) came and made the sea dry...you should know these earthly things...I know these earthly things and I know heavenly things which I ca not tell you...
>
> ...Nicodemus was a man, but no man has ascended to heaven except the man who came down from heaven...like Moses who was a man and came down from the mount to give the law...he who comes from above, born from above, is above all, but Nicodemus, like Aaron, wonders about the earthly things...but what Christ has seen and heard, as in a mountain, he testifies about this...but no one in Israel

receives this...except those like the Levites who did believe that God - he is the true God (as Elijah and the prophets of Baal)...for these Levites Moses (and Christ) ascended the mountain heaven but for the others there was and is only wrath...

Although there is the clear type of Moses in John 3, there are other types present in the narrative as well. This is a feature of the NT — its language can be drawn from a number of places. Another type concerns the Angel of the Lord.

Expositions of John 3 often refer to the language of theophany, and it is right to focus on the expression '...come *down*' in John 3:13. However, an appeal to the general language of theophany (e.g. Babel (Gen 11:5) or at Sodom (Gen 18:21)) is not sufficient to explain how Christ came down from heaven. We need to be more specific and home in on a specific act of deliverance. What is the language of 'coming down' in the OT underpinning John 3? The exodus deliverance seems the most likely:

> And I am come down to deliver them out of the hand of the Egyptians... Exod 3:8, cf. Exod 19:11 Num 11:17, Acts 7:34

Jesus' conversation with Nicodemus concerned birth of water and birth of the spirit (*entry* into the kingdom of God is paralleled with *entry* into the land). Nicodemus had puzzled over these statements. He may have been taking them at face value, but in a context where birth of water and birth of the spirit is treated, John chips in with '...except he that came down from heaven...' and details Christ's method of deliverance in the next verse (v. 14) using a different wilderness type.

Jesus came down to deliver those in captivity out of bondage. The Angel of the Lord delivered Israel through the plagues and particularly the last one, and he delivered them through the Red Sea. At the Red Sea Israel were baptised into Moses in the cloud and in the Sea. The deliverance there involved light - the angel stood as a pillar of light to Israel and a pillar of cloud and darkness to Egypt (Exod 14:20). During the night Moses stretched his hand over the Red Sea and Israel were baptised unto Moses in the cloud and in the sea (1 Cor 10:2).

We should not therefore be surprised to find a reference to light in the context: "this is condemnation—that the light is come into the world, and men loved darkness rather than light" (John 3:19, 20, and 21).

307

They wanted to return to Egypt as always. Furthermore we should not be surprised if there is also a reference to a name (Exod 23:20). They refused to believe in the name which was shared by the Father, Son, and Angel of the Presence (John 3:18).

7. Ascending back to Heaven?

At the end of Christ's debate with the Jews in John 6, the disciples murmur at the hard sayings. To this Christ responds, 'What and if ye shall see the Son of Man ascend up where he was before?'. He does not say 'ascend back up to heaven', but this reading has been assumed by commentators. Christ has certainly used 'heaven' a lot in the dialogue so far, but not here where we might expect it on a pre-existence reading. This may indicate that Christ's point here is a different one.[1]

Christ talks of ascending up to some place where he was before. He had previously been *up a mountain*, where he had fed the Five Thousand. He had fed them in an area of grassland (i.e. it was not a wilderness). As a result of this, they would have made him king (John 6:15). As Christ observes a day or two later after the miracle, 'Ye seek me, not because ye saw the miracles, but because ye did eat of the loaves, and were filled' (John 6:26).

This feeding on a grassy mountain slope is the backdrop to the *whole* talk about the feeding of the people in the wilderness. In this dialogue Jesus directs the people away from the physical realm to the spiritual realm, and he does this by identifying himself as the bread that came down from heaven. In this context, at the end of the dialogue, and when his disciples also start to be offended by his doctrine, he rebukes them with the words, 'What and if ye shall see the Son of Man ascend up where he was

---

[1] The Greek active participle 'ascend' does not settle anything about the focus of Jesus' proposal. An active participle does not necessarily indicate that an *activity* is the focus of what is being said; the focus could be on the *place* — in our case a previous place where Christ proposes to go. The elements of John 6:62 are, (i) ascension, (ii) prior place, and (iii) the disciples seeing the ascension to a prior place. Unfortunately the word 'ascension' is a theological word, and can make a reader think of the Ascension, but we ought to be more neutral and say that the elements in John 6:62 are a 'going up' to a prior place and the disciples seeing such. The Greek for 'where' here is often used in John of geographical place, and the Greek for 'before' is used in clauses about previous circumstances.

before'.[1] This comment of Jesus looks back to when he was on the mountain and had fed the 5000. He had certainly been there before (πρότερον), and instead of the people hearing hard sayings, they had wanted to make him king. This backdrop explains the contrast in his question: what if, instead of hearing these words of life in Capernaum, you see me going up to where I was before and feeding the flesh? It is the spirit that quickens and not the bread that feeds the body.

Jesus mentions life and a quickening spirit, and he links these to his words, i.e. his message. He contrasts these with the unprofitable flesh. This contrast is the same as that found in vv. 26-27 between the perishing manna and the life that Jesus offered. The people sought him because of the loaves and fishes, but Jesus wanted them to take the real food he offered - his message. With his disciples balking at his message, Jesus makes the same contrast in order to stress that it was the message that would give life.

8. Conclusion

We have looked at some of the OT types behind the 'coming' language of John, in order to illustrate *why* the narrative is cast in its distinctive way. In all cases a pre-existence reading is completely foreign to the text, and alien to a reading that immerses the text in the OT *Jewish* background. This approach can be profitably followed with all the 'coming' verses (coming *down*, coming *into*, coming *forth*, coming *from above*), although we have only examined the main texts.

---

[1] The disciples were questioning Jesus' sayings in John 6. Jesus' response is one that is made towards allaying doubt. At this time the disciples did not understand that Jesus was to die, so how is a reference to a future ascension to heaven of any value in allaying their fears? Jesus' assurance is contained in the words 'It is the spirit that quickeneth; the flesh profiteth nothing: the words that I speak unto you, they are spirit and they are life' (v. 63). The assurance is not contained in the words 'What and if ye shall see the Son of Man ascend up where he was before?', because this 'if' is contrasted by an 'it is' in the next sentence: i.e. 'It is the spirit that quickeneth [etc.]'. A reference to Christ's ascension to heaven does not fit this contrast, because such an ascension would be faith-confirming and there would not be a basis for the contrast.

309

CHAPTER ELEVEN
Jewish Monotheism

1. Introduction

In 1 Cor 8:6, Paul states that "to us there is one god, the Father, out of whom are all things, and we for him, and one lord, Jesus Christ, through whom are all things, and we through him". This assertion at once delineates our topic: it affirms monotheism in relation to the Father, and is thus consistent with the Judaism of Paul's day, as well as the Hebrew Scriptures;[1] but it juxtaposes Jesus Christ alongside the Father, which would not be acceptable to devout Jews of the first century. Our questions then are: What was Jewish monotheism in the first century? Is this different from the monotheism in the Hebrew Scriptures? Does Christian belief about Jesus change either or both of these two belief systems such that Christianity should be seen as different in its monotheism?

These are important questions because Trinitarians today affirm that their doctrine is a **form of monotheism**. Our objective in this chapter is to evaluate how Jewish monotheism is analysed and handled by Trinitarian NT scholars. We will counter-argue that Jewish 'monotheism' is about *what there is*—one God, the Father—and that this is not a doctrine which the apostles and prophets of the first century church could have or would have changed in a direction leading to Trinitarianism.

2. Context

Our topic is Jewish monotheism in the first century and we should distinguish this from the monotheism to be found in the Hebrew Scriptures. Jewish scriptural writings contribute to the picture of Jewish monotheism, but they are only one component in the picture that the historian draws. This may seem like a neutral point to make, but it is often made in an historically positivist[2] way in relation to tracing the sources of

---

[1] We use the term 'Hebrew Scriptures' to refer to those Scriptures of Jesus' day that became the Masoretic Text that we have in our Hebrew Bibles. This includes the Aramaic portions, but we are obviously excluding any translations extant in Jesus' day when we use this term, for example the Old Greek or any Aramaic Targums.

[2] For an account of 'positivism' in the philosophy of historiography see D. Bebbington, *Patterns in History* (Leicester: Inter-varsity Press, 1979), chap. 7.

Christian ideas. This positivism is seen when the teachings and ideas expressed in the NT are just sourced in a Palestinian Jewish environment, the nature of which is determined by the surviving literature of the period, only one part of which were the Jewish Scriptures. (A second source is the wider Greco-Roman world including the Diaspora.) However, in explaining the teaching of the Christian writers without reference to the phenomenon of the bestowal of the Spirit, the historical account is irredeemably positivist. (Instead, a naturalistic category such as 'religious experience' will be deployed.)

Historical explanation that works with only the human dimension is positivist when divine agency is excluded. It looks upon events and circumstances and the expression of ideas in a *closed* way; the bestowal of the Spirit, necessarily, is an input from the 'outside' and historical explanation that admits of divine agency sees history as *open* to God. If we take up this latter stance as historians, the writings of the NT become 'of the Spirit' because they are the writings of apostles and prophets (Eph 2:20). This requires us, in practice, to privilege the Hebrew Scriptures when identifying textual affinities with the NT because they were, according to apostles and prophets, likewise 'of the Spirit' (John 10:35; 2 Tim 3:16; 1 Pet 1:21). The intertextuality of the NT writings is dense in respect of the OT and this is proof of a use by the Spirit of writing engendered under earlier bestowals, for example, such as that in the days of the eighth century Hebrew prophets BCE.

The use of Jewish writings other than scriptural ones is very sparse in the NT (or absent or unrecoverable depending on your view). While we are interested in the broad historical context of Jewish monotheism, we take the view that the dense intertextuality that the NT writings have with the OT directs our historical analysis to see the monotheism of the Hebrew Scriptures as the primary context for any understanding of the monotheism of the apostolic church. In this way we can take on board the parallels offered by scholars between the NT writings and the Judaism of their day (if they are worth noticing), but still give priority to the Spirit as the source of ideas about the exaltation of Jesus alongside God in heaven and the consequent expression of monotheism.

3. Jewish Monotheism
It is not difficult to enumerate texts[1] that illustrate Jewish monotheism and/or the monotheism of the Hebrew Scriptures. Here our principal and

---

[1] We are restricting our examples to *discursive* textual evidence rather other kinds of textual and non-textual data. How broadly you define a 'text' is

312

unexceptionable result is that there is one god but that he has agents that do his will. The one god is worshipped but agents are not worshipped (they may be venerated). This framework is often dubbed as 'inclusive monotheism' by scholars because it countenances divine beings alongside God.[1] However, this is not how the Hebrew Scriptures[2] set up monotheism. This result does not mean that all Jews (Diasporan or those living in the homeland) held this view; the Jewish writings from the Second Temple period illustrate diverse ideas in this area. For example, some Jews were syncretistic in their approach—they saw commonalities between their tradition and the gods of other ethnic groups.[3]

Above, we have offered a definition of Jewish monotheism. How a scholar defines monotheism affects his analysis of the situation in the first century. We have offered a metaphysical definition: monotheism is about *there being* one God. We could change the basis of our definition and say that monotheism is the *belief* that there is one God. This changes our perspective from metaphysics to epistemic states and epistemology. If we do, we draw in the human being to our definition: monotheism is about what he or she believes. We could also change our definition again and say

---

moot for our purposes, since we are selecting *discursive* texts; a text could, for example, be a short inscription, but by choosing discursive texts we gain more ready access to the *thinking* of the day. Or again, the burying of coins with the dead is an example of non-textual data that we are not using here, but nevertheless relevant to popular beliefs about gods/demons that escort the dead, see J. Magness, *The Archaeology of Qumran and the Dead Sea Scrolls* (Grand Rapids: Eerdmans, 2003), 175.

[1] M. Mach, "Concepts of Jewish Monotheism during the Hellenistic Period" in *The Jewish Roots of Christological Monotheism* (eds. C. C. Newman, J. R. Davila & G. S. Lewis; Leiden: E J Brill, 1999), 21-42 (24); W. Horbury, "Jewish and Christian Monotheism in the Herodian Age" in *Early Jewish and Christian Monotheism* (eds. W. E. S. North and L. T. Stuckenbruck; London: T & T Clark, 2004), 16-44 (17); R. Bauckham, *The Climax of Prophecy* (Edinburgh: T & T Clark, 1993), chap. 4.

[2] We are not considering the development of Israelite thinking about God on the basis of 'evidence' in the Hebrew Scriptures; rather, we are taking the Hebrew Scriptures as an authoritative collection with a single theology about God—an holistic way of reading common enough in Jesus' day.

[3] This was a common Hellenistic attitude to the gods—that local ethnic gods were to be equated across ethnic boundaries, so that, for example, the Greek Zeus was another name for the Roman Jupiter or, vis-à-vis the Jews, Yahweh; see J. D. G. Dunn, *The Partings of the Ways* (London: SCM Press, 1991), 19.

that monotheism is about what or who is worshipped. This definition draws in the human being but it is not so much concerned with intellectual belief as with religious practices.

Hurtado defines monotheism in this way:

> I suggest that in the interests of historical accuracy and clear communication the term 'monotheism' should be used only to describe **devotion to one god** and the rejection of the pantheon of deities such as were reverenced throughout the Greco-Roman world.[1]

This may appear a neutral and accurate definition but it is a self-serving definition. If we define monotheism in relation to devotion (or loyalty), then as soon as we observe that Jesus is part of the pattern of Christian devotion, then either we have included him within a monotheistic pattern or we have to abandon 'monotheism' as a term for Christianity. Since the earliest Christians[2] did not consider themselves to be anything other than monotheists (as evidenced in texts such as Mark 12:32; 1 Cor 8:6; Eph 4:6; 1 Tim 2:5; Jms 2:19), we are forced to see a 'binatarian' (two-ness) pattern in Christian 'monotheistic' devotion.

This is a self-serving definition because the orthodox NT scholar is seeking a beginning in the NT for the Trinitarian view of God. If s/he can *include* Jesus within a monotheistic frame of reference on the basis of NT evidence, then a start has been made for Trinitarianism. It is important though to realise that this strategy depends on first defining Jewish monotheism in relation to devotional practices. If instead we define monotheism in terms of **what there is**, i.e. there is one God, the Father (following 1 Cor 8:6), or in terms of **belief**, i.e. the belief that there is one God, the Father, then this particular 'beginning' for Trinitarianism is blocked.[3] G. F. Moore correctly observed,

---

[1] L. W. Hurtado, *One God, One Lord* (2nd ed.; London: T & T Clark, 2003), 129 n. 1; my emphasis.

[2] While there are many texts outside of the NT that also purport to be Christian, their date and provenance tends to be later than NT writings; on the questions of date see, respectively, H. Klauck, *Apocryphal Gospels* (London: T & T Clark, 2003) and Robinson, *Redating the New Testament*.

[3] Scholars use the language of a 'trajectory' to root Trinitarianism in the devotional practices of the apostolic church; see W. E. S. North and L. T. Stuckenbruck, "Introduction" in *Early Jewish and Christian Monotheism* (eds.

The exclusive worship of one God, whether by the choice of
individuals or by the law of national religion, is not
monotheism at all in the proper and usual meaning of the
word, namely, the theory, doctrine, or belief that there is but
one God.[1]

Jewish monotheism is not about devotion; it is about *what there is* or what
Jews thought there was with regard to gods.[2] So, Paul can affirm of Jesus
that "God also hath highly exalted him" and that "every tongue should
confess that Jesus Christ is Lord, to the glory of God the Father" (Phil
2:9-11), and monotheism is here clearly maintained, while at the same time
devotional practices for Christians have been enlarged, naturally, to
include *confession* about Christ. The obvious historical construction to put
upon the evidence in the NT is to say that **Christian devotional
practices were not monotheistic** because they included Jesus, but that
Christian beliefs about gods were monotheistic because they believed, like
the Jews, that there was only one God, the Father. As A. Marmorstein
observes,

> The common Jew, as well as the ordinary Jewish Christian,
> found the deification of a human being in general
> unbearable, if not abominable. Both saw in such a doctrine
> an unpardonable falsification of the pure Jewish
> monotheism.[3]

W. E. S. North and L. T. Stuckenbruck; London: T & T Clark, 2004), 1-
13 (3).
[1] G. F. Moore, *Judaism in the First Centuries of the Christian Era* (2 vols;
Reprinted—Peabody: Hendrickson, 1997), 1:222-223. Moore is writing in
1927 what would become a standard handbook about Judaism, and so he
could go on and say then of 'monotheism' that, "This is the only sense in
which the term has hitherto been used of Judaism, Christianity, and
Mohammedanism". Hurtado, writing in 1998, is introducing 'religious
practices' (worship) as the defining context for 'monotheism' so that he
can retain the *kudos* of this term for orthodox Trinitarian Christianity.
[2] Jesus' controversy with the Jews in John 10 (vv. 34-35) shows that Jews
felt no problem for monotheism with humans being 'called gods' because
of texts like Ps 82:6.
[3] A. Marmorstein, "The Unity of God in Rabbinic Literature" in *Studies in
Jewish Theology* (eds. J. Rabbinowitz and M. S. Lew; Oxford: Oxford
University Press, 1950), 72-105 (101). Marmorstein's essay is a review of
the Tannaim and Amoraim.

Above, we introduced the term 'inclusive monotheism'. This is a term of art used in the analysis of first century Jewish monotheism. It is applied to texts that speak of there being one God, but which include information about other exalted heavenly figures, such as angels, the Word, Wisdom, Enoch, the Son of Man, or the patriarchs. The expression 'exclusive monotheism' is applied to texts that do not affirm anything in particular about divine/heavenly figures.[1] The value in such an analysis for a Trinitarian scholar lies in what it allows: it facilitates the use of 'monotheism' to describe the *inclusion* of Jesus within a monotheistic framework. This may appear a neutrally descriptive thing to do, but it becomes less so when the expression 'inclusive monotheism' is applied to Trinitarianism and the three-in-one.

The term 'inclusive monotheism' does not have to be used to describe the monotheism of first century Judaism (or that of the Hebrew Scriptures). To do so is a choice made by the historian to configure the data and steer the understanding of his or her readers. In contrast, we would say that the etymology of '/mono/theism/' makes it an unsuitable term for such usage. The term 'monotheism' is about what there is or what is believed about the gods, viz. that there is only one God. If, in addition, you believe in demons, spirits or angels (or any other divine beings), then this is something to be characterized separately as an additional part of your overall beliefs, unless you are a polytheist or henotheist. Jewish monotheism of the first century is not an inclusive monotheism precisely because there is nothing else included within what is otherwise said to be one; further, there is no differentiation of the one for us to identify that something has been included in that one. Thus, 'monotheism' is not descriptive of Jewish cosmology; it is descriptive of what Jews thought about the category of 'god'. Accordingly, we would eschew the use of the expressions 'inclusive monotheism' and 'exclusive monotheism' when describing either Jewish monotheism (or that of the Hebrew Scriptures); they mislead the reader in widening the scope of 'monotheism' to embrace cosmology and confuse the picture of what Jews said was one. Instead, when Jews elaborate upon their cosmology, they use terms like 'angel', 'spirit' and 'demon', and they refer to divine attributes as agents of divine action.

It is not difficult to enumerate Jewish texts extant in the first century that enunciate the view that there is one God; in this they are consistent with

---

[1] This consequence of monotheism—the denial of deity to other divine beings—led to the charge of atheism being levelled against Jews (Josephus, *Contra Apion* 2.148).

the Hebrew Scriptures. The basis of Jewish devotional practices in respect of gods was the belief that there was one God, i.e. loyalty to the one God arose from the concomitant belief that that there was one God. For this reason, 'monotheism' is more descriptive of *belief* rather than the extent of any religious devotions. Thus, some Jews evidently had devotional practices in respect of angels (Col 2:18), but this does not mean that such Jews were not monotheists in respect of 'the gods'; in the case of Colossae, we do not know.

4. Illustrating Jewish Monotheism

Judaism in the first century was, no doubt, a varied religion, allowing us to speak of Judaism**s** as well as Judaism; it would make little sense to speak of the plural while denying the singular. We can illustrate its monotheism from a variety of texts. In doing this, we are not saying that some assertions are true and some false, or that only some writings are definitive of Judaism; the texts are just illustrations of monotheism.

(1) Philo (50 BCE to 50 CE) might not be paradigmatic for the religion of the common man of his times or the religious groups in Judaism based around the synagogue, but he does illustrate a philosophical Judaism. He grounds monotheism in the beliefs of Abraham:

> But this man, having formed a proper conception of him in his mind, and being under the influence of inspiration, left his country, and his family, and his father's house, well knowing that, if he remained among them, the deceitful fancies of the polytheistic doctrine abiding there likewise, must render his mind incapable of arriving at the proper discovery of the one true God, who is the only everlasting God and the Father of all other things, whether appreciable only by the intellect or perceptible by the outward senses; while, on the other hand, he saw, that if he rose up and quitted his native land, deceit would also depart from his mind, changing his false opinions into true belief. *Vir.* 1:214; cf. *Leg.* 3:4, 82; *Decal.* 65

This text illustrates a common apologetic stance in Judaism: to contrast its monotheism with the polytheism of the nations (contemporary or historical). Nevertheless, Philo also has a particular view of the Word (*logos*) as *second* to God:

> Why is it that he speaks as if of some other god, saying that he made man after the image of God, and not that he made

him after his own image? Very appropriately and without any falsehood was this oracular sentence uttered by God, for no mortal thing could have been formed on the similitude of the <u>supreme Father</u> of the universe, but only after the pattern of the <u>second deity</u> (*ton deuteron theon*), who is the Word of the supreme Being; since it is fitting that the rational soul of man should bear before it the type of the divine Word; since in his first Word God is superior to the most rational possible nature. But he who is superior to the Word holds his rank in a better and most singular pre-eminence, and how could the creature possibly exhibit a likeness of him in himself? *Quaest.* 2:62

Is Philo a monotheist? The answer depends wholly on *our* analysis. The Father is supreme but the Word is a second god. We could say that he is a monotheist in respect of his view of the Father because the Word is evidently not equal to the Father. Or, we could say that he is not a 'strict' monotheist; perhaps he is an 'inclusive' monotheist? Certainly, his views about the Word go beyond anything in the Jewish Scriptures, and so we might legitimately affirm that he is not true to his own traditions. The answer to our question, therefore, as to whether Philo was a monotheist, depends on how we are using the term. Is it a term for a broad cosmology with a supreme deity, or is it a term for statements that use adjectives like 'one' or 'only' or 'unique' in relation to gods to affirm there is one God?[1]

(2) In the *Letter to Aristeas* (2c. BCE) we read,

> Our Lawgiver first of all laid down the principles of piety and righteousness and inculcated them point by point...For he proved first of all that there is <u>only one God</u> and that his power is manifested throughout the universe...Beginning from this starting point he went on to show that <u>all mankind except ourselves</u> believe in the existence of many gods...For when they have made statues of stone and wood, they say that they are the images of those who have invented something useful for life and they worship them, though

---

[1] This issue in Philo is introduced by K. Schenck, *A Brief Guide to Philo* (Louisville: WJK Press, 2005), 43-44; it is further discussed as a "fourth sphere of ambiguity" in Philo's thought in R. Radice, "Philo's Theology and Theory of Creation" in *The Cambridge Companion to Philo* (ed. A. Kamesar; Cambridge: Cambridge University Press, 2009), 124-145 (128-129).

they have clear proof that they possess no feeling. *Letter to Aristeas*, 131-135[1]

This is a strong statement of the exclusivity of Jewish views. It affirms the existence of only one God (the metaphysical dimension) and then describes what Jews *believe* in contradistinction to 'all mankind' (the epistemic dimension).

(3) Josephus (30 CE – 100 CE) gives expression to the Jewish monotheism in several places in his *Antiquities of the Jews*, for instance,

> ...he [Abraham] was the first that ventured to publish this notion: That there was but one God, the Creator of the universe; and that, as to other [gods], if they contributed anything to the happiness of men, that each of them afforded it only according to his appointment, and not by their own power. *Ant*. 1:155

> The first commandment teaches us that there is but one God, and that we ought to worship him only... *Ant*. 3:91

> And let there be neither an altar nor a temple in any other city; for God is but one, and the nation of the Hebrews is but one. *Ant*. 4:201

> Now when the Israelites saw this, they fell down upon the ground, and worshipped one God, and called him The great and the only true God; but they called the others mere names, framed by the evil and vile opinions of men. *Ant*. 8:343[2]

The doctrine here is serving Josephus' nationalism: God is one and so he has only one favoured nation, the Jews (*Ant*. 4:201). He sees a spectacular demonstration of the doctrine in the contest between Elijah and the prophets of the Tyrean Baal (*Ant*. 8:343).

---

[1] Text taken from R. H. Charles, *The Apocrypha and Pseudepigrapha of the Old Testament in English* (2 vols; Oxford: Clarendon Press, 1913).
[2] Texts are taken from W. Whiston, *Complete Works of Josephus* (Peabody: Hendrickson, 1987).

The above examples, (1)–(3), are not illustrations of 'Exclusive Monotheism'—just 'Monotheism'.[1] This belief is presented alongside a broader cosmology of other divine beings (spirits, angels, and divine agents like Wisdom and the Word). The texts do not centre their monotheistic statements upon devotional practice but instead *derive* the principle of what/who to worship from the theory.

The claim to be stating the truth is an important characteristic of Jesus as well as the first Christians (e.g. John 14:6; 16:13; Acts 26:25; Gal 2:5; 2 Pet 1:12; Jms 5:19). Historians may well treat all groups within Judaism on an equal footing without regard to any distinction between truth and falsity in respect of 'the faith' of the Jewish Scriptures. All groups contribute to the complex phenomenon that is the Judaism of the first century. However, this does not answer the question of who was a 'true Jew' (Rom 2:29; Rev 2:9) in respect of the traditions of the Fathers (Acts 26:6; Gal 1:14). If we have a paradigm of the faith in the Law and the Prophets, then we can offer an historical judgment as to whether this or that Jewish writer or group is faithfully following their Scriptures.

5. Scriptural Monotheism

This chapter, so far, has been concerned with the use of the term 'monotheism' by scholars to describe Judaism in the first century. Today, the term is valued by Jews, Christians and Muslims, but Trinitarianism is not obviously a monotheistic system (it is more obviously a tri-theistic doctrine). Consequently, orthodox Christians use 'monotheism' to embrace the Jewish cosmological beliefs about angels, other divine agents, and exalted heavenly figures alongside the one God. This allows them to dub Trinitarianism a type of monotheism, even though the analogy with 'inclusive monotheism' is weak (there being no comparable internal distinctions within the Godhead in Judaism). In any event, this isn't an analytical strategy deployed by OT prophets, who do not use an abstract noun like 'monotheism', but do inveigh against the gods of the nations. The book of Isaiah is the classic source, for example,

> I *am* the Lord, and *there is* none else, *there is* no God beside me: I girded thee, though thou hast not known me... Isa 45:5 (KJV)

---

[1] For other texts that stress there is *one* God, or that the God of Israel is the *only* God, or that there is no god *besides* God, see 2 Macc 1:14; Wisd 12:13; Jdt 8:20; 9:14; Bel 1:41; Sir 18:2-3; 24:24; 36:5; *Sib. Or.* Frg 1:7-8; Frg 3:3-4; and *2 Enoch* 33:7-8; 36:1; 47:3.

This statement is addressed to Cyrus, a pagan potentate, and so it is a claim made in an international context with regard to the gods of the nations; it is a claim that Yahweh is the only God. It reflects the *Shema* of Deut 6:4 which is likewise made in the context of having no other gods (from the Canaanite nations) before God (Deut 6:14). While we do not have the abstract noun 'monotheism' in the Hebrew Scriptures, we do have this analysis: there is one God (ours) in contradistinction to the gods of the nations. We use the term 'monotheism' to describe this contrasting analysis rather than the cosmological analysis that there is one God who has angels and other agents that do his will. When scholars and theologians use 'monotheism' to describe a first century cosmology of at least God and his angels, they are not capturing what the Hebrew Scriptures are presenting in their emphasis of what it means to say that there is one God.

The basic doctrine that there is one God does not mean that the Hebrew Scriptures do not reference gods or position God in relation to gods. For example, God is a 'God of gods' (Deut 10:17; Ps 95:3; 136:2; Dan 2:47; 11:36). Yahweh is a great God above all gods, but to say so isn't an admission that other gods exist and that therefore you are a polytheist or henotheist. It is, rather, recognition that there are many gods and lords (1 Cor 8:5) 'out there' among the nations and that your god is the only real God. So, for example, this rhetoric is taken up by Philo in his treatise, *On the Confusion of Tongues*,

> Some persons therefore, admiring exceedingly the nature of both these worlds, have not only deified them in their wholes, but have also deified the most beautiful parts of them, such as the sun and the moon, and the entire heaven, which, having no reverence for anything, they have called gods. But Moses, perceiving their design, says, "O Lord, Lord, King of the gods", in order to show the difference between the ruler and those subject to him. *Conf.* 173

The point here is that *within* Israel, and for the faithful, there was one God and not many, but *outside* Israel among the nations (and within Israel among the unfaithful), there were many gods to which God was as a king by comparison. There were polytheists and henotheists among the people, as shown in the Law and the Prophets, but the witness of the Jewish Scriptures taken up by Jews in Jesus' day was that there was one God, Yahweh, and the gods of the nations were not to be called 'God'.

6. Angels, Divine Agents and Exalted Figures

In the Jewish writings around in the first century there are angels, various exalted figures such as the patriarchs, Enoch or the Son of Man, and divine agents such as the Word or Wisdom; there is also a world of demons and a prince of demons. Do such define Jewish monotheism or are they complementary to that monotheism? Scholars might say that Jews countenanced a variety of intermediaries because God was seen as completely transcendent; there needed to be such beings to make contact with humanity. Whether this is true or not for some of the implied authors of first century Jewish writings is not our concern; certainly, it is not a particularly OT picture, which has Yahweh immanent with his people. Our question is *whether Jewish intermediaries characterize monotheism*.

6.1 Angels

Angels are well known from the Hebrew Scriptures,[1] but until Daniel they are not differentiated by name. Further, until Daniel they are not given any individual back-story, but rather they are the transparent agents of God's will. In Jewish writings, following Daniel, there is more information about angels and more are named. For instance, God is praised as the 'prince of gods and the king of glorious ones, lord of every spirit, ruler of every creature' (1QH 18.8) and a 'ruler of the spirits' (2 Macc 3:24). The argument to consider here is that, whether 'angels' or 'spirits', they are heavenly beings that have oversight of the affairs of humanity (Sir 17:17; *Jub.* 15.31), and as such they are lesser 'gods' under a high God, and that this is an *inclusive* monotheism.

A variation of this argument surrounds the figure of the Angel of the Lord[2] who appears in the Hebrew Scriptures as well as Jewish literature of the first century. The speech and action of the Angel of the Lord appears to be identical to the speech and action of Yahweh. In contradistinction, other materials present an angel simply in the role of a messenger, an intermediary, or an agent of Yahweh. The prominence afforded to a persistent figure such as the Angel of the Lord raises the question in another way of whether angels are part of an *inclusive* monotheism.

The problem with this argument is the **lack of parity**. Angels are generally called such in Jewish writings, distinct from God, and subordinate agents. We might say that they manifest God in action and

---

[1] W. G. Heidt, *The Angelology of the Old Testament* (Washington: Catholic University Press, 1949), 69-101.

[2] For a diachronic introduction see W. Eichrodt, *Theology of the Old Testament* (trans. J. Baker; 2 vols; London: SCM Press, 1961-67), 2:23-29.

show certain attributes of God, but to say this still places God at the centre of our cosmology as a distinct being. In terms of choosing between two terms—'monotheism' or 'inclusive monotheism' to describe this cosmology, there doesn't seem to be anything in the model of a divine council with a 'king' (God) and his servants (angels) to merit the word 'inclusive'—a more accurate word would be 'associative': there is one God (monotheism) and he has an **associated divine council of angels**.

6.2 Exalted Figures

Various exalted figures feature in Jewish writings about the 'last days'; these are given the role of someone acting directly for God, but someone without peer among the angels or other heavenly agents. For example, the Son of Man from Daniel is such a figure that appears as a 'messianic' figure in the last days. One text identifies this figure as Enoch of the seventh generation from Adam, who was widely assumed to have been taken to heaven:

> And he (i.e. the angel) came to me and greeted me with His voice, and said unto me: 'This is the Son of Man, who is born unto righteousness, and righteousness abides over him, and the righteousness of the Head of Days forsakes him not'. And he said unto me: 'He proclaims unto thee peace in the name of the world to come; for from hence has proceeded peace since the creation of the world, and so shall it be unto thee for ever and for ever and ever. And all shall walk in his ways since righteousness never forsaketh him: With him will be their dwelling-places, and with him their heritage, and they shall not be separated from him for ever and ever and ever. And so there shall be length of days with that Son of Man, and the righteous shall have peace and an upright way in the name of the Lord of Spirits for ever and ever.' *1 Enoch* 71:14-17; cf. *1 Enoch* 46:1; 48:5; 62:9[1]

The exaltation of Jesus in NT writings is predicated upon various OT prophecies, for example Ps 2:2 or 110:1; Jesus' use of 'Son of Man' in reference to himself is based on Daniel 7, as is Stephen's vision of Christ in Acts 7. This is not out of step with Judaism insofar as there were contemporary visionary texts which portrayed an exalted figure acting with and on behalf of God. The difference with the Christian view lies in the fact that Jesus was a recent historical person who had been exalted,

---

[1] Text is taken from Charles, *The Apocrypha and Pseudepigrapha of the Old Testament in English.*

whereas Jewish apocalypses referred to historical figures like Enoch. The exaltation of Jesus to a position next to God is shocking if you have a low estimate of humanity. The purpose of man was to be an image of God and to exercise dominion (Gen 1:26-27). The exaltation of Jesus is a fulfillment of this divine intention. Theologians use the expression 'high Christology' for views that see Jesus in exalted heavenly terms; what they have is a correspondingly low anthropology. Rather, we should have a high anthropology in terms of the intended destiny of man. The conviction that Jesus was exalted to heaven, or that Jews believed figures such as Enoch had been so exalted, does not give us grounds for defining monotheism to include whoever has been exalted; such individuals were men and the visions that describe them distinguish them from God (this is true for Jesus in say, the *Letters to the Ecclesias* as well as for Enoch in *1 Enoch*).

6.3 Divine Agents

Whereas angels and exalted figures are less plausibly made part of a definition of monotheism, the divine attributes are an integral part of the divine nature: God is wise and has wisdom; God speaks and his word is powerful. If the Hebrew Scriptures use personification or linguistic hypostatization in respect of God's wisdom and his word, this is not inclusive monotheism; God's attributes are essential to his nature. Furthermore, if Jewish writings of the first century hypostasize divine attributes as beings, they are not *being inclusive* in their presentation of monotheism but **composite**—they are presenting God and his attributes in a composite way. The divine attributes are separated off from God and referenced independently and this is the opposite of what is happening when figures are exalted and included among the heavenly beings.

7. Devotion

We began this chapter with a rebuttal of the argument that monotheism should be defined in relation to devotional practices. As we draw the chapter to a close, we will briefly consider the question of the 'worship' of Jesus. Dunn observes,

> 'Worship' as such is a term rarely used in reference to Christ...Cultic worship or service (*latreuein, latreia*) as such is never offered to Christ, and other worship terms are used only in relation to God. In the case of the most common

words for praise and thanksgiving (*eucharistein*), they too are never offered to Christ.[1]

Dunn counsels here that a Bible reader needs to be aware of distinctions among the Greek words translated as 'worship' because not all are used in relation to Jesus. The argument, "Jesus was worshipped and only God should be worshipped, therefore Jesus is God", is popular, but too simplistic because 'worship' is too imprecise a word. Jesus states that, "Thou shalt worship the Lord thy God, and him only shalt thou serve" (Luke 4:8), but the 'worship' word is *proskunein*, a word meaning 'to bow, give obeisance'. He does not say that it is only to God that you should bow and give obeisance, but rather that that it is only God that you should 'serve'. The word used for 'serve' is *latreuein* which Dunn observes is never used in relation to Christ. Instead, we find that NT writers use *proskunein* in respect of Jesus, for example, when the author of Hebrews states, "Let all the angels of God worship him" (Heb 1:8).

With the exaltation of Jesus, the role of Jesus as a high priest, and with his future role in establishing the kingdom of God, it should occasion no surprise that Jesus is integral to the devotions of the apostolic church: veneration given his exalted heavenly position beside God; reverence and respect for him as lord; and obeisance (*proskunein*) towards him as the 'image of God' (Col 1:15; Heb 1:3). These attitudes express themselves in the devotional life of a Christian, but they do not arise from an inclusion of Jesus within a monotheistic pattern of *latreuein*.

R. J. Bauckham affirms of first century Jews that,

> Their self-conscious monotheism was not merely an intellectual belief about God, but a unity of belief and praxis, involving the exclusive worship of this one God. Monolatry (the worship of only the one God) as the corollary of monotheism (belief in only the one God) is an important aspect of Jewish monotheism...[2]

Bauckham illustrates the mistake in analysis that we have been highlighting. He treats 'monotheism' as a term embracing belief and praxis (worship), but he does so without arguing that 'monotheism' as a term

---

[1] J. D. G. Dunn, *Did the first Christians worship Jesus?* (London: SPCK, 2010), 27.

[2] R. J. Bauckham, *Jesus and the God of Israel* (Milton Keynes, Paternoster, 2008), 5.

should pick out a kind of worship. He makes this move because he wants to argue that the worship of Jesus is evidence that he was included in the divine identity of the one God. We should not grant his premise that worship of one God is an *aspect* of Jewish monotheism, but rather insist that worship of one God is a *corollary* of Jewish monotheism. Since actions (praise, prayer) flow from beliefs, it is natural to see them as corollaries to belief; in fact, beliefs distinguish actions, so that we can distinguish the praise of a polytheist from the praise of a monotheist. The quote above seems to point in two directions and is inconsistent. What he offers for Jewish worship is the term 'monolatry', which is derived from the Greek *latreuein*, which as Dunn observed is used only of God and never of Christ.

8. Conclusion

The Hebrew Scriptures present God in singular terms: he speaks with one voice; intentions, attitudes and emotions are attached to one subject; the singular pronoun is used. In terms of the *genus*, there is said to be one God and that God is presented as a person with the personal qualities that are illustrated in human beings. The nature of God is not particularly described; rather, his character is emphasized in his dealings with men and women. There is nothing in the data to suggest differentiation in the Godhead or that God is anything other than a single person, the Father.

First century Jewish monotheism is broadly in line with the scriptural tradition; there may be writings that reference a number of divine agents, but this is data that makes up a rich Jewish cosmology rather than describes an inclusive monotheism. The singular emphasis in Jewish texts that reference God, even when there are other divine agents in the surrounding verses, needs to be given due weight in our historical description of Judaism. The best term for this singular emphasis is just 'monotheism'.

The reverence of Jesus, the acknowledgement and honour ascribed to him, and the obeisance, the calling upon him, and the remembrance of him—all these actions are part of Christian devotion and reflect Jesus' exaltation as 'lord' and Davidic king. Whilst this belief was no doubt rejected by Jews in the first century, it is entirely compatible with the Jewish monotheism of the time, because it is the Father who is said to be the one God by Jews and the earliest Christians alike, different from angels, exalted patriarchs, and the heavenly divine agents.

CHAPTER TWELVE
Monotheistic Christology

1. Introduction

Erik Waaler notes "It has been argued that 1 Cor 8:1-6 is the earliest NT text testifying to the pre-existence of Christ and His participation in the act of creation."[1] C. Fletcher-Louis says that 1 Cor 8:6 is a "key text for the emerging consensus" of Christological Monotheism and that it "places Jesus squarely within the identity of the one God of Israel."[2] N. T. Wright says that it has an "apparently extraordinary 'high' christology" and it is a "Christian redefinition of the Jewish confession of faith, the *Shema*".[3] This remark shows that Wright (and it is true of others[4]) is conducting his analysis within the socio-historic context of Jewish Monotheism in the Second Temple period. He (and it is true of others) is not considering the text just within the context of inspired Scripture, i.e. what text means within the context supplied by the Spirit alone. This narrower and different context of appraisal generates the questions: does **the Spirit** present Deut 6:4 as a 'Jewish' confession of faith or rather a proclamation of divine revelation? Would the Spirit 'redefine' its own presentation in Deut 6:4? Was it a definition only for its time? These are unfashionable questions but is as well to advertise them here even though we do not deploy an 'evangelical' argument against Christological Monotheism.

Waaler reviews the history of scholarship[5] and it is worth noting that there has been a shift in the last century from seeing 1 Cor 8:6 against a Hellenistic backdrop to one that is primarily Jewish. Both exercises are a

---

[1] E. Waaler, *The Shema and the First Commandment in First Corinthians* (Tübingen: Mohr Siebeck, 2008), 4.

[2] C. Fletcher-Louis, *Jesus Monotheism* (Eugene, OR: Cascade Books, 2015), 8-9.

[3] N. T. Wright, *The Climax of the Covenant* (London: T&T Clark, 1991), 121. Hurtado, *One God, One Lord*, 97-98, says that it is a "binary mutation" of Jewish Monotheism. Bauckham, *Jesus and the God of Israel*, 100, 101, says 1 Cor 8:6 is a "remarkable rewriting of the Shemaʿ…this unprecedented reformulation of the Shemaʿ." Dunn, *Christology in the Making*, 180, says Paul "splits the *Shema*"; Waaler, *The Shema and the First Commandment in First Corinthians*, 433, says "Paul in 1 Cor 8:6 divided the *Shema* in two".

[4] For example, Hurtado, *One God, One Lord*, 161, justifies a Jewish focus, but we go further and restrict our data to Jewish Scripture.

[5] Waaler, *The Shema and the First Commandment in First Corinthians*, 4-27.

matter of bringing parallels to bear on the NT text, and the resulting proposals are beyond our scope for discussion. The intertextuality of the NT with the OT is so vast and any intertextuality with contemporary Jewish and non-Jewish literature so tiny that the method of bring extra-Biblical parallels to bear must take second place.

The flow of ethical argument in this part of the Corinthians' letter is also not essential for a discussion of how Christological Monotheism reads 1 Cor 8:6. The situation in Corinth and the teaching about *knowledge* which Paul was opposing is addressed by a statement with **two main clauses**:[1] one that is monotheistic and one that is about the Lord Jesus Christ. To say that there are two clauses, only one of which is monotheistic, is to take the opposite position to Christological Monotheism, and it doesn't depend on any particular view about the situation in Corinth regarding food offered to idols. This is our 'critical' argument against Christological Monotheism. Hence, we have given the title of this chapter as 'monotheistic Christology'.

The nature of the exegesis offered by Christological Monotheism on 1 Cor 8:6 is **largely declarative**. For example, Wright says that for Paul "the allegiance of local paganism to this or that 'god' and 'lord' must be met with nothing short of the Christian version of Jewish-style, *Shema*-style, monotheism."[2] Bauckham's declaration is, "Paul has taken over all of the words of this Greek version of the Shema', but rearranged them in such a way as to produce an affirmation of both one God, the Father, and one Lord, Jesus Christ."[3] The question to challenge Wright and Bauckham with is to ask whether this is actually what Paul is doing with the two clauses: are both clauses jointly expressing monotheism? Has Paul taken over *all* the words of the Hebrew version of the Shema in his Greek;[4] in

---

[1] Both main clauses are set off against the declaration in v. 5 about many gods and many lords and each has a subordinate clause concerning all things. The two clauses are joined by a conjunction but the implied verb 'there is' joins the two clauses as a single statement.

[2] Wright, *The Climax of the Covenant*, 128; Wright follows the same approach in his recent *The Paul Debate* (London: SPCK, 2016), 22-24.

[3] Bauckham, *Jesus and the God of Israel*, 101. It's an exaggeration to say that Paul has taken over *all* of the words of the Shema: the verb 'to be' is formally absent from the Greek of 1 Cor 8:6.

[4] It is superficial to observe that the OG of the Shema (insofar as we have it in the LXX) has *kyrios* and so does Paul; the *kyrios* of the OG Shema relates to 'Yhwh' in the Hebrew and so the question is whether Paul's use of *kyrios* has that relation.

particular has he taken over 'Yhwh'? This is the crux of the argument and to determine this question, logico-linguistic analysis of the text is required.

We will also need to examine Paul's use of other OT texts with 'Yhwh', as this is important for deciding whether Paul has taken over 'Yhwh' from the Shema in 1 Cor 8:6. Here the work of D. B. Capes is often cited.[1] Hence, we will jump from our exegesis/analysis of 1 Cor 8:6 into these texts in order to appraise the question of how many 'Yhwh' texts used by Paul refer to Christ. We shall find that an analysis of such texts (which includes 1 Cor 8:6), when informed by logico-linguistics, yields a much smaller list than that proposed by scholars such as Capes, who carry out more theologically driven exegesis. Accordingly, such a list does not offer much support for the view that 'Yhwh' has been quoted from Deut 6:4 in 1 Cor 8:6.

Finally, we will examine what Paul means by saying 'all things' are from the Father and through the Son. Commentators take two approaches to these two ideas: cosmological and soteriological. It is either all things of the created order or all things in the new creation that are from the Father and through the Son. Which is correct?[2]

This then is the scope of this chapter; we are not discussing the flow of Paul's argument about food offered to idols; the cultural situation in Corinth; the general Hellenistic and/or Jewish background of monotheistic belief;[3] how and when Paul uses either the Hebrew or Greek

---

[1] D. B. Capes, *Old Testament Yahweh Texts in Paul's Christology* (Tübingen: Mohr (Paul Siebeck), 1992). S. B. Nicholson notes the influence of Capes' study on Yhwh texts with scholars in an unpublished doctoral thesis, "Dynamic oneness: The significance and flexibility of Paul's one-God language" (Durham, 2007, online).

[2] T. Gaston, "Some Thoughts on 1 Cor 8:6 and the Shema" *CeJBI* 10/1 (2016): 65-70 (68), says, "The fact that Paul includes these clauses is another indication that he does not specifically have the *Shema* in mind." The counter-argument would be that the allusion to the Shema in the first clause of 1 Cor 8:6 is mediated by conventional ways known to Paul – such as affirmations of 'one God' in Jewish texts.

[3] On the question of the background and how to distinguish Jewish Monotheism from Jewish Cosmology see chap. 1.

Scriptures;[1] or sundry literary matters to do with composition or style. Our focus is just on the textual relationship of 1 Cor 8:6 to the Shema.

2. Analysis

The text is fairly straightforward, and we have translated the prepositions with the most likely meanings,

> But to us *there is* one God, the Father, out of whom *are* all things, and we to/for him; and one Lord Jesus Christ, through/by whom *are* all things, and we through/by him. 1 Cor 8:6 (KJV revised)

> ἀλλ' ἡμῖν εἷς θεὸς ὁ πατὴρ ἐξ οὗ τὰ πάντα καὶ ἡμεῖς εἰς αὐτόν, καὶ εἷς κύριος Ἰησοῦς Χριστὸς δι' οὗ τὰ πάντα καὶ ἡμεῖς δι' αὐτοῦ.

This statement is compared to the Shema,

> Hear, O Israel: Yhwh our God, Yhwh *is* one. Deut 6:4 (KJV revised[2])

> שׁמע ישׂראל יהוה אלהינו יהוה אחד

> ἄκουε Ισραηλ κύριος ὁ θεὸς ἡμῶν κύριος εἷς ἐστιν

and the **proposal** is made that, "Any Greek-speaking Jew who hears a Christian say what 1 Cor 8:6 says is bound to hear those words as a claim that Yhwh is now somehow identified with Jesus Christ."[3] Such a proposition, without evidence in Second Temple writings from Greek-speaking Jews, is of little value as it stands. Commenting on Paul's use of Deut 6:4, Wright says: "What Paul seems to have done is as follows. He has expanded the formula, in a way quite unprecedented in any other texts known to us, so as to include a gloss on θεός and another on κύριος..."[4]

---

[1] This is discussed in A. Perry, "Did the NT Writers Quote the LXX?" *CeJBI* 7/2 (2013): 59-78 [Online at www.academia.edu]. This paper considers the question of *kyrios* as a replacement for the Tetragrammaton.
[2] There are issues of translation that could be discussed, but Waaler, *The Shema and the First Commandment in First Corinthians*, 49-50, 101-105, supplies the supporting argumentation.
[3] Fletcher-Louis, *Jesus Monotheism*, 10.
[4] Wright, *The Climax of the Covenant*, 129; the lack of exegesis is astonishing.

Wright notes that there is a paucity of Second Temple evidence for this proposal because there are no other texts known to us like 1 Cor 8:6.[1]

A more plausible proposal would be that a Greek-speaking Jew would see an *allusion* in Paul's words to the Shema in, for example, 'God', 'us/our' and 'one',[2] but it is not obvious that Yhwh is to be identified with Jesus Christ.[3] Rather, the descriptive aspect of 'our God' and 'one' is picked up by 'to us...one God', which therefore in turn identifies 'the Father' as Yhwh rather than Jesus Christ. Further, the counting aspect of Paul's conjoined statements, 'one...and one', rather militates against the interpretation that Christ is being placed **within** the identity of the one God of Israel. The Shema has a single occurrence of 'one' whereas 1 Cor 8:6 has two occurrences. Finally, if we accept Wright's claim, we still have to do the work of saying what we mean by 'included within the identity of the one God of Israel' – this could be explained as simply as the indwelling of God's Spirit rather than anything more complicated, say, such as a recognition of an incarnation.[4]

Wright asserts that Paul has taken κύριος from Deut 6:4, but offers no argumentation for this proposal. He then concludes, "There can be no mistake: just as in Philippians 2 and Colossians 1, Paul has placed Jesus *within* an explicit statement, drawn from the Old Testament's quarry of emphatically monotheistic texts...producing what we can only call a sort of christological monotheism."[5] We have criticized Wright's exegesis of Colossians 1 and Philippians 2 in previous chapters, but only Philippians 2 uses a characteristic monotheistic OT text (Isa 45:23). We might agree that Phil 2:10 places Jesus *within* the same eschatological **situation** as Yahweh in Isa 45:23, but placement within a situation is not the same as

---

[1] Dunn, *Christology in the Making*, 179, makes the same point, "no real parallel".

[2] It is important to note that the Shema is not providing the phrase 'one God' to Paul.

[3] Gaston, "Some Thoughts on 1 Cor 8:6 and the Shema", 67, expresses doubt on whether there is an allusion, but we see the three elements in common as sufficient to give an allusion.

[4] The analysis is sorely lacking. Do we mean 'within the *personal* identity' or just 'within the identity' of the God of Israel? There are differences to mark between the identity of God (a god) and the personal identity of God (a god).

[5] Wright, *The Climax of the Covenant*, 129. In 1991, Wright was able to say that this fact was becoming more widely recognised in scholarship.

inclusion within the divine identity and so Wright's comparison is false.

The case for the christological monotheist is based around the claim that *kyrios* is picking up 'Yhwh' from Deut 6:4 and using this name for Christ, thus identifying Jesus with Yhwh in some sense. **The first counter-argument** to this claim is that, even if Paul is picking up 'Yhwh' from Deuteronomy, *bearing* the name 'Yhwh' doesn't imply an identification of Jesus with Yhwh. This is shown in two ways: first, the name that is above every name was *given*[1] to Christ by God (Phil 2:9); and secondly, the name was also given to the Angel of the Lord who led Israel through the wilderness ("My name is in him", Exod 23:21).

The Angel of the Lord is a type of Christ leading his people through the wilderness. In the same way that he bore the name, so too Christ bears the name. Hence, any basis there might be in the possession of this name for identifying Jesus with Yhwh would also apply to the Angel of the Lord.[2] Yet the Angel of the Lord is distinguished from Yhwh in the same way that Paul distinguishes 'one…and one' in 1 Cor 8:6.

However, before we reach this conclusion, we should ask, **as a second counter-argument**, whether *kyrios* in 1 Cor 8:6 is actually picking up 'Yhwh' from Deut 6:4 in the first place. 'Yhwh' is a proper name, but *kyrios* in 1 Cor 8:6 is not being used here as a proxy[3] for this proper name

---

[1] Bauckham, *Jesus and the God of Israel*, 24-25. The unanswered question for a christological monotheist is why this name was 'given' to Christ. Did the Son not have it at the time of the exodus?

[2] The 'identity' metaphysics should accommodate this fact. It's not clear that such a metaphysics would be a single dyadic arrangement (which is what christological monotheists want), but rather a varying dyadic arrangement in which Yhwh chooses to be **who** he chooses to be ('I will be **who** I will be', Exod 3:14).

[3] Gibson, *Biblical Semantic Logic*, 154, notes proper names are usually transliterated into language B from language A; hence, we describe *kyrios* as a proxy use for 'Yhwh'. Gibson calls this "exegetical replacement" and not translation; see also J. W. Adey, "One God: The Shema in Old and New Testaments", in *One God, the Father* (ed. T. Gaston; Sunderland: Willow Publications, 2013), 26-39 (33), "The truth of God is 'Christianised in so far as there is this replacement of 'Yahweh', Israel's God's personal name (the only proper noun) in the Hebrew *Shema*, for (the common noun) 'Lord' (Gk: κύριος/kurios) of the NT. This divine name-absent or alternative ('Lord') mode of presentation of God is a NT

precisely because it is modified by 'one'.[1] The 'one' is in a semantic contract with the 'many' of v. 5, which in turn has the plural of *kyrios*. This in turn brings that plural into a semantic contract with the singular of v. 6. Thus, because the plural is functioning as a descriptive title, so too *kyrios* in v. 6 is functioning as a title and not as a proxy for the name 'Yhwh'. Accordingly, we can observe a symmetry between the two clauses: just as 'God' is not a proper name in 'one God' so too 'Lord' is not serving as a proxy for a proper name in 'one Lord'.

In a contiguous reproduction of a Yhwh text, *kyrios* without an article is a fairly clear proxy replacement for the name and it carries some functionality of that name. In freer quotations and allusions of/to Yhwh texts, *kyrios* may be used with an article as an exegetical replacement for 'Yhwh', but where the reference is to Christ, the use of the article makes it unlikely that *kyrios* is being used as a proxy for the name 'Yhwh', and this is because *kyrios* is being modified by the article.[2]

Given that *kyrios* is generally used to describe or address lords, masters, owners, deities, rulers, persons of rank, as well as the God of Israel, we need to know which use of *kyrios* we have in 1 Cor 8:6. If *kyrios* is being used **descriptively** of Jesus Christ, then it is not representing the name 'Yhwh'. Indeed, we might well argue that since 'Jesus' means 'Yah saves' or 'Yah is salvation', it is the name 'Jesus' which picks up 'Yhwh' from

---

theological convention in the light of Jesus' advent." In fact, various devices were used in OG to *represent* the divine name. The logico-linguistics of Gibson and Adey stands opposed to the loose analysis of Capes who talks of the divine name being 'translated' by *kyrios* and that Yhwh texts in the Hebrew Bible "refer" to the divine name; see his summary essay for his book, "YHWH texts and Monotheism in Paul's Christology" in *Early Jewish and Christian Monotheism* (eds. L. T. Stuckenbruck and W. E. S. North; London: T & T Clark International, 2004), 120-137 (120, 127).

[1] The philosophical logic for this argument is set out in M. A. E. Dummett, *Frege: Philosophy of Language* (2nd ed.; London: Duckworth, 1981), chap. 4. It is rare to have numbers and articles modify names, and this can be seen by looking at usage. For example, a teacher commenting on her class might say, "We have three Andrews in this class", or in talking about a pupil to another teacher, she may remark, "The Andrew in my class is disruptive". This is highly specific usage.

[2] N. Turner, *Grammatical Insights into the New Testament* (Edinburgh: T & T Clark, 1965), 127, says that *kyrios* with the article is normally Christ and without it is proxy for 'Yhwh'.

Deut 6:4, but this obviously is just a general pick-up of 'Yhwh' common to many Hebraic names.

If the first clause, 'there is one God, the Father', is monotheistic, what type of clause is 'there is one Lord, Jesus Christ'?[1] Is it possible to have a god and a lord within a scriptural faith? Is this conjoining of the Father and the Son so innovative that it redefines Scriptural Monotheism and Jewish Monotheism? Is the associative partnership implicit in 'of whom are all things' (the Father) and 'by whom are all things' (the Son) actually (or still) monotheistic?[2]

Our **two-clause** reading of 1 Cor 8:6 is immune to Bauckham's reasoning for Christological Monotheism. He says, "there can be no doubt that the *addition* of a unique Lord to the unique God of the Shema' would flatly *contradict* the uniqueness of the latter...The only possible way to understand Paul as maintaining monotheism is to understand him to be including Jesus in the unique identity of the one God affirmed in the Shema'."[3] All we have to observe here is that the second clause is not 'adding to' the 'one' of the monotheism in the first clause and that 'one...and one' does add up to two! We do not have to maintain Paul's monotheism by deploying a late-20c. theological construct like 'included in the divine identity'. We can maintain his monotheism by confining his avowal of monotheism to the first clause.

The questions we pose go to the heart of the matter and their answer is that a **son** of God is precisely the person who can be in partnership with God without any confusion of persons or change to monotheism; **this is not a High Christology but a High Anthropology**.

---

[1] At least one commentator tries 'monokurism'.

[2] G. D. Fee, *1 Corinthians* (NICNT; Grand Rapids: Eerdmans, 1987), 375, claims "Although Paul does not here call Christ God, the formula is so constructed that only the most obdurate would deny its Trinitarian implications...the designation 'Lord' which in the OT belongs to the one God, is the proper designation of the divine Son." This illustrates typical theological linguistics: we should rather insist that 'Yhwh' is a name given to the Son (Phil 2:9-11) and has no implication as regards the Trinity or divinity.

[3] Bauckham, *Jesus and the God of Israel*, 101. Bauckham's error lies in his use of the concept of 'addition'. Dunn, *The Partings of the Ways*, 189, is better in talking of a **parallel** between one Lord and one God.

3. The Shema

J. W. Adey comments, "The 'one God' of Biblical revelation is a *single* 'person' God, the Father only, unambiguously unitarian or monotheistic…".[1] The Shema would seem to be a clear expression of that monotheism. The singleness of God is **not about his (compound) unity**, but about there being a sole God.

Christological Monotheism holds that Jesus is included within the divine identity of the God of Israel. As a second move it affirms a continual adherence on the part of Paul to Jewish Monotheism. The two propositions introduce a confusion into the definition of monotheism between *what is one* and *unity*. Jewish (as well as scriptural) Monotheism is not about unity but about there being a single God. The compound unity of the Father and the Son is not informative for Paul's use of the Shema.

This observation introduces a requirement for Christological Monotheism: it needs to show that 'inclusion within the divine identity' is actually *relevant* to a characterization of 'monotheism'. The contrary challenge is that we can characterize Jewish Monotheism, Scriptural Monotheism and Pauline Monotheism, referring to the singleness of God, as well as showing that Jesus is included within the divine identity of the God of Israel – but without this being a matter of monotheism and instead being a matter of **cosmology**.[2] The drive to have 'inclusive identity' part of a definition of monotheism seems anachronistic and based in the needs of Christian theology rather than an accurate description of NT history.

If we want to be faithful to the etymology 'mono/theism' (μόνος/θεός), then we should include the following Pauline 'mono' texts '*only* God' (1 Tim 1:17; cf. Jude v. 25) and '*only* Sovereign…who *only* has immortality' (1 Tim 6:15-16). These texts, coupled with the distinction between the Son and the invisible God in Colossians, gives us a consistent monotheistic pattern in Paul's thought that **doesn't include** the Son.

Is Paul (or the Spirit) rewriting or rearranging the Shema? If the 'one' and 'God' of the Shema is used in the first clause in 'one God' and the sense of 'to us' is reproduced in the 'our' of the first clause, then the Shema is partly quoted. 'Yhwh' is absent but we have 'the Father' in an analogous position in the first clause to give us the reference of that name.

---

[1] J. W. Adey, "One God: The Shema in Old and New Testaments", 27.
[2] Scholars traditionally include angels, exalted patriarchal figures and demons in discussions of Jewish Cosmology.

If the 'one' of the Shema has been used in the first clause, can we say that it is also used in the second clause and for a different person? The point here is that the referent of 'Yhwh' has been brought into the first clause under the reference of 'the Father'. The available sense of 'one' in the Shema as it is related to Yahweh has therefore been used up in the first clause. The alternative analysis therefore is that we have a **corresponding use** of 'one' in the second clause, a use that is modelled on the first clause (and the two clauses do have a similar structure).[1]

A correct analysis of the first clause disallows the possibility of *kyrios* being used from the Shema in the second clause. The argument is that the semantic resources of the Shema are used up in the first clause. This argument supplements the earlier argument above that *kyrios* is not functioning as a proxy for the name 'Yhwh' in the second clause.[2]

We should ask *whether it is possible* for the Shema to be rewritten or rearranged so as to include Jesus Christ within the divine identity of the God of Israel. The question here is whether the semantics of 'one' (אחד, 'eḥāḏ) in the Shema allow this possibility. Our argument is that they do not, because 'one' is about singleness and not unity whereas 'inclusion within the divine identity' is about unity, i.e. requires a sense corresponding to 'unity' in the Shema.[3]

A quotation of the Shema in Zech 14:9 assists this analysis.

> And Yahweh shall be king over all the earth: in that day shall there be Yahweh <u>one</u>, and his name <u>one</u>. Zech 14:9 (KJV revised)

---

[1] Hence, the second clause is 'one Lord, Jesus Christ' and not 'one Lord Jesus Christ'; *contra*, Gaston, "Some Thoughts on 1 Cor 8:6 and the Shema", 69, and with Waaler, *The Shema and the First Commandment in First Corinthians*, 428-429.

[2] The methodological weakness of Christological Monotheism's treatment of 1 Cor 8:6 is that its exegesis is not informed by the distinctions in logico-linguistics.

[3] The semantics are fully set out in J. W. Adey, "Is the Shema's 'one' ('eḥāḏ) one or more?" in *One God, the Father* (ed. T. Gaston; Sunderland: Willow Publications, 2013), 290-311 (290). Adey says, "My aim is to confirm that no other semantic value is possible for the *Shema's* 'ḥd than as a cardinal number *counting* 'one'."

Adey comments on this text, "the way *ʾḥd* qualifies Yahweh and 'Yahweh' in Zech 14:9, *classifying* but not (it is said) identifying, connects and complies syntactically and semantically with reading *ʾḥd* as a numeral 'one' in the *Shema*."[1] And a further quotation,

> Have we not all <u>one</u> father? Hath not <u>one</u> God (*ʾēl*) created us? (Mal 2:10 KJV)

Adey's comment on this text is, "The singularity of 'God' is further emphasized by the grammatically singular form *ʾēl*".[2] The singleness of Yahweh is also seen in the complementary statements that God is alone God or that Yahweh is alone Yahweh (2 Kgs 19:15, 19; Neh 9:6; Ps 83:18).

Where *ʾeḥād* might be used for 'oneness' or 'unity', then there is a two that remains two, as for example in the case of "the two shall be one flesh" (Gen 2:24). Adey observes,

> "…whilst 'one' in the appropriate context may be transposed into a metaphoric sense as 'unity' ('one*ness*'), dismantling 'one' as 'unity' does not end up with 'one' (thing). 'Unity' requires at least two (parts or persons) for its meaning. In Deut 6:4 the only theistic party is Yahweh. The text has none other that is God but He, and this justifies asserting that the given four semantic units in the *Shema* statement are insufficient to provide for or even evoke the concept of (some plural *oneness* as) unity.[3]

In summary: Christological Monotheism needs to argue that the Shema *can* be rewritten and that its singleness in respect of Yahweh can be divided. It also has to show that 'Yhwh' is actually being picked up in the second clause of 1 Cor 8:6; it needs to argue the case that the semantic properties of *kyrios* in Corinthians are consistent with such a pick-up. Bauckham and Wright certainly make the exegetical **claim** that Paul is re-writing the Shema, but have they been misled by the 'surface grammar' of the appearance of *kyrios* in the NT and the OG to think there has been a pick-up of 'Yhwh'?

---

[1] Adey, "Is the Shema's 'one' (*ʾeḥād*) one or more?", 293.

[2] Adey, "Is the Shema's 'one' (*ʾeḥād*) one or more?", 293.

[3] Adey, "Is the Shema's 'one' (*ʾeḥād*) one or more?", 297.

4. Yhwh-Kyrios Identity

'Yhwh' is represented by '*kyrios*' in Pauline NT texts that quote the OT. This is not controversial.[1] To give one example,

> Blessed *is* the man to whom *kyrios* will not impute sin. Rom 4:8 (KJV revised)

> Blessed *is* the man unto whom Yhwh imputeth not iniquity, and in whose spirit *there is* no guile. Ps 32:2 (KJV revised)

The question is whether there are quotations of texts that have 'Yhwh', but which are used of Christ. The argument put by Christological Monotheism is that there are such texts and they are an "emerging pattern".[2] This pattern is used to support the interpretation that Paul included Jesus Christ within the identity of the God of Israel (in 1 Cor 8:6). Dunn asks,

> "Should we therefore conclude that in making such use of such scriptures Paul was equating or even identifying Jesus with God, with the one God of Jewish monotheism? Such a development would seem to go well beyond anything within the current diversity of first-century Judaism and constitute such a radical revision of the dogma of monotheism as to make a parting of the ways inevitable and in fact already irretrievable."[3]

Dunn's doubt is well-placed. The first problem facing commenters is that many of the NT texts proposed[4] can be read solely with reference to Yahweh. The second problem is how to derive an 'inclusive' identity

---

[1] See also Rom 9:28-29 (Isa 1:9); Rom 10:16 (Isa 53:1); Rom 11:34 (Isa 40:13); Rom 15:11 (Ps 117:1); 1 Cor 3:20 (Ps 94:11); for more quotations see Bauckham, *Jesus and the God of Israel*, 189-190; Capes, "YHWH texts and Monotheism in Paul's Christology", 125; and Waaler, *The Shema and the First Commandment in First Corinthians*, 429-432.

[2] Fletcher-Louis, *Jesus Monotheism*, 11.

[3] Dunn, *The Parting of the Ways*, 190, 191; he adds "To call Jesus 'Lord', therefore, was evidently not understood in earliest Christianity as identifying him with God."

[4] See Capes, "YHWH texts and Monotheism in Paul's Christology", 125, for a table; and Capes, *Old Testament Yahweh Texts in Paul's Christology*, 90-114, for exegesis. Capes would be the starting point for researching scholarship on this question.

characterization from texts that use 'Yhwh' of Christ. Examples of these texts are worth discussing in order to tease out what conditions must be satisfied in order for Paul to be making some sort of 'including identification' between the God of Israel and Christ.

There are two common logical notions of identity to distinguish from inclusive identity.[1] An **absolute identity** such as 'a=b' gives no priority to either 'a' or 'b' and offers no basis for saying that 'a is included within the identity of b' instead of 'b is included within the identity of a'. Indeed, 'within' is problematic. If we try and use the preferred language of Christological Monotheism, 'a=b' would translate as the proposition " 'a' is included **in** an identity **with** 'b' " which doesn't give you a notion of 'inclusion within'. How we explain the cognitive difference between 'a=b' and 'a=a' is not important for our purposes.[2] What absolute identity requires is that if two are identical, then whatever is true of one is true of the other.[3] Given the different things Paul says about God and Jesus, it seems clear he did not presuppose or make an absolute identification between the two; rather the opposite – 1 Cor 8:6 is not, formally, an identity statement.

If we consider **relative identity** ('a is the same F as b'),[4] it doesn't seem that this framework will give us an understanding for inclusive identity. Logically, two are one (*the same*) relative to their satisfying a categorical predicate ('the same *F*'; Fido and Pooch are the same breed'). Does Paul think that Jesus is the same god as Yahweh? One doubt would be that he distinguishes them in terms of 'God the Father and the Lord Jesus Christ'. However, putting this doubt aside, if Paul believed that they were the same god, this doesn't necessarily imply that he is 'including' Jesus in the divine identity of Yahweh/God of Israel.

There are problems with thinking of 'inclusive' identity as a relative identity. Exponents of Christological Monotheism don't use the technical

---

[1] S. J. Wagner, "Identity" in *The Cambridge Dictionary of Philosophy* (2nd ed.; Ed. R. Audi; Cambridge: Cambridge University Press, 1999), 415-416.

[2] In proper name theory, this is a debate between Fregean and Kripkean semantics; see S. Haack, *Philosophy of Logics* (Cambridge: Cambridge University Press, 1978), 57-65.

[3] D. Wiggins, *Sameness and Substance Renewed* (Cambridge; Cambridge University Press, 2001), 5. This is Leibniz' principle of the identity of indiscernibles.

[4] P. Geach, *Reference and Generality* (New York: Cornell University Press, 1962), 39; Gibson, *Biblical Semantic Logic*, 140.

vocabulary of relative identity. Furthermore, relative identity (or qualitative identity) maintains that *a* and *b* are at least numerically unique.[1] Again, as with the notion of absolute identity, to say that Jesus and the God of Israel are *the same* god doesn't give any priority to either in terms of inclusion.

If we think of **shared identity** or **group identity**, these are examples of 'inclusive' identity. We might say 'a is a member of the same class as b'. There are many gods and many lords and these would be classes in which we might place the God of Israel and the Lord Jesus Christ. Putting it in this way, doesn't obviously include Jesus in the class of many gods, but rather the class of many lords. In fact, 1 Cor 8:6 doesn't lend itself to an inclusivity thesis, since Paul would seem to affirm that the "to-us" class of gods has only one member and likewise the "to-us" class of lords.[2] He assigns deity to the Father and lordship to Jesus.

It is one thing to *claim* that Paul includes Jesus within the divine identity of the God of Israel; it is another thing to show this *worked out* in his writing. We have noted the declarative quality of Christological Monotheism. For example, we might ask whether (for Paul) it was God the Father[3] that included Jesus within his identity. If this were the case, and suppose that he did so through the bestowal of his Spirit upon Jesus, does this have any implication as regards intrinsic deity in respect of Jesus? If Jesus is included within the divine identity of the God of Israel, is the identity nevertheless still retained by the God of Israel as *his* identity in such an inclusion?

In a rough and ready way we might say, "A criterion of identity for something is that criterion by means of which we can individuate something, specify which one it is, tell where it begins and another leaves off; in short, by means of which we can pick something out or tell that it is the same one again."[4] In the writings of Paul, the use of 'the Father' in

---

[1] Gibson, *Biblical Semantic Logic*, 140-143. `
[2] Gaston, "Some Thoughts on 1 Cor 8:6 and the Shema", 68, insightfully notes that because the context is one of pagan lords and gods, Paul is not redefining Christianity over against Judaism. The pagan classes of gods and lords each have many members; the class of the Jewish God has a sole member and the class of the Christian Lord has a sole member.
[3] If we were discussing Luke 1:35, we might ask whether God the holy Spirit did the including.
[4] A. C. Grayling, *An Introduction to Philosophical Logic* (Brighton: Harvester Press, 1982), 40.

constant conjunction with 'God' serves as one criterion for individuating God, of which there is only one ('To us there is one God, the Father'). Any inclusion of Jesus within this identity doesn't change that criterion of identity which is not satisfied by Jesus (he is the Son). Paul doesn't give us any language to change the criterion.

5. Representative Identity

The best sense for 'included within the divine identity' is **representative identity** – i.e. where someone represents (acts for) someone else.

> Wherefore God also hath highly exalted him, and given him a name which is above every name: that at the name of Jesus every knee should bow, of *things* in heaven, and *things* in earth, and *things* under the earth; and *that* every tongue should confess that Jesus Christ is *kyrios*, to the glory of God the Father. Phil 2:9-11 (KJV revised); cf. Rom 14:11

The name given to Jesus that is above every name is not the common Jewish name of 'Jesus' but that of 'Yhwh'. As we have noted above, the type for this is the giving of the name to the Angel of the Lord. This framework of name-bearing is indicative of representation (acting/speaking[1] in someone's name). This is clear from the example of the Angel of the Lord where God instructs that the people were to obey his voice because "my name is in/with him" (Exod 23:21). The identity here is representative, one in which someone represents the authority and the will of another. As such, it does not confuse the persons of God and the Angel of the Lord. We can, if we want, gloss this kind of identity as an 'inclusive' identity: the representative is *part of* the identity of the one represented.

Paul quotes Isa 45:23 in Phil 2:9-11 which, while 'anthropomorphic', is quite specific in its personal language: 'my mouth' and 'unto me' – this singular language doesn't seem to offer much room for *others* to receive obeisance.

> I have sworn by myself, the word is gone out of my mouth
> *in* righteousness, and shall not return, that unto me (כי לי)

---

[1] On representative speaking, see Wolterstorff, *Divine Discourse*, chap. 2. A prophet representing Yahweh is a 'same-sayer' with Yahweh ('Yahweh and Isaiah are same-sayers'). There is a level of description of what the prophet is doing that corresponds to what God is doing through the prophet—whether speaking or acting.

every knee shall bow, every tongue shall swear. (Isa 45:23 KJV)

Commentators assume that bowing 'at the name of Jesus' is equivalent to bowing before Jesus alone. It is as if their exegesis drops 'the name' from their consideration of what Paul is saying. However, if you bow 'at the name' and that name is 'Yhwh', then Yahweh is involved as an indirect recipient of the obeisance when the one being bowed to is a representative.[1]

The bowing goes hand in hand with the confession that Jesus Christ is *kyrios*. Is this a confession that Christ is 'Yhwh', a bearer of the divine name; is it a confession that Jesus is Yahweh; or is it a confession that he is the believers' lord?

Christ is not only given a name; he is highly exalted, an elevation which is all about 'lordship' (quoting Isa 52:13-15 – a position of authority over kings). Exegetically, *kyrios* ('Jesus Christ is Lord'[2]) could be a proxy for 'Yhwh'; however, since *kyrios* is not being quoted from a Yhwh text, we have no prompt for this reading. The sense of *kyrios*, which we noted above, includes ideas of lordship and being a master or ruler, and this fits with the obeisance in the act of bowing. Is it likely that Paul is saying that confession to God's glory is a matter of acknowledging Jesus bears the divine name or that he is the believer's lord? To state the question is to answer it.

How do we account for the use of Isa 45:23 in Phil 2:9-11? The simplest and most Jewish explanation is that the identity implied by name-bearing is **representative**. Jesus represents Yahweh (as a name-bearer of 'Yhwh'), so that bowing to him is bowing to Yahweh. Hence, bowing and confessing is to/for[3] the glory of God the Father and not the glory of Jesus. Rather than placing Christ on an equal footing,[4] first his exaltation, and then the believer's glorifying of God through him, define his position as subordinate.

---

[1] It is worth noting that obeisance is not worship.

[2] This 'identity' is attributive, not representative.

[3] Paul picks up on 'unto me' from Isa 45:23 and translates this with 'to' the glory of God the Father

[4] *Contra* Capes, *Old Testament Yahweh Texts in Paul's Christology*, 159, who claims that Jewish believers in Paul's day "would probably assume that Jesus reigns, not as a second God but as One who shares full equality and divinity with God". This is wishful thinking.

342

The situation in which someone represents the identity of another person is a common occurrence in diplomatic contexts, in government, and in legal settings.[1] The example of Isa 45:23 and Phil 2:9-11/Rom 14:11 suggests that Jesus Christ is a plenipotentiary representing Yahweh (cf. Joseph and Pharaoh).[2]

It should be noted that the use of Isa 45:23 in Rom 14:11 is more formal than that in Phil 2:9-11,

> For it is written, "As I live, says *kyrios*, to me every knee shall bow and every tongue confess to God."

The differences here with Isa 45:23 are the change from 'By myself have I sworn' to 'As I live' and the addition of 'says *kyrios*'. The lack of the article, and the conventional formula 'thus says the Lord (God)' in the Prophets,[3] particularly Ezekiel, suggests that *kyrios* in Rom 14:11 is standing proxy for 'Yhwh' and refers to Yahweh. This is clear from the fact that what is said was said *back then* and Christ is not a figure back then – just Yahweh.

Romans 14:11 is about what was written; it is not about something being said contemporaneously. We might ask why Paul dropped 'By myself have I sworn' and used 'As I live'. To this we can say, first, the 'As I live' Yhwh texts are pronouncements and commands, but mostly **judgments**. This accounts for Paul's composite quotation: he is relating the pronouncement of Isa 45:23 to the **judgment** seat of Christ; secondly, the first person of 'By myself have I sworn' is kept in 'As I live'; and thirdly, 'As I live' evidently has the same force as the speech act of swearing reported in Isaiah.[4]

---

[1] Critically, for our discussion of Christological Monotheism, this doesn't collapse the distinction of persons involved in the representative situation.
[2] Other examples in which prophecies that refer to Yahweh have their fulfilment with Christ include Rom 9:33 (Isa 8:14; 28:16).
[3] The declaration 'As I live' tends to go with 'Adonai Yahweh' e.g. Ezek 5:11; 14:16-20; 16:48; 18:3; 20:33; 33:11; but Num 14:28; Isa 49:18; Jer 22:24 have 'Yhwh'.
[4] On speech act theory see Searle, *Speech Acts*. The point here is that conventionally we associate quotation with textual material, but Isaiah reports an act of swearing, where Romans is a speech act of swearing (written down).

Isaiah 45:23 is quoted in Romans in support of the proposition that all must appear before the judgment seat of God; hence, all confess to God. However, because the judgment seat of God is the judgment seat of Christ, all will bow the knee to God by bowing the knee to Christ. In Isaiah's day, the expectation was that the people would bow the knee to the Arm of the Lord.[1]

In general, insofar as Christ does the same thing his father does, the same action predicates are applied to them both. For example,

> To the end he may stablish your hearts unblameable in holiness before God, even our Father, at the coming of our Lord Jesus Christ with all his saints. 1 Thess 3:13 (KJV)

> ...and *kyrios* my God shall come, and all the saints with thee. Zech 14:5 (KJV)

This allusion seems clear: Zechariah is typical language for God acting on behalf of his people ('come') manifest in an individual. The context is the Last Days and the Day of the Lord (Zech 14:1, 3, 4). Yahweh goes forth into battle and 'his feet' shall stand on the Mount of Olives.

This allusion is an example of Yhwh texts that describe God acting on behalf of his people in the land. The language of Yahweh coming in the person of another is seen, for example, in the case of the Arm of the Lord (Isa 40:3; 10; 51:9; 53:1; John 12:38). This is God being manifest in the flesh (1 Tim 3:16) and fulfilling his own declaration, 'I will be **who** I will be' (Exod 3:14[2]). That God is manifest in someone on the ground is indicated by the prediction that 'his feet' would stand on the Mount of

---

[1] Capes, "YHWH texts and Monotheism in Paul's Christology", 129, interprets *kyrios* as referring to Christ in Rom 14:11, so that it is Christ who says, 'As I live' (reflecting the fact of his resurrection). This exegesis fails to see that 'As I live' is an act of swearing by oneself and not an affirmation of being alive, which Jesus would make as one raised from the dead: 'I am alive for evermore' (Rev 1:18).

[2] For the justification of this translation see Albrektson, "On the Syntax of *'ehyeh 'asher 'ehyeh* in Exodus 3:14", 15-28; and A. Perry, "The Translation of Exodus 3:14a" *CeJBI* 3/4 (2009): 39-64; (Available on www.academia.edu).

Olives. As Adey observes, "A Biblical criterion of being the true God is that God's identity can be depicted by another".[1]

The predicates of action are equally applicable to Yahweh as they are to the person on the ground.[2] There are criteria of application[3] for these predicates which are satisfied by Yahweh and the person on the ground. The point here is not that the person bears the name 'Yhwh', nor that they necessarily represent Yahweh (*pace* foreign potentates brought against Israel), though this may be true: the point is that God is manifesting himself in someone through the Spirit – their actions are the actions of God. In this sense, that person is included in an identity with God (and vice-versa) but without any confusion of persons.

Fletcher-Louis states, "Time and again we find divine *action* or *functions* ascribed to Christ in a way that now makes sense if Christ belongs within the divine identity and if he fully participates in the divine nature."[4] What we need to question here is the 'fully participates in the divine nature'. This sounds like theologically motivated eisegesis designed to support later church doctrine.

The framework for understanding the same divine action being attributed to God and to Christ is **representative**. This is clear from the use of 'parentheses' in Paul,

> Now God himself and our Father, (even our Lord Jesus Christ), <u>direct</u> our way unto you. 1 Thess 3:11 (KJV revised); cf. 2 Thess 3:5

The singular verb 'to direct' is attached to the subject 'God' as shown by the emphasis 'himself', but the guidance is through the Lord Jesus, as

---

[1] Adey, "One God: The Shema in Old and New Testaments", 31. S. B. Nicholson, "Dynamic oneness: The significance and flexibility of Paul's one-God language", comments "If the identity of the One God may include anyone who participates in the mighty acts, then what is to prevent more than Jesus and the Holy Spirit from being described as part of Yahweh's deity?" (p. 15). Quite!

[2] Hence, it is not enough to aver that does things in person, because this doesn't distinguish the theologies of incarnation and manifestation; see Wright, *The Paul Debate*, 33.

[3] Dummett, *Frege: Philosophy of Language*, 74-76, distinguishes criteria of identity and criteria of application.

[4] Fletcher-Louis, *Jesus Monotheism*, 14.

shown by the 'even' sense of the conjunction. Paul uses the same construction for emphasis in 1 Thess 5:23, "May the God of peace himself (Αὐτὸς δὲ ὁ θεὸς) sanctify you wholly", and 1 Cor 8:6 makes the relationship clear: spiritual things are *of* the Father but *through* the Son (see below).[1]

The singular verb attaches to the emphasized subject, God the Father, but the parenthesis provides a substitution for the reader, a device which therefore does not contravene the normal grammar of noun-verb agreement.[2] Fletcher-Louis' grammatical analysis is therefore wrong "*two* persons grammatically expressed as *one* acting subject".[3] It is rather, *two* grammatical subjects (one primary, one secondary) available for *one* action verb.

6. Typological Identity
It might be argued that we should eschew metaphysical questions on how Paul included Jesus within the divine identity of the God of Israel and assert instead that this is a literary idea. The problem with this proposal is that language use is referential, and the difficult metaphysical questions cannot be avoided.

There are however literary identities. One kind is a **typological identity**.

---

[1] *Contra* Fletcher-Louis, *Jesus Monotheism*, 14, who reverts to the normal device of 'mystery' when he comments, "the prayer in 1 Thess 3:11…nicely illustrates the conscious ambiguity of a God who is *one*, yet now, for Paul and his fellow Christians, mysteriously *two*."

[2] W. J. Perschbacher, *New Testament Greek Syntax* (Chicago: Moody Press, 1995), 41, comments, "Two articular subjects joined with a singular verb indicate a special unity, the nature of which is determined by context." D. B. Wallace, *Greek Grammar Beyond the Basics* (Grand Rapids: Zondervan, 1986), 482, states, "There may be some significance in the use of a singular verb with this compound subject." One of his suggestions is that "the optative is uniting the Father and the Son in terms of purpose". Both grammarians don't take into account the 'himself' and the 'even' in tying the verb more closely to the singular subject of the Father. They are correct to see a unity – it is a unity that allows a substitution of subject from a parenthesis to go with the verb. Obviously, it is no objection to say that Greek does not have brackets, since parentheses are a function of sense.

[3] Fletcher-Louis, *Jesus Monotheism*, 14.

Nevertheless, when it [the heart, v. 16] shall <u>turn</u> to *kyrios*, the veil shall be taken away. Now the Lord is the Spirit: and where the Spirit of the Lord *is*, there *is* liberty. 2 Cor 3:17 (KJV revised)

And when Aaron and all the children of Israel saw Moses, behold, the skin of his face shone; and they were afraid to come nigh him. And Moses called unto them; and Aaron and all the rulers of the congregation <u>returned</u> unto him: and Moses talked with them...And till Moses had done speaking with them, he put a veil on his face...But when Moses went in before Yhwh to speak with him, he took the veil off, until he came out. Exod 34:30-34 (KJV revised)

The comparison here is with Moses 'going in' before Yhwh without a veil. The use of the verb 'to turn' picks up the children of Israel 'outside' who 'turned away' from Moses (Exod 34:31 – they turn back, same verb in the LXX). Paul is saying that when the heart of the Jews *turns* to Yhwh, the veil will be taken away, i.e. they will then be like Moses.[1]

Paul's first exegetical comment upon the incident is that 'The Lord is the Spirit'. The identity here is **typological**; Yahweh in Moses' day stands for 'the Spirit' in Paul's day.[2] That Paul is thinking in terms of typological comparison is shown by his earlier remarks. The Corinthians were not a letter written in 'tablets' of stone but one that was written in the 'tablets' of the heart with the Spirit of the living God (2 Cor 3:3). In order for the Jews to be such a letter, they would have to 'turn' to the Spirit. Paul is stating this imperative by his assertion that 'the Lord' (Yahweh) is 'the Spirit'.[3]

---

[1] *Contra* Capes, *Old Testament Yahweh Texts in Paul's Christology*, 155, but with J. D. G. Dunn, "2 Corinthians 3:17 'The Lord is the Spirit'" makes the same identification of *kyrios* with Yahweh in his *The Christ and the Spirit, Volume 1, Christology* (Grand Rapids: Eerdmans, 1998), 115-125 (122); however, he fails to make the intertextual link with the 'turning' of the children of Israel.

[2] Capes, *Old Testament Yahweh Texts in Paul's Christology*, 156, fails to see that the identity is typological and thus argues that *kyrios* in v. 16 refers to Christ. Dunn, "2 Corinthians 3:17 'The Lord is the Spirit'", 119, says that identifying *kyrios* with Yahweh has been a minority opinion amongst commentators. However, he doesn't express it as a 'typological' identity.

[3] Another example of typological identity is 1 Cor 10:4 ('the rock was Christ'). Here the typological identity is with Yahweh (Deut 32:3-4);

Paul's second exegetical comment is 'where the Spirit of the Lord is, there is liberty'. This is about the ministry of the Spirit (2 Cor 3:8) and it echoes Jesus' words, "The Spirit of the Lord is upon me…to proclaim liberty to captives" (Luke 4:18; Isa 61:1). The ministry of the Spirit was through Paul to those who would respond (2 Cor 3:1). Jesus spoke of liberty as a release from captivity (Assyrian deportation), a metaphor for forgiveness of sins. Paul varies this in terms of a freedom from bondage (Egypt; cf. Gal 2:4; 5:1). This second comment reinforces the implication of the first comment - that *kyrios* is going proxy for 'Yhwh' in v. 16 and refers to Yahweh. This is because, for Jesus, the Spirit is the Spirit of the Lord.

The above two comments are bound by the connection between Moses and the Spirit of the Lord in Isaiah 63. The use of 'Spirit of the Lord' alludes to the judges who (like Moses) delivered the people (e.g. Jud 3:10; 6:34; 11:29; 13:25; 14:6). The Spirit of the Lord in Moses caused the people to rest, and it was in this way that Yahweh led the people (Isa 63:14). This rest was the Promised Land to which they had been led (Ps 95:11).

The last comment made by Paul is that believers behold 'the glory of the Lord' and are 'changed into the same image from glory to glory' (v. 18). The glory of Yahweh is Christ, a point made clear in John (John 13:32; 17:1, 5) as well as Paul (2 Cor 8:19, 23). This 'glory' is therefore also an 'image' to which believers are conformed (Rom 8:29). This last comment further shows that *kyrios* in v. 16 is referring to Yahweh.[1]

Capes says that "the most convincing evidence that κύριος in [2 Cor] 3:16 refers to Jesus comes from [2 Cor] 4:5",[2]

> For we preach not ourselves, but Christ Jesus as Lord; and ourselves your servants for Jesus' sake. 2 Cor 4:5 (KJV revised)

Bauckham, *Jesus and the God of Israel*, 100, doesn't distinguish the typological basis of the identity.

[1] Capes, *Old Testament Yahweh Texts in Paul's Christology*, 157, is not sufficiently precise in his exegesis to distinguish the reference of 'the glory of the Lord' (which is Christ) from the reference of 'the Lord' in this expression (which is Yahweh).

[2] Capes, *Old Testament Yahweh Texts in Paul's Christology*, 157.

This illustrates the problem confronting exegetes; κύριος is used to refer to Yahweh and Jesus Christ and commentators can get confused over usage. Paul's point here in v. 5 is about the **content** of preaching, whereas in the previous chapter, his concern has been with understanding the driving force of preaching – the Spirit. Paul's teaching about the Spirit takes the form of a typological comparison with Yahweh. Capes is therefore simply mistaken. With typological identity, the type may have the same role, status or function as the anti-type. In the comparison between Yahweh and the Spirit, both are the source of instruction.

7. Mistaken Identity

The problem facing exegetes is when to know that *kyrios* is being used to refer to Christ and when to Yahweh. Examples of **commentators mistaking identity** include the following:

(i) The use of Joel 2:32 in Rom 10:13.

> That if thou shalt confess with thy mouth, 'Lord Jesus', and shalt believe in thine heart that God hath raised him from the dead, thou shalt be saved…For there is no difference between the Jew and the Greek: for the same lord over all is rich unto all that call upon him. Whosoever shall call upon the name *kyrios* shall be saved. Rom 10:9-13 (KJV revised)

On the basis of the mention of the Lord Jesus in v. 9, it is assumed that 'same lord over all' and 'call upon the name *kyrios*' equally refer to Jesus. Hence, Capes avers, "Since κύριος refers to Jesus in 10:9, he probably had Jesus in mind here also."[1]

An allusion or echo of Joel 2:32 exists in, "with all that in every place call upon the name of Jesus Christ our Lord" (1 Cor 1:2). This places Jesus into the position of the saviour that Yahweh occupies in the 'calling' of Joel 2:32. It could be used to support the claim of Capes about Rom 10:13 but, equally, we should observe that the name 'Yhwh' is not referenced in 1 Cor 1:2. Since salvation is a matter of God working through Jesus, the appeal for salvation can be described directly in terms of Joel 2:32 and Yahweh or in allusive terms referring to Christ.

The expression 'lord of all' evokes God's rule over the nations (Jew and Greek). In 1 Chron 29:11-12, Yahweh is 'head above all' (LXX has, differently, 'lord of all') and 'riches' are also said to come from him in this

---

[1] Capes, *Old Testament Yahweh Texts in Paul's Christology*, 119; also 127, 128.

text. These two points of contact suggest that Paul is quoting from this prayer, but it is also common enough to address Yahweh in these terms (e.g. 2 Chron 20:6).

This in turn suggests that the use of Joel 2:32 is also a reference to Yahweh – 'calling upon the name of the Lord'. This is a specific refrain[1] in the Jewish Scriptures for invoking God to act as a **saviour**, see the table below for examples.

Ps 79:6	Wrath will be poured out on those who do not call on God's name.
Ps 80:18	Time of destruction; the people will call on the name of the Lord and be saved.
Isa 64:7	Time of wrath, but no one was calling upon the name of the Lord.
Jer 10:25	Fury to be poured out on those who do not call upon the name of the Lord.
Zeph 3:9	Time of indignation and judgement; the way of service is to call upon the name of the Lord.
Zech 13:9	Time of war and destruction; a third brought through fire, calling upon the name of the Lord.

This pattern[2] fits with Paul's use of Joel 2:32, which in Joel's day was likewise a time of war and the need for salvation: with the forthcoming destruction of Jerusalem and time of trouble, Paul preached that men and women had to believe with their heart and confess with their mouth and call upon the name of the Lord **in order to be saved**. Hence, we find the expression also being used in Peter's Pentecost address, again quoting Joel (Acts 2:21), offering **salvation** from the great and notable Day of the Lord. More generally, as the disciples and apostles preached a message of salvation, the expression is used to describe the response of (some) people to this message (Acts 9:14, 21; 22:16; 1 Cor 1:2; 2 Tim 2:22). 'Calling upon the name of the Lord' is an expression for invoking God to act as a saviour; it is not an expression denoting everyday personal or cultic prayer.[3]

---

[1] This is why it should not be seen as a general expression for prayer.
[2] Josephus, *War* 2.294 also uses the pattern.
[3] *Contra* Capes, *Old Testament Yahweh Texts in Paul's Christology*, 120, who says, "Evidently, it indicates that Paul thought believers should offer prayers to the Lord Jesus who would respond by bestowing on them

(ii) Another example of commentators mistaking identity is the quotation of Jer 9:23-24 in 1 Cor 1:31,

> That, according as it is written, 'He that glorieth, let him glory in *kyrios*'. 1 Cor 1:31 (KJV); cf. 2 Cor 10:17

> Thus saith <u>Yhwh</u>, 'Let not the wise *man* glory in his wisdom, neither let the mighty *man* glory in his might, let not the rich *man* glory in his riches: But let him that glorieth glory in this, that he understandeth and knoweth me, that I *am* <u>Yhwh</u> which exercise lovingkindness, judgment, and righteousness, in the earth: for in these *things* I delight', saith <u>Yhwh</u> Jer 9:23-24 (KJV revised)

The principal actor in Paul's treatise in 1 Cor 1:19-31 is God: God destroys (v. 19); he brings to nothing (v. 19); he has made (v. 20); he saves (v. 21); he chooses (vv. 27-28); and he makes (v. 30). Christ is the 'object' in the discourse – the 'Wisdom of God'. It follows that v. 31 is a simple use of *kyrios* for 'Yhwh' and that the believer is to boast in God's acts. Accordingly, Capes is simply wrong to conclude, "As indicated by his description of Christ's work in 1:30, Paul quoted this Yahweh text (κύριος in LXX, יהוה in the Hebrew text) and applied it to Christ."[1] On the contrary, in v. 30 Christ is God's work! The boasting is related to the acts of God.

This is clear from Paul's other use of Jer 9:23-24 in 2 Cor 10:17. In this part of his letter, he is concerned with the work of preaching, a work he attributes to God by saying, "But we will not boast beyond our measure, but within the measure of the sphere which God apportioned to us as a measure, to reach even as far as you" (2 Cor 10:13 NASB). This is the context for his quotation, "But he who boasts, let him boast in *kyrios*" (2 Cor 10:17 NASB revised).

The mistake commentators make[2] is to disregard v. 13 and look at v. 18 which says, "For not he who commends himself is approved, but whom

---

divine riches." Fletcher-Louis, *Jesus Monotheism*, 10, makes the use of Joel 2:32 his main example of a 'Yhwh-kyrios' text being applied to Christ.

[1] Capes, *Old Testament Yahweh Texts in Paul's Christology*, 134, who cites scholarship following our interpretation; Fletcher-Louis, *Jesus Monotheism*, 10, follows Capes.

[2] See Capes, *Old Testament Yahweh Texts in Paul's Christology*, 135-136.

the Lord commends" (2 Cor 10:18 NASB). They assume that 'the Lord' is a reference to Christ as the one who commended Paul. However, in vv. 12-13, Paul contrasts those who commend themselves with God who 'apportioned' a ministry to Paul. It follows then that 'the Lord' is a reference to God and not Christ.

(iii) Another example of commentators mistaking identity is,

> For who has known the <u>mind</u> of *kyrios*, that he may instruct him? But (δὲ) we have the mind[1] of Christ. 1 Cor 2:16 (KJV revised)

This is a quotation of Isa 40:13,

> Who hath directed the Spirit of the Lord, or *being* his <u>counsellor</u> hath taught him? Isa 40:13 (KJV)

Within Isa 40:12-13, the variation of 'mind' for 'Spirit' by Paul makes sense, since the argument in Isaiah is all about counsel and the thinking that is being offered about policy and direction in the affairs of state (Isa 5:19; 8:10; 14:26; 16:3; 19:11; 29:15; 30:1; 36:5). Those who have the Spirit of the Lord have the counsel of Yahweh to offer the king. The argument in Paul is equally about the possession of the Spirit (1 Cor 2:4-15). The rhetorical question that Paul uses from Isaiah invites the answer – no one instructs the Spirit of the Lord in his prophets. This answer applies to those who have the mind of Christ through the Spirit – no one can instruct them.

---

[1] This word is in the LXX of Isaiah, which Paul is conventionally taken to cite, but as R. R. Ottley observes, Paul's use of Isaiah is sometimes closer to the Hebrew and sometimes the LXX—*The Book of Isaiah according to the Septuagint* (2 vols; Cambridge: Cambridge University Press, 1906), 2:298. We also need to be aware of the possibility that agreement between the NT and the LXX may be due to harmonization carried out by Christian scribes, and take note of the Greek versions of Aquila and Symmachus which render the Hebrew literally. Given Paul's knowledge of Greek and Hebrew, the interesting question is how his quotation relates to the Hebrew original (as we have it in the MT) rather than any Greek translation. For a discussion see, R. T. McLay, *The Use of the Septuagint in New Testament Research* (Grand Rapids: Eerdmans, 2003), 150-152; K. H. Jobes and M. Silva, *Invitation to the Septuagint* (Grand Rapids: Baker Academic, 2000), 198.

The adversative (δέ) is used by Paul to equate the situation in Isaiah's day, where the prophets had the Spirit of the Lord, with believers in his day who had the Spirit – *but* as the mind of Christ. He makes the equation by re-using 'mind of' but with 'Christ' and not *kyrios*. Accordingly, *kyrios* in his citation does refer to Yahweh precisely because believers have the mind of Christ.[1] This use of Isa 40:13, keeping the reference of *kyrios* as Yahweh, is the same as in Rom 11:34.

(iv) In his consideration of food offered unto idols, Paul quotes Ps 24:1, "The earth is the Lord's, and the fulness thereof" (1 Cor 10:26). The argument for reading *kyrios* here as a reference to Christ is nothing more than the use of *kyrios* in the context for Christ. Thus, we have 'cup of the Lord', 'table of the Lord' (v. 21), and 'provoke the Lord' (v. 22). Capes claims that "the most significant evidence that in this Yahweh text κύριος refers to Christ regards the structure of Paul's argument on eating idol meat"[2] and he cites 1 Cor 8:6 on 'one Lord'.

The problem with this argument is that it doesn't respect the difference between a quotation of a scriptural text with 'Yhwh' and the non-quoting use of *kyrios* for Christ that we have in the immediate context of vv. 21-22. Given that *kyrios* can be used to refer to the God of Israel and Jesus, we need a theological reason for Paul to be using *kyrios* for 'Yhwh' referring to Christ in his use of the Psalm.

Appealing to the Lord as the possessor of the earth is an argument rooted in the Jewish Scriptures (e.g. Ps 89:11) and it is an obvious argument to make in support of the view that food bought in the market, even if previously offered to idols, is acceptable. This argument from Scripture is not made in support of Paul's earlier point about fellowshipping the table of demons in which he uses *kyrios* for Christ. This supports the interpretation that *kyrios* in his quotation refers to Yahweh as the provider of all food.

The quotation is used to bolster a point about eating food, idols and conscience. If we look at Capes' "most significant evidence", we find that this cluster of points is related to 'God' and not 'the Lord'.

- An idol is nothing in the world, for there is only one God (1 Cor 8:4).

---

[1] *Contra* Capes, *Old Testament Yahweh Texts in Paul's Christology*, 136-140, who claims, "Paul took Isa 40:13, an Old Testament Yahweh text, and applied it to Jesus as κύριος" (139).
[2] Capes, *Old Testament Yahweh Texts in Paul's Christology*, 144.

- There is one God, the Father (1 Cor 8:6).
- Food does not commend us to God (1 Cor 8:8)

1 Corinthians 8:6 distinguishes God the Father and the Lord Jesus Christ with its prepositional statements. If we compare these to 1 Cor 10:26, they disambiguate Paul's quotation: the earth is 'of the Lord' (τοῦ κυρίου) and it is God the Father 'from whom' or 'out of whom' are all things (ἐξ οὗ).

(v) The use of the Jewish Scriptures may be more a matter of influence, an echo and an allusion, rather than citation or quotation This makes the use of *kyrios* for 'Yhwh' more difficult to determine. The following text looks to be dependent in some way on Mal 1:7, 12 and Deut 32:21,

> Ye cannot drink the cup of the Lord, and the cup of devils: ye cannot be partakers of the table of the Lord, and of the table of devils. Do we provoke the Lord to jealousy? Are we stronger than he? 1 Cor 10:21-22 (KJV)

> Ye offer polluted bread upon mine altar; and ye say, 'Wherein have we polluted thee?' In that ye say, 'The table of Yhwh *is* contemptible.' ...But ye have profaned it, in that ye say, 'The table of Yhwh *is* polluted; and the fruit thereof, *even* his meat, *is* contemptible'. Mal 1:7, 12 (KJV revised)

> They have moved me to jealousy with *that which is* not God; they have provoked me to anger with their vanities: and I will move them to jealousy with *those which are* not a people; I will provoke them to anger with a foolish nation. Deut 32:21 (KJV)

The Corinthians were provoking the Lord to jealousy (i.e. Christ, vv. 16, 22), but there is no quotation of a 'Yhwh' text in the allusion to Deut 32:21. Bauckham states,

> "But since 'the cup of the Lord' and 'the table of the Lord' in the preceding verse must refer to Christ, this must be one of those quite frequent occasions on which Paul interprets the *kurios* of an Old Testament YHWH text as Jesus. The implication for Jewish monotheism and Christology is remarkable: the exclusive devotion that YHWH's jealousy requires of his people is required of Christians by Jesus

Christ. Effectively he assumes the unique identity of YHWH."[1]

The use of 'table of the Lord' alludes to Mal 1:7, but there it is the altar, the table of Yhwh. The question is whether this is a use of *kyrios* for 'Yhwh' **bringing** 'Yhwh' **into** the Corinthians' text by proxy. The alternative suggestion is that 'table of the Lord' **varies** the Malachi text with a use of *kyrios* with the Christian sense of 'lord' determining a reference to Christ; this would give a uniformity of use of *kyrios* across vv. 21-22 – 'cup of the Lord' and 'table of the Lord'.

The expression 'the table of the Lord' is a metonymy for the Lord's Supper – believers partook of the Supper and this is expressed as partaking of the table of the Lord. In Malachi, 'table of the Lord' is not a metonymy but refers literally to the altar-table upon which the bread was placed. The defiled bread that was placed upon the altar-table defiled that table. This difference between the reference of a metonymy and a literal reference in the two uses of the expression means that *kyrios* in Corinthians is not functioning as a proxy for 'Yhwh': the Lord's Supper is not 'the Supper of Yahweh'. The principle that this example illustrates is that in a use of a 'Yhwh' text for Christ, with *kyrios* going proxy for 'Yhwh', **there should be correspondence in the kind of use**.

The same analytical choice confronts us with the allusion inherent in 'provoke the Lord'. Is this **bringing** 'Yhwh' from the Deuteronomy context **into** the Corinthians text by proxy or is it **varying** that text with a use of *kyrios* for Christ. This would continue the use of *kyrios* across vv. 21-22. In effect, then, v. 16 with its 'cup of blessing...fellowship of the blood of Christ' is setting the reference of *kyrios* in 'the cup of the Lord' to be Christ, and then the following 'table of the Lord' and 'provoke the Lord' continues this usage.

This is the simpler interpretation and the alternative would need a theological reason as to why Paul might want to use *kyrios* for 'Yhwh' of Christ at this point in his discourse (i.e. bring 'Yhwh' under proxy into his allusion); it is not enough to assert that this is what he has done.[2] The problem for this claim is that an allusive use of language is not a citation or quotation in which *kyrios* stands proxy for 'Yhwh' in a contiguous and more formal reproduction of a Jewish scriptural text. What we simply

---

[1] Bauckham, *Jesus and the God of Israel*, 100.
[2] Capes, *Old Testament Yahweh Texts in Paul's Christology*, 144, 149-150, makes the claim, as does Bauckham, ibid.

have, *contra* Bauckham, is the jealousy of Christ; there is no reason for Paul to draw in the name 'Yhwh' under proxy.

A principle of exclusive devotion is illustrated in the example of Yahweh's jealousy over Israel's sacrificing to that which was not God. It's an obvious example from the Law to teach an exclusive devotion to Christ in respect of table fellowship. Does such exclusive devotion imply or presuppose that Jesus is included in the divine identity of Yhwh? It's rather odd to read such a heavy piece of theology into the simple use of an example. Jewish Christians in Jerusalem, after all, still used the temple as well as breaking bread in houses. Does exclusive devotion to Yahweh in certain practices and exclusive devotion to Christ in **other** practices require a particular theological harmonization such as 'included in the divine identity'? It is doubtful.

(vi) A second example of an allusion to a Yhwh text is,

> That no man go beyond and defraud his brother in any matter: because that *kyrios* is the avenger of all such, as we also have forewarned you and testified. 1 Thess 4:6 (KJV revised)

> O Lord God, to whom vengeance belongs; O God, to whom vengeance belongs, shew thyself. Ps 94:1 (KJV revised); cf. Deut 32:35

The allusion here is clear and, equally, it is clear that *kyrios* is not referring to Christ but to God. The absence of the article is one indicator, but the context also shows that it is God's will that Paul is presenting (vv. 1, 3, 5, 7, 8, 9). The commandments of the Lord Jesus are mentioned (v. 2) but the use of *kyrios* there is distinguished by the article. What we have here is **a corresponding kind of usage** of *kyrios* in the allusion and no reason to see a change of reference.

8. All Things and Wisdom
The most common interpretation of 'all things' in 1 Cor 8:6 is that this embraces the Genesis creation and that the Son is being placed as the one through whom that creation came into being – "through/by whom are all things".[1]

---

[1] Fletcher-Louis, *Jesus Monotheism*, 12, "Paul ascribes to the Lord Jesus Christ a role in creation."; Hurtado, *One God, One Lord*, 21, on which see J. Murphy-O'Conner, *Keys to First Corinthians: Revisiting the Major Issues*

But to us *there is* one God, the Father, out of whom *are*[1] all things, and we to/for him; and one Lord Jesus Christ, through/by whom *are* all things, and we through/by him. 1 Cor 8:6 (KJV revised)

J. Murphy-O'Conner discusses **cosmological** readings of 1 Cor 8:6, showing how they are often based on extra-Biblical comparisons with parallel texts that have 'all things' being *of* one God but through an agent such as Wisdom or *the Logos*. He notes example philosophical texts from the Stoics and Philo, but several Second Temple religious texts can be adduced for Wisdom having a role in creation. One argument for a cosmological reading is that all things come from God, and so food comes from God, and is acceptable. The problem with the argument is that vv. 1-7 is directed to those who already have this knowledge; it is not directed to those who need persuasion.[2] Another argument is a comparison with 1 Cor 11:12 where Paul states "but all things are of God". However, it is not certain that Paul is making a point here about creation; he could be making a contrast with the new creation as with 2 Cor 5:18 ("But all things are of God, who hath reconciled us to himself by Jesus Christ"). If we exclude creation as the topic of v. 6, then the parallel between Christ and Wisdom vis-à-vis creative agency is diminished.[3]

The competing interpretation is **soteriological**. Within 1 Corinthians, Paul uses 'all things' to embrace different concepts. First, he says that the spiritual man judges all things (1 Cor 2:10-16). Such a person is the recipient of the Spirit from God who works 'all things in all' (1 Cor 12:6; Eph 1:23) – all these things are distributed throughout the body in terms of the spiritual gifts ('spiritual things', 1 Cor 12:1ff). All things are for the believers so that the abundance of grace might be spread to all (Rom 8:28, 31-32; 2 Cor 4:14-15). This is why all things are 'new' in the new creation (2 Cor 5:17-18). Secondly, and politically, the day will come when God will put all things under the feet of Christ, and after fulfilling his work,

---

(Oxford: Oxford University Press, 2009), 58-75, in which he updates an older *Revue Biblique paper* of his arguing for a soteriological reading and critiquing the cosmological reading.

[1] The implied verb need not be static, though this is the usual choice. Murphy-O'Conner, *Keys to First Corinthians: Revisiting the Major Issues*, 73, argues for 'through whom all things came'. Waaler *The Shema and the First Commandment in First Corinthians*, 412-413, disagrees.

[2] Murphy-O'Conner, *Keys to First Corinthians: Revisiting the Major Issues*, 68.

[3] Hurtado, *One God, One Lord*, 98, 162.

Christ will deliver all things to the Father (1 Cor 15:27-28; Eph 1:10-11). Of these two uses of 'all things', 1 Cor 8:6 would fall into the first category of 'spiritual things' because Paul is talking about **knowledge** in 1 Corinthians 8.[1] Christians judge, not according to the flesh, but according to the Spirit.

The underlying point here is that 'all things' is a common enough way to talk generally. Elsewhere, Paul will refer to thrones, rulers, lordships and authorities as 'all things' (Col 1:16); he will comment that he has suffered the loss of all things (Phil 3:8); and in his Mars Hill speech, Paul declares that God gives all things to all. The 'all things' of 1 Cor 8:6 are the gifts of the Spirit which are 'of' the Father but 'through' Jesus Christ (e.g. Eph 2:18; Tit 3:5-6).

There is a further point of contrast with the cosmological reading. Paul states that believers are 'through/by' Jesus Christ - this is a reference to the new creation of men and women in Christ (Rom 6:11, 23; 2 Cor 5:17; Col 1:20; Gal 3:14; 6:15), who in turn receive the spiritual gifts. Paul's point is based *in the present* and not the *past* of the Genesis creation.

Murphy-O'Conner argues for a soteriological reading close to our position, but he has still not let go entirely of the cosmological reading. He says,

> Creation is evoked, not in or for itself, but because of the inconceivable power therein displayed. Believers are to understand that power of some magnitude is at work in their lives.[2]

There is no need for a reference to creation. The context and the intertextual links surrounding 'all things' shows a present-tense soteriological sense related to the spirit gifts.[3]

Nevertheless, even if we exclude creation as the reference of 'all things' in 1 Cor 8:6 (the cosmological reading),[1] a parallel with Wisdom can still be

---

[1] The 'things' (εἰδωλοθύτων) offered to idols are not the 'things' of 1 Cor 8:6; *contra* Dunn, *Christology in the Making*, 180.

[2] Murphy-O'Conner, *Keys to First Corinthians: Revisiting the Major Issues*, 74.

[3] *Contra* Waaler, *The Shema and the First Commandment in First Corinthians*, 415-416. He offers five reasons for the difficulty of the soteriological reading (which we have addressed at various points in this chapter), but he doesn't rebut the intertextual argument we present.

upheld insofar as Wisdom is the source of knowledge. Paul's argument is centred on knowledge and various behaviours arising from what is known, and so a correlation between Wisdom and the Spirit is valid.

Wright makes a comparison with the personified and pre-existent Wisdom of God,[2] but Paul doesn't use σοφία at this point in his letter. He does compare Christ to the wisdom of God earlier (1 Cor 1:24), but he isn't thinking of Christ as the personified Wisdom of God at that point in his letter. A comparison with the wisdom of God fits the context of 1 Corinthians 8 because Paul is concerned with gifts and knowledge, but this concern shows that he is not thinking of Christ as the pre-existent and personified Wisdom of God because the gifts ('all things') were of the present. Wright's pre-existent reading requires 'all things' to be the 'all things' of creation.[3] Dunn is closer to the truth of the matter when he says, *"Christ is being identified here not with a pre-existent being but with the creative power and action of God."*[4]

9. Conclusion

In view of the above discussion, is 1 Cor 8:6 evidence that Paul thought of Jesus as having a divine nature and/or identity? Better evidence would be statements to the effect that Jesus *was God* (from GJohn, following Dunn). Bearing the divine name is not sufficient to give us a divine nature. Does the bearing of the divine name include Jesus within the divine identity? We might say this, but it doesn't seem enough. Rather, we need God to include his son within his identity through the bestowal of his Spirit. This exegesis does not confuse the persons of the Father and the Son, nor does it allow us to say that Jesus had divine nature. Furthermore, we don't have to attribute to Paul the re-writing of the Shema, something unconscionable for a Jew, let alone the inspiration of the Spirit in Paul; and so, we can uphold both Jewish and Scriptural

---

[1] Hurtado, *One God, One Lord*, 98, 162.

[2] Wright, *The Climax of the Covenant*, 130, "Jesus, in this newly coined formula…takes the place of κύριος within the *Shema*, and also takes the place of σοφία within the hypothetical Hellenistic Judaism."

[3] Wright, *The Climax of the Covenant*, 131, "pre-existent activity, mediating the creation". Instead, we partly agree with Dunn, *Christology in the Making*, 181, "Paul is not making a statement about the act of creation in the *past*, but rather about creation as believers see it *now*". We would qualify Dunn by saying that Paul is making a statement about the new creation in which believers experience spiritual things.

[4] Dunn, *Christology in the Making*, 182, (his italics).

Monotheism in the first clause of 1 Cor 8:6. Rather than proposing Christological Monotheism, we can have **monotheistic Christology**.

CHAPTER THIRTEEN
God-Language

The Christian world is divided into hundreds of denominations and sects, but the overwhelming majority believe in the doctrine of the Trinity, which is a doctrine that says that God is three persons in one Godhead: — God the Father, the Son, and the Holy Spirit are three persons that have always constituted *what God is* in his very essence.[1] If you examine the doctrine of the Trinity, you soon realise that it is expressed in rather abstract and technical words. This kind of language is not found in the Bible, which is instead comprised of the everyday language of letters, history books, poetry, and prophetic oracles. Let's look at the everyday language of the NT letters, language that isn't complicated or 'theological', and see why the doctrine of the Trinity is not a Bible teaching.

In today's scientific world, evidence is all important. Had the Trinity been a Biblical teaching it would be reasonable to expect plenty of evidence, after all there can be no more fundamental aspect of faith than what you believe about God and Jesus. However, the 'evidence' that is usually put forward consists of only a few passages that are highly debateable. In contrast, the evidence against the doctrine of the Trinity is quite widespread and readily understood, because it is everywhere present in the language that believers used to refer to God and Jesus.

Let me give a quick example of what I mean by the questionable evidence. If Jesus was an integral part of a Trinity, you would expect him to have been called 'God' many times in the Bible. However, whereas the Father of Jesus is repeatedly called 'God', Jesus is called 'God' on only a handful of occasions. The ratio in the NT is around 1180:5, depending on exactly how many texts we interpret as applying the title 'God' to Jesus. This ratio is an astonishing piece of evidence, and it begs the question as to why Jesus is called 'God' in those few places that he is so-called. We aren't going to examine these passages again, because our purpose is to show overall why the doctrine of the Trinity is not a true Bible teaching. In lieu of what we have said in earlier chapters, I would offer one quick thought: surprisingly, Jesus is not the only man to be called 'God'. Moses is called 'God' (Exod 4:16; 7:1) and the leaders of Israel are also called 'God' (Ps 82:1)—but it's a rare occurrence in the OT as in the NT.

---

[1] This chapter first appeared as an article in *Glad Tidings* magazine but the formulation derives from Bro. J. H. Broughton.

Let's now look at the everyday language of the first century church. Traditional church creeds put God the Father and Jesus on an equal plane. In contrast, the ordinary letters of the apostles contain many statements that God the Father is the God of Jesus. This should be quite astonishing for a Trinitarian, let's look at the evidence:

The God and Father of our Lord Jesus Christ... 2 Cor 11:31

Blessed [be] the God and Father of our Lord Jesus Christ... Eph 1:3

That the God of our Lord Jesus Christ, the Father of glory... Eph 1:17

We give thanks to God and the Father of our Lord Jesus Christ... Col 1:3

Blessed [be] the God and Father of our Lord Jesus Christ... 1 Pet 1:3

And hath made us kings and priests to God and his father... Rev 1:6

All these fragments from the NT letters and the book of Revelation refer to the Father as the God of Jesus Christ, and they refer to the Father in this way with Jesus in heaven seated at his right hand side.

Not only do the letters of Paul and Peter refer to the Father as the God of Jesus, *Jesus himself referred to his father in this way*:

My God, my God, why hast thou forsaken me? Mark 15:34

...I have not yet ascended to my Father: but go to my brethren, and say to them, I ascend to my Father, and your Father; and [to] my God, and your God. John 20:17

Him that overcometh will I make a pillar in the temple of my God, and he shall go out no more: and I will write upon him the name of my God, and the name of the city of my God, [which is] new Jerusalem, which cometh down out of heaven from my God... Rev 3:12

Here Jesus refers to his father as his God both while he was on earth, and after he had ascended to heaven. There was no change in Jesus' relationship with his father, he was always *his God*, and with Mary, Jesus tells us he is also *our God*.

The doctrine of the Trinity places Jesus on an equal plane with his father in the sense that the Son of God is equally God in all aspects—equally eternal with his father, equally of the same nature, equally all-powerful and equally all-knowing. Such a view doesn't square with the apostle's teaching which is that the Father is the God of Jesus and ourselves - if we are true followers of Christ we *share the same God with the Lord*.

Our argument up till now has been that the Father is the God of the Lord Jesus and the God of his followers. If this is so, we would expect the natural everyday language of the first century believers to be saturated with this basic recognition of the Father as God. And indeed this is what we find, for example, in the way they greeted one another. In these greetings, the apostles refer to the Father and Jesus in the same sentence but always differently: they refer to the Father always as 'God', and they refer to Jesus always as 'Lord'. I will list three examples (others are given in footnote (1)):

> To all that are in Rome, beloved of God, called [to be] saints: Grace to you and peace from God our Father, and the Lord Jesus Christ. Rom 1:7
>
> Grace [be] to you, and peace, from God our Father, and [from] the Lord Jesus Christ. 1 Cor 1:3
>
> Grace [be] to you and peace from God our Father, and[from] the Lord Jesus Christ... 2 Cor 1:11

The argument here is that the *natural everyday language* of the church was not Trinitarian — the Father was always regarded as God. This is true not only in the greetings but also in the 'goodbyes' and the incidental expressions of love and regard for others (again there are too many to quote, so I list more in footnote (1) on the next page:

> Giving thanks always for all things to God and the Father in the name of our Lord Jesus Christ... Eph 5:20

---

1 See also Gal 1:1, 3; Eph 1:2; Phil 1:2; Col 1:2; 1 Thess 1:1; 2 Thess 1:1-2; 1 Tim 1:2; 2 Tim 1:2; Tit 1:4; Phile v. 3; 1 Pet 1:2; 2 John v. 3; Jude v. 1.

Peace [be] to the brethren, and love with faith, from God the Father and the Lord　Jesus Christ. Eph 6:23

And whatever ye do in word or deed, [do] all in the　name of the Lord Jesus, giving thanks to God and the Father by him. Col 3:17

Remembering without ceasing your work of faith, and labour of love, and patience of hope in our Lord Jesus Christ, in the sight of God and our Father... 1 Thess 1:3

Now our Lord Jesus Christ himself, and God, even our Father, who hath loved us, and hath given [us] everlasting consolation and good hope through grace... 2 Thess 2:16[1]

Always the distinction in these expressions of love is that the Father is God and Jesus is Lord. The apostle Paul expresses it this way, 'every tongue should confess that Jesus Christ [is] Lord, to the glory of God the Father' (Phil 2:11). If we want to believe the same things as the first century Christians and use the same everyday language of love, we have to recognise that there is only one God the Father and one Lord Jesus Christ (John 17:3, 1 Cor 8:6, Eph 4:6).

What have we done? We've carried out a scientific enquiry into what the first century church believed about God and about Jesus. We haven't concentrated on the plain statements of their doctrine, (although we have quoted John 17:3, 1 Cor 8:6 and Eph 4:6, which are very plain statements of doctrine). Instead we have tried to show what their everyday language pre-supposes about God. This language - of greetings, of saying 'goodbye', of hoping for the best, of saying thank you — this language establishes beyond doubt that the first century Christians believed that the Father of Jesus Christ is the one true God.

---

[1] Rom 15:6; 2 Cor 1:3; Phil 4:20; Col 2:2; 1 Thess 3:11, 13; Jms 1:27; 3:9.

APPENDIX A
The Nicene Creed

1. Introduction[1]

The first milestone in the establishment of the doctrine of the Trinity is the Council of Nicaea's formulation of that doctrine in 325 CE; the next milestone is the expanded formulation of the doctrine at the Council of Constantinople in 381 CE; this appendix reviews the history of this period in church history. The story begins with Arius, a minor theologian of the early 4c.

The theological debate that was precipitated by Arius in the 4c., and which led to the formulation of the Nicene Creed in 325 CE at the Council of Nicaea, revolved around the issues of the Son's eternity and divinity. Earlier Christological debates had settled the question of the pre-existence of the Son as the Word of God, and it fell largely to the Eastern 4c. church Fathers to make the choice: was the Son existent with the Father from eternity, and if so, what does this imply with regard to the divinity of the Son and the unity of God. The answers that emerged during the course of the 4c. resulted in what might be regarded as the first formulations of the doctrine of the Trinity, but the process was not without sharp theological conflict. The theological matrix of the East was complex with differing approaches to these issues centred on important sees such as that of Alexandria, Caesarea and Antioch.

There are two possible approaches to an evaluation of the Nicene Creed: historical (concentrating on church politics) and theological (concentrating on doctrinal conflict). An historical appraisal might consider such questions as,

- Did the Council and its creed settle the Arian controversy in the view of participants and their respective churches?

---

[1] This appendix is included as a standard introduction to the history of the doctrine of the Trinity in the 4c.; it is also included to form a stark contrast with the alternative doctrine and way of thinking illustrated in the body of this book.

- Did the Council and its creed provide a suitable foundation for unity in the church and allow the church to conduct its mission on the basis of an agreed doctrine?

- Did the Council meet Constantine's wider political objectives – the consolidation and stability of the empire?

The answers to these questions are not unequivocal. Although the Council was virtually unanimous in adopting the creed, the Arian controversy was by no means settled. Theological views labelled as "Arian"[1] kept on emerging in forceful and significant ways in the years following Nicaea. Successive councils were to affirm or contradict the formulations of Nicaea, and Arianism (so-called) was often in the ascendant. For example, Jerome was to famously remark of the Council of Constantinople held in 360 CE that "The whole world groaned and was astonished to find itself Arian."[2] In fact, rather than settle the Arian controversy, it can be plausibly argued that the Eastern Church was never fully Nicene until after 381 CE (and even then there were pockets of "Arian" churches). The Council which met in Constantinople in that year brought the Arian controversy to a formal close. Of itself, this Council did not settle the Arian dispute; by 381 CE the tide of Arianism had dissipated for a variety of reasons, both ecclesiastical and theological. In particular, the work of the Cappadocian Fathers had proved decisive in providing an underpinning "Nicene" metaphysical framework for the relations in the Godhead, not only of the Father and the Son, but also of the Holy Spirit. Nevertheless, Constantinople represents the closure of a period in the church's history dominated by the Arian controversy. Constantinople endorsed Nicaea and enlarged the Nicene Creed, producing a fuller

---

[1] M. Wiles discusses the labelling of opponents as "Arian" in "Attitudes to Arius in the Arian Controversy" in, *Arianism after Arius* (ed., M. R. Barnes D. H. and Williams; Edinburgh: T&T Clark, 1993). The evidence he adduces shows that the term was polemical. It was used as a term of approbation by those who supported the Nicene Creed against their opponents. However, those who opposed the formulae of Nicaea disavowed Arius. Consequently, while the disputes of the 340s and the 350s have become known as subsequent "phases" of the Arian controversy, it should not be thought that the "Arian" theology was simply that of Arius.

[2] Jerome, *Dial. Contra Lucif.* 19; this extract is cited in J. Stevenson and W. H. C. Frend, eds., *Creeds, Councils and Controversies* (London: SPCK, 1989), 32. Hereafter, we will refer to this source of primary texts as *CCC*; each text is referenced according to Stevenson and Frend's numbering system.

Trinitarian doctrine reflecting the debates of the previous sixty years. It is for this reason that 381 CE represents a watershed in the development of the doctrine of the Trinity, and can be taken as a *terminus ad quem* for understanding the foundation stones of the doctrine of the Trinity.

If the Council of Nicaea and the Nicene Creed did not settle the Arian controversy, did it provide a suitable foundation for unity in the church, (thereby adding to the peace of the empire), and allow the church to conduct its mission on the basis of an agreed doctrine? From Constantine's perspective, the answer is probably a qualified affirmative one.[1] Arius and a few supporters were anathematized, powerful Arian sympathizers like Eusebius of Nicomedia and Eusebius of Caesarea were persuaded that the creed could be interpreted in accordance with their own ideas, the overwhelming majority of bishops subscribed to the creed and its anathemas, and the Council's creed and canons allowed Alexander of Alexandria to maintain his stance against Arius in Egypt. Perhaps the lasting ecclesiastical achievement of the Council, however, was to firmly establish the principle of "majority rule" among the bishoprics as a principle for conflict resolution. The canons that were agreed at Nicaea formalised a growing organisational and hierarchical structure among the Eastern churches.

However, the ecclesiastical peace was short-lived. H. Chadwick observes in his history that as long as Constantine was alive, the Nicene Creed remained unquestioned, but after his death in 337 CE, a "second phase" of the Arian Controversy began, which coincided with the reign of Constantius (337-361 CE).[2] The question raised by the course of the Arian Controversy in this second phase is this: *how did the Nicene Creed survive a period when there were such powerful political and ecclesiastical forces arraigned against it?* As an historical event, Nicaea did not settle the Arian controversy, but as a theological instrument, the Nicene Creed survived a period of intense hostility. If we can understand why it survived such hostility, we will have opened a door to understanding its theological achievement. The

---

[1] Constantine's desire for church unity is seen in his initiative in sending Ossius, Bishop of Cordova, prior to Nicaea to sort out the conflict between Alexander and Arius in Alexander; and in his letters, after Nicaea, commending its decisions to the churches of Alexandria and Nicomedia. The letters are reproduced in J. Stevenson and W. H. C. Frend, eds., *A New Eusebius* (London: SPCK, 1987), 287, 293, 294. Hereafter, we will refer to this source of primary texts as *NE*; each text is referenced according to Stevenson and Frend's numbering system.

[2] H. Chadwick, *The Early Church* (London: Penguin, 1967), 133-136.

historical achievement of the Nicene Creed is that it survived and served as a rallying point for a school of thought during the reign of Constantius. One of the reasons for its persistence is to be found in its theology and in particular its theological framework.[1]

In this appendix then, our concern is not to map out the ecclesiastical and political impact of the creed, nor its historical vicissitudes, but to try and identify the reasons why it survived and hence why the doctrine of the Trinity became orthodoxy.

2. Methodology

It cannot be doubted that politics and rhetoric[2] played a full part in Nicaea achieving the status of orthodoxy. Our method will be to trace how certain key theological clauses in the Nicene Creed fared in fourth century church history.

The premise upon which we will look at this history is that orthodoxy emerged through a process of trial and error. We will not assume that Arianism was a "heresy" that sought to overturn orthodoxy; rather, we will assume that it was not clear before the fourth century how the divinity of the Son and the unity of God were to be expressed in a coherent theology. Consequently, it was inevitable that there would be doctrinal conflict in this area.[3] Furthermore, the stance we will adopt is that of an outsider looking at this period of church history. Orthodoxy is that which *became* the dominant opinion and enshrined in what were eventually judged to be decisive and authoritative councils, and heresy is that opinion that fell by the wayside.

---

[1] This is an abstract way of construing history. Of course, the Nicene Creed survived because it had powerful advocates in figures such as Athanasius and Basil of Ancyra in the East and Hilary of Poitiers in the West; their arguments fleshed out the spirit of the creed, and these arguments prevailed despite ecclesiastical politics.

[2] For an overview of how rhetorical labels were used in the Arian controversy, see R. Lyman, "A Topography of Heresy: Mapping the Rhetorical Creation of Arianism" in *Arianism after Arius* (eds. M. R. Barnes and D. H. Williams, eds., Edinburgh: T&T Clark, 1993), 45-62.

[3] The arguments supporting this premise are set out by Hanson, "The Achievement of Orthodoxy in the Fourth Century AD", in *The Making of Orthodoxy* (ed., R. Williams; Cambridge, Cambridge University Press, 1989), 142-156.

It is important to note that we are using the concepts of "orthodoxy" and "heresy" as a kind of meta-language commenting on the history of the period. Those who aligned themselves with Nicaea did use the language of heresy to describe Arius and his followers.[1] However, this is a use of the term inside the language-game of doctrinal dispute, and it reflects the rhetoric and polemics of that dispute. From our perspective, all parties to the Arian dispute claimed to be orthodox and uphold the "catholic" faith.[2] R. Williams, in the introduction to his study on Arius comments, "We need to give full weight to the fact that 'Arians' and 'Catholics' were conducting a debate within a largely common language, acknowledging the same kind of rules and authorities".[3] Williams makes this plea in the context of an extended evaluation of past scholarship on Arius and the Arian Controversy in which he illustrates that 19c. and early 20c. scholarship approached the subject from the standpoint of the successful party – the orthodox – and moreover, in some cases, (Williams particularly discusses the work of Newman, Harnack and Gwatkin), scholars were anachronistically constructing the failure of Arianism and the success of orthodoxy in terms of the 'liberal' or 'conservative' theologies of their own day.

Williams takes a more sympathetic approach to Arius than previous scholars, but he still works within the language-game of the doctrinal dispute. He approaches Arianism from the position of the orthodox party (that is, as an heir of Nicaea); it is just that his method is more careful in its appraisal and he acknowledges that orthodoxy was shaped by Arianism.

The notions of "orthodoxy" and "heresy" that we are deploying in this appendix are then terms of art in an historical premise; we are not using these terms as they have been used by scholars working *within* the Nicene tradition. We are giving a weak statistical or majority sense to the notion

---

[1] For example, see the letters of Eusebius of Nicomedia and Theognius of Nicaea, written c. 327CE in which they seek to rehabilitate themselves within the church, disavowing "the suspicion of heresy", cited in *NE* 296. No doubt Arius and his supporters used the same rhetoric, but our Arian materials are sparse and the historical documents we have are preserved by the victors.

[2] For example, Arius' letters to Alexander (*NE* 284), Eusebius of Caesarea (*NE* 283), or to Constantine (*NE* 295) show an attachment to the "catholic faith", while affirming his understanding of Christ.

[3] R. Williams, *Arius* (London: SCM, 2001), 24.

of "orthodoxy".[1] Orthodoxy is that which *became the dominant opinion*.[2] We are therefore looking at the theology of the orthodox in order to determine why it survived instead of the heresy.

3. Thesis

An evaluation of the Nicene Creed has three dimensions:

- Theological – was the creed in keeping with tradition, not only in respect of Christology, but also with regard to Soteriology and Cosmology? Insofar, as the creed took Trinitarianism forward, are the arguments that were used to support this development well founded?

- Philosophical – was the creed influenced by neo-Platonist thinking and consistent with common views of the day? Insofar as the creed used the notions of *ousia* and *hypostasis*, was its use of this terminology philosophically coherent?

- Biblical – was the creed consistent with Biblical language? It was a particular aim of the 4c. Fathers that creeds express doctrine in Biblical language, and it was a sharp criticism when a creed was not Biblical in its phraseology.[3]

---

[1] This is not to say that a notion of "orthodoxy" is *not* constitutive of the religion of Christianity. This is illustrated in such phenomenon as baptismal creeds, catechetical instruction, liturgy and Scripture; these instruments in their turn are part of the wider missionary and teaching character of the religion. The documentary evidence shows that both sides subscribed to the goal of conformity to an "orthodox" tradition. Rowan Williams illustrates this sense of orthodoxy in relation to the pre-Nicene period in his essay, "Does it make sense to speak of Pre-Nicene Orthodoxy?" in *The Making of Orthodoxy* (ed., R. Williams; Cambridge, Cambridge University Press, 1989), 1-23.

[2] It should be noted that our definition of orthodoxy is retrospective. It takes the state of affairs that existed at the *end* of a period (325-381CE) and uses this to characterize the parties during that period. Strictly, on a definition of 'orthodoxy' as "majority view", the Eastern Church bishoprics (as measured by the councils of the period) were at times "Arian" (according to the West) and perhaps only "Nicene" in the immediate years after Nicaea.

[3] For example, see Athanasius' defence of Nicaea, *De Decretis* and section 18, reproduced in P. Schaff and H Wace, eds., *Nicene and Post-Nicene Fathers*, Series 2, Vol. 4, (Edinburgh: T&T Clark, 1976); hereafter, this series will be referred to as *NPNF*.

Our main interest is in the systematic theology of the creed rather than its philosophical or Biblical foundations. Our guiding question is: *What did the Nicene Creed achieve in respect to the Arian controversy during the period 325-381 CE?* There are four strands to our answer of this question:

1) The theological achievement of the creed lies in its programmatic character. In its positive clauses and anathemas it sets down a framework for defining the relationship of the Father and the Son that is austere.[1] In particular, it provides a framework for checks and balances to be added to or deleted from the creed. Nicaea was the first ecumenical council, (co-incident with the emergence of Christianity as a state religion), and it illustrates an evolutionary step in the way doctrine was developed: a gentle pun of its achievement might be that it was a "clause balancing act".

2) The Nicene Creed blocked certain theologies that explained the Son in creaturely terms. [2,3] It did this by affirming the Son's eternity, the Son's begettal from the substance of the Father, and the Son's sharing of the substance of the Father. In particular, it blocked a "creature" view of the Son in favour of "divine substance" metaphysics. Its use of "substance" (*ousia*) proved to be pivotal in controlling future Arian debates.

3) The creed supplied (the beginnings of) an ontological explanation of the divinity of the Son and the relation of the Son to the Father, and in doing this it moved forward the development of the doctrine of the Trinity. In particular, it brought the Father and the Son into an *internal* relationship within the Godhead. In doing this, it moved Trinitarian thinking away from expressing the internal relations of the Godhead in terms of Father and Word (*logos*), and from over-dependence on the external metaphor of an economy.

---

[1] Hanson makes a similar point when he says that "though the language of the Nicene Creed may be obsolete, the shape is not", *Achievement of Orthodoxy*, 155. Such an observation makes Hanson's earlier dismissal of Nicaea as a "disastrous failure" puzzling, as the metaphysical "shape" of the creed is an achievement, even if the metaphysics has to be enlarged, "Achievement of Orthodoxy", 146.

[2] As such it also blocked "creature models" of the Holy Spirit in disputes after 361CE

[3] P. Tillich describes this blocking as "the truth and the greatness of the Council of Nicaea", *A History of Christian Thought* (New York: Touchstone, 1968), 72.

4) The creed affirmed and circumscribed the boundaries of an acceptable anthropomorphism - an acceptable religious language about God. This intention is seen particularly in the pro-Nicene supporting argument about the ineffability of God. The creed affirms the principle that what can be said about God, albeit in the anthropomorphic terms of a substance metaphysics, *has to be* irredeemably austere; richer anthropomorphisms misrepresent God.

If this is the theological achievement of the Nicene Creed, (1)-(4), it is not without shortcomings. The notions of *hypostasis* and *ousia* are not clearly defined and their use in relation to the Father and the Son was a source of theological conflict in the decades following Nicaea. Further, while the creed expresses something of the unity of the Godhead in respect to the Father and the Son (particularly in its deployment of the notion of 'homoousios'), it does not adequately express the separateness of the Son in relation to the Father – an ontological category is not supplied that can carry how the Son and the Father are distinct within the Godhead. Further, theological conflict was to arise over whether and how the Father and the Son were actually of the "same substance" ('homoousios'). Finally, there is nothing in the creed describing the Holy Spirit.

These strengths and weaknesses in the Nicene Creed set a theological agenda that pre-dominated until 381 CE The creed was the first instrument specifically designed as an oecumenical test of orthodoxy,[1] and its model, (positive affirmations combined with anathemas), was designed to forestall division and unite the bishoprics.

4. Arius
Our source materials[2] for Arius' thought are limited and largely confined to quotations by his opponents. A convenient summary of Arius' theology

---

[1] Kelly presents the consensus view that Nicaea was a new development in the development of creeds. It initiated the use of creeds as "tests of orthodoxy", albeit at the level of the bishopric. The Nicene Creed did not usurp the pastoral role and function of local baptismal creeds; its purpose was designed to superintend over these creeds. The subsequent impact of the creed on local creeds seems to have been one of augmenting the local creed with Nicene phrases rather than replacing such creeds. See his *Early Christian Creeds*, ch. 7.

[2] The principal materials are the church histories of Socrates, Sozomen and Theodoret which record various letters of Arius and offer historical detail and comment; and Athanasius who was an attendant at Nicaea and who, in addition to recording letters of Arius, historical detail and

is preserved in a "confession of faith", which he made in a letter (c. 320 CE) to his bishop, Alexander of Alexandria:

"We acknowledge one God, alone unbegotten, alone everlasting, alone unbegun, alone true, alone having immortality, alone wise, alone good, alone sovereign; judge governor and administrator of all, unalterable and unchangeable, just and good, God of Law and Prophets and New Testament; who begat an Only begotten Son before eternal times, through whom he has made both the ages and the universe; and begat him not in semblance, but in truth: and that he made him subsist at his own will, unalterable and unchangeable; perfect creature of God, but not as one of the creatures; offspring, but not as one of the things that have come into existence; nor as Valentinus pronounced that the offspring of the Father was an issue; nor as Manichaeus taught that the offspring was a portion of the Father, consubstantial ['homoousios']; or as Sabellius, dividing the monad, speaks of a Son-and-Father; nor as Hieracas, of one torch from another, or as a lamp divided into two; nor that he who was before, was afterwards generated or new-created into a Son…but, as we say, at the will of God, created before times and before ages, and gaining life and being and glories from the Father, who gave real existence to those together with him. For the Father did not, in giving to him the inheritance of all things, deprive himself of what he has ingenerately in himself; for he is the fountain of all things. Thus there are three subsistences ['hypostasis']. And God, being the cause of all things, is unbegun and altogether sole but the Son being begotten apart from time by the Father, and being created and found before the ages, was not before his generation; but, being begotten apart from time before all things, alone was made to subsist by the Father. For he is not eternal or co-eternal or co-unoriginate with the Father, nor has he his being together with the Father, as some speak of relations, introducing two ingenerate beginnings, but God is before all things as being Monad and Beginning of all.[1]

---

comment, quotes from Arius' only known theological work, *Thalia*. For an assessment of the historical veracity of these materials see Hanson, *The Search for the Christian Doctrine of God*, 5-15.

[1] Cited in *NE* 284.

The main points of this "confession" are as follows:

- It is a clear statement of the transcendence of the Father and the preservation of this transcendence is a key factor in Arius' theology.

- The principal difference between the Father and the Son is that the Father is un-originated whereas the Son was "not" before his generation. The Son was brought into existence from non-existence solely by the will of the Father.

- The Son is a "creature", but not as the other creatures.

- There are three *hypostases* – Father, Son (and Holy Spirit).

The other main source of Arius' views is his poetic work *Thalia* (c. 323 CE),[1] extracts of which are preserved by Athanasius in *Orationes contra Arionos* I.5-6 and *De Synodis* 15.[2] The patristic scholar R. P. C. Hanson[3] paraphrases Athanasius' extracts of *Thalia* from *Orationes contra Arionos* I.5-6 and attributes the following theological propositions to Arius:

- God was solitary and the Word and Wisdom did not yet exist. Next, when he wanted to make us, he then made a certain person and called him Word and Spirit and Son so that he could make us.

- The Word is, like everybody, changeable in his nature and he remains good in his own freewill as long as he chooses, but when he wishes he too can be changed as we can, for his nature is alterable.

- As everything else is alien to and unlike God in substance, so 'the Word is different from and in all points unlike the Father's substance and individual character'.

---

[1] Williams proposes this date on the grounds that *Thalia* was constructed after Arius' excommunication and on the suggestion of the followers of Eusebius of Nicomedia and as part of Arius' approaches to Eusebius. See his *Arius*, 62-66.

[2] These extracts are cited in *NE* 286.

[3] Hanson thinks that Athanasius' reproduction of *Thalia* in *Orationes contra Arionos* I.5-6 is reliable because it is consistent with extracts in *De Synodis* 15 which preserve Arius' metrical form. Hanson believes that it is unlikely that the *De Synodis* extract is unfaithful because it preserves a metrical form, *The Search for the Christian Doctrine of God*, 12-15.

- The substances (*ousiai*) of the Father, the Son and the Spirit are divided, alienated and separated in nature and they differ from and do not participate in each other: 'They are unlike (*anomoioi*) altogether in their substance (*ousiai*) and levels of glory infinitely'. [1]

There are further subtleties and nuances in Arius' theology, but this Athanasian paraphrase is sufficient to understand how the Nicene Creed addressed Arius and his supporters.[2] Arius' confession of faith to Constantine after Nicaea (c. 327 CE) must be discounted as it is evidently an innocuous piece designed to facilitate his rehabilitation.[3] We can make the following observations about Arius' doctrine:

- Arius' Christology is cosmological rather than soteriological in focus; he is concerned with the relation between the Father and the Son.[4]

- Arius is bumping up against the limits of language: he wants to place the creation of the Son "before eternal times", "before ages" and "before times", (and make the Word the creator of time), and yet use the temporal relation 'before' to express this point.[5]

- Arius is very aware of the dangers of material anthropomorphic metaphors that cluster around the concept of "begettal" when applied

---

[1] These four propositions are taken exactly from Hanson's paraphrase of Athanasius' extracts of *Thalia*, *The Search for the Christian Doctrine of God*, 13-14.

[2] It is beyond the scope of this appendix to consider the relationship between Arius and his early supporters. Hanson covers the ground in his history, *The Search for the Christian Doctrine of God*, ch. 2.

[3] Cited in *NE* 295.

[4] This is a controversial point. Our argument is that a) Arius' surviving writings illustrate a cosmological focus, and b) the Nicene Creed, viewed as a rebuttal of Arius, has a cosmological focus. The argument for a soteriological focus in Arius' thought is an argument from other and later Arian writers.

[5] The relation of God to time and "timelessness" or "eternity" is a complex philosophical topic. For a recent treatment, see B. Leftow, *Time and Eternity* (New York: Cornell University Press, 1991). Arius' remarks show that he accepts the logic of a "before-after" series in speaking of divine action, but that this is logically distinct from the creation of time in which it makes sense to identify a past, present and future. On this see A. N. Prior, *Past, Present and Future* (Oxford: Oxford University Press, 1967), ch. 1.

to the Son; he distances himself from earlier heretics and circumscribes his claims in ways that are common at this time.

- Arius wants to affirm that the Son is a "creature of God, but not as one of the creatures"; in making this qualification, he recognises the danger in deploying a creature anthropomorphism to describe the Son, but it can be legitimately asked: if the Son is completely unlike the creatures, what semantic content is left in the creature metaphor?

- Arius gives expression to there being three subsistences, but there is nothing conceptually in his surviving writings that can mediate the ontological unity of this trinity. His picture of the trinity is purely a construct of economic external relations.

- Arius doesn't give expression to a Logos theology such that *the Logos* became immanent in a Son; he opposes the view that *the Logos* was "generated or new-created into a Son". For Arius, the correct starting point for Christology is the generation of the Son-Word, not the pre-existence of the Word.

Arius' doctrinal motivation is complex,[1] but several strands can be identified from his surviving writings. Firstly, it is clear that there is a

---

[1] Hanson discusses the motivation of Arius on the premise that later Arian theology can be used to flesh out Arius' thinking. Following this approach, Hanson makes soteriology the "heart of Arianism", *The Search for the Christian Doctrine of God*, 112. Given Arius' own emphasis on the transcendence of the deity, we can legitimately speculate that he would have proposed that it was necessary that there be a lesser divinity to become incarnate for the salvation of men. Or, in short, that he would have under-pinned his cosmology with a soteriological necessity. Paul Tillich makes the same point: "The really decisive issue, its basic meaning and permanent significance, had to do with the question: How is salvation possible in a world of darkness and mortality?", *History*, 70. Tillich however argues this point, not from later Arians, but from Athanasius' later response to Arianism, and in particular Athanasius' soteriology. Williams puts Athanasius' argument this way, "...the Word cannot deify if he is not God...", but the deification is not a sharing of divine substance, it is the enjoying of the divine *relation* of Son to Father, hence there is an eternal relation in the Godhead, see his *The Wound of Knowledge* (London: DLT, 1990), 51. We can't explore this approach here: our interest in Arius is confined to documenting how he is the theological catalyst for the

Biblical motivation[1] – Arius believed Scripture supported the view that the Son was the beginning of God's creation. Secondly, there is a manifest desire to protect the deity from any hint of physicality. Arius says in his *Letter to Alexander*, "But if the terms 'from him' and 'from the womb' and 'I came forth from the Father and I come' be understood by some to mean as if a part of him, being consubstantial, or as an issue, then the Father is according to them [Arius' opponents] compounded and divisible".[2] Lastly, there is a desire to preserve the transcendence of God - this is the dominant theme of *Thalia*. Arius secures this goal by making the Son different in key respects: the Father is the only unoriginate; the Son is created from the will of the Father (out of nothing) and not his substance; the Father is fundamentally unknowable; and the Son is creator and intermediary between the Father and the world.

5. Nicaea and the Nicene Creed

The Nicene Creed is a framework for balancing clauses that affirm and delimit aspects of "orthodoxy" in opposition to Arius;[3] it is a short instrument:

> "We believe in,
>
> One God, the Father, Almighty, Maker of all things visible and invisible.
> And in One Lord Jesus Christ, the Son of God, begotten of the Father, Only begotten, that is, from the substance [*ousia*] of the Father; God from God, Light from Light, Very God from Very God, begotten not made, Consubstantial ['*homoousios*'] with the Father, by whom all things were made, both things in heaven and things in earth; who for us men and for our salvation came down and was incarnate, was made man, suffered, and rose again the third day, ascended into heaven, and is coming to judge the living and the dead.
> And in the Holy Spirit.

Nicene Creed. The emphasis of that creed is *cosmological* rather than soteriological.

[1] Williams details the evidence for Arius' self-perception as a "Biblical theologian" in his *Arius*, 107f.

[2] Cited in *NE* 284.

[3] It is evident that it is not intended to be a comprehensive symbol of the faith – it lacks clauses on the Paraclete, baptism, forgiveness, salvation, resurrection, and eternal life.

And those who say, 'There was when he was not', and 'Before his generation he was not', and 'he came to be from nothing', or those who pretend that the Son of God is 'of other *hypostasis* or substance [*ousia*]', or 'created', or 'alterable', or 'mutable', these the Catholic and Apostolic church anathematizes."[1]

The creed takes over some of the clauses from earlier local baptismal and catechetical creeds and inserts clauses to handle Arius' theology. Athanasius in *De Decretis* 25[2] claims that none of the phrases are absolutely innovative but re-use Scriptural language and concepts found in earlier Fathers of the church.

Appended to the positive affirmations of the creed was an anathema directed against Arius and his supporters, which identified them by typical slogans from their doctrine. Three points need to be observed about these slogans:

- Most of the slogans are about the "temporal" begettal of the Son, which indicates where most of the controversy was situated.

- There is condemnation of those who deny that the Son is of the same substance as the Father, but, crucially, two terms for "substance" are used (*hypostasis* and *ousia*) as synonyms.

- The Arian view that the Son is "mutable" or "alterable" is condemned.

---

[1] No "Acts" from the Council of Nicaea recording the creed remain. The primary sources are Eusebius and Athanasius. Our version is taken from the *Letter of Eusebius of Caesarea to his Church on the Creed of Nicaea* cited in *NE* 291. There are small textual variations among the primary sources recording Eusebius' letter (the histories of Socrates, Theodoret, and Athanasius' *De Synodis*), but a discussion of these is beyond the scope of this appendix. For a discussion, see T. H. Bindley, *The Oecumenical Documents of the Christian Faith* (London: Methuen, 1906), 19-20. Kelly, *Early Christian Creeds*, 227-230, reviews the possible pro-genitors of the creed following the hypothesis that anti-Arian clauses have been added to an existing model; again a consideration of this issue is beyond the scope of this appendix.

[2] Reproduced in *NPNF* Series 2, Vol. 4.

The "anti-Arian" positive clauses of the Nicene Creed are discussed in the following table.

Clauses		Comment
begotten of the Father	γεννηθεντα εκ του Πατπρος	This clause was taken to express the eternal generation of the Son. It was held that generation from an eternal Father must itself be eternal because the one generated must share the same nature. The clause was often ended with "before the ages" in other 4c. creeds, e.g. Eusebius' Caesarean creed, Alexander's Alexandrian creed and Cyril's Jerusalem creed. The omission here is probably a counter-weight to the Arian *temporal* emphasis on the Son's begettal.
only begotten	Μονογενη	This word was used to specify the uniqueness of the Son, but it was equally used by Arians who interpreted the generation of the Son to be synonymous with his creation.
that is, from the substance of the Father	τουτ' εστιν εκ της ουσιας του Πατρος	This is the first key anti-Arian clause and explains the Son's begettal according to Athanasius, *De Decretis* 19.[1] It was designed to express the Son's origination from God's substance as unique and separate from the way in which "all things" have their origination in God.
True God from True God	Θεον αληθινον εκ θεου αληθινου	Arians insisted on the uniqueness of the Father in several respects; this clause was intended to express the equal deity of the Son and oppose the subordinationism of Arius.

---

[1] Reproduced in *NPNF*, Series 2, Vol. IV.

Clauses		Comment
Light from Light	Φως εκ Φως	This was a common simile for expressing the community of substance between Father and Son.
begotten not made	γεννηθεντα ου ποιηθεντα	This is the second key anti-Arian clause. Arius contended that the Son was a creature, something made, albeit unlike other creatures, and the creed opposes the Son's begettal to what can be considered to be made.
of one substance with the Father	ομοουσιον τω Πατπρι	This is the third key anti-Arian clause, as con-substantiality was explicitly denied by Arius. For the orthodox, sonship implied community of nature and not creatureship.
was incarnate, was made man	σαρκωθεντα εναινθρωπησαντα	These two clauses express the union of the two natures. Although we have no record of Arius' views on the incarnation, it is possible that he held the later Arian view that Christ was not fully human, but God inhabiting a human body.

Table 1 - Anti-Arian Clauses in the Nicene Creed

As a framework for the expression of doctrine, the creed proved flexible and the subsequent era of creed-making that followed (principally, 341-361 CE) showed how the creedal structure was flexed respectively in "Arian" and Orthodox directions. For example, the creed associated with Constantinople 381 (the formal end of the Arian controversy) reflects the Nicene tradition, but makes key deletions and additions.[1] It adds that the Son was begotten of the Father "before all ages", a creedal formula that pre-dates Nicaea, but which had strong Arian overtones in 325 CE (see Table 1); the Nicene clause, "both things in heaven and things in earth" is deleted; the incarnation is specifically linked to the Holy Spirit and the Virgin Mary; and a clause about the everlasting kingdom is added to rebut

---

[1] Cited in *CCC* 90.

an heretical view of Marcellus of Ancyra. The main addition is a substantial expansion of the clause about the Holy Spirit. This last addition makes the "Constantinopolitan" creed the first "proper" oecumenical Trinitarian formulation.

This short review of the Nicene Creed illustrates the first two of the four parts to our thesis (see above): i) the creed has a *programmatic character* – it puts clauses into a sequence and an evolving explanatory order and sets an agenda for controlling orthodox thinking on the question of the eternity and being of the Son; and ii) the creed *blocks certain Arian theologies*.

In order to evaluate the last two parts to our thesis (see above): i) that the creed supplies the *beginnings of an ontology of the Trinity*; and ii) that it *circumscribes the boundaries of an acceptable anthropomorphism*, certain key concepts require an extended discussion; and a review of the conciliar use of Nicaea is also necessary.

6. Technical Theology
The controversy engendered by Arius was on two levels: firstly, it was about the nature of the Son's existence, and secondarily it was about the character of the being of the Son.

6.1 The Existence of the Son (Begettal)
In scholastic terms, Arius' theology makes the existence of the Son *contingent*. The orthodox response to Arius did not deploy the notion of *necessary existence*, but the insistence that the Son is co-eternal with the Father can be construed as a paraphrase of the idea that the Son has necessary existence.[1] Athanasius addresses the question of the nature of the Son's existence in *Orationes contra Arionos* III.62-66. His argument is expressed in relation to the Arian doctrine that the Son came to be through the will of the Father, and he concludes his point in these words:

> "For to say, 'Of will He came to be,' in the first place implies
> that once He was not; and next it implies an inclination two

---

[1] The notion of necessity that we assume here is a metaphysical *de re* necessity. A modern treatment can be found in Swinburne, *The Christian God*, 116-122. Classical philosophy of religion would discuss the necessary existence of God without taking into account any internal distinction of the Godhead such as Christianity's Father, Son, and Holy Spirit. Swinburne offers a subtle analysis of metaphysical necessity that allows Father, Son, and Spirit to have necessary metaphysical existence, and he applies his philosophical treatment to the Nicene Creed, 180-186.

ways, as has been said, so that one might suppose that the Father could even not will the Son."1

Athanasius is opposing here the development of the notion of begettal in connection with the will of the Father. In effect, by rejecting the development of the notion of begettal using substance metaphysics (for fear of materialism), Arians had nowhere else to go but to employ an "event" metaphysics. Their question became: what is it for an event to exist, and in particular, what is it for a divine begettal[2] to exist as an event. Their answer was that such an event was an expression of divine will which, in addition, they viewed as a contingent expression of that will. (In theory, they could have argued that the begettal of the Son was a *necessary* expression of the will of the Father.)

Athanasius' rebuttal is by analogy: the Father's begettal of the Son is not "by will" but "by nature":

> "A man by counsel builds a house, but by nature he begets a son; and what is in building began to come into being at will, and is external to the maker; but the son is proper offspring of the father's essence, and is not external to him; wherefore neither does he counsel concerning him, lest he appear to counsel about himself. As far then as the Son transcends the creature, by so much does what is by nature transcend the will."3

Athanasius is rejecting the "event" based model for understanding the begettal of the Son. He is insisting that the notion of "divine substance" is the proper category with which to enlarge an explanation of divine begettal.[4]

---

[1] *Orationes contra Arionos* III.66, *NPNF*, Series 2, Vol. 4.

[2] The typical Arian proposal would be that the Son was created out of nothing by the will of the Father.

[3] *Orationes contra Arionos*, III.62.

[4] It should be noted that the polarity suggested here between an "event" model and a "substance" model is the underlying metaphysical conflict between Athanasius and Arianism. Athanasius' particular argument in *Orationes contra Arionos* III.62-66 is that the Son, as Word, is the "Living Counsel" of the Father, and as such it is contradictory to affirm that the Father could exercise his counsel and bring the Son into existence. This argument (from attributes) is one way in which Athanasius affirms the co-eternality of the Son.

382

Arius had correctly seen the "material" anthropomorphic dangers in talking about the generation of the Son (in keeping with standard concerns of the day), and for this reason shied away from the concept of divine substance. However, the application of a temporal concept "before", (and an "event" model), in a description of the generation of the Son (the Son is begotten before time) is itself an anthropomorphism which implies the notion of contingent existence. The orthodox response to Arius perceived that a more austere and less anthropomorphic characterization of the Son's generation was both possible and necessary if the full deity of the Son was to be preserved – and this was to affirm that the Son was of the same substance as the Father and *eternally* begotten.[1]

The issue between Arius and Athanasius can be characterized in terms of how the religious language of sonship is to be understood. Both sides are approaching the concept as a model for understanding deity, but each side is circumscribing the anthropomorphic implications to a different level of precision. Arius is prepared to affirm that "there was when he was not", which brings contingency into the frame, while excluding more material overtones. Athanasius thinks that this is still too anthropomorphic and has unacceptable implications. Thus he would qualify the model of sonship with the insistence of eternal generation, as a way of blocking even more unacceptable anthropomorphic implications.[2]

Much of the debate at Nicaea was evidently about the "eternal" status of the Son. However, it can be plausibly argued that this issue was to prove

---

[1] Arius would argue that the Son was begotten "in truth" and not "in semblance" – see his *Letter to Alexander* cited in *NE* 284. Arius thought that the orthodox position did not have a real begettal because they taught an "eternal begettal". Theodoret in his history records the argument of Eusebius of Nicomedia, "We have not heard of two unbegotten beings..." (*HE* 1.6.3, cited in *NE* 285), which is a rhetorical expression of the same point: an eternal begettal is a chimera and not real. The Arian argument is that 'begettal' language is irreducibly "event-like" - to take this away, is to turn the divine begettal into a "semblance". The orthodox response is more austere and less anthropomorphic: begettal is intrinsically *theomorphic*, and begettal in creation is an analogical model of the "true" divine *eternal* begettal.

[2] The 'model-qualifier' approach to religious language is set out by I. T. Ramsey, *Religious Language* (London: SCM Press, 1957). Ramsey discusses the application of his approach in connection with the eternal generation of the Son and the concept of divine substance – see 158-159.

less controversial than the issue of the Son's being. The question of what the Son can be said to *be* in being begotten is an issue about how the Son relates to the substance that is God. This issue divided the church long after the co-eternal status of the Son was settled. For example, we can see this in the fact that whereas the Homoean "Dated Creed" (359 CE) proscribes the concept of substance, it affirms the Son's co-eternality.

6.2 Ousia and Hypostasis

These two terms carry the ontology of the Nicene Creed. In the positive affirmations of the creed, the Son is "of the substance (*ousia*) of the Father"; and "consubstantial ['*homoousios*'] with the Father". In the anathemas, it is denied that the Son is "of other *hypostasis* or substance [*ousia*]". Exactly what was meant by these affirmations at the time of Nicaea is a matter of scholarly dispute. Hanson describes the Arian Controversy as a period of "semantic confusion"[1] over these terms, confusion exasperated by typical opposing Eastern and Western preferences for their usage. His conclusion about how these terms might have been understood at Nicaea shows the possibility for confusion:

> "The state of affairs as regards the use of hypostasis and ousia at the outset of the search for the doctrine of God occasioned by the Arian Controversy can therefore be stated thus: several alternative ways of treating these terms were prevalent. They could be regarded as synonymous and used either to describe what God is as Three or what he is as One; or hypostasis could be used to describe the 'Persons' of the Godhead and ousia either ignored or rejected; or hypostasis could be used for 'distinct existence' and ousia for 'nature'; or a general state of indecision and uncertainty as to how either of them should be used could exist in a writer's mind. We can find examples of all these alternatives."[2]

G. C. Stead's discussion of both *ousia* and *hypostasis* shows that their diachronic semantic domains overlap. He notes that at the time of Nicaea, theologians drew no clear-cut distinction between the terms in their application, and that the scholarly consensus today is that in the Nicene Creed they are used as synonyms.[3] However, Stead's discussion is

---

[1] Hanson, *The Search for the Christian Doctrine of God*, ch. 7.

[2] Hanson, *The Search for the Christian Doctrine of God*, 184-5.

[3] G. C. Stead, *Philosophy in Christian Antiquity* (Cambridge: Cambridge University Press, 1994), chs. 14, 15. Stead summarizes, "…we have listed

principally concerned with the use of *ousia* and *hypostasis* at the time of the Cappadocian Settlement rather than Nicaea. G. L. Prestige's proposal[1] on the meaning of *hypostasis* and *ousia* at Nicaea is that they connote the "individual objective source" that is the Father, rather than any generic substance that is the Father. Prestige's argument for this reading is that it is suggested by the complementary denial that the Son is not of any other *hypostasis* or *ousia* (than the Father[2]) or out of the non-existent. The contrary emphasis to the idea that the Son was created out of non-existence or that he has a different *hypostasis* or *ousia* to the Father would be that the Son was out of the existent objective reality that is the Father. This persuasive argument, proposed by Prestige, is that the contextual rhetoric of the Arian controversy suggests that *hypostasis* and *ousia* were understood in the sense of an "existent objective reality".[3]

Even though the Nicene Creed implies that the Father is an *hypostasis*, there is no comparable expression defining that the Father and Son (or the Holy Spirit) are distinct individual realities – *hypostases* in the Eastern Origenist tradition. On the other hand, neither is there any explicit affirmation that God is one *ousia* or *hypostasis* – which would be a characteristic Western insistence. The emphasis is on derivation of the Son from the substance of the Father. We have already noted above Arius' teaching in *Thalia* that the "substances (*ousiai*) of the Father, the Son and the Spirit are divided, alienated and separated in nature and they differ from and do not participate in each other". Clearly, the Nicene clause 'of the substance (*ousia*) of the Father' directly opposes this teaching.

---

the basic sense of *ousia* under seven headings: A, existence; B, category; C, the category of substance; D, stuff or material; E, form; F, definition; and G, truth. It seems to me that 'hypostasis' can be an exact equivalent of *ousia* in sense A and D, and sometimes comes close to it in sense B and E; sense C and F are only occasionally represented by 'hypostasis', but it is nearly equivalent in a few phrases assignable to G...", 178.

[1] G. L. Prestige, *God in Patristic Thought* (London: SPCK, 1952), 177. Hanson follows Prestige, *The Search for the Christian Doctrine of God*, 189.

[2] It should be noted that the anathema, 'of other *hypostasis* or substance [*ousia*]', doesn't mention the Father and that we are inferring that it is the Father who is excluded by the contrary preference for another *hypostasis* or *ousia*.

[3] For an Aristotelian discussion of the notion of "substance" in a Nicene context, see W. P. Alston, "Substance and the Trinity" in *The Trinity* (eds., S. T. Davis, D. Kendall, and G. O' Collins; Oxford: Oxford University Press, 1999), 179-201.

The creed is not deploying a concept of "species" or "nature" in respect of the Godhead; neither is it deploying the later Cappadocian concept of an "individual". The distinction of Father, Son, and Holy Spirit is presupposed, but there is no ontological framework carrying this distinction. The objective of the creed is limited to a rebuttal of Arius. However, there is clearly the beginning of an ontology. The creed does not disallow a future proposal that the Son is an *hypostasis* (or that there are three *hypostases* in the Godhead) – the creed has an open place for such an elaboration. Neither does it exclude a future elaboration of the ontological unity of the Godhead; in fact, as we shall argue below, the use of *homoousios*, (however vague or ambiguous this term was at the time of Nicaea), is a significant placeholder for developing an expression of the ontological unity of the Godhead. (Indeed, it expresses something of an ontological unity.) All that the creed prohibits is the derivation of the Son from any other *ousia* than the Father.

6.3 Homoousios (Consubstantial)

This term is probably the most contentious of the terms in the Nicene Creed for a variety of reasons. There is evidence for contention at the time of Nicaea and later during the doctrinal debates of the 350s CE It is a key ontological claim that the Son is consubstantial with the Father, but exactly how the term was understood at Nicaea in the light of both its secular and religious usage is unclear. The later 4c. debates surrounding the term can be viewed as an exercise in trying to pin down an acceptable semantic content that did not lead to erroneous material or modalist anthropomorphisms. Judged in this light, at the time of Nicaea, the term can be seen as a placeholder in a creed awaiting substantive theological content. The theological conflict over the term in the 350s can be seen as a process of trial and error in supplying an acceptable content. The term survived and was included in the creed associated with Constantinople 381 CE; in a sense, then, it proved an effective placeholder for a theology that finally emerged at Constantinople.

The term has little documented theological usage prior to 325 CE Prestige concludes that prior to Nicaea this term conveyed a metaphor drawn from material objects meaning "of one stuff", and that when applied to divine nature it had to be couched with reservations in order to safeguard the unity of God.[1] The most significant pre-Nicene occurrence of the term is its condemnation by the Synod of Antioch in 268 CE Prestige's discussion of this council follows Athanasius' report in *De Synodis* 45:[2] the

---

[1] *Fathers*, 197-209.

[2] The relevant extract is cited in *CCC* 31 and in *NE* 230.

Council were opposing Paul of Samasota,[1] and in the course of doing this, opposed the use of 'homoousios', if by this it was implied that the Father and the Son were of the same *antecedent* substance. In terms of our thesis, Antioch was circumscribing a use of the 'homoousios' anthropomorphism.

Arius had specifically rejected 'homoousios' as being applicable to the Son. He comments in *Thalia* of the Son, "He has nothing proper to God in his essential property, for neither is he equal nor yet consubstantial with him".[2] Arius also condemns the term in his letter to Alexander as "Manichaean"; he says that his teaching is "[not] as Manichaeus taught that the offspring was a portion of the Father consubstantial".[3] Arius' condemnation shows a rejection of the metaphor of a "shared substance" because its material overtones can lead to ideas of the Son as a "part" of the Father separated off from his substance. The Council no doubt had an eye on Arius' explicit theology when they included the homoousion posit.[4] However, it is also certain that they did not therefore mean the Father and the Son were of the same *material* substance.

The non-material sense of 'homoousios' is illustrated in Eusebius' report on the Council. He records Constantine's interpretation as follows: "The Son is not to be called 'consubstantial' according to what happens to bodies, nor is he constituted by a division or some kind of cutting up of the Father, nor can the immaterial and intellectual and bodiless nature undergo what happens to bodies, but these things must be conceived of in divine and ineffable terms".[5] Constantine's appeal to ineffability (a common appeal) is the typical way in which 4c. theology advertises that it is dealing with anthropomorphisms that need to be circumscribed.

Eusebius adds his own explanation of 'homoousios': the Son is consubstantial with the Father, but not "by any suffering or alteration or change of the essence [substance] and power of the Father". The Son is not like the creatures and "not of any other hypostasis or essence

---

[1] There is no documentary evidence that Paul of Samasota used 'homoousios'.

[2] *Thalia* 9, cited in *NE* 286

[3] *Letter to Alexander*, cited in *NE* 284.

[4] Eusebius claims that it was the addition of this one word to his own baptismal creed that constituted the difference between the two creeds; see the *Letter of Eusebius to Caesarea*, cited in *NE* 291.

[5] Cited in *NE* 337.

[substance], but of Father."[1] Eusebius is seeking to preserve the impassibility of the Father in any link between the Son and the substance of the Father, but more importantly, he sees the term as a key block to the creaturely view of the Son, which was Arius' doctrine. For Arius, the Son was a creature and not of the same substance as the Father. Eusebius' remarks position the homoousion posit over against Arianism; his report does not suggest that the rejection by Antioch 268 is an issue. He doesn't qualify 'homoousios' by blocking the idea that the Father and Son share an *antecedent* substance. However, Eusebius' report does not indicate *positively* what it means to say that the Son is consubstantial with the Father. Instead, we have illustrated the (Scholastic) *negative method* in defining God – the Son is *not* of any other substance than the Father and God is *not* a material substance.

Hanson notes that scholars have been puzzled by the relative lack of the use of the term 'homoousios' (both in the East and the West) immediately after Nicaea. Hanson's conclusion is that the term did not have any crucial importance for those at Nicaea.[2] The significance of 'homoousios' at Nicaea lies in its opposition to Arius' creature anthropomorphism; this is an important aspect of the achievement of the Nicene Creed. The inclusion of the term in the Nicene Creed was innovative, and the innovation was viewed with suspicion. The fact that the term was included, despite this suspicion (illustrated by Eusebius), is a measure of its importance. However, as Eusebius' remarks suggest, in the theological context of Nicaea, it is not clear what 'homoousios' adds over and above "of the substance of the Father".[3]

The defence of 'homoousios' did not erupt until the late 350s CE It was then that the more extreme forms of "Arian" thinking caused pro-Nicenes to insist on this term. It is at this time that the Antioch 268 condemnation is used rhetorically by the anti-Nicene groups at the Sirmium councils of 357-358 CE, arguing that the Antioch decision should bind the church. The difficulty that was felt by the pro-Nicenes, and which is illustrated in Athanasius' defence of Antioch 268, is that to find fault with one respected council cast doubt on reliability of other respected councils. Hence, in Athanasius' view, it was essential that the

---

[1] Cited in *NE* 339.

[2] Hanson, *The Search for the Christian Doctrine of God*, 437.

[3] It is a separate study to consider who promoted the term at Nicaea. For example, it is beyond the scope of this appendix to consider the possibility that the term is motivated by the Western doctrine of *una substantia*. On this see Prestige, *Fathers*, 219-221.

term be defended, both in its exclusion at Antioch, and its inclusion at Nicaea.[1] The defensive strategy was to argue that the use of a term cannot be divorced from its context. At Antioch the context of exclusion was inadmissible material implications; at Nicaea the context of inclusion was an opposition to an Arian creature anthropomorphism. Athanasius' interpretation of the theological context at Nicaea is telling:

> "But the bishops who anathematized the Arian heresy, understanding Paul's craft, and reflecting that the word 'co-essential' ['homoousios'] has not this meaning when used of things immaterial, and especially of God, and acknowledging that the Word was not a creature, but an offspring from the essence, and that the Father's essence was the origin and root and foundation of the Son, and that he was of very truth his father's likeness, and not of different nature, as we are, and separate from the Father but that, as being from him, he exists as Son indivisible, as radiance is with respect to light, on these grounds reasonably asserted on their part, that the Son was 'co-essential' ['homoousios']."[2]

Of course, Athanasius may here be placing a positive spin on Nicaea; the Nicene Fathers may not have had such a harmonious view of their theology. Doubtless, the rhetorical demands of the 350s and the opposition of the Homean party required such a spin. Nevertheless, Athanasius' recollection of Nicaea may be justified as an historical reconstruction of what was going on between the lines of the Council. In the face of a creature anthropomorphism, the Council deployed the category of (divine) substance to describe the nature of the Son, and 'homoousios' followed as an amplification of that deployment. We can conclude that even if the Nicene Fathers did not have a clear understanding of the unity of substance of the Father and Son, nevertheless they did put the category of "substance" central to an expression of the unity of the Godhead, and in the Eastern (largely Origenist) theological context of the early 4c., this is no mean theological achievement for the Western-Alexandrian axis of the church.

---

[1] Hanson comments that the condemnation by Antioch must have caused "considerable embarrassment" to the theologians who wanted to defend the term in any later conciliar creed, *The Search for the Christian Doctrine of God*, 195.

[2] *De Synodis* 45, cited in *CCC* 31.

If the homoousion posit was initially directed against creature anthropomorphism,[1] it was later held to harbour modalist views of the Godhead. Prestige notes[2] that Sabellian modalist views were not a factor at Nicaea, but by the 350s and particularly because of the thinking of Marcellus of Ancyra, a large body of the Eastern church felt that to affirm that the Son was of the "same" substance as the Father was to espouse a modal view of the Godhead. A critical point in evaluating the achievement of the Nicene Creed therefore is whether it should have affirmed that the Son was "of the same substance" as the Father or whether it should have affirmed that the Son was "of *like* substance" with the Father. A consideration of this issue requires that we investigate later developments in the Arian controversy.

7. Arianism

One measure that we can apply in our assessment of the Nicene Creed is to examine how its creedal formulations fared during the period 341-361 CE This was a period during which "Arianism", in one form or another, was in the ascendant, and creeds were drawn up expressing different doctrine and emphases to that expressed at Nicaea. Pressure was brought to bear by various parties in the East and West on the orthodox doctrine, and the survival of the Nicene Creed during this period is therefore a good indication of its rationale.

The consensus of scholarship is that Arius formed no party in the church neither did he form a school. His theology was a catalyst for a controversy that assumed a life beyond Arius. Arius sought support against Alexander, and received support from figures such as Eusebius of Nicomedia[3] and Eusebius of Caesarea.[4] That Arius himself was not a party leader is illustrated by the opening words of the "Dedication Council" in 341 CE, "We have neither become followers of Arius – for how should we who

---

[1] Arians may have eschewed using the notion of substance to enlarge upon the nature of divine begettal, but their creature anthropomorphism is nevertheless a "substance" metaphysics; the Nicaea Council could have eschewed the notion of substance in the definition of the Godhead, but it did not – it countered one type of substance metaphysics with another substance metaphysics.

[2] Prestige, *Fathers*, 211.

[3] Eusebius subscribed to the Nicene Creed, but not the anathematizing, see his *Letter from Exile*, cited in *NE* 296.

[4] It should not be assumed that Arius' supporters (great or small) subscribed to all of his doctrinal position. For a list and evaluation see Hanson, *The Search for the Christian Doctrine of God*, ch. 2.

are bishops follow a presbyter – nor have we embraced any other faith than that which was set forth from the beginning".[1] Instead, Athanasius ascribes leadership of the Arians to Eusebius of Nicomedia,[2] and Chadwick observes in his history that Eusebius dominated the East up until his death in 341 CE[3]

Given the ascendance of Eusebius of Nicomedia and the Syrian church, the theological views of the East between 325-341 C.E are probably more realistically expressed in the statements delivered by the Dedication Council than by Nicaea. After the death of Constantine and the accession of Constantius, a growing split between East and West developed, deriving from Rome's continued support for Athanasius and Marcellus. The objective of the Dedication Council was to affirm the orthodoxy of the East over against Western opinion. Four documents (conventionally known as Antioch 1-4) are associated with the Council, although not all emanate from its proceedings. The documents illustrate ambivalence in respect to both Arian and Nicene views.

In Antioch 1, the bishops affirm "one only begotten Son of God before all ages, subsisting and co-existing with the Father who begat him", which is more sympathetic to Arian thought than to the Nicene Creed. It reintroduces the clause "before all ages" and drops the category of substance in relation to the assertion of the Son's begettal. In Antioch 2, the same emphasis can be seen: "only begotten God, by whom are all things, who was begotten before the ages from the Father" – where again a mention of the substance of the Father is absent.

Furthermore, Antioch 2 affirms, "exact image of the Godhead, substance (*ousia*), will power, and glory of the Father", which weakens the "identity of substance" in the Nicene Creed to "exact image". (The council do not use the term 'homoousios'). The patristic scholar, Stuart Hall, comments that the council "...expressed well the beliefs later held by the party labelled 'homoiousian'...",[4] and this is shown by the fact that the Seleucia Council of 359 CE wanted to affirm Antioch 2.

---

[1] Cited in *CCC* 6 – all subsequent citations from the Antioch Documents are from *CCC* 6.

[2] *Apologia contra Arianos* 59, cited in *NE* 298.

[3] *History*, 133-136.

[4] S. G. Hall, *Doctrine and Practise in the Early Church* (London: SPCK, 1992), 142.

Antioch 2 also expands the doctrinal statements about the Holy Spirit and offers a Trinitarian formula: it affirms of the Father, Son, and the Holy Spirit (and opposing Marcellus of Ancyra) that "the names not being given without meaning or effect, but denoting accurately the peculiar subsistence (*hypostasis*), rank and glory of each that is named, so that they are three in subsistence, and in agreement one". This statement gives a classic Origenist *economic* expression to the unity of the trinity - (they are one in agreement) and is in keeping with the typical Eastern emphasis on the Threeness of the Trinity. Such a statement pulls back from the beginnings of the ontology that was expressed at Nicaea.

However, even though the Dedication Council did not re-affirm Nicaea, it did not subscribe to Arianism. Antioch 2 denounces those who hold "creature" views of the Son, or who say that there was "time or season or age" before the generation of the Son.[1] Antioch 4 goes further and denounces Arian clauses related to among other things the Son's *hypostasis*: "But those who say that the Son is from nothing, or is from another *hypostasis* and is not from God; and that there was a time when he was not, the Catholic Church regards them as alien."[2] This excludes, in a more definite way, any creature model of divine begettal, but *against Nicaea* it substitutes *hypostasis* for *ousia* in any implication about that from which the Son is derived.

What we see in the documents of the Dedication Council is a middle way. We noted above that the controversy engendered by Arius was on two

---

[1] As with other clauses in the creeds of the period, this clause could be interpreted in a *pro* or *anti* Arian light. One of the drivers for the multiplication of explanatory clauses in the typical creedal framework is the attempt to overcome ambiguity in clauses. On the other hand, it should be remembered that the standard way to achieve unity in an ecumenical context is to express doctrine at a suitable level of generality so that all parties can agree the formula. Whereas the Nicene Creed illustrates the attempt to exclude Arianism, it is likely that the Dedication Creed (Antioch 2) was designed to unite the Alexandrian and Syrian groupings of the East, with the hope that the West would acquiesce to the symbol.

[2] This document was issued later than Antioch 2, and it illustrates a more decisive condemnation of Arianism than the anathemas in Antioch 2, and it removes the statement about the subsistence of the three *hypostases* of the trinity. It was designed to promote East-West unity and its publication probably indicates that Antioch 2 had gone too far in appeasing any Arian faction in the East.

levels: firstly, it was about the nature of the Son's existence, and secondarily it was about the character of the being of the Son. The Dedication Council illustrates that the East were prepared to settle the question of the co-existence of the Father and Son, but they were unwilling to embrace the ontology (however indeterminate) of the Nicene Creed. By 341 CE, we can say that one of Arius' two theological planks had failed to carry the East, and the conservative majority of the church had settled the question of the co-eternity of the Son. The middle way offered to the West was that the Son was *like in substance* to the Father. Kelly comments on this creed that it "was a faithful replica of the average theology of the Eastern Church".[1] If this is true, it shows that we can measure the theological achievement of the Nicene Creed as "mixed". It had carried the East on the question of the Son's necessary co-eternal existence, but it had failed to convince on the matter of the Son's sharing of the substance (*ousia*) of the Father.

The creedal position of this council is significant as a benchmark. It is referenced by a number of later councils. As such, although the development of doctrine subsequent to 361 CE moved on and re-affirmed the Nicene position, in the period 341-361 CE, the Dedication Council is more representative of Eastern opinion. For example,

- The Philippopolis council of 342/3 CE uses Antioch 4 as its creed, and appends further anathemas denying that there are three gods, and that the Father, Son and Holy Spirit are "one and the same".[2]

- The creed of the "Long Lines"[3] (345 CE) incorporates Antioch 4; however, it defends the concept of the trinity as three real persons (πρόσωπα), not as three *hypostases*, and it eschews the "substance" concepts of *hypostasis* and *ousia* in its description of the unity of the Godhead; it affirms instead that the Father and Son exist together in an inseparable unity.

- The first creed of Sirmium (351 CE) affirmed Antioch 2/4 and appended a list of twenty-six additional anathemas[4] condemning typical Arian and Marcellian views; some anathemas are interesting

---

[1] Kelly, *Early Christian Creeds*, 274.

[2] The text of the additional anathemas is given by Kelly, *Early Christian Creeds*, 276.

[3] Cited in *CCC* 10.

[4] These are conveniently reproduced by Hanson in his history, *The Search for the Christian Doctrine of God*, 326-328.

for the light they shed on how the concept of divine substance was being understood, for example, anathemas nos. 6 & 7 deny that the *ousia* of God is extended or that the Son is an extension of the *ousia* of God.

- Basil of Ancyra, reacting to the "Anomoean" doctrine in the "Blasphemy of Sirmium", called a council at Ancyra in 357 CE and affirmed Antioch 2, stipulating that the Son was *like in substance* to the Father.

- The Council of Seleucia 359 CE wanted to affirm Antioch 2, but because of conflict over the application of the concept of substance in describing the relationship of the Father and Son, acquiesced and adopted a "Homoean" stance.

If we are measuring the theological achievement of the Nicene Creed and using the creeds during the period 341-361 CE as a primary source, it would have to be admitted that Eastern theology did not subscribe to the homoousion posit.[1] This limits the theological achievement that we can ascribe to Nicaea, but, crucially, their creedal formulations still retain an ontological expression, and to this extent it can be argued that Nicaea was successful: it had carried[2] the church in recognising the need for such an expression. This conclusion supports our thesis that the theological achievement of Nicaea lies in the first step it makes towards a Trinitarian ontology. Athanasius' view[3] of the Homoiousian grouping in the church was that they were essentially batting on the same side as the

---

[1] It should be noted that the rejection of the homoousion posit was not influenced by any Arian distaste, but because of the Sabellian and Marcellian modalist thinking that clustered around the idea that the Father and Son shared the same substance.

[2] The contrary trend up until the rise of the Western Anomoeans in the late 350s was for the West to re-affirm Nicaea. For example, Socrates reports (cited in *CCC* 7) that the Westerns ratified the Nicene Creed and the doctrine of consubstantiality at the Sardicia council of 342/3CE; at the Council of Milan (355CE), Hilary records (cited in *CCC* 21) that Paulinus of Trier and Eusebius of Vercellae used the Nicene Creed as a litmus of orthodoxy; and finally, it was during the mid-350s that Athanasius began defending Nicaea with a vengeance and insisting on the necessity of the homoousion posit; he was supported at this time by key western theologians such as Hilary of Poitiers.

[3] *De Synodis* 41, cited in *CCC* 31.

Homoousions. It would fall to the Cappadocian Fathers to develop the thinking that would carry the church on this question.

7.1 Anomoean Arianism and the Homoean Reaction

It is questionable whether the average Eastern theology represented by the Dedication Council can be fairly classified as "Arian" in any legitimate sense. The fact that this term was used at the time to describe such Eastern thinking should be treated as rhetoric. The same cannot be said for the "Anomoeans", who were a full-blooded revival of Arian thinking in the late 350s. This is shown by their common view with Arius that the Son is *unlike* the Father. We have observed above that this was a view of Arius: the Son was alien in substance in respect of the Father.

The response to this revival of Arianism was very different to that illustrated at Nicaea. Instead of affirming Nicaea, or instead of affirming that the Son was like the Father in substance, the church espoused a "Homoean" view – that the Son was merely like the Father. The difficulties that had been experienced over the category of substance influenced creeds such as the "Dated Creed" and the creed of Constantinople (360 CE). As Kelly observes, although Jerome might have called the Homoean response "Arian", this is really a misnomer, for the "creed asserts none of the articles of the old heresy".[1] The short-lived nature of the Homoean response illustrates that it wasn't a deep-rooted development in church doctrine, and therefore although it might be used in evidence to show that the Nicene Creed had "failed" to carry the church even in respect to the importance of the category of substance, this would be a superficial reading of the facts. The fact that Nicaea was taken up after this Homoean interregnum is a significant measure of its theological achievement.

8 Towards Constantinople and 381

The councils in our period illustrate two polarities in what we might characterize today as the doctrine of divine substance.

The first opposition was whether it was correct to talk of three *hypostases* in the Godhead or just one *hypostasis*. The Dedication Council affirmed three *hypostases*, but the Philippopolis 342/3 Council denied that this meant that there were three Gods. The Sardicia 342/3 Council affirmed that the Godhead was "one *hypostasis*, which is termed 'essence (*ousia*)' by

---

[1] Kelly, *Early Christian Creeds*, 294.

the heretics".[1] This council followed Nicaea, treating *hypostasis* and *ousia* as synonyms.

The second opposition was whether it was correct to talk of the Son as of the same substance (*ousia* or *hypostasis*) as the Father, or *like* in substance to the Father, or even *unlike* to the Father in substance. The question here is whether substance is a category that ought to be used in the description of the Trinity. For example, the Second Creed of Sirmium 357 states that there "ought to be no mention" of *ousia*, *homoousion* or *homoiousion*.[2] The "Dated Creed" 359 CE states that "whereas the term 'essence (*ousia*)' has been used by the Fathers in simplicity…it has seemed good to remove it, that 'essence' be never in any case used of God".[3]

In effect, the issue at stake was whether and how a doctrine of divine substance could be used to describe how God is as one *as well as* how he is as three: the Eastern emphasis on the individual *hypostases* of the Father, Son, and Holy Spirit was often joined with an affirmation of their economic Trinitarian unity; the Western emphasis on the unity of the Father, Son, and Holy Spirit in terms of a single *hypostasis*, did not carry with it a corresponding expression of their separateness in terms of a substance metaphysics. The Cappadocian settlement applied the concept of substance to both aspects of the Trinitarian formulation: it affirmed that there is a proper sense in which God is one substance and a proper sense in which God is three substances. It employed the two common terms for 'substance' - *hypostasis* and *ousia* - to achieve this resolution.

We have observed that the Nicene Creed gives no explicit expression to how the Father, Son, and Holy Spirit have distinction of substance, but this does not mean that the creed is marked by failure in this regard. It is evident that Nicaea and its symbol is very much the creature of its times – it is a reaction to Arius' theology. Instead, the creed ought to be measured on whether it was correct to place a "unity of substance" doctrine at the heart of its statements on the relation between the Father and the Son. We have discussed four aspects in regard to the question: *What is the theological achievement of the Nicene Creed?* – but if there is just a single measure of this creed (among the four canvassed), it has to concern how we view the foresight that led to the statement that the Son was of one substance with the Father.

---

[1] Cited in *CCC* 7.
[2] Cited in *CCC* 27.
[3] Cited in *CCC* 33.

The proposition that there are three *hypostases* in the Godhead is intuitively easier to comprehend. This emphasis is necessary to protect against a variety of conceptions that viewed the Son and the Holy Spirit as properties, accidents or modes of the Father, or along with the Father as "names" of presentations or manifestations of the one God.[1] Instead it is affirmed that there is a substantial and distinct identity to each of the three *hypostases*. The proposition that the three *hypostases* are one substance is however less easy to grasp.[2]

The most common metaphor for expressing the unity of substance (*ousia*) and the distinction of the three *hypostases* is that between a "common nature" and individuals that instantiate that nature. However, this is an anthropomorphic metaphor and acknowledged as such by the Cappadocians. For example, Gregory of Nazianzus argues,

> "What was Adam? A creature of God. What, then, was Eve? A fragment of the creature. And what was Seth? The begotten of both. Does it, then, seem to you that creature and fragment and begotten are the same thing? Of course it does not. But were not these persons consubstantial? Of course they were. Well, then, here it is an acknowledged fact that different persons may have the same substance. I say this, not that I would attribute creation or fraction or any property of a body to the Godhead...but that I may contemplate in these, as on a stage, things which are objects of thought alone."[3]

It is important to interpret Gregory's remark in an anthropomorphic light: Gregory is not saying that the persons of the Trinity are only one substance in the sense that they have a common nature. Though they do have a common nature, this does not adequately express the numerical identity of substance implied by 'homoousios'. According to the analogy of "nature", there is no stronger sense of unity between the persons than

---

[1] This series of denials illustrates the important negative method used to define divine substance.

[2] Prestige's observes this distinction in this way, "...to assert the equality of the three persons is a very different thing, as history had proved, from showing in what sense Christianity can interpret the affirmation, to which it is absolutely bound, that the three are one God.", *Fathers*, 87.

[3] Gregory of Nazianzus, *Theological Orations*, 5.11, reproduced in *Christology of the Later Fathers* (ed., E. R. Hardy: Grand Rapids: WJK Press, 1954).

that between members of a species.[1]   To employ another common material metaphor, the unity of substance shared by the persons of the Trinity was also pictured as a participation of the "same stuff". Gregory puts it in this way,

> "To us there is one God, for the Godhead is one, and all that proceeds from him is referred to one, though we believe in three persons…but the Godhead is, to speak concisely, undivided in separate persons…"[2]

These explanations of the unity of the Godhead involve the negative circumscribing of various anthropomorphic analogies. This strategy is complemented by the careful and austere circumscription of how the separate *hypostases* are distinct as persons. For the Cappadocians, such a complementary strategy was necessary if the unity of the Godhead was not to be divided asunder; hence, their austere and minimalist proposal for distinguishing the persons:

> "…while we confess the invariable character of the nature, we do not deny the difference in respect of cause, and that which is caused, by which alone we apprehend that one person is distinguished from another…and again in that which if of the cause, we recognize another distinction…"[3]

In making the distinction between *ousia* and *hypostases* in this way, the Cappadocians developed Nicaea. They rejected the Nicene treatment of these terms as synonyms, restricted *ousia* as to an expression of unity, and clarified the distinction of Father Son and Holy Spirit as separate *hypostases*. In this sense, Nicaea falls short in the quality of its theological achievement; however, it remains true that in expressing a unity of substance, Nicaea represents a significant evolutionary step in church doctrine. It provided the beginnings of a metaphysics that would underlie the economy of the divine Trinity.

---

[1] The same observation would be applicable if we to use the category of genus rather than species, or for that matter any other class-member analogy such as "natural kind".

[2] Gregory of Nazianzus, *Theological Orations*, 5.14.

[3] Gregory of Nyssa, *Quod non sint tres dii*, reproduced in Hardy, ed., *Fathers*, 266.

9. Conclusion

The doctrine of the Trinity is a philosophical doctrine; it is an exercise in philosophical theology. Its categories are philosophical (even if its words are Biblical) and its main concern is to express how men can speak of God. It seeks to preserve the impassibility of God, the uniqueness of God, and the non-anthropomorphic nature of God. Its problem is how to speak of God with human language. Hence, its formulations are austere. The 4c. Fathers wanted to place the Father, Son, and Holy Spirit into a relationship within the framework of one Godhead, while maintaining a non-anthropomorphic purity. The various creeds of the 4c. are successive attempts to achieve this objective.

APPENDIX B
Matthew 28:19

1. Introduction

The triadic formula of Matt 28:19, 'in the name of the Father, and of the Son, and of the Holy Spirit' (KJV) is a trinitarian 'proof text', but it has been suspected[1] by New Testament (NT) scholars precisely because of its Trinitarian overtones, although not by textual critics. A quick search on Google will produce websites and downloadable PDF files for and against the **originality** of this formula. However, the main starting point for anyone's investigation should be the 'New Testament Virtual Manuscript Room' of the University of Muenster, which will yield the academic sources for the text-critical discussion along with the occasional NT commentator listed as well.[2]

Within text-critical scholarship, the modern classic (1901) statement raising the question of originality (and voicing doubts) is that by F. C. Conybeare,[3] but his doubts were soon 'answered' by E. Riggenbach[4] in German and J. Lebreton in French;[5] and then in the English language journals by F. H. Chase[6] (1905). Thereafter, there has been a succession of

---

[1] Hence, O. Michel stated, "Admittedly this missionary charge of Matthew is open to critical suspicions of having been liturgically enlarged or worked over." "The Conclusion of Matthew's Gospel" in *The Interpretation of Matthew* (ed., G. Stanton; London: SPCK, 1983), 30-41 (34). This remark doesn't imply that he himself was suspicious. Or again, S. K. Wood observes, "Scripture scholars are generally agreed that this represents a later development of the text and clearly reflects a liturgical tradition already in place in the Matthean community." in her essay "The Trinity in the Liturgy, Sacraments, and Mysticism" in *The Cambridge Companion to The Trinity* (ed. P. C. Phan; Cambridge: Cambridge University Press, 2011), 381-397 (384).
[2] http://ntvmr.uni-muenster.de/home. A search on the website for the conjectures about Matt 28:19 will yield a table of scholars, papers and books for and against the genuineness (originality) of the triadic formula.
[3] F. C. Conybeare, "The Eusebian Form of the Text Matth. 28, 19," *ZNW* 2 (1901): 275-288; "Three Early Modifications of the Text of the Gospels," *Hibbert Journal* 1 (1902): 96-113.
[4] E. Riggenbach, „*Der Trinitarische Taufbefehl*" *BFCT* 7 (1903): 7-103.
[5] J. Lebreton, *Histoire du dogme de la Trinité* (Paris, 1910).
[6] F. H. Chase, "The Lord's Command to Baptize," *JTS* 6 (1905): 481-517.

papers, for and against, but the triadic formula has not been dislodged from its position in the standard Greek text.

The first full-length thesis to set out the case for the originality of the triadic formula was that of B. H. Cuneo,[1] which in turn received a critical review from Conybeare.[2] Within NT scholarship, throughout the twentieth century, commentaries have lined up for and against, with those against usually preferring the shorter variant 'in my name' (or just nothing) as original to Matthew.[3] A variety of arguments have been used in the 'against corner' with the evidence of the fourth century church historian, Eusebius (265-339 CE), being the main plank of the case; hence, the shorter reading is known as the 'Eusebian' reading.

In this Appendix, our objective is to set out the data for and against the originality of the triadic formula, which we do in **Section Two**. Whether it is original is a 'balance of probabilities' argument; it involves the textual tradition, considerations of NT history, and questions of style.[4] We will argue that it is original to Matthew.

Once we have settled that it is original to Matthew, and indeed the words of Jesus, we can enquire as to its meaning. Is it incipient Trinitarianism? Why does Jesus associate the Father, the Son and the holy Spirit in this way? Why is such an association rare in the NT writings and why does Jesus do it at the time of his final ascension to heaven? These are questions we cover in **Section Three** of this Appendix.

Finally, in **Section Four** of the Appendix we will look at some objections to our interpretation.

---

[1] B. H. Cuneo, *The Lord's Command to Baptise* (Washington DC: Catholic University of America, 1923). [Online].
2 F. C. Conybeare, "The Lord's Command to Baptise, being No. V of the N. T. Studies of the Catholic University of America by Bernard Henry Cuneo," *JTS* (1924): 191-197.
[3] For a review of scholarship, see B. H. Green, "Matthew 28:19, Eusebius, and the *lex orandi*" in *The Making of Orthodoxy* (ed., R. Williams; Cambridge: CUP, 2002), 124-141.
[4] Whatever the judgment, it will be clear from the data that this is not an issue of the 'corruption of Scripture'. B. D. Ehrman, *The Orthodox Corruption of Scripture* (Oxford, OUP, 1993), doesn't include the text.

2. Manuscript Evidence

Today's standard Greek New Testament (GNT) does not offer 'in my name' as a variant for Matt 28:19, but it did feature in the apparatus of the standard Greek text of the early part of the twentieth century – that of Nestlé. As B. H. Green notes, "The Eusebian reading, after featuring in previous editions of Nestlé's Greek Testament from 1927 to 1963, disappeared from the apparatus in the Aland's recension of 1979 (Nestlé-Aland[26])."[1] It didn't feature in editions of GNT from the first 1966 edition onwards under the lead editorship of K. Aland, and hence Metzger doesn't discuss the variant in his commentary on the GNT.[2] With the recension of Nestlé under the leadership of Aland from 1979, and the effective merger of the Nestlé and GNT editions, it disappeared.

The issue is a simple one. T. Wasserman has recently described the earliest papyri witnesses to the text of Matthew and he documents the fact that Matt 28:19 does not occur in any of the early papyri up to the mid-4th century CE.[3] The manuscript evidence for the longer text of Matt 28:19 begins with era of the uncials in the late 4th century and it is ubiquitous. The older evidence for the shorter reading as well as the longer reading comes from patristic citations, starting in the sub-Apostolic era up to and including the Nicene Fathers and particularly Eusebius. The editors of GNT have generally given priority to the witness of the manuscripts over

---

[1] Green, "Matthew 28:19, Eusebius, and the *lex orandi*", 138. For a history of the standard editions of the Greek New Testaments and the relationship of the Nestle-Aland editions, see K. Aland and B, Aland, *The Text of the New Testament* (Grand Rapids: Eerdmans, 1989), 20-36. J. Verheyden notes that the variant appeared in 'old' Nestle from 1906 onwards and not just 'new' Nestle (1927 onwards) as Green implies, i.e. just after Conybeare's paper had appeared – "The Gospel Text of Eusebius of Caesarea" in *Philohistôr* (eds., A. Schoors and P. Van Deun; Leuven: Peeters Press, 1994), 35-70 (69). The history of the Nestle is divided into 'old' and 'new' periods in Aland and Aland, *The Text of the New Testament*, 20.

[2] Metzger, *A Textual Commentary on the Greek New Testament* – commenting on the third edition.

[3] T. Wasserman, "The Early Text of Matthew" in *The Early Text of the New Testament* (eds., C. E. Hill & M. J. Kruger; Oxford: OUP, 2014), 83-107 (86-87 has the table of manuscript contents). This is just happenstance because what is missing is not just Matt 28:19 but various parts of Matthew. Only a conspiracy theorist would say Jesus' words were removed deliberately.

patristic citation in determining the text of the New Testament, and hence they have regarded the longer reading as original.

The question, though, is what we do with the patristic data as this is the **oldest data** we have for this text. Here, we have data for both readings and we need to explain them in their patristic setting. Can we say either is original to Matthew? If we decide that the shorter reading is original, why is this not reflected in the later manuscripts? If the longer reading is original, why do we have the shorter reading at all? What textual 'story' do we tell for both readings, or was there a combined text which the Fathers cut and pasted for their particular purposes?

The patristic data suggests 'in my name' existed in the manuscript traditions before the mid-4c., but the total absence of any shorter reading in our extant manuscripts requires an explanation, and here various hypotheses have been suggested. The explanation we will pursue is that the shorter reading is from a **Hebrew Matthew** and the triadic reading is from a **Greek Matthew**. There are in effect two books and not one; the Greek Matthew was widespread, and **the Hebrew Matthew had already substantially fallen away by the time of Eusebius**. The two gospels are related by author, but the Greek Matthew is not an exact translation of the Hebrew Matthew but a derivative work (with Hebrew Matthew a source); they are two gospels by the same author and hence equally authoritative. What motivates this hypothesis is the evidence for the shorter reading and the need to explain the source of that reading. We cannot say that 'in my name' is the church father summarising the triadic formula or that the triadic formula is expanding 'in my name'; both clauses have different functions.

Again, theoretically, we might suppose the readings were combined in an original single reading of 'Go make disciples in my name, baptising them in the name of the Father and of the Son and of the holy Spirit'. However, not only is there no manuscript evidence for this *combined* reading, there is no patristic evidence either, so we can reject this proposal. Apart from this though, the combination doesn't cohere well since a person becomes a disciple through baptism, and the 'making' and the 'baptising' would have different name specifications in a combined reading – invoking the authority of Jesus with the 'in my name' specification, and then *nominating* (or naming) disciples with the triadic formula in baptism.

Or again, we might suppose that the shorter reading is just the relevant church father missing out the baptismal clause because he doesn't need it for the point that he wants to make clear. This explanation doesn't work because it's not so much the absence of the baptismal clause from a shorter quotation but the *presence* of the 'in my name' in the first place that requires explanation.

Finally, we might say that the 'in my name' has just been added by the relevant church father by way of merging Matt 28:19 with Luke 24:47 or the general testimony of Acts. So, not only does the church father miss out the triadic clause, he is doing harmless assimilation of scriptural texts through an addition. Again, when we look at the actual texts of Eusebius, this hypothesis doesn't provide a satisfactory explanation. We cannot say that the shorter reading is Eusebius' own expansion because he relies on it *as Scripture*.

The last two hypotheses are the most common ones in papers that defend the originality of the triadic formula.[1] However, the underlying assumption on the part of scholars is that 'Matthew' is **one book** and we need to determine the original text (and for some conservative scholars, this will give the original words of Jesus). Our competing hypothesis is that 'Matthew' was **two books**. We need to explain the origin of both readings as separate texts; we cannot reduce one reading to the other or side-line the shorter reading.[2]

2.1 Eusebius' Citations

Patristic citations may be from memory or a text; the text may be varied by the church father or be identifiable as from a type of text known to textual critics; the writings of the church father may have been altered later by copyists. Hence, in J. Verheyden's review of scholarship on the Gospel text handled by Eusebius he says "...it is clear that the reconstruction of a Father's Bible text can be a complex undertaking."[3]

Eusebius of Caesarea had available to him an extensive (and recently restored) Christian library from which he had access to Gospel texts. Jerome (c. 345-419 CE) mentions the library in connection with the Gospel of Matthew,[4]

---

[1] For example, this is why the approaches of F. H. Chase and B. H. Cuneo are unsatisfactory; see below.

[2] When evaluating patristic evidence for whether a text preserves the original of a NT writing, we have to satisfy ourselves that a church father is quoting an actual text and not just doing his own thing with a text.

[3] Verheyden, "The Gospel Text of Eusebius of Caesarea", 45.

[4] J. R. Edwards, *The Hebrew Gospel & The Development of the Synoptic Tradition* (Grand Rapids: Eerdmans, 2009), 28-37, discusses Jerome's testimony.

Matthew, also known as Levi, a tax-collector who became an apostle, was the first in Judea to compose a Gospel of Christ in Hebrew letters and words, on whose account those of the circumcision believed, although it is not certain who later translated the Gospel into Greek. Indeed, the Hebrew itself was diligently brought out by Pamphilus the Martyr and is still to this day in the library of Caesarea. *Vir. Ill.* 3

The point in this testimony is important for our assessment of Eusebius' use of Matthew: it establishes the background for his citing Matt 28:19 – he had access to Hebrew and Greek texts of Matthew. Our hypothesis immediately suggests itself: the shorter Matt 28:19 reading comes from the Hebrew and the longer reading comes from the Greek. This would explain why only the triadic baptismal formula is found in the later manuscript tradition. The more commonly used Greek manuscript tradition **had always been triadic**, and it was only in the dusty libraries of Palestine and a Hebrew edition of Matthew that a shorter reading was preserved.

Scholars tend to operate with a binary approach: either the long or the short reading is original to Matthew. Hence, they argue for their preferred alternative. They explain how either the longer or shorter form is secondary and later. The proffered explanations cancel each other out and don't explain how Eusebius could use both texts **as authoritative Scripture**. The better hypothesis is that both the Hebrew and the Greek Matthew were regarded by him as Scripture.

Eusebius cites Matt 28:19 in his writings several times in the longer and shorter forms and we will first describe texts with the short form.[1]

2.1.1 Shorter Form
Examples with (or alluding to) "Go ye and make disciples of all nations in my name" include,[2]

Jerome is merely repeating the testimony of Papias' record by Eusebius (*Ecc. Hist.* iii 39.16) that Matthew wrote his *logia* in Hebrew.
[1] Green's statistics for the two readings are: shorter (16 or which 3 are duplicates); longer (5); and for neither (9); the 'neither' reading would be a use of Matthew where there is just a mention of going to all nations - "Matthew 28:19, Eusebius, and the *lex orandi*", 125.
[2] Cuneo, *The Lord's Command to Baptise*, 41-42, tabulates the data.

(1) *Commentary on the Psalms* 59, 9,[1]

> He said, "I have not come except to the lost sheep of the
> house of Israel" [Mt. 15:24]. And he exhorted his disciples
> to preach the gospel to them [the Jews] first, saying, "Go
> nowhere among the Gentiles, and enter no town of the
> Samaritans, but go rather to the lost sheep of the house of
> Israel" (Mt. 10:5-6]. Then after these [were evangelized] he
> <u>commanded</u> his disciples to preach the good news to all
> nations <u>in his name</u>.[2]

The basis for seeing here an allusion to Matt 28:19 is, first, Eusebius refers
to a situation where Jesus gave a *command* (a speech act) and, secondly, he
uses the expression 'all nations' (πάντα τὰ ἔθνη) which is used in Matt
28:19. On the other hand, Eusebius may also be alluding to Luke 24:47
where 'all nations' occurs along with 'in his name'. However, Luke uses
the preposition *epi* whereas Eusebius quotes Matthew with *en* (and the
triadic formula uses *eis*) This makes it unlikely that Eusebius is conflating
Matthew with Luke.

If Eusebius is running his allusions together, we cannot be certain he is
using a short text of Matt 28:19, although we should note that Luke 24:47
does not record a speech act of commanding. Nevertheless, E J Hubbard
is wrong to regard such allusiveness as an "inexact quoting of Scripture";[3]
Eusebius may well have been alluding to Scripture in *exactly* the manner he
wanted, and this is the point. The use of a notion of inexactitude doesn't
explain the use of a shorter Matthew text because we know Eusebius
respects and reveres Scripture. Obviously, we can't say that Eusebius is
alluding to 'in the name of the Father, and of the Son, and of the Holy
Spirit' inexactly with 'in my name'; rather, he is likely using a short form of
Matt 28:19 as well as alluding to Luke 24:47.

---

[1] The other examples of the short form in Eusebius' commentaries are
Commentary on the Psalms are Ps 65, 6; 67, 31-36; 76, 20; in his *Commentary on
Isaiah*, 18, 2; 34, 16; see Conybeare, "The Eusebian Form of the Text
Matth. 28, 19," 276.

[2] Conybeare, "The Eusebian Form of the Text Matth. 28, 19," 275-276
gives the Greek text and this translation is from B. J. Hubbard, *The
Matthean Redaction of Primitive Apostolic Commissioning: An Exegesis of Matthew
28:16-20* (Atlanta: Scholars Press, 1974), 155.

[3] Hubbard, *The Matthean Redaction of Primitive Apostolic Commissioning: An
Exegesis of Matthew 28:16-20*, 156.

(2) *History of the Church* 3, 5,

> But to teach their message they travelled into every land in
> the power of Christ, who had said to them: 'Go and make
> disciples of all nations in my name.'[1]

This is a clear quotation of Matt 28:19, and whether from memory or
from sight, the question is what text underlies the citation. This evidence
provides a foundation for reading the 'in his name' in his commentary on
the Psalms 59, 9 (see above) as from a short Matt 28:19 rather than Luke
24:47. On the other hand, we should bear in mind that a mind infused
with Scripture is likely to allude to multiple texts.

(3) *Oration of Praise to Constantine* 16, 8,

> Surely none save our only Saviour has done this, when, after
> his victory over death, he spoke the word to his followers,
> and fulfilled it by the event, saying to them, 'Go ye, and
> make disciples of all nations in my name.'[2]

This is another clear quotation. There is no reason why Eusebius should
have not used the triadic formula in making his point. The question is why
he is using 'in my name'. Is he quoting a short text of Matt 28:19 from a
manuscript to which he has access?

What we can note from this example, and the previous one, is that 'in my
name' is associated with the verb 'to make disciples' whereas the triadic
formula is associated with the verb 'to baptise'.

(4) *Demonstratio Evangelica* 3, 6-7,

> For he did not enjoin them 'to make disciples of all nations'
> simply and without qualification, but with the essential
> addition 'in his name.' For so great was the virtue attaching
> to the appellation that the apostle says, God bestowed on
> him the name above every name, that in the name of Jesus
> every knee shall bow of things in heaven and on earth. It
> was right therefore that he should emphasize the virtue of
> the power residing in his name but hidden from many, and

---

[1] Translation from *Eusebius: The History of the Church* (trans., G. A.
Williamson; rev. ed., A. Louth; London: Penguin, 1989).
[2] Translation from *NPNF*[2].

therefore say to his apostles, 'Go ye and make disciples of all nations in my name'.[1]

...they could only have succeeded in their daring venture, by a power more divine, and more strong than man's, and by cooperation of him who said to them: 'Make disciples of all nations in my name.'[2]

This example demonstrates Eusebius' **exegetical interest in the actual text**, so that we can be certain 'in my name' is in a text he knows.[3] The question is whether he is focussing on one part of a text which has a following clause reading, 'baptizing them in the name of the Father, and of the Son, and of the Holy Spirit', or whether he just has a short text with only 'in my name'. As far as textual criticism goes, this would appear to be undecidable. It is not enough to hypothesize with Cuneo that his argument had no need of the baptismal clause and this explains its absence.[4] The text-critical matter to be explained is the presence of 'in my name' and not the absence of the baptismal clause. Hence, the same applies for Eusebius' other citation in *Demonstratio* 9.

At this point, an historical consideration can be suggested. What would Jesus have said? Could he just have said 'make disciples in my name', to which Luke 24:47 gives support (along with Acts and Paul); or could he have said, 'make disciples in my name, baptizing them in the name of the Father, and of the Son and of the Holy Spirit'? Or, did he just say, 'make disciples, baptizing them in the name of the Father, and of the Son and of the Holy Spirit'? These questions do not exhaust the situation: Jesus might have uttered his command in the same conversational exchange in more than one way and at different points in that exchange. We can often form a larger picture of Jesus' conversations when we compare the Synoptic Gospels, and a Hebrew Matthew and a Greek Matthew might have recorded two different parts of the Great Commission. One part has an

---

[1] Translation from Conybeare, "Three Early Modifications of the Text of the Gospels," 105; the Greek text is in Conybeare, "The Eusebian Form of the Text Matth. 28, 19," 277.

[2] Translation from Hubbard, *The Matthean Redaction of Primitive Apostolic Commissioning: An Exegesis of Matthew 28:16-20*, 154; the Greek text is in Conybeare, "The Eusebian Form of the Text Matth. 28, 19," 277.

[3] *Contra* Chase, "The Lord's Command to Baptize", 492, who wants us to believe that Eusebius adds in 'in my name' of his own invention and then relies on the phrase in his argument.

[4] Cuneo, *The Lord's Command to Baptise*, 75.

emphasis on 'making' and the other on 'baptizing'. If this is the case, our hypothesis of a Hebrew and a Greek text at Caesarea would explain mixed usage on the part of Eusebius.

In any event, it seems clear that Eusebius has in mind just a short text (and as we will see below, he knows the triadic text also) rather than a combined text. We do not need to agree with Eusebius' exegesis,[1] but clearly Jesus' name is central, and the actual presence of 'in my name' in his text is essential to his point; if he had added 'in my name' as a gloss of his own, by way of summary or paraphrase, it would subvert the point of quoting Jesus' *own* words.[2]

(5) *Theophania* 5, 46,

> For it was not that he <u>ordered</u> them simply and without discriminating, 'to go and make disciples of all peoples', but with this important addition, that he said 'in my name'…[3]

The observation to make here is the same as before: **Eusebius is relying on reporting a speech act of Jesus that is a command or order** and his point rests on giving the correct words of that speech act. We cannot explain his use of Scripture as one where he assimilates Matt 28:19 with the testimony of Mark, Luke or Acts. For example, Luke 24:47 is not a speech act of commanding, but a third person description by Jesus of what would happen to 'the Christ'. Rather, we have to concede that Eusebius has a text with a speech act of commanding that has 'in my name'.

2.1.2 Longer Form
Eusebius also uses the longer reading in writings from later in his life (c. 336-340 CE). Conybeare makes heavy weather of this fact, and argues Eusebius only uses the triadic formula after the trinitarian decision of Nicea (325 CE). This is an implausible strategy to follow, and assuming these later writings are all Eusebius' hand, they show his respect for the triadic formula.

---

[1] It is unclear whether Eusebius thinks 'in my name' is about authority or about something more mystical – incorporation into a name.
[2] *Contra* Hubbard, *The Matthean Redaction of Primitive Apostolic Commissioning: An Exegesis of Matthew 28:16-20*, 154.
[3] Translation from Conybeare, "The Eusebian Form of the Text Matth. 28, 19," 278; other examples are *Theophania* 4, 16; 5, 17; 5, 46; and 5, 49.

(1) *Against Marcellus of Ancyra* 1, 1,

> What was this Gospel? The same which our Saviour is said to have given to his disciples, when he said to them: 'Going make disciples of all the nations, baptising them in the name of the Father and of the Son and of the Holy Ghost.' For he alone has favoured us with the grace of knowing the Holy Trinity by means of the mystical regeneration...[1]

The reason for the use of the longer form of Matt 28:19 is clear; Eusebius is making a point about baptism and knowing the Trinity. This trinitarian use of the baptismal formula of Matthew is common amongst the church Fathers, but it doesn't mean that Jesus' triadic formula is trinitarian. To establish Jesus' meaning, we just have to consider his teaching about the Father and the Spirit in his Upper Room discourse in John. Similarly, to appreciate how Jesus spoke of himself as 'the Son', we have to consider his teaching in John, rather than the Synoptics. What Jesus is doing with the third person impersonal form of address, 'the Son', **is to create what will be the new structural relationship for a believer to relate to God, his father.** It is John, rather than the Synoptics, which brings out this teaching, but there are the occasional examples of the teaching in the Synoptics like Matt 28:19.[2] This teaching is not trinitarian because it is subordinationist; the Son is subordinate to the Father and an intercessor between God and human beings.[3]

(2) *Ecclesiastical Theology* 3, 5,

> None of these spirits can be compared to the Comforting Spirit. Therefore this one alone is comprised in the holy and thrice-blessed Trinity, as also our Lord in commanding his disciples to administer baptism to all the nations who would believe in him did not order them to administer it in any

---

[1] Translation from Hubbard, *The Matthean Redaction of Primitive Apostolic Commissioning: An Exegesis of Matthew 28:16-20*, 157; see also Cuneo, *The Lord's Command to Baptise*, 82.

[2] In Matthew, Jesus usually speaks of himself in the third person with 'the Son of Man'; the only other text with 'the Son' is Matt 11:27.

[3] Certain theologians have talked of an 'economic Trinitarianism' in relation to the New Testament, but this is misleading and bad history-writing. Trinitarianism should be defined by the theological concerns of the fourth century which were to define the ontology of the Godhead and the relationships of the Father, Son and Spirit.

other way than by baptising them in the name of the Father, and of the Son, and of the Holy Ghost.[1]

The reason for the triadic formula is clear in this example: it functions as a proof text for the Trinity and particularly the inclusion of the holy Spirit.

(3) *Theophania* 3, 8,

> That at the outset he said that he would make them fishers of men, and in the end openly after his example they should make disciples of all peoples together with his peculiar aid. From the Gospel of Matthew, '…Go ye and make disciples of all peoples, and baptise them in the name of the Father and Son and Holy Ghost…'[2]

This text in *Theophania* should be read alongside the earlier text at 5, 46, which has only the short form of Matt 28:19. Together they acutely raise the question of what text or texts Eusebius is citing.

2.1.3 No Short or Long Form
Eusebius quotes Matt 28:19 without either 'in my name' or the longer triadic formula, for example,

(1) *Demonstratio Evangelica* 1, 3,

> Accordingly, when our Saviour and Lord, Jesus, the Son of God, after his resurrection from the dead, said to his disciples, 'Going make disciples of all nations', he added, 'teaching them to keep all that I have commanded you.' He did not command them to teach the nations the Mosaic observances…[3]

Eusebius' quotation here has neither the triadic baptismal formula nor the 'in my name' expression because his point is about the superior status of

---

[1] Translation from Hubbard, *The Matthean Redaction of Primitive Apostolic Commissioning: An Exegesis of Matthew 28:16-20*, 157; see also Cuneo, *The Lord's Command to Baptise*, 83.
[2] Translation from Conybeare, "The Eusebian Form of the Text Matth. 28, 19," 279.
[3] My translation. The Greek text is in Conybeare, "The Eusebian Form of the Text Matth. 28, 19," 276; Cuneo, *The Lord's Command to Baptise*, 72, has another English translation.

Jesus' commands. Other examples of his use of Matt 28:19 in this cut-down form and for this or similar reasons are his *Demonstratio Evangelica* 1, 4 and 6, as well as 3, 6-7; and his *Commentary on the Psalms*, 46, 4 and 95, 3.[1] However, what these examples do not tell us is what Eusebius is cutting out in his citation – whether the triadic clause of the 'in my name' expression – or both.

(2) *Ecclesiastical Theology* 3, 3

> For the Saviour said to his holy fountains: 'Going make disciples of all nations'. Therefore it is entirely clear that the holy Apostles are figuratively called fountains by the prophet [Solomon].[2]

This is an even shorter citation of Matthew, but the same point applies as with (1) - we can't tell what is missing.

(3) *Theophania* 3, 14,

> Who, of those that ever existed, is the mortal man, ...who bore all this pre-eminence...and could effect so much, that he should be preached throughout the whole earth? And that his name should fill the hearing and tongues of every people upon the face of the whole earth? But this no man has done excepting our Saviour alone, who said to his disciples by word and fulfilled it be deed, 'Go and teach all peoples' ...

Eusebius does not use the 'in my name' expression here or the triadic clause, but his concern is with the name of Christ being preached and we might have expected 'in my name' or the triadic clause (or both), and so we don't know what he is omitting. On the other hand, a very similar point almost word for word is made in his *On Praise of Constantine*, 16, which does include 'in my name'.[3]

These examples, (1) - (3), have led commentators to argue that Eusebius quotes Scripture inexactly. So, E. J. Hubbard concludes, "He clearly is capable of quoting the NT inexactly and of combining or at least grouping in close proximity passages which in some way relate to each other. These

---

[1] For English translations see Cuneo, *The Lord's Command to Baptise*, 72-73.

[2] Translation from Cuneo, *The Lord's Command to Baptise*, 74.

[3] Cuneo, *The Lord's Command to Baptise*, 76.

tendencies of his argue for the conclusion that the shorter reading is not based upon textual evidence, but represents a free use of 28:19 combined with 'in my name', a phrase widely used in the NT."[1]

Such tendencies exist in many of the church Fathers (and Bible students down the ages), and the explanation works for the omission of parts of a *known* verse. But we have no evidence that the triadic clause and 'in my name' *were ever present together* in Matt 28:19 – either in a manuscript or a patristic citation. And so, the strategy of explaining the absence of either doesn't work for our text – what we need first is evidence of their presence together. A notion of inexactitude may help explain the omission of something from a known and established text, although the notion is being badly applied by the scholar (a notion of shortening is more accurate), but it doesn't explain the absence of things never found together when those things *look like* competing alternatives.

For example, Chrysostom in his Homilies (*NPNF*) quotes the triadic form of Matt 28:19 in his exposition of Heb 2:18, but in his exposition of Eph 2:10 he merely cites the text as "Go and make disciples of all nations, teaching them to observe all things whatsoever I commanded you". This is no different from Eusebius' omission of the triadic formula in *Demonstratio Evangelica* 1, 3, cited above. We cannot infer on this basis of omission that Chrysostom or Eusebius do not know the triadic formula. However, Eusebius' singular use of 'in my name' cannot be described as an example of omitting the triadic name clause, because it is not known that Matt 28:19 ever had both the triadic clause and 'in my name' together. The inclusion of a shorter 'name' authority expression *looks like* a competing alternative to a 'naming' baptismal clause. It is this that requires explanation, and any appeal to the common practice of omission is a red herring.[2] Or again, we might say that what we are trying to explain in the Eusebian data or the Patristic data is why there is no combined reading.

2.2 Other Patristic Citations and Allusions

The longer and shorter forms of Matt 28:19 (as well as neither) are referenced through citation or allusion in other patristic texts, but evidence of the use of or allusion to the shorter form is **much more limited** than that of the longer form. We can take this as evidence for

---

[1] Hubbard, *The Matthean Redaction of Primitive Apostolic Commissioning: An Exegesis of Matthew 28:16-20*, 161; see also Cuneo, *The Lord's Command to Baptise*, 95-110.

[2] *Contra* Chase, "The Lord's Command to Baptize", 487-488; 492.

Greek Matthew superseding the Hebrew Matthew because of the Gentile expansion of the church. We will first describe texts with the shorter form.

2.2.1 Shorter Form

(1) The *Didache* is usually dated around c. 100-150 CE,[1] and it has evidence of the shorter text,

> But let no one eat or drink of your Thanksgiving (Eucharist), but they who have been <u>baptized into the name of the Lord</u>; for concerning this also the Lord hath said, 'Give not that which is holy to the dogs'. *Did.* 9:5[2]

This instruction about the Eucharist reflects the testimony of Acts – that baptism was into or to (*eis*) the name of the Lord. It states the rule the table of the Lord was not an 'open' one to those who had not been baptised.

(2) Justin Martyr (100-165 CE) may allude to the shorter form of Matt 28:19,

> Therefore, just as God did not inflict his anger on account of those seven thousand men, even so he has now neither yet inflicted judgment, nor does inflict it, knowing that daily some [of you] <u>are becoming disciples in the name of Christ,</u> and quitting the path of error; who are also receiving gifts, each as he is worthy, illumined through the name of this Christ. *Dialogue with Trypho* 39 (c. 130-140 CE)[3]

The case here for an allusion to a short text of Matthew ('in my name') rests on the use of the same verb for 'make disciples' (μαθητεύω), and to bring out the connection we could translate this text as 'being made disciples in the name of Christ'. We might dismiss this from being an allusion and see Justin's language just as a general description of the making of disciples based on his reading of Acts. However, Acts doesn't

---

[1] See J. A. T. Robinson, *Redating the New Testament* (London: SCM Press, 1976), 324-327, who argues for a date 40-60 CE. This is too early, and most scholars date the document c. 100-150 CE.

[2] Translations of the *Didache* are from J. B. Lightfoot & J R Harmer, *The Apostolic Fathers* (2nd ed: London: Macmillan, 1926).

[3] Translation from *ANF*; see Conybeare, "Three Early Modifications of the Text of the Gospels," 106, for a discussion of the Greek.

use the verb μαθητεύω in its examples of conversion and initiation, and it only uses the verb 'to baptize' (βαπτίζω) in connection with the 'in the name of' formula. So, while 'in the name of Christ' could be picking up any of 'in my name' (Matt 28:19, short text), 'in the name of Jesus Christ' (Acts 2:38), 'in the name of the Lord Jesus' (Acts 8:16; 19:5), or 'in the name of the Lord (Acts 10:48), the concept of 'being made a disciple' is informed by Matthew's gospel.[1]

(3) *Shepherd of Hermas Similitudes* 9, 17.4

> Because, he said, <u>all the nations</u> that dwell under heaven were called by hearing and <u>believing upon the name of the Son of God</u>. Having, therefore, received the seal, they had one understanding and one mind; and their faith became one, and their love one, and with the name they bore also the spirits of the virgins. On this account the building of the tower became of one colour, bright as the sun.[2]

The possible allusion to a short form of Matt 28:19 here is even weaker than that of Justin Martyr. It rests on the mention of 'all the nations' and the belief 'upon the name of the Son of God'; but this is so general as to be of no value in establishing a Hebrew Matthew with the short text.[3]

2.2.2 Longer Form
Examples of the use of the longer form of Matt 28:19 in the church Fathers before Nicea **are plentiful**. What they show is that we can't really explain the long text as originating in a particular region such as West rather than the East (which Conybeare suggested[4]). For example,

(1) The *Didache* also takes pride of place in the list of patristic testimony to the longer form.

> But concerning baptism, thus shall ye baptise: having first recited all these things, baptise in the name of the Father, and of the Son, and of the Holy Spirit, in living [running] water. But if thou hast not living water, baptise in other

---

[1] See the discussion in Chase, "The Lord's Command to Baptize", 489-490 who says (490) the evidence is "very slight"; this seems correct.
[2] Translation from *ANF*.
[3] Chase, "The Lord's Command to Baptize", 490, reasonably concludes that this evidence can be "set aside".
[4] Verheyden, "The Gospel Text of Eusebius of Caesarea", 69.

water; and if thou art not able in cold, then in warm. But if
thou hast neither, then pour water on the head thrice in the
name of the Father and of the Son and of the Holy Spirit.
Did. 7:1-3

This adds an additional option for baptism of pouring water in the
absence of running water (a river), but our interest is in its triadic formula
fitting Greek Matthew. Of course, some scholars have suggested that both
Mathew and the *Didache* reflect later liturgical practice in the church rather
than the words of Jesus. But there is little value in just asserting that
something has been interpolated when the only *alleged* problem is that it
doesn't fit Jesus' way of speaking or the examples in Acts.

It might be argued[1] that *Did.* 7:1-3 is inconsistent with *Did.* 9:5, noted
above, which only mentions 'baptized into the name of the Lord', and it
might be concluded that *Did.* 7:1-3 has had the triadic formula added. But
this observation of inconsistency could support our saying either of these
parts of the *Didache* has been interpolated, since we know that in the 3c.
certain sects practised a singular baptism, and it was a matter of
controversy whether they were to be accepted without re-baptism. It
would serve a purpose if an instruction about the Eucharist was altered to
accommodate sectarians just as it might serve a purpose to insert a
trinitarian clause into the instructions for baptism to support the
development of the doctrine of the Trinity.

(2) Justin Martyr also alludes to the longer form,

Then they are brought by us where there is water, and are
regenerated in the same manner in which we were ourselves
regenerated. For, in the name of God, the Father and Lord
of the universe, and of our Saviour Jesus Christ, and of the
Holy Spirit, they then receive the washing with water. *First
Apology* 61 (c. 160 CE)[2]

Given his use of the tradition of 'making disciples in the name of Christ'
in his earlier writing, *Dialogue with Trypho* (see above), we should ask
whether he thought there was a need to reconcile the tradition of
baptising in the threefold name and the tradition of making disciples in

---

[1] For example, F. J. Foakes Jackson & K. Lake, *The Beginnings of Christianity*
(5 vols; London: Macmillan, 1920), 1:336.
[2] Translation from *ANF* and updated following Whittaker, *Documents of the
Baptismal Liturgy*, 2.

the singular name. If scholars and commentators in recent times have seen a tension, this does not mean that Justin or others in his era saw one. The existence of both traditions in different Hebrew and Greek gospels by Matthew might not have been an issue and the question of originality might not have been raised (in much the same way that the Synoptic accounts were harmonized). Indeed, with Justin Martyr, the sub-Apostolic church may have seen a Hebrew and a Greek Matthew as equally authoritative and recording different aspects of the Great Commission – one with an emphasis on the command to make disciples and the other with an emphasis on baptism.

(2) Clement of Alexandria (c. 150-215 CE) cites the longer form from a Gnostic heretic, Theodotus (c. 160 CE),

> And to the apostles he gives the command. "Going around preach ye and baptise those who believe in the name of the father and son and holy spirit". *Excerpta ex Theodoto* 76[1]

The interesting point about this example is that baptism using the triadic formula was not confined to just those who would become orthodox, although as example (4) below shows, heretical groups also baptised in the singular name.

(3) Tertullian (160-225 CE) uses the longer form twice and alludes to it once,

> For the *law* of baptizing has been *imposed*, and the formula prescribed: "Go," *he* saith, "teach the nations, baptizing them into the name of the Father, and of the Son, and of the Holy Spirit". *On Baptism* 13

> Accordingly, after one of these had been struck off, he commanded the eleven others, on his departure to the Father, to "go and teach *all* nations, who were to be baptized into the Father, and into the Son, and into the Holy Spirit. *The Prescription Against Heretics* 20

> After His resurrection He promises in a pledge to His disciples that He will send them the promise of His Father; and lastly, He commands them to baptize into the Father

---

[1] Translation from Conybeare, "Three Early Modifications of the Text of the Gospels," 106.

and the Son and the Holy Ghost, not into a unipersonal God. *Against Praxaeas* 26[1]

In the last two references, Tertullian does not include 'in the name of' as part of his usage of Matthew.

(4) Cyprian (early to mid 3c. CE, d. 258) uses the triadic formula several times and in particular it is deployed by several attendees of the Seventh Council of Carthage (258 CE) which was held to pronounce that only the church had the authority to carry out valid baptisms in the triune name. For example,

> The Lord, when after his resurrection he sent forth his apostles, charges them, saying, "All power is given unto me in heaven and in earth. Go ye therefore, and teach all nations, baptizing them in the name of the Father, and of the Son, and of the Holy Spirit: teaching them to observe all things whatsoever I have commanded you." *Epistles of Cyprian* 24[2]

This position was maintained against heretics who baptised only in the name of Jesus Christ, for example, some of the Marcionites.[3] What this shows for our purposes is that both the triadic formula and the singular formula were in use in the third century by groups professing to follow Christ (orthodox or heretic). However, this evidence doesn't identify the basis for the singular approach to baptism that 'heretics' were taking; we don't know if they drew upon Matthew, or were just following the examples of Acts.

2.3 The Baptismal Rite

As far as the evidence in Acts and Paul's letters goes, the baptismal rite was singular; people were baptised 'in/to the name of' Jesus (Acts 2:38; 8:16; 10:48; 19:5; 1 Cor 1:13, 15). Following the example of John the Baptist, individuals were baptised once in water (Matt 3:16; Acts 8:38), and Paul's metaphor of burial shows that the baptism was by full

---

[1] Translations from *ANF*; see Conybeare, "Three Early Modifications of the Text of the Gospels," 107, for a discussion of the Latin.

[2] Translation from *ANF*; see also letters 62 and 72 and the report of the council in *ANF* for the use of the triadic formula in relation to the Trinity.

[3] Cuneo, *The Lord's Command to Baptise*, 6-8.

immersion (Rom 6:4).[1] But it is worth noting that the examples of Acts do not record any formula (in a speech act) used during the act of baptism. For example, when Peter says, "Repent, and be baptized every one of you in the name of Jesus Christ for the remission of sins, and ye shall receive the gift of the holy Spirit". (Acts 2:38), he doesn't record the form of words used upon baptism; they might have been a triadic formula.

At some point in the sub-Apostolic era the rite became more varied and some churches practised a three-stage rite according to Justin Martyr. Whether we find the triadic formula intact in a text describing the baptismal rite, those texts that just describe a three-fold rite are also evidence for the antiquity of the triadic formula. However, the relationship of the triadic formula to the three-fold baptismal rite is not clear, because an utterance of the triadic formula would be just as applicable in a single-step act of baptism, whereas a three-stage baptism might require three utterances of the triadic formula or indeed break that formula up into three parts. The historical data is set out by E. C. Whittaker.[2] The question why this change from apostolic practice occurred is beyond the scope of this chapter.

Justin Martyr gives his reasoning for the threefold invocation of the names in his *First Apology*,

> And for this [rite] we have learned from the apostles <u>this reason</u>. Since at our birth we were born without our own knowledge or choice, by our parents coming together, and were brought up in bad habits and wicked training; in order that we may not remain the children of necessity and of ignorance, but may become the children of choice and knowledge, and may obtain in the water the remission of sins formerly committed, there is pronounced over him who chooses to be born again, and has repented of his sins, the name of God the Father and Lord of the universe; he who <u>leads</u> to the laver the person that is to be washed calling him by this name alone. For no one can utter the name of the ineffable God; and if any one dare to say that there is a name, he raves with a hopeless madness. And this washing is

---

[1] It is beyond the scope of this chapter to review the meaning of the Greek verb 'to baptise' — as to whether it is a verb used for 'immersing/dipping'.

[2] E. C. Whittaker, *Documents of the Baptismal Liturgy* (London: SPCK, repr., 2001).

called illumination, because they who learn these things are illuminated in their understandings. And in the name of Jesus Christ, who was crucified under Pontius Pilate, and in the name of the holy Spirit, who through the prophets foretold all things about Jesus, he who is illuminated is washed. *First Apology* 61[1]

The rite describes the utterance of the name of the Father during a procession to the laver, and the mention of the names of Jesus Christ and the holy Spirit presumably also occur at this time in that procession but the text is unclear.

2.4 Explaining the two forms of Matt 28:19

The patristic evidence for the longer form of Matt 28:19 far outweighs the evidence for the shorter form. This is to be expected for several reasons. First, the longer form is in the second gospel written by Matthew and this edition would naturally supersede the earlier Hebrew one. Secondly, as the church progressively became more Gentile, we should expect copies of the Hebrew Matthew to decrease in number. Thirdly, the longer form of the text is important for the ritual of baptism and teaching novitiates; the shorter form of Matthew is only significant for teaching a theological point about the making of disciples in all nations. Finally, the longer form of the text fits the developing doctrine of the Trinity and this became orthodoxy.

Hence, the preponderance of evidence for the longer text of Matthew does not count against the originality of the shorter reading. The problem we have is not to explain the longer text but to explain the existence of the shorter reading and the absence of a combined reading. Does the patristic usage of a shorter form of Matt 28:19 indicate that there was an actual text with the reading, or is it just down to the church father? If there is a text, is this from a Greek or Hebrew manuscript tradition?

Eusebius' writings are the main evidence for the short reading. The hypothesis that we have put forward is that Eusebius knows the shorter text from an earlier Hebrew Matthew rather than the later Greek Matthew. Other competing explanations of Eusebius' use of a shorter text that have been put forward include:

---

[1] Translation from *ANF* and updated following Whittaker, *Documents of the Baptismal Liturgy*, 2.

(1) The church practised a 'rule of secrecy' which forbad the disclosure of formula and rites associated with the sacraments such as baptism.[1] It is hypothesised that Eusebius omitted the triadic baptismal formula in keeping with this tradition. The problem with the hypothesis is that it doesn't fit the nature of Eusebius' material – it is not for the wider populace, but for initiates.[2] Rather, Eusebius is using a short form of Matt 28:19 because his point is about preaching and not baptism.

(2) Conybeare's explanation is that "It is evident that this [shorter form] was the text found by Eusebius in the very ancient codices collected fifty to a hundred and fifty years before his birth by his great predecessors. Of any other form of text, he had never heard, and knew nothing until he had visited Constantinople and attended the council of Nice."[3] This argument places the origin of the longer form in the West, with Eusebius encountering it from the western Fathers at Constantinople. Conybeare's argument is that Eusebius only uses the triadic formula in his later writings and in trinitarian controversy and that this is because he came to know of it in later life. This explanation seems implausible given Eusebius' access to an extensive Christian library, his experience of other churches on any travels in his early life, and his interaction with those who would come to visit and use the library.[4]

(3) It has been observed that Eusebius quotes the longer form when he is talking about baptism and the shorter text when baptism is not the focus but rather the authority of Christian preaching. This is fair enough, but it doesn't explain the *existence* of the 'in my name' clause, since we can't explain the clause away as Eusebius' own gloss on the triadic formula (it has a different function).[5] We might be tempted to see Eusebius' shortening and summarising Matthew, perhaps loosely saying that Eusebius quotes Matthew inexactly, influenced by his knowledge of other Scripture. However, this seems too convenient a strategy to explain away

---

[1] Kelly, *Early Christian Creeds*, 168-172 for an introduction.
[2] Riggenbach put forward the argument - „*Der Trinitarische Taufbefehl*", 10-32; see Verheyden, "The Gospel Text of Eusebius of Caesarea", 69, for comment; Cuneo, *The Lord's Command to Baptise*, 71, knows this argument.
[3] Conybeare, "Three Early Modifications of the Text of the Gospels," 105.
[4] Caesarea was a Scriptorium where codices of the Scriptures were copied and distributed to churches; see B. M. Metzger, *The Text of the New Testament* (2nd ed.; Oxford: Oxford University Press, 1978), 7.
[5] For this strategy see Chase, "The Lord's Command to Baptize," 486-487.

an uncomfortable fact.[1]   This might be a reasonable approach in an odd case, but Eusebius' uses the shorter clause thirteen times *as Scripture*, and in some cases, he comments on the exact wording. His use of Matt 28:18-20 always puts the shorter 'in my name' in the right sequence of that passage and this points to usage of an actual text rather than his adding to a text. The evidence really points to Eusebius knowing a text of Matthew with the shorter form of words.

(4) If Matthew is using an actual text, is this Hebrew or Greek? Is the short text from the Western text type or the Alexandrian? Chase offers the hypothesis that Eusebius gets his short text from a Western text,[2] observing that this text is known for adding clauses to the Gospels. However, the lack of evidence of such a reading among the Fathers who quote Matt 28:18-20 from a Western text casts doubt on this Greek text-type being the source. The **rarity** of the shorter reading is best explained as local to Palestine and a Hebrew Matthew.

Without setting up (1) – (4) above in order to knock down straw men, the hypothesis which we have presented is that Eusebius had sight of an earlier Hebrew text of a gospel by Matthew with the shorter 'in my name'. He also knew of a Greek text of a gospel by Matthew with the longer clause. Jerome knows of a translation of the former, but our existing Greek text of Matthew doesn't look like a translation of a Hebrew precursor. Given that we do not have a Hebrew Matthew, we cannot determine the precise relationship with our Greek Matthew. We cannot say, for example, that Matthew did not write a Hebrew gospel. It's entirely possible that a Hebrew gospel by Matthew was translated (by whoever) and that it was a different volume to the Greek gospel written by Matthew that has come down to us. Matthew may not have translated his Hebrew gospel, preferring to write a new gospel in Greek based on his earlier Hebrew work.[3]

---

[1] Cuneo, *The Lord's Command to Baptise*, 95-110, follows this approach arguing that Eusebius quotes his text of Matthew 'inexactly'; see Verheyden, "The Gospel Text of Eusebius of Caesarea", 69, for comment.

[2] Chase, "The Lord's Command to Baptize", 488. Metzger, *The Text of the New Testament*, 132-133, describes the early evidence for a 'Western' text in the writings of Justin, Irenaeus, Tertullian and others.

[3] That authors might write in their first language and then in the lingua franca of the day is seen in Josephus and the introduction to his *The Wars of the Jews*: "I have proposed to myself, for the sake of such as live under the government of the Romans, to translate those books into the Greek

The two textual traditions had equal authority for Eusebius, but the preservation of a Hebrew Matthew with a short clause as far as the fourth century doesn't settle the question of what Jesus said upon the occasion of the Great Commission. Here, we can hypothesize that Jesus instructed the apostles to make disciples in his name, and as he developed the detail of the commission, he instructed them to baptise individuals using the triadic formula. Matthew records different elements of the commission, as did the now lost Hebrew Matthew. This hypothesis is no different from what we see in the different Synoptic Gospels as they record different words for Jesus in the same conversational situation. Harmonies of the Synoptic Gospels typically merge the records to produce an overall account.

Since both forms of Matt 28:19 are original to Matthew's gospels, and represent Jesus' words on the occasion of the Great Commission, the reason why we only have the longer form in the manuscripts is down to the apostolic authority of the Greek Matthew. This gospel superseded the Hebrew Matthew and became canonical. Hence, it was copied. The Caesarean copies of the Hebrew Matthew were destroyed by the Muslims when they destroyed the library (see Wikipedia), and any other copies have not survived.

3. What does the triadic formula mean?
We can now turn to a consideration of what the triadic formula would have meant in Jesus' teaching and the first Jewish-Gentile Christian communities.

πορευθέντες οὖν μαθητεύσατε πάντα τὰ ἔθνη, βαπτίζοντες αὐτοὺς εἰς τὸ ὄνομα τοῦ πατρὸς καὶ τοῦ υἱοῦ καὶ τοῦ ἁγίου πνεύματος,

(Matt. 28:19 BGT)

The preposition used in the commission is *eis* which often carries a sense of 'to/into', although this Greek preposition casts a wide net with its

---

tongue, which I formerly composed in the language of our country, and sent to the Upper Barbarians; {b} I, Joseph, the son of Matthias, by birth a Hebrew, a priest also, and one who at first fought against the Romans myself, and was forced to be present at what was done afterward, [am the author of this work.] (*War* 1:3). On this question see the discussion in Edwards, *The Hebrew Gospel and the Development of the Synoptic Tradition*, 174-182.

range of meanings. It's all a matter of seeing what vocabulary is being used with the preposition when determining its meaning. Translations usually opt for 'in' with our text – 'in the name of' but, for example, Heb 6:10 has been translated with 'toward': "For God is not unjust so as to forget your work and the love which you have shown toward his name, in having ministered and in still ministering to the saints" (Heb 6:10 NASB).

The two most common suggestions made by scholars for this preposition in Matt 28:19 are that Jesus either commands his disciples to baptise 'in' i.e. on the authority of the Father and the Son and the holy Spirit, or he commands his disciples to baptise 'into' the name of the Father and the Son and the holy Spirit.

Elsewhere in Matthew, Jesus speaks of those who act on his behalf or represent him in some way, but in such cases Matthew uses the preposition *epi*, for example, "For many shall come in (*epi*) my name, saying, I am Christ; and shall deceive many" (Matt 24:5 KJV). Similarly, Mark uses *epi* for where the authority of Christ is invoked, and/or someone is acting instead of Christ (e.g. Mark 9:39, 41). But the preposition *en* is also used in this way as in Mark 16:17, "And these signs will accompany those who have believed: in (*en*) my name they will cast out demons, they will speak with new tongues" (NASB). The pattern is the same for Luke and John and this makes the use of *eis* in Matt 28:19 stand out.

If we now consider the examples of Acts, the difficulty is a different one. Acts uses *epi* (Acts 2:38) and *en* (Acts 10:48) as well as *eis* (Acts 8:16; 19:5) in relation to baptism. The difference between these examples is that Acts 2:38 and 10:48 are **speech acts**; Acts 2:38 is an exhortation to individuals to be baptised in the name of Christ and Acts 10:48 is instructing others to baptise individuals in the name of Christ. In each case, 'in the name of' expresses the authority for the baptism. In the case of Acts 8:16 and 19:5, however, we have **the narrator describing** a baptism, what it was, and here we find that it was '*to* the name of the Lord Jesus'. Obviously, the use of *eis* in these last two examples directly compares with Matt 28:19.

Paul's teaching about baptism does not support the view that baptism was 'into' a name, whether that be 'the name of the Lord Jesus' or 'the name of the Father, Son and holy Spirit'. In Romans, he states, "Or do you not know that all of us who have been baptized into (*eis*) Christ Jesus have been baptized into (*eis*) his death?" (Rom. 6:3 NASB). Here *eis* is construed as 'into' but it is not 'into a name' but into a **person** and his death. Baptism into Christ places a person in Christ; the aspect of Christ into which an individual is baptised is his death.[1]

It would seem then from Paul's teaching that Matt 28:19 should not be construed as 'into the name of the Father and of the Son and of the holy Spirit'. Paul's own remarks about baptising *to* his own name reinforce this conclusion. He says, "Has Christ been divided? Paul was not crucified for you, was he? Or were you baptized to (*eis*) the name of Paul? I thank God that I baptized none of you except Crispus and Gaius, that no man should say you were baptized to (*eis*) my name" (1 Cor. 1:13-15). This brings out the sense of the preposition *eis* but only as part of the whole expression: Paul is disavowing any claim to glory on his part because individuals were not *attached* to his name in their baptism.

Returning now to Matt 28:19, what does Jesus mean by baptising *to* the name of the Father and of the Son and of the holy Spirit? The **type** in Scripture to which he is alluding is that of building the temple:

> Now set your heart and your soul to seek the Lord your God; arise therefore, and build ye the sanctuary of the Lord God, to bring the ark of the covenant of the Lord, and the holy vessels of God, into the house that is to be built to the name of the Lord. (1 Chron 22:19 KJV); cf. 2 Chron 2:4; Jer 3:17; 7:14

> ...**to the name of** the Lord
> ...**to the name of** the Father, the Son and the holy Spirit

Here we have an obvious principle about temples: they are not just a dwelling for a deity; they also give glory to the deity and are *identified* with that deity – i.e. we have a temple *of Yahweh*. Jesus is quoting Chronicles and 'to the name of' when he commands 'baptising them to the name of the Father and of the Son and of the holy Spirit'. In the same way that a temple was *made* for Yahweh, a disciple was *made* through baptism for the Father, the Son and the holy Spirit.

The reason why Biblical unitarians are suspicious of the triadic formula in Matt 28:19 is that it 'looks too trinitarian'. What they fail to appreciate is

---

[1] Baptism is described in terms of incorporation as in Gal 3:27, "For as many of you as have been baptised *into* (*eis*) Christ". It is a mistake to equate incorporation into Christ with the baptism *to* (*eis*) the name of Christ; *contra* Chase, "The Lord's Command to Baptise," 501.

the wider context of Jesus' Passion week with the disciples and his teaching in that week. This is mainly recorded by John and it particularly features the holy Spirit. So, whereas reading Matthew alone can engender the impression that Matt 28:19 is out of place, reading the Great Commission with the Gospel of John correctly contextualises Jesus' last command.

> And I will pray the Father, and he shall give you <u>another</u>
> <u>Comforter</u>, that he may abide with you for ever; Even the
> Spirit of truth; whom the world cannot receive, because it
> seeth him not, neither knoweth him: but ye know him; for
> he <u>dwelleth</u> with you, and shall be in you. John 14:16-17
> (KJV)

> Jesus answered and said unto him, 'If a man love me, he will
> keep my words: and my Father will love him, and we will
> come unto him, and make our <u>abode</u> with him'. John 14:23
> (KJV)

> But the <u>Comforter</u>, which is the holy Spirit, whom the
> Father will send in my name, he shall teach you all things,
> and bring all things to your remembrance, whatsoever I have
> said unto you. John 14:26 (KJV)

Here Jesus teaches the disciples that he and his father will make their 'abode' (μονή) with them; he also teaches them that the holy Spirit will 'dwell' (μένω) with them.

This temple teaching is found in Paul,

> But ye are not in the flesh, but in the Spirit, if so be that the
> Spirit of God <u>dwell</u> in you. Now if any man have not the
> Spirit of Christ, he is none of his. Rom 8:9 (KJV)

> Know ye not that ye are the <u>temple</u> of God, and that the
> Spirit of God dwelleth in you? 1 Cor 3:16 (KJV)

> ...for ye are the <u>temple</u> of the living God; as God hath said,
> I will dwell in them, and walk in them; and I will be their
> God, and they shall be my people. 2 Cor 6:16 (KJV)

> In whom all the building fitly framed together groweth unto
> an holy <u>temple</u> in the Lord...Eph 2:21 (KJV)

The role of believers to be a temple carries forward to the kingdom,

> Him that overcometh will I make a pillar in the <u>temple</u> of
> my God, and he shall go no more out: and I will write upon
> him the <u>name</u> of my God, and the name of the city of my
> God, which is new Jerusalem, which cometh down out of
> heaven from my God: and I will write upon him my new
> <u>name</u>. Rev 3:12 (KJV)

> And I saw no <u>temple</u> therein: for the Lord God Almighty
> and the Lamb are the temple of it. Rev 21:22 (KJV)

What we see here is an association of temple and name, along with a
teaching about the dwelling of God with believers through the Spirit.
Coupled with Jesus teaching in John about the coming of the holy Spirit
and his dwelling with the disciples, we have the key to unlock the meaning
of the triadic formula: this is a command to build the temple – i.e. the
temple that comprises believers is made through baptism and this temple
is **to** the name of the Father, the Son and the holy Spirit.

What is the name of the Father, the Son and the holy Spirit?
Commentators talk of 'the three-fold name'; some discuss whether there
is one name or three names. Again, Paul helps the exegesis. Jesus was
given a name above every name (Phil 2:9), and the highest name is that of
'Yahweh'. A baptism to the name of the Father and the Son is therefore
entirely explicable. What of the holy Spirit – why should the holy Spirit be
associated with the Father and the Son in terms of a name? Here the
precedent is the giving of God's name to the Angel of the Presence (Exod
23:20-21; Isa 63:9). This angel mediated God's presence in the tabernacle
and led Israel through the wilderness. The connection between the
presence of God in a believer and the holy Spirit is made by David (Ps
51:11). Hence, as well as vexing the Angel of the Lord at Meribah (Ps
78:40), the people grieved the holy Spirit in Moses (Isa 63:10). Hence,
Paul warns his converts to be careful not to grieve the holy Spirit of God
(Eph 4:30) and Peter questions Ananias and Saphira as to why they had
lied to the holy Spirit. Baptising believers to the name of the Father, the
Son and the holy Spirit is about how the presence of the Father and the
Son is mediated through the Spirit. Individually and collectively, believers
are named 'of Yahweh' (see Isa 55:13; 63:19) because they are a temple.

4. Objections
We have set out the patristic data for the two textual traditions of Matt
28:19. New Testament scholars operate with hypotheses about the

development of Matthew in the first century. They have been suspicious of the originality of the triadic formula whereas textual critics, working with the manuscripts handed down to us, have not generally doubted the originality of the text. The sort of considerations that NT scholars focus upon are *internal* to Matthew and more broadly the New Testament. They basically claim that what we know about Jesus' pattern of speaking, Matthew's audience, and the history in Acts and Paul, counts against the triadic formula as the genuine words of Jesus. It is to these arguments that we now turn.

(1) That individuals might be baptised to the name of the Father is uncontroversial; that they might be baptised to the name of the Father and of the Son is more innovative and distinctive within the context of Second Temple Judaism. However, that Jesus might refer to himself as 'the Son' fits his language in John, and this is the gospel which most often records Jesus' *close working relationship* with 'the Father', for example,

> Then answered Jesus and said unto them, Verily, verily, I say unto you, The Son can do nothing of himself, but what he seeth the Father do: for what things soever he doeth, these also doeth the Son likewise. For the Father loveth the Son, and sheweth him all things that himself doeth: and he will shew him greater works than these, that ye may marvel. For as the Father raiseth up the dead, and quickeneth them; even so the Son quickeneth whom he will. For the Father judgeth no man, but hath committed all judgment unto the Son: That all men should honour the Son, even as they honour the Father. He that honoureth not the Son honoureth not the Father which hath sent him. John 5:19-23 (KJV)

Would evangelists and apostles have baptised to the name of the holy Spirit? Here, Jesus' presentation of the holy Spirit as a 'Comforter' or 'Advocate' or 'Helper' (translations vary) is a natural personification given the operation of the Spirit through the apostles. Their authority was confirmed by their possession of the Spirit. Hence, to lie to them was to lie to the holy Spirit. The dwelling of the holy Spirit with believers along with the Father and the Son is the basis upon which believers are pictured as a temple, and so we can see how apostles and evangelists would baptise to the name of the Father and the Son and the holy Spirit.

We should not therefore discount the triadic formula on the grounds that it cannot have arisen in a first century pre-dominantly Jewish setting. On the basis of what we have said so far, the triadic formula is explicable as original to Jesus; we shouldn't doubt it because it 'looks trinitarian'. Indeed, when it is explained by Acts and John, it *doesn't* support the doctrine of the Trinity. The relationship between the Father and the Son and the holy Spirit in those books is clearly *not* trinitarian (but unitarian and subordinationist), but that is another topic. Suspecting the formula to be 'trinitarian' is anachronistic and it is better to think of it as 'triadic'.

(2) Mark 16:15-16[1] is the parallel 'Great Commission' to that of Matthew and it includes a reference to baptism but without the triadic formula. Further, there is no reference to the 'making' of disciples nor a reference to carrying this out in the name of Jesus. However, Mark doesn't record the same occasion and we have evidence with Matthew and Mark of a *series of* occasions in which Jesus gave a commission.[2] Jesus addressed the disciples on these occasions and from these talks, the two gospels pick out different aspects of the commission; there is no reason to suppose that Jesus did not repeat himself in his talks with his disciples when giving his commission, nor is there any reason to say that Jesus' commission did not include different emphases which Matthew and Mark record from separate occasions. We should distinguish the circumstance and occasion of the commission from the content of the commission. There's no reason in Mark to doubt either the longer of the shorter text of Matthew; rather, Mark's record shows that commissioning the disciples was a repeated matter and with broad content.

(3) Likewise, Luke 24:47 records yet different words from an occasion of a commission. Here, Jesus does not mention 'making' disciples nor baptizing them, but there was to be preaching 'in his name'. We should however note that Luke records Jesus' mention of the disciples being endued with 'power from on high' which quotes Isa 32:15 and an expectation that this power would be the Spirit. This is important for our deliberations because it shows that in commissioning the disciples Jesus does talk about the holy Spirit and this supports a mention of the holy Spirit in a triadic formula by Jesus.

(4) The evidence of Acts and Paul, that the apostolic church baptised in the name of Jesus, has been taken to imply that the triadic formula is late and not used by the apostles and evangelists in the early decades of the

---

[1] On the authenticity of Mark 16:9-20 see N. P. Lunn, *The Original Ending of Mark* (Wipf & Stock, 2014).

[2] The narrative intent is to record a commission within the genre of presenting the earthly ministry of Jesus; whether a mountain in Galilee (Matthew) or an urban setting (Mark and Luke).

church. However, the historical records we have do not report any form of words that was used in a speech act of baptising, whether singular or triadic. This absence allows commentators to suppose that the triadic formula is a later creation by Matthew or an editor and that we should infer a singular formula was used in a baptismal speech act in the early church. But all sorts of speculation are possible, for example, that the singular form was used for Jews in the early days and the triadic formula was used for Gentiles as the church became dominated by non-Jews. Such speculation contains the seeds of its own defeat: it is difficult to see how a triadic formula would gain traction if it was *not rooted* in Jesus' words and accepted on the basis of apostolic authority.

The point here is that the supposed new triadic formula would have to gain traction in a supposed context where it was already the practice to baptise with the words 'in the name of Christ'. The theology of the triadic formula would need a catalyst other than Jesus' original words, and the theology arising out of such a catalyst would need to be superior to the theology of baptising in the name of Christ in order to get going and be adopted. Furthermore, this catalyst cannot be late and situated in the third century with the development of the doctrine of the Trinity, because the evidence for the triadic formula is earlier than that development.

Contrawise, if the triadic formula is original to Jesus, along with the shorter commission in a Hebrew Matthew, there isn't a need for a catalyst or a superior theology. As the church progressively became more Gentile and parted from Judaism, the Greek Matthew naturally got copied and distributed rather than an older gospel.

(5) The shorter text certainly fits the flow of Matthew, "All power is given unto **me** in heaven and in earth. Go ye and make disciples of all nations in **my** name…". However, equally, the longer text flows, 'Going therefore, make disciples of all nations, baptising them in the name of…'. Scholars might object to the triadic formula on stylistic grounds and its use of a participle ('baptising') following on from a participle ('Going'), but the case that is made seems somewhat subjective. And the fact that Jesus has shown concern on previous occasions with what is done *in* his name doesn't necessarily count against the uniqueness of the triadic formula because Jesus is uniquely instructing his disciples about baptism.

(6) The general pattern in Acts is that believers were baptised with the holy Spirit after conversion and baptism with water. This seems to have been mainly through the laying on of hands (Acts 8) although the Spirit could fall on individuals directly (Acts 10). There is no form of words or

instruction about such a baptism. Jesus states that the Father would send the holy Spirit *in his name* (John 14:26), but this may relate to the bestowal of the Spirit at Pentecost rather than any procedure of the laying on of hands. We can't therefore argue by analogy that water baptism would only have been in Jesus' name because the Spirit was sent only in Jesus' name.

The objections, (1) – (6), attempt to show that the triadic formula is not original to Jesus and/or Matthew on internal grounds of consistency with NT evidence which shows actions being done in the name of Jesus. The principle is stated by Paul, "And whatever you do in word or deed, do all in the name of the Lord Jesus, giving thanks through him to God the Father" (Col 3:17 NASB). Everything should be done on the authority of Christ or as his representative, but since this is not the meaning of 'baptising…to the name of' in Matt 28:19, making believers into a temple for the name of God does not contradict the general principle of doing things in the name of Jesus.

5. Conclusion
Modern English readers are used to literal and free versions of the Bible. This is not the explanation for Eusebius' texts of Matt 28:19. His writings show knowledge of two textual traditions, but we don't need to decide which is original to Matthew or which represents the original words of Jesus. These two binary choices have structured scholarship, but the existence of a Hebrew and a Greek gospel written by Matthew (the Hebrew now lost) is the best explanation of the existence of two traditions. The manuscripts naturally represent the Greek Matthew, but the current GNT should reinstate a marginal variant for the text to document the Eusebian reading. The patristic evidence for the shorter text is not evidence for a competing reading of the original text of a Greek Matthew; it is evidence of an original Hebrew Matthew.

BIBLIOGRAPHY

Primary Texts

Alford, H., *The Greek Testament* (4 vols; London: Rivingtons, 1859). (Alford)

Bettenson, H. D., ed., *Documents of the Christian Church* (Oxford: Oxford University Press, 1944

Beyerlin, W., ed., *Near Eastern Religious Texts relating to the Old Testament* (London: SCM Press, 1978).

Bindley, T. H., ed., *The Oecumenical Documents of the Christian Faith* (London: Methuen, 1906).

Charles, R. H., ed., *The Apocrypha and Pseudepigrapha of the Old Testament in English* (2 vols; Oxford: Clarendon Press, 1913).

Charlesworth, J. H., ed., *The Old Testament Pseudepigrapha* (2 vols; New York: Doubleday, 1983-1985). (OTP)

Eusebius: The History of the Church (trans., G. A. Williamson; rev. ed., A. Louth; London: Penguin, 1989).

Field, F., ed., *Origenis Hexaplorum quae supersunt* (Oxford: Clarendon Press, 1875).

Gilbey, T., ed., et al; *St Thomas Aquinas: Summa Theologica, Latin Text and English Translation* (London: Blackfriars, 1964).

Grossfield, B., ed., *Targum Onqelos* (Edinburgh: T&T Clark, 1988).

Harmer, J. R., ed., *The Apostolic Fathers* (London: Macmillan, 1926).

Rubinkiewicz, R., *Apocalypse of Abraham* in *The Old Testament Pseudepigrapha* (ed. J. H. Charlesworth; 2 vols; New York: Doubleday, 1983-1985), 681-705.

Schaff P., and H. Wace, eds., *Nicene and Post-Nicene Fathers* (Edinburgh: T&T Clark, 1976).

Whiston, W., ed., *Complete Works of Josephus* (Peabody: Hendrickson, 1987).

Yonge, C. D., ed., *The Works of Philo* (New York: Hendrickson, 1993).

Scriptural Texts

Biblica Hebraica Stuttgartensia (eds., K. Elliger and W. Rudolph; 4th Ed.; Deutsche Bibelgesellschaft, 1990).

Septuaginta (ed., A. Rahlfs; 2 vols; Stuttgart: Deutsche Bibelgesellschaft, 1979).

Dictionaries, Grammars

Abbott-Smith, G. A., *A Manual Greek Lexicon of the New Testament* (3rd ed.; repr.; Edinburgh: T & T Clark, 1948). (Abbot-Smith)

Arnold, B. T., and J. H. Choi, *A Guide to Biblical Hebrew Syntax* (Cambridge: Cambridge University Press).

Arndt W. F., and F. W. Gingrich, *A Greek-English Lexicon of the New Testament and Other Early Christian Literature* (Cambridge: Cambridge University Press, 1957). (BAGD)

Audi; R., ed., *The Cambridge Dictionary of Philosophy* (2nd ed.; Cambridge: Cambridge University Press, 1999).

Blass, F., and A. Debrunner, *A Greek Grammar of the New Testament* (Chicago: University of Chicago Press, 1961).

Brown, F., S. R. Driver and C. A. Briggs, *A Hebrew and English Lexicon of the Old Testament* (Oxford: Oxford University Press, 1907). (BDB)

Danker, F. W., *The Concise Greek-English Lexicon of the New Testament* (Chicago: University of Chicago Press, 2009). (Danker)

Friberg, B, T. Friberg and N. F. Miller, *Analytical Lexicon of the Greek New Testament* (Grand Rapids: Baker, 2000). (Friberg)

Gesenius, W., *Hebrew Grammar* (ed. E. Kautzsch; trans. A. E. Cowley; 2nd ed.; Oxford: Oxford University Press, 1910).

Lambdin, T. O., *Introduction to Biblical Hebrew* (London: Darton, Longman and Todd, 1971).

Lust, J., E. Eynikel and K. Hauspie, *Greek-English Lexicon of the Septuagint* (Stuttgart: Deutsche Bibelgesellschaft, 2003). (LEH)

Liddell, H. G. and R. Scott, *An Intermediate Greek-English Lexicon* (Oxford: Clarendon Press, 1889). (L&S)

Moulton, J. H. & G. Milligan, *The Vocabulary of the Greek Testament* (London: Hodder & Stoughton, 1930).

Perschbacher, W. J., *New Testament Greek Syntax* (Chicago: Moody Press, 1995).

Sawyer, J. F. A., *A Modern Introduction to Biblical Hebrew* (London: Oriel Press, 1976).

Van der Merwe, C. H. J., and J. A. Naudé and J. H. Kroeze, *A Biblical Hebrew Reference Grammar* (Sheffield: Sheffield Academic Press, 2002).

Wallace, D. B., *Greek Grammar Beyond the Basics* (Grand Rapids: Zondervan, 1986).

Weingreen, J., *A Practical Grammar for Classical Hebrew* (Oxford: Oxford University Press (Clarendon), 1939).

Winer, G. B., *A Treatise on the Grammar of New Testament Greek* (2nd ed.; Ed. W. F. Moulton; Edinburgh: T & T Clark, 1877).

Secondary Literature

Ackroyd, P., *Words and Meanings* (Cambridge: Cambridge University Press, 1968).

Adey, J. W., " 'In the Beginning' of John 1:1: A New View Examined" (Unpublished paper supplied by the author).

— "One God: The Shema in Old and New Testaments" in *One God, the Father* (ed. T. Gaston; Sunderland: Willow Publications, 2013), 26-39.

— "Is the Shema's 'one' (ʾeḥād) one or more?" in *One God, the Father* (ed. T. Gaston; Sunderland: Willow Publications, 2013), 290-311.

Aland, K., "Eine Untersuchung zu Johannes 1, 3-4. Über die Bedeutung eines Punktes" *ZNW* 59 (1968): 174-209.

Aland, K., and B, Aland, *The Text of the New Testament* (Grand Rapids: Eerdmans, 1989).

Albrektson, B., "On the Syntax of אהיה אשר אהיה in Exodus 3:14", in *Words and Meanings* (ed., P. Ackroyd; Cambridge: Cambridge University Press, 1968), 15-28.

Alston, W. P., "Substance and the Trinity" in *The Trinity* (eds., S. T. Davis, D. Kendall, and G. O' Collins; Oxford: Oxford University Press, 1999), 179-201.

Ashton, J., *Studying John* (Oxford: (Oxford University Press, 1994).

— ed., *The Interpretation of John* (2nd ed.; Edinburgh: T&T Clark, 1997).

— *Understanding the Fourth Gospel* (2nd ed.; Oxford: Oxford University Press, 2007).

Barnes, M. R., and D. H. Williams, eds., *Arianism after Arius* (Edinburgh: T&T Clark, 1993).

Barr, J., *The Semantics of Biblical Language* (Oxford: Oxford University Press, 1961).

Barrett, C. K., *The Gospel According to St John* (London: SPCK, 1955).

Bauckham, R., *The Climax of Prophecy* (Edinburgh: T & T Clark, 1993).

— *Jesus and the God of Israel* (Milton Keynes: Paternoster, 2008).

Beasley-Murray, G. R., *John* (WBC36; Waco: Word, 1991).

Bebbington, D., *Patterns in History* (Leicester: Inter-varsity Press, 1979).

Bernard, N., "BEFORE ABRAHAM WAS, I AM" *The Testimony* (1993): 196.

Black, D. A., ed., *Rethinking New Testament Textual Criticism* (Grand Rapids: Baker House Academic, 2002).

Booker, G., *Psalm Studies* (Austin, Texas: Booker Publications, 1988).

Borgen, P., "Observations on the Targumic Character of the Prologue of John" *NTS* 16 (1970): 288-295.

— "Creation, Logos and the Son: Observations on John 1:1-18 and 5:17-18" *Ex Auditu* 3 (1987): 88-97.

— "Logos was the True Light: Contributions to the Interpretation of the True Light" *Nov. T.* 14/2 (1972): 115-130.

Børreson, K., ed., *The Image of God: Gender Models in Judaeo-Christian Tradition* (Minneapolis: Fortress Press, 1991).

Briggs, R. S., Words in Action: Speech Act Theory and Biblical Interpretation (Sheffield: Continuum, 2001).

Brown, R. E., *The Gospel According to John I-XII* (Anchor Bible 29; New York: Doubleday, 1966).

Bruce, F. F., *The Gospel of John* (Grand Rapids: Eerdmans, 1994).

Buber, M., and F. Rosenzweig, *Scripture and Translation* (Bloomington: Indiana University Press, 1994).

Bultmann, R., *The Gospel of John* (Oxford: Basil Blackwell, 1971).

— "The History of Religions Background of the Prologue to the Gospel of John" in *The Interpretation of John* (ed., J. Ashton; 2nd ed.; Edinburgh: T&T Clark, 1997), 27-46.

Burgon, J. W., *The Causes of the Corruption of the Traditional Text of the Holy Gospels* (London: Geo. Bell & Sons, 1896).

Capes, D. B., *Old Testament Yahweh Texts in Paul's Christology* (Tübingen: Mohr (Paul Siebeck), 1992).

— "YHWH texts and Monotheism in Paul's Christology" in *Early Jewish and Christian Monotheism* (eds. L. T. Stuckenbruck and W. E. S. North; London: T & T Clark International, 2004), 120-137.

Carter, J., *The Gospel of John* (Birmingham: CMPA, 1972).

Carter, W., *John* (Peabody: Hendrickson, 2006).

Chadwick, H., *The Early Church* (London: Penguin, 1967).

Chambers, T. W., *A Companion to the Revised Old Testament* (London: H. E. Jerrard, 1885).

Chase, F. H., "The Lord's Command to Baptize," *JTS* 6 (1905): 481-517.

Childs, B. S., *Exodus* (OTL; London: SCM Press, 1974).

Coloe, M., "The Structure of the Johannine Prologue and Genesis 1" *Australian Biblical Review* 45 (1997): 40-55.

Comfort, P., *Early Manuscripts and Modern Translations* (Cambridge: Tyndale Press, 1990).

— *New Testament Text and Translation Commentary* (Carol Stream: Tyndale House Publishers, 2008).

Conybeare, F. C., "The Eusebian Form of the Text Matth. 28, 19," *ZNW* 2 (1901): 275-288.

— "Three Early Modifications of the Text of the Gospels," *Hibbert Journal* 1 (1902): 96-113.

— "The Lord's Command to Baptise, being No. V of the N. T. Studies of the Catholic University of America by Bernard Henry Cuneo," *JTS* (1924): 191-197.

Cross, F. M., *Canaanite Myth and Hebrew Epic* (Cambridge: Harvard University Press, 1973).

Culpepper, R. A., "The Pivot of John's Prologue" *NTS* 27 (1980): 1-31.

Cuneo, B. H., *The Lord's Command to Baptise* (Washington DC: Catholic University of America, 1923). [Online].

Dahms, J. V., "Isaiah 55:11 and the Gospel of John" *EQ* 53.2 (1981): 78-88.

Daniélou, J., *The Theology of Jewish Christianity* (London: Darton, Longman and Todd, 1964).

Davis, S. R., 'Jesus is Light: The Meaning of Light in the Gospel of John' (MA Thesis; Reformed Theological Seminary; 2018).

Davis, S. T., D. Kendall, and G. O' Collins, eds., *The Trinity* (Oxford: Oxford University Press, 1999).

— *The Incarnation* (Oxford: Oxford University Press, 2002).

Dahms, J. V., "Isaiah 55:11 and the Gospel of John" *EQ* 53.2 (1981): 78-88.

Dodd, C. H., *The Fourth Gospel* (Cambridge: Cambridge University Press, 1953).

— *The Interpretation of the Fourth Gospel* (Cambridge: Cambridge University Press, 1953).

Dummett, M. A. E., *Frege: Philosophy of Language* (2nd ed.; London: Duckworth, 1981).

Dunn, J. D. G., *Christology in the Making* (1st ed.; London: SCM Press, 1980; 2nd ed.; 1989).

— *The Partings of the Ways* (London: SCM Press, 1991).

— *The Christ and the Spirit, Volume 1, Christology* (Grand Rapids: Eerdmans, 1998).

— *Did the first Christians worship Jesus?* (London: SPCK, 2010).

— "2 Corinthians 3:17 'The Lord is the Spirit'" in *The Christ and the Spirit, Volume 1, Christology* (Grand Rapids: Eerdmans, 1998), 115-125.

Edersheim, A., *The Temple* (Repr. Ed.; London: Angus Hudson, 1997).

Edwards, J. R., *The Hebrew Gospel and the Development of the Synoptic Tradition* (Grand Rapids: Eerdmans, 2009).

Eichrodt, W., *Theology of the Old Testament* (trans. J. Baker; 2 vols; London: SCM Press, 1961-67).

Ehrman, B. D., *The Orthodox Corruption of Scripture* (Oxford, OUP, 1993).

Ehrman, B. D., and D. B. Wallace "The Textual Reliability of the New Testament" in *The Reliability of the New Testament* (ed., R. B. Stewart; Minneapolis: Fortress Press, 2011), 13-60.

Elowsky, J. C., and T. C. Oden, *John 1-10 4a Ancient Commentary on Scripture* (Downer Grove: IVP Academic, 2007).

Endo, M., *Creation and Christology: A study on the Johannine Prologue in the Light of Early Jewish Creation Accounts* (Tübingen: Mohr-Siebeck, 2002).

Epp. E. J., and G. D. Fee, *New Testament Textual Criticism, its Significance for Exegesis* (Cambridge: Cambridge University Press, 1981).

Evans, C. A., *Word and Glory: On the Exegetical and Theological Background of John's Prologue* (JSNTS 89; Sheffield: Sheffield Academic Press, 1993).

Fee, G. D., *1 Corinthians* (NICNT; Grand Rapids: Eerdmans, 1987).

Fennema, D. A., "John 1:18: 'God the Only Son'" *NTS* 31 (1985): 124-135.

Fletcher-Louis, C., *Jesus Monotheism* (Eugene, OR: Cascade Books, 2015).

Foakes, F. J. Jackson, and K. Lake, *The Beginnings of Christianity* (5 vols; London: Macmillan, 1920).

Fortana, R. T., and T. Thatcher, eds., *Jesus in Johannine Tradition* (; Louisville; WJK Press, 2001).

Gasque, W. Ward, and R. P. Martin, eds., *Apostolic History and the Gospel* (Exeter: Paternoster Press, 1970).

Gaston, T., ed., *One God, the Father* (Sunderland: Willow Publications, 2013), 26-39.

— 'Why Three? An Exploration of the origins of the doctrine of the Trinity with reference to Platonism and Gnosticism' (DPhil Thesis, Oxford University, 2013).

— "The Son of Man" *CeJBI* (Oct 2007): 3-17.

— "Some Thoughts on 1 Cor 8:6 and the Shema" *CeJBI* 10/1 (2016): 65-70.

Gaston, T., and A. Perry, "Christological Monotheism: 1 Cor 8:6 and the Shema" *HBT* 39 (2017): 176-196.

Geach, P., *Reference and Generality* (New York: Cornell University Press, 1962).

Gibson, A., *Biblical Semantic Logic* (Oxford: Basil Blackwell, 1981).

— "Our Man in Hell (1)" *The Testimony* (1971): 348-352.

— " 'I AM' AND 'I AM HE' " *The Testimony* (1975): 94-95.

Gieschen, C. A., *Angelomorphic Christology* (Leiden: E. J. Brill, 1998).

Glasson, T. F., *Moses in the Fourth Gospel* (London: SCM Press, 1963).

Goutsos, D., *Discourse Analysis: An Introduction* (Edinburgh: Edinburgh University Press, 2004).

Grant, R. M., *Jesus after the Gospels* (London: SCM Press, 1990).

— *Heresy and Criticism* (Louisville: WJK Press, 1993).

Green, B. H., "Matthew 28:19, Eusebius, and the *lex orandi*" in *The Making of Orthodoxy* (ed., R. Williams; Cambridge: CUP, 2002), 124-141.

Guthrie, D., *New Testament Theology* (Leicester: Intervarsity Press, 1981).

Haack, S., *Philosophy of Logics* (Cambridge: Cambridge University Press, 1978).

Hall, S. G., *Doctrine and Practise in the Early Church* (London: SPCK, 1992).

Hanson, A. T., "John 1:14-18 and Exodus 34" *NTS* 23 (1976): 90-101.

Hanson, R. P. C., *The Search for the Christian Doctrine of God* (Edinburgh: T & T Clark, 1988).

— "The Achievement of Orthodoxy in the Fourth Century AD", in *The Making of Orthodoxy* (ed., R. Williams Cambridge, Cambridge University Press, 1989), 142-156.

Hardy, E. R., *Christology of the Later Fathers* (Grand Rapids: WJK Press, 1954).

Heidt, W. G., *The Angelology of the Old Testament* (Washington: Catholic University Press, 1949).

Hill, C. E., and M. J. Kruger, eds., *The Early Text of the New Testament* (Oxford: OUP, 2014).

Hodgkin, A. M., *Christ in All the Scriptures* (London: Pickering & Inglis, 1922).

Hooker, M., "The Johannine Prologue and the Messianic Secret" *NTS* 21 (1974): 40-58.

Horbury, W., "Jewish and Christian Monotheism in the Herodian Age" in *Early Jewish and Christian Monotheism* (eds. W. E. S. North and L. T. Stuckenbruck; London: T & T Clark, 2004), 16-44.

Hoskyns, E. C., and F. N. Davey, *The Fourth Gospel* (2nd ed (rev).; London: Faber & Faber, 1957)

Hubbard, B. J., *The Matthean Redaction of Primitive Apostolic Commissioning: An Exegesis of Matthew 28:16-20* (Atlanta: Scholars Press, 1974).

Hurst, L. D., and N. T. Wright, eds., *The Glory of Christ in the New Testament* (Oxford: Oxford University Press, 1984).

Hurtado, L. W., *One God, One Lord* (2nd ed.; London: T & T Clark, 2003).

Irving, S., *Studies in John's Gospel* (Nottingham: Dawn Publications, 2015).

Jackman, G, *The Word Became Flesh* (Pub. By the Author, 2016).

Jeremias, J., "The Revealing Word" in his *The Central Message of the New Testament* (London: SCM Press, 1965), 71-90.

Jobes, K. H., and M. Silva, *Invitation to the Septuagint* (Grand Rapids: Baker Academic, 2000).

Kamesar, A., ed., *The Cambridge Companion to Philo* (Cambridge: Cambridge University Press, 2009).

Käsemann, E., "The Structure and Purpose of the Prologue to John's Gospel" in his *New Testament Questions of Today* (London: SCM Press, 1969), 138-167.

Kelly, J. N. D., *Early Christian Doctrines* (London: A & C Black, 1977).

— *Early Christian Creeds* (London: Longman, 1972).

Kenny, A., *The Metaphysics of Mind* (Oxford: Oxford University Press, 1992).

Klauck, H., *Apocryphal Gospels* (London: T & T Clark, 2003).

Kline, M. G., *Images of the Spirit* (Grand Rapids: Baker, 1980).

Lamarche, P., "The Prologue of John" in *The Interpretation of John* (ed., J. Ashton; 2nd ed.; Edinburgh: T&T Clark, 1997), 47-65.

Lebreton, J., *Histoire du dogme de la Trinité* (Paris, 1910).

Leftow, B., *Time and Eternity* (New York: Cornell University Press, 1991).

Lightfoot, R. H., *St. John's Gospel: A Commentary* (Oxford: Oxford University Press, 1956).

Lindars, B., *The Gospel of John* (London: Oliphants, 1972).

— *John* (Sheffield: Sheffield Academic Press, 1990).

Longenecker, R. N., *The Christology of Early Jewish Christianity* (Grand Rapids: Baker Book House, 1981).

Lunn, N. P., *The Original Ending of Mark* (Wipf & Stock, 2014).

Lyman, R., "A Topography of Heresy: Mapping the Rhetorical Creation of Arianism" in *Arianism after Arius* (eds. M. R. Barnes and D. H. Williams; Edinburgh: T&T Clark, 1993), 45-62.

Macdonald, S., "The Divine Nature" in *The Cambridge Companion to Augustine* (eds. E. Stump and N. Kretzmann; Cambridge: Cambridge University Press, 2001), 71-90.

McCarthy, D. J., "Exod 3:14: History, Philology and Theology" *CBQ* 40 (1978): 311-322.

Mach, M., "Concepts of Jewish Monotheism during the Hellenistic Period" in *The Jewish Roots of Christological Monotheism* (eds. C. C. Newman, J. R. Davila and G. S. Lewis; Leiden: E J Brill, 1999), 21-42.

Magness, J., *The Archaeology of Qumran and the Dead Sea Scrolls* (Grand Rapids: Eerdmans, 2003).

Marmorstein, A., "The Unity of God in Rabbinic Literature" in *Studies in Jewish Theology* (eds. J. Rabbinowitz and M. S. Lew; Oxford: Oxford University Press, 1950), 72-105.

Marsh, J., *Saint John* (London: Penguin, 1968).

Marshall, I. H., "Incarnational Christology in the New Testament" in Donald Guthrie's festschrift *Christ the Lord: Studies in Christology Presented to Donald Guthrie* (ed. H. H. Rowdon; Leicester: Intervarsity Press, 1982), 1-16.

McNamara, M., "Logos of the Fourth Gospel and Memra of the Palestinian Targum (Ex 12:42)" *ExpT* 79 (1967-68): 115-117.

McLay, R. T., *The Use of the Septuagint in New Testament Research* (Grand Rapids: Eerdmans, 2003).

McReynolds, P. R., "John 1:18 in Textual Variation and Translation" in *New Testament Textual Criticism, its Significance for Exegesis* (eds., E. J. Epp and G. D. Fee; Cambridge: Cambridge University Press, 1981), 105-118.

Metzger, B. M., *The Text of the New Testament* (2nd ed., Oxford: Oxford University Press, 1968).

— *A Textual Commentary on the Greek New Testament* (London: United Bible Societies, 1971).

Michel, O., "The Conclusion of Matthew's Gospel" in *The Interpretation of Matthew* (ed., G. Stanton; London: SPCK, 1983), 30-41.

Miller, E. L., "*The Logos* was God" *EQ* 53.2 (1981): 65-77.

Moody, D., "God's Only Son: The Translation of John 3:16 in the Revised Standard Version" *JBL* 72/4 (1953): 213-219.

Moore, G. F., *Judaism in the First Centuries of the Christian Era* (2 vols; Reprinted—Peabody: Hendrickson, 1997).

Moule, C. F. D., "Further Reflexions on Philippians 2:5-11" in *Apostolic History and the Gospel* (eds. W. Ward Gasque and Ralph P. Martin; Exeter: Paternoster Press, 1970), 264-276.

Mullen, N., "Philippians 2:6-11 – A Study in History and Exposition 2. *Harpagmos*: 'Robbery' or 'Something to be Grasped'?" *The Testimony* 56 (1986): 25-29.

Murphy-O'Conner, J., *Keys to First Corinthians: Revisiting the Major Issues* (Oxford: Oxford University Press, 2009).

Newman, C. C., J. R. Davila and G. S. Lewis, eds., *The Jewish Roots of Christological Monotheism* (Leiden: E J Brill, 1999).

Nicholson, S. B., "Dynamic oneness: The significance and flexibility of Paul's one-God language" (PhD Thesis; Durham, 2007, online).

Norris, A. D., *Acts and Epistles* (London: Aletheia Books, 1989).

North, W. E. S., and L. T. Stuckenbruck, eds., *Early Jewish and Christian Monotheism* (London: T & T Clark, 2004).

— "Introduction" in *Early Jewish and Christian Monotheism* (eds. W. E. S. North and L. T. Stuckenbruck; London: T & T Clark, 2004), 1-13.

Ogden, G. S., "Time, and the Verb *hyh* in O. T. Prose" *VT* 21 (1971): 451-469.

Ottley, R. R., *The Book of Isaiah according to the Septuagint* (2 vols; Cambridge: Cambridge University Press, 1906).

Painter, J., *The Quest for the Messiah* (Edinburgh: T & T Clark, 1991).

Pákozdy, L. M., "I shall be that which I shall be" *The Bible Translator* 7 (1956): 146-148.

Paxson, J., *The Poetics of Personification* (Cambridge: Cambridge University Press, 1994).

Payne, J. Barton, "Eighth Century Israelitish Background of Isaiah 40-66" *WTJ* 29 (1966-1967): 179-190; 30 (1968): 50-58; 185-203.

Peltier, R. V., ' Christology in the Prologue of John: A Rejection of Philo of Alexandria's Logos Philosophy' (M.Th. Thesis, Univ. of South Africa, 2019).

Perkins, P., *Gnosticism and the New Testament* (Minneapolis: Fortress Press, 1993).

Perry, A., "The Translation of Exodus 3:14a" *CeJBI* 3/4 (2009): 39-64; (Available on www.academia.edu).

— "Did the NT Writers Quote the LXX?" *CeJBI* 7/2 (2013): 59-78 [Online at www.academia.edu].

— *Beginnings and Endings* (2nd ed. Rev. 3; Sunderland: Willow Publications, 2018).

Peterson, W. L, *Tatian's Diatessaron: Its Creation, Dissemination, Significance, & History in Scholarship* (Leiden: E. J. Brill, 1994).

Phan, P. C., ed., *The Cambridge Companion to The Trinity* (Cambridge: Cambridge University Press, 2011).

Phillips A. and L. Phillips, "The Origin of 'I Am' in Exodus 3.14" *JSOT* 78 (1998): 81-84.

Porter S. E., and C. A. Evans, eds., *The Johannine Writings* (Sheffield: Sheffield Academic Press, 1995).

Prestige, G. L., *God in Patristic Thought* (London: SPCK, 1952).

Prior, A. N., *Past, Present and Future* (Oxford: Oxford University Press, 1967).

Pryor, J. W., "Jesus and Israel in the Fourth Gospel – John 1:11" *Nov. T.* 32/3 (1990): 201-218.

Radice, R., "Philo's Theology and Theory of Creation" in *The Cambridge Companion to Philo* (ed. A. Kamesar; Cambridge: Cambridge University Press, 2009), 124-145.

Ramsey, I. T., *Religious Language* (London: SCM Press, 1957).

Riggenbach, E., „*Der Trinitarische Taufbefehl*" *BFCT* 7 (1903): 7-103.

Robinson, J. A. T., *Redating the New Testament* (London: SCM Press, 1976).

— *The Priority of John* (London: SCM Press, 1985).

Rowdon, H. H., ed., *Christ the Lord: Studies in Christology Presented to Donald Guthrie* (Leicester: InterVarsity Press, 1982).

Rowe, K. C., *Early Narrative Christology* (Grand Rapids: Baker Academic, 2009).

Rowland, C., *Christian Origins* (London: SPCK, 1985).

Sanders, J. N., *The Fourth Gospel in the Early Church* (Cambridge: Cambridge University Press, 1943).

Schenck, K., *A Brief Guide to Philo* (Louisville: WJK Press, 2005).

Schild, E., "On Exodus iii 14 — 'I am that I am'" *VT* 4 (1954): 296-302.

Schoors A., and P. Van Deun, eds. *Philohistôr* (Leuven: Peeters Press, 1994).

Scott, M., *Sophia and the Johannine Jesus* (JSNT 71; Sheffield: Sheffield Academic Press, 1992).

Searle, J., *Speech Acts* (Cambridge: Cambridge University Press, 1969).

Segal, A. F., *Two Powers in Heaven: Early Rabbinic Reports about Christianity and Gnosticism* (Repr.; Waco, TX: Baylor University Press, 2012).

Shaker, C., 'The Lamb of God Title in John's Gospel: Background, Exegesis and Major Themes' (MA Thesis; Seton Hall University; Online).

Smalley, S., *John – Evangelist and Interpreter* (Exeter: Paternoster, 1978).

Sproston, W. E., "Witnesses to what was ἀπ' ἀρχῆς: 1 John's Contribution to our Knowledge of Tradition in the Fourth Gospel" in *The Johannine Writings* (eds. S. E. Porter & C. A. Evans; Sheffield: Sheffield Academic Press, 1995), 138-160.

Stanton, G., ed., *The Interpretation of Matthew* (London: SPCK, 1983).

Stead, G. C., *Philosophy in Christian Antiquity* (Cambridge: Cambridge University Press, 1994).

Stevenson, J., and W. H. C. Frend, eds., *Creeds, Councils and Controversies* (London: SPCK, 1989).

— *A New Eusebius* (London: SPCK, 1987).

Stuckenbruck, L. T., and W. E. S. North, eds., *Early Jewish and Christian Monotheism* (London: T & T Clark International, 2004).

Stump, E., and N. Kretzmann, eds., *The Cambridge Companion to Augustine* (; Cambridge: Cambridge University Press, 2001).

Swete, H. B., *An Introduction to the Old Testament in Greek* (Rev. Ed.; Cambridge: Cambridge University Press, 1914).

Swinburne, R., *The Christian God* (Oxford: Oxford University Press, 1994).

Tillich, P., *A History of Christian Thought* (New York: Touchstone, 1968).

Thompson, M. M., *The God of the Gospel of John* (Grand Rapids: Eerdmans, 2001).

Turner, N., *Grammatical Insights into the New Testament* (Edinburgh: T & T Clark, 1965).

Valentine, S. R., "The Johannine Prologue—A Microcosm of the Gospel" *EQ* 68:3 (1996): 291-304.

Verheyden, J., "The Gospel Text of Eusebius of Caesarea" in *Philohistôr* (eds., A. Schoors and P. Van Deun; Leuven: Peeters Press, 1994), 35-70.

Waaler, E., *The Shema and the First Commandment in First Corinthians* (Tübingen: Mohr Siebeck, 2008).

Wagner, S. J., "Identity" in *The Cambridge Dictionary of Philosophy* (2nd ed.; Ed. R. Audi; Cambridge: Cambridge University Press, 1999), 415-416.

Wallace, D. B., ed., *Revisiting the Corruption of the New Testament* (Grand Rapids: Kregel Publications, 2011).

Wasserman, T., "The Early Text of Matthew" in *The Early Text of the New Testament* (eds., C. E. Hill & M. J. Kruger; Oxford: OUP, 2014), 83-107.

Watson, F., "Is John's Christology Adoptionist?" in *The Glory of Christ in the New Testament* (eds. L. D. Hurst and N. T. Wright; Oxford: Oxford University Press, 1984), 113-124.

Weigle, L. A., et al, *An Introduction to the Revised Standard Version of the Old Testament* (London: Thomas Nelson & Sons Ltd, 1952).

Whittaker, E. C., *Documents of the Baptismal Liturgy* (London: SPCK, repr., 2001).

Whittaker, H. A., *Abraham Father of the Faithful* (Birmingham: CMPA, 1966).

— *Studies in the Acts of the Apostles* (Cannock: Biblia, 1985).

— *Studies in the Gospels* (Cannock: Biblia, 1988).

— *Bible Studies* (Cannock: Biblia, 1987).

Wiggins, D., *Sameness and Substance Renewed* (Cambridge; Cambridge University Press, 2001).

Wiles, M., "Attitudes to Arius in the Arian Controversy" in, *Arianism after Arius* (ed., M. R. Barnes D. H. and Williams; Edinburgh: T&T Clark, 1993).

Williams, C. H., " 'I Am' or 'I Am He'? Self-Declaratory Pronouncements in the Fourth Gospel and Rabbinic Tradition" in *Jesus in Johannine Tradition* (eds. R. T. Fortana and T. Thatcher; Louisville; WJK Press, 2001), 343-352.

Williams, R., ed., *The Making of Orthodoxy* (Cambridge: Cambridge University Press, 1989).

— *Arius* (London: SCM Press, 2001).

— *The Wound of Knowledge* (London: DLT, 1990).

— "Does it make sense to speak of Pre-Nicene Orthodoxy?" in *The Making of Orthodoxy* (ed., R. Williams Cambridge, Cambridge University Press, 1989), 1-23.

Wolterstorff, N., *Divine Discourse* (Cambridge: Cambridge University Press, 1995).

Wood, S. K., "The Trinity in the Liturgy, Sacraments, and Mysticism" in *The Cambridge Companion to The Trinity* (ed. P. C. Phan; Cambridge: Cambridge University Press, 2011), 381-397.

Wright, B. J., "Jesus as ΘΕΟΣ: A Textual Examination" in *Revisiting the Corruption of the New Testament* (ed., D. B. Wallace; Grand Rapids: Kregel Publications, 2011), 229-265.

Wright, N. T., *The Climax of the Covenant* (London: T&T Clark, 1991).

— *The Paul Debate* (London: SPCK, 2016).

Wyns, P., "John 1:3-4" in *The Christadelphian EJournal of Biblical Interpretation Annual 2010* (ed., J. Adey et al; Sunderland: Willow Publications, 2010), 7-12.

Yuile, G., *Pragmatics* (Oxford: Oxford University Press, 1996).

www.ingramcontent.com/pod-product-compliance
Lightning Source LLC
Chambersburg PA
CBHW060322100426
42812CB00003B/852